THE BUSINESS
OF MANAGEMENT

Also by Derek Torrington and published by
Prentice-Hall International:

PERSONNEL MANAGEMENT (with John Chapman)

FACE-TO-FACE IN MANAGEMENT

STEVENSON COLLEGE EDINBURGH

THE BUSINESS
OF MANAGEMENT

Derek Torrington and Jane Weightman

University of Manchester Institute of Science and Technology

Prentice/Hall PHI International

Englewood Cliffs, NJ   London   Mexico   New Delhi   Rio de Janeiro
Singapore   Sydney   Tokyo   Toronto   Wellington

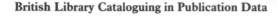

British Library Cataloguing in Publication Data

Torrington, Derek
  The business of management.
  1. Management
  I. Title II. Weightman, Jane
  658 HD31

  ISBN 0–13–104928–3

ISBN 0–13–104928 3

Prentice-Hall Inc., *Englewood Cliffs, New Jersey*
Prentice-Hall International, UK Ltd, *London*
Prentice-Hall of Australia Pty, Ltd, *Sydney*
Prentice-Hall Canada, Inc., *Toronto*
Prentice-Hall Hispanoamericana, SA, *Mexico*
Prentice-Hall of India Private Ltd, *New Delhi*
Prentice-Hall of Japan, Inc., *Tokyo*
Prentice-Hall of Southeast Asia Pte, Ltd, *Singapore*
Editora Prentice-Hall do Brasil Ltda, *Rio de Janeiro*
Whitehall Books Ltd, *Wellington, New Zealand*

Typeset by Multiplex (medway) Ltd, Maidstone, Kent
Printed in the United Kingdom by A. Wheaton & Co., Exeter

CONTENTS

13   COACHING AND TEACHING   183

14   TEAM WORKING   198

15   AUTHORITY, LEADERSHIP AND AUTONOMY   215

16   PERFORMANCE APPRAISAL   229

PREFACE

Management textbooks do not impress students unless they seem practical, but practical books are of little value without a satisfactory theoretical framework. We have tried to write a practical book that will gain the assent of practising managers as a realistic explanation of what they are doing, but which will also be convincing to students: "this could be your life". We have been careful to examine not management but managing, seeking not detachment from, but identification with, the life that managers lead and the problems they face.

Our material has come from various sources. First there has been the staple diet of academics: the literature and the research studies; secondly has been a programme of interviews carried out by Jane Weightman with managers in a wide variety of organisations; thirdly has been the reactions and criticisms of students on courses, ranging from twenty years of age to sixty, from undergraduate to post-graduate, from first line supervisor to managing director. Our own experience has provided some input, but the most important moderating influence has been a panel of advisers who have commented on and discussed both our ideas and our typescript. We especially acknowledge their help: Jan Czerski, Technical and Commercial Manager, BASF Ltd; Christina Deegan, Personnel Officer, H.R. Howard & Sons Ltd; Mike Gore, Adviser for Special Education, Cheshire County Council; Donald Hood, General Manager, Marconi Space and Defence Systems; John Ithell, Personnel and Administration Manager, BBC Northern Region; and Geeti Khastgir, Divisional Nursing Officer, North West Regional Health Authority.

We should acknowledge our considerable debt to those managers who were interviewed by Jane in the course of her work and who provided many of the practical examples we have been able to use. Arthur Maddocks gave us considerable literary help.

Our publisher has obtained much critical comment for us from those who were willing to read drafts of the book without the impediment of knowing us too well. We should mention especially the comments made by Charles Handy and Rosemary Stewart. We also acknowledge the assistance of Margaret Lees in typing and editing, which gets better and better. As always the editorial and production personnel at Prentice-Hall have carried out thorough market research and provided invaluable advice on presentation and content, as well as maintaining production schedules that deliver exactly what they promise on exactly the day for which it was promised. All the mistakes and misunderstandings are our fault.

The example of self-assertion in everyday life is reprinted, with permission from *Person to Person* by Michael Argyle and Peter Trower, Harper & Row, London, 1979. "The General Technique of Skimming" is reprinted by permission of Penguin Books Ltd from *Read Better: Read Faster* by Manya and Eric de Leeuw, Pelican Books, 1965, p.105.

Universty of Manchester
Institute of Science & Technology
PO Box 88
Manchester M60 1QD

Derek Torrington
Jane Weightman
September 1984

THE BUSINESS
OF MANAGEMENT

Chapter One

INTRODUCTION TO MANAGEMENT

Mankind survives and operates through organisation. Organisation is needed to provide us with our motor cars and cultural amenities; our health care and education; our consumer goods and information services. For all these things we have to work together — to organise. We also *are* organised. Organisational life is the setting in which most of us spend our working hours and at least part of our leisure. A day at the office may well be followed by an evening with the amateur dramatic society or a weekend with the hockey team.

This book concentrates on the role of manager in contemporary organisation. It is about management as a job to be done by people with a wide range of specialist reponsibilities. It is not just about those who are ultimately in charge, but mainly about those who cope with bits of organisational functioning rather than with the grand design. We try to get inside the mind of the individual manager and answer questions like: How do I understand what is going on around me? Why do people behave this way? Why is my undertaking organised differently from the one in which my neighbour works? How do I cope with this situation? Do I understand the structure properly? Can I make a better contribution? Am I secure? How do I resolve this problem? How do I get things done? How do I meet my responsibilities?

Although there has been some reaction against very large scale and impersonal bureaucracy, working in concert rather than working alone seems to be a pervasive feature of our lives. The feats of David Livingstone or Francis Chichester are famed because of the courage and skill of individuals triumphing over formidable obstacles, but when Neil Armstrong walked on the surface of the moon it was the triumph of thousands who had contributed to the co-operative venture of the NASA space programme. Marie Lloyd or Harry Lauder were solo performers of great popularity, but the contemporary rock star travels with an entourage of thirty or forty people, all of whom are needed to put together the eventual performance. Individuals will continue to make great contributions to society on their own, but the major achievements that are often needed come from managed organisations; not only factories, offices and commercial undertakings, but hospitals and research centres, government departments and charitable bodies, schools and

1

colleges. For every novel representing the creative output of an individual there will be a hundred newspapers representing the creative accomplishment of a managed team. Management is not just a job done by people called "manager"; it is an aspect of the job done by all those who have to cope with the problems and opportunities of organisation: social workers, editors, ward sisters, chefs, housewives, engineers, school teachers, clergymen, administrators and many more.

There are many challenges to mankind that require a management contribution for their resolution. We have to learn to manage problems such as atmospheric pollution and the shortage of energy; technological innovation and the obsolescence of traditional skills; poverty in the third world and unemployment in the west. Few of these problems have a simple solution requiring no more than the necessary political will, and few of them depend on the intuitive insight of an individual. Managed activity is needed both to produce the solutions and to implement the programmes for those solutions to be put into operation.

Trewatha and Newport (1982) quote the late President J.F. Kennedy, writing in 1963:

> Much of the free world's success in using its human resources fully and with dignity can be laid to enlightened and progressive management. . . . It is to managers who grow with the needs and resources of their time that we must continue to look for the new ideas and their implementation to meet the challenges of the future.

1. THIS BOOK AND THE CONTEMPORARY MANAGEMENT SCENE

We have written this book in the hope of meeting a number of needs, based on work we have been doing with managers and management students in the last few years.

Managerial uncertainty. Large numbers of people have management jobs, or jobs with a management component, and most of them seem uncertain of what they are doing. For some this is caused by disappointment on finding out how little managers can achieve. Believing that managers make decisions, solve problems and shape the future, they find in practice that their scope is limited and that only a portion of their time is spent in these exciting activities. Other people are frustrated by problems of structure or policy within their organisation that they feel helpless to remedy. We have, however, found the most common reason to be uncertainty about simple things, like the nature of managerial work, the basic methods of working that are available, and the difference between different types of managerial role. In reading books about organisation, or participating in management courses, managers and aspiring managers frequently find the material fascinating but insufficient as it deals with what they see that others *ought* to do rather than what they personally *can* do.

Review Topic 1.1

To what extent are managers in control of the areas of the organisation for which they are responsible, and to what extent are they are the mercy of external factors?

Numbers and changing circumstances of managers. One carefully researched estimate is that the number of managers in Britain is now over 2¼ million, or ten per cent of the working population (Manpower Research Group, 1980 and Whiteley *et al.*, 1980). This does not include the many more who have a management dimension to their work without being regarded as managers.

The management career is changing also. In the expanding organisations that were the norm of industrialised societies until the middle 1970s there was at least the assumption that most managers would eventually be promoted to senior posts, and middle management positions were used as training posts for senior management. This was never really true, but it was believed widely enough for it to become a valid operating assumption. Increasingly middle management is a whole career for many people, and a respondent in one of our research studies described it as "terminal management". In another very large and *expanding* company we obtained comprehensive manpower information of the average age at which managers reached the grade at which they eventually retired. For senior managers this was between 46 and 53, but for middle managers it was between 43 and 48, so when middle managers retire they have been in their final grade for longer than senior managers, with all the problems of frustration and lack of fresh opportunity. Also, however, the job of the manager is typically described in terms of the job of the chief executive delegated in different-sized parcels to others and therefore similar to his. In fact the job of the chief executive is quite different from all other management jobs and it is unrealistic for managers at other levels to model their behaviour on that example.

Organisational size. Management and management ideas have both developed during the last fifty years against a background of increasing organisational size and an expanding number of jobs classified as managerial, bringing greater problems of co-ordination and communication and an emphasis on the administration of stable environments rather than dealing with the risks and uncertainty which are the reality of the modern organisation. Middle managers have been identified as the administrators of the stable state and with a vested interest in resisting change. White (1981) conducted a study in a south coast electrical company and explained middle managers' resistance to innovation by the fact that they are structurally dissociated from the satisfactions of ownership, technically dissociated from the process of production and socially dissociated from the work force.

The move to ever-increasing size has halted, especially in the number of people employed. Most large organisations have reduced the number of employees and many have decentralised their management operations so that only a small number of matters are reserved for resolution at the centre while operating units are managed with increased autonomy. A further aspect of this trend is that managers are finding their sphere of operations to be more compact. Some forecasters also think that the number of small, independent companies will increase. At the same time there is the growth of the employment complex, like the airport, shopping centre, or construction site or science park, where a large number of independent organisations share a common location, facilities and some aspects of co-ordination.

The Move to Specialisation Slackens.   With increasing organisational size came specialisation, much encouraged by two sets of interest groups: professional bodies and academic institutions. Professional bodies exist to serve the interests of those who share a specialised bit of the management action, such as purchasing or personnel. Once created, the professional body then has to strengthen and expand that specialised interest in order to exist itself. Higher education has adopted management with enthusiasm during the 1960s and 1970s in order to meet the demand from large numbers of students seeking an entry to the apparent joys of managerial life and a company car. The essence of academic study is the specialisation within academic disciplines, so both universities and the professional bodies have developed interest in the special interest manager. Between them they provide the most common entry ticket: qualification, so that people coming in to management have a developed specialisation.

One of the effects of the economic recession in the 1980s appears to be a move away from specialisation towards flexibility. The self-justifying specialised function that Parkinson (1957) caricatured so vividly is losing ground so that individual managers are rediscovering a need to operate in all areas of the business, which was regarded as the prime attribute of those who first experienced business school training.

This book is not about those specialised activities, but about the things that most managers do. It is, for example, about influencing people, but not about marketing; it is about selecting team members, but not about personnel management. Similarly it is about the majority of management work; not about the top manager making strategic decisions, but about the work of other managers in influencing those decisions and making them work.

2.   RECENT DIRECTIONS IN MANAGEMENT LITERATURE

In 1976 Rosemary Stewart published a slim volume about her research on management jobs. This won a management award for excellence and provided a practical method of categorising management jobs according to their content. This is considered more fully in Chapter 4, but is mentioned here because it marked a breakaway from the normative assumptions that had previously dominated management ideas.

Alistair Mant (1977) further shook the foundations by calling into question most of the status-ridden ideas about management and suggesting that we needed to refresh our memories about some very simple aspects of tough but fair leadership, and structures which clarify roles and allow people to have a say in things.

> We do not, it seems to me, require one penny more spent on fundamental research into the "unknown", but to understand why we are so bad at putting to use what we already know. (p. 207)

Charles Handy (1976) wrote a book about organisations that comes nearer than any other in recent years to being a British book about management as a job to be done, although there were only twenty pages out of four hundred with the title "On Being a Manager". The popularity of this work in comparison with the more clinical and often disdainful texts on organisation theory and organisation behaviour shows the interest in this sort of approach.

Working in North America Henry Mintzberg has been very influential with his book (1973) on the nature of managerial work, and his later analysis of the structuring of organisations (1979) that emphasises both the vertical and horizontal nature of co-ordination that managers need to consider.

This book concentrates on the job to be done, with methods that can be applied. We attempt to give reasoned arguments for those methods, demonstrating the logic of doing something and helping to analyse which methods are appropriate for which settings. Too often only the academic or only the practical is available. Where a bridge can be made between the two, a more forceful method is developed, as it has to stand the test of both logic and use.

Review Topic 1.2

Think of one or two methods of managing that are *only* academic and one or two that are *only* practical. What are their shortcomings?

---

3. A WORKING DEFINITION

Probably the best-known definition of management is that of Mary Parker Follet, who described it as:

> The art of getting things done through people.

This is neat but insufficient as the emphasis is solely on getting other people to do things, without giving due weight to other tactics and resources. It also implies that the "other people" are subordinates, although they are frequently peers, outsiders or superiors in a hierarchical sense.

The sales manager aiming to increase sales may achieve that by getting the salesmen to work harder or more effectively, but he may also achieve the objective by altering the advertising policy. We suggest five headings for the dimensions of management as a job to be done:

a)   Managers have conflicting *goals*. They have to meet production targets
     at the same time as keeping costs down. They achieve profit margins
     but also satisfy the needs of subordinates. They seek to use economic
     methods of production but also satisfy environmental controls. They
     are always seeking for a balance to ensure that one goal is not attained
     at the expense of another.

b)   Managers are held *responsible* for results, not only their own results,
     but also the results of others. The branch bank manager is held
     responsible for everything that happens on his premises. If there are
     mistakes, he takes the blame from his superiors, from his staff and from
     the customers, all of whom have a touching faith in his ability to satisfy
     their various expectations.

c)   Managers work in *organisations*, with all the resources, opportunities
     and frustrations that such a setting provides. The complexity of the
     organisation provides a wide range of skills and facilities that can be
     deployed, but it also requires co-operation, synchronisation and
     communication. Enabling the complex organisation to perform is a
     crucial part of the manager's job that makes it distinctive from some
     other leadership functions like, for instance, captaining a cricket team.

d)   The stable state for managers is *uncertainty*. There will be planning and
     procedures to reduce the level of uncertainty, but the unexpected
     problem, the unprecedented situation is the realm of the manager.
     Generally the operators in an organisation are able to cope with
     predictable situations as a result of their training, information and
     authorisation, but have to call on managerial assistance to deal with the
     unfamiliar, either because the manager has more technical
     understanding and experience or because the manager has an element
     of hierarchical authority to take certain decisions which have not been
     delegated to the operators.

e)   Managers work with and through other *people*. Here we are not quite
     back to Mary Parker Follet, because the people are not only
     subordinates but also organisational peers, customers, clients, suppliers
     and other outsiders who provide goods or services to the organisation,
     or who use its products or services.

The initial letters of the key words above produce the mnemonic
GROUP, and increasingly managers find all those five aspects of
management are being mediated through groups. There is the group
decision-making of boards of directors and senior management teams,
planning conferences in advertising and the media, autonomous working
groups in factories, joint production committees in industrial democracy
exercises, selection panels, suggestion committee meetings, staff meetings
and all the other ways in which managing becomes a corporate activity rather
different from the emphasis on individuals that until recently was the sole
focus for management work.

We use the term "manager" throughout this book, but the comments are not only relevant to those who carry that formal title. Most of those who work in organisations have a management dimension to their lives, although those with the formal title may be more fully occupied with such activities.

4. THE STRUCTURE OF THIS BOOK

We draw on the resources of varying strands of research, mostly from those working on the subjects of organisation, but from other fields as well within the broad spectrum of management investigation.

The book is organised in four sections:

Management and Organisation

Here we present an account and interpretation of how management has developed from various sources and how emphasis and method have changed in recent years, followed by an account of the different types of organisation and the types of management jobs within them. The section closes with an analysis of management work that forms the basis of our thinking in the remainder of the book.

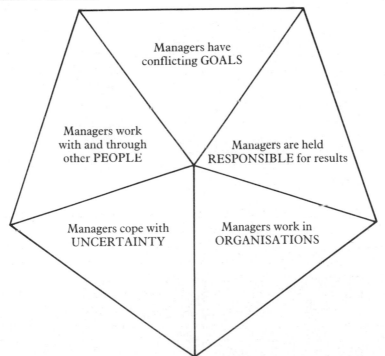

Managers have
conflicting GOALS

Managers work
with and through
other PEOPLE

Managers are held
RESPONSIBLE for results

Managers cope with
UNCERTAINTY

Managers work in
ORGANISATIONS

Figure 1.1   Five Dimensions of the Manager's Job

Working in the Organisation

All managers to some extent have to cope with the organisational context and the network of relationships in which they are enmeshed. They will be a part of a political system, both formal and informal, that has to be understood by its members. The mechanics of these systems are the channels of communication between individuals and groups, the administrative procedures through which action takes place and the committees in which decisions are made, information disseminated and possibilities explored. To operate in these situations the manager is helped if he can understand and predict the behaviour of those around him. In this context he has little power to instruct others, but he will frequently need the support and compliance of others. So we consider ways in which it is possible to win the consent of others without having formal, hierarchical authority "over" them.

The Working Team

Most managers have subordinates and are expected, both by their superiors and by their subordinates, to be responsible for the work that the subordinates do and to integrate the activities of several into a coherent whole. To do this the manager depends on various types of authority and an understanding of the need for autonomy by individual team members if there is to be effective working together. Some of the members will be selected for team membership by the manager and he will either coach them in their role or teach them the job they have to do. Many of the managers to whom we have spoken, talk wryly about the problem of the team member who has *not* been selected, but inherited by the manager. All too often the working relationship is unsatisfactory to both the manager and the team member. It may, however, be possible to tailor the job in some way to fit the potential and expectations of the incumbent while still eliciting from him the necessary contribution.

Planning, Problem-Solving and Decision-Making

Managers have to plan the work of their team and the contribution made to the overall organisation, although this has to fit within other, all-embracing planning and must not be so detailed as to remove reasonable and necessary initiative from team members in planning their own work. Within the planning framework there are problems to be solved and decisions to be made.

Personal Effectiveness

Any professional training involves developing features of self-discipline and method to make the individual effective. In this section of the book we examine the methods of self-organisation that the manager needs to become effective, including material on effectiveness in reading and writing, presenting ideas to groups of people orally, and creative innovation.

To ensure that all the material is as accurate and up-to-date as possible, we have based the book not only on the knowledge and experience of the authors and a detailed review of the literature, but also on a programme of empirical investigation among managers in varied organisations.

There are five recurring aspects of presentation of the material to explain here. There are many *references*, so that the reader can follow up particular features of the book about which he needs a deeper understanding. We have also given separate treatment to *interactions*. Most important incidents in management life have a face-to-face encounter at the centre, where the manager meets with one or more people to settle something or move forward with a project in a way which is not possible without that meeting, which requires careful preparation and management to produce results. The marketing expert spends weeks in preparation and planning, but the crucial event is the meeting with the customer. We have picked interactive situations that are widely used or relevant and provide detailed comment on them. We have also singled out administrative *drills* that are widely needed by managers and give detailed models of those. In each chapter there are *review topics* to assist the reader to reflect on the issues presented. Finally we conclude each chapter with one or more *summary propositions* that are working formulations stemming from the chapter material.

SUMMARY PROPOSITIONS

1.1. Although managing the work of organisations is a widespread activity, many managers lack understanding of their role and knowledge of simple methods that can be used in managerial work.

1.2. The main dimensions of the manager's job are that they have conflicting goals, are held responsible for results, work in organisations, cope with uncertainty, and work with and through other people.

REFERENCES

Handy, C.B. *Understanding Organizations*, Penguin Books, Harmondsworth, Middlesex, 1976.

Manpower Research Group, "Occupational Change in the British Economy" in *Employment Gazette*, vol. 88, no. 12, December 1980, pp. 1204–1208.

Mant, A. *The Rise and Fall of the British Manager*, Macmillan, London, 1977.

Mintzberg, H. *The Nature of Managerial Work*, Harper & Row, New York, 1973.

Mintzberg, H. *The Structuring of Organizations*, Prentice Hall Inc., Englewood Cliffs, New Jersey, 1979.

Parkinson, C.N. *Parkinson's Law*, John Murray, London, 1957.

Stewart, R. *Contrasts in Management*, McGraw Hill, Maidenhead, 1976.

Trewatha, R.L. and Newport, M.G. *Management*, 3rd edition, Business Publications, Plano, Texas, 1982.

White C. "Why Won't Managers Co-operate?" in *Industrial Relations Journal*, March/April 1981, pp. 61–72.

Whiteley, J.D., Wilson, R.A., Smith, D.J.E., "Industrial and Occupational Change" in Lindley, R.M., *Economic Change and Employment Policy*, Macmillan, London, 1980, pp. 68–140.

Part I

MANAGEMENT AND ORGANISATION

The context in which he works is more important to managers than it is to most working people, and management cannot be understood without seeing how ideas about it have developed.

This part of the book first reviews how management ideas have been developing since the earliest days of civilisation, with elements from antiquity blending with those of recent years. Different types of organisation structure currently in use are considered before examining how management jobs differ with function and place in the hierarchy. The closing Chapter of this section tries to answer the questions: "What do managers actually do?" and "What makes management work different from the work that other people in the organisation do?"

At the end of Chapter 5 there is a figure (*5.4 The dynamics of management*) that shows the interdependence of the first five chapters.

Chapter Two

THE DEVELOPMENT OF MANAGEMENT

Although management is a relatively recent notion in human affairs, it is but a specialised development in the long-running saga of human organisation. Our understanding of modern management phenomena is enlightened by searching in the past to see how the process evolved.

1. THE EGYPTIANS AND THE SUMERIANS

The modern nation state evolved 4,500 years ago and was brought into being by the building of the great pyramids at Giza, near Heliopolis in Egypt. The pyramids exercise a strange fascination over the minds of modern men and women. We marvel at the largest stone structures in the world, each containing enough stone to build a wall all the way round a country the size of France. The technological achievement of building with such precision and durability was extraordinary, but the reason for their being built is even more intriguing. Mendelssohn (1974) has argued that the great pyramids were built as a method of creating an integrated human community the size of a state. Previously man had lived in communities no larger than a tribe or village, but the increasing size of the Egyptian population required a larger-scale pattern of organisation in order to make optimum use of the resources of the Nile, the sole source of water to irrigate the land on which the food was grown. Not only was the water seasonal, with inundation followed by drought, but the level varied from year to year, as is mentioned in the Old Testament prophecy of Joseph about seven fat years being followed by seven lean years.

For the people to be fed there had to be co-operation, not just between families and within the local village, but between villages that were widely dispersed. That sort of co-operation depends on social organisation to bring about commitment, obedience and sacrifice for the sake of benefit. People learn to co-operate because they want to; no system of imposing authority on the unwilling can operate unless either the majority are willing or the leaders have exceptional coercive power at their disposal. The Pharaohs did not have exceptional coercive power, so a mode of co-operation had to be devised, and the pyramid project — that was to last for a hundred years — came into existence.

For three months each year 100,000 to 120,000 men were gathered together on the Giza plateau to co-operate on this immense task. These men left their families and their homes for three reasons. First the pyramids were great projects on which to be engaged, providing an experience quite different from the limited routine of village agriculture. Secondly, the resurrection of the Pharaoh, after a suitable burial, was essential to the afterlife of the common man. You ensured your own afterlife by contributing to the appropriate interment of your Pharaoh. Thirdly, the surrounding system of social organisation provided the Pharaoh with centralised stocks of grain for distribution during the lean years.

This project achieved a number of outcomes:

A Civil Service Infrastructure.   If 100,000 men were to work on the arduous physical labour of cutting and manhandling blocks of stone weighing fifteen tons each, they had to be not only organised, but fed and housed. This required a large number of administrators and a bureaucratic system.

A Sense of Nationhood.   The workers developed a sense of commitment to, and membership of, the nation as well as their family and village, because of the common task on which they were engaged. Patriotism was born.

Dependence on the Centre.   The Pharaoh had the grain. So the common people were economically dependent on him for survival, and the central administration acquired a steadily increasing hold over the population as a whole.

Hierarchy.   The organisation and co-ordination of such a large labour force produced a hierarchy of authority as the logical means of integrating dispersed effort. There is an echo of this in an often quoted passage from the Old Testament where Moses, having led the exodus of the Jewish people out of their bondage in Egypt, is counselled by his father-in-law Jethro to set up a system of delegation that must have been very similar to that which they had experienced at the hands of the Pharaoh:

> ... search for capable, God-fearing men among all the people, honest and incorruptible men, and appoint them over the people as officers over units of a thousand, of a hundred, of fifty or of ten. They shall sit as a permanent court for the people; they must refer difficult cases to you but decide simple cases themselves. In this way your burden will be lightened, and they will share it with you.
>
> (New English Bible, Exodus, ch. 18, vv. 19–22).

The pyramid project provided the pattern for the nation state, which was not only successful in Egypt, but was taken as the pattern for succeeding nations and other large-scale organisations like armies and the Roman Catholic Church. In turn it became the pattern of schools, hospitals, local government and business.

The principle was simple and logical, and it worked because the task facing the organisation was relatively simple once the original design and technological work had been done. After that the project required small expertise and huge labour.

The main features of the pyramid organisation are to be found in all large-scale contemporary enterprises. The hierarchy and the "civil service infrastructure" of central administration binds the dependent employee to the corporation. Wages, salaries and fringe benefits have replaced the stock of corn and the employing organisation may well be one in which the employee takes great pride, but the company pension scheme for support in the afterlife of retirement is a poor substitute for the eternity with Osiris that Pharaoh could offer. Furthermore the modern-day corporation will seldom have a single undertaking for its employees of the simplicity of pyramid building. So the pattern of human organisation that has been with us since antiquity is no longer sufficient.

The earliest civilisation known in the fertile crescent of the Middle East was that of the Sumerians, slightly before the early Egyptians. Their main contribution is that they invented writing, because their priests kept business and legal records on clay tablets.

Woolley (1963) excavated extensively in the area of Ur of the Chaldees and demonstrated how priests in Sumer achieved great power. The ordinary Sumerians did not anticipate the blissful afterlife that was the expectation of the Egyptian pyramid-builders; they expected it to be at best a dismal reflection of their time on earth and their apprehension led them to offer constant propitiation to the Gods. The agents of this propitiation were the priests, who were the only ones able to carry out the ritual. The ritual involved sacrifices with the quality of the propitiation being related to the volume of sacrifice that had been made. It was also the priests who kept the records of what sacrifices had been offered and by whom.

Records were the basis of control and became the avenue to an elite position of power. As organisations have developed and evolved, the need for centralised information has remained and carried with it the power to control. The main contemporary examples are the accountancy profession and the computer, which are used to control complex organisations, and which are shrouded in mysteries which their practitioners use to maintain their exclusive access to the data banks.

Cleverly (1971) has described a number of instances in contemporary organisational life where there are clear rituals, and has shown the way in which management specialists establish themselves as a quasi-priesthood in becoming the sole custodians and interpreters of their specialised mysteries;

although these mysteries will be those of cost centres and management development rather than the more urgent concerns of the Sumerians.

2. MACHIAVELLI

As the western world grew up the ideas and methods produced by the Egyptians and Sumerians were refined in the Greek city states, the Roman Empire and the Roman Catholic Church, described by one pair of contemporary management writers as "the most effective formal organisation in the history of western civilisation" (Koontz & O'Donnell, 1976).

A novel and original contribution came in the writings of a disgraced Florentine civil servant of the late fifteenth century. Niccolo Machiavelli served as secretary to the Florentine Republic from 1498 until 1512, when he was dismissed and imprisoned on the charge of conspiring to overthrow the Medici family, who had returned to power. When he was released he started writing, but his classic *Il Principe* was not published until 1532, five years after his death. In this book Machiavelli makes a clear distinction between ethics and politics, which brought him long-running notoriety, although many statesmen have followed the spirit of this concept by not allowing objection on ethical grounds to interfere with political and diplomatic goals. It is an easier notion for managers to accept as they can argue that social responsibility is drawn from them by legislation, government policy, employee resistance, union power or consumer choice, so that their task is to get on with running the business as effectively as possible within those constraints.

The main interest in Machiavelli's ideas lies, however, in his analysis of how the prince (or leader, or manager) meets his obligations. These have been resurrected for the management audience by Jay (1967) and the main points are:

Cohesive Organisation.   The prince should maintain the cohesiveness of his organisation by binding to him his friends and those on whom he will depend. This will involve giving them rewards for their contribution and making sure that they know what the prince expects and what they can expect from him.

Mass Consent. However cohesive the power structure of the organisation, the prince has to maintain the consent of the governed, as this is the source of his authority. Not only does it give him authority over the governed, it also gives him authority over his 'courtiers'.

Leadership. Cohesive organisation and mass consent can only be achieved if the prince is a leader and example-setter for his people, being wise and tempering necessary justice with mercy.

Review Topic 2.1

Think of contemporary examples of cohesive organisation, mass consent, leadership and toughness, as defined by Macchiavelli.

Toughness.   There will be attempts to unseat the prince, so he must have the toughness to resist any such attempts and be ruthless with the instigators.

This cool appraisal of what is involved has given our language the word *Machiavellian*, to mean cunning, amoral and opportunist. It is interesting that the word "management" is derived from the Italian sixteenth century word *maneggiare*, meaning to control or train, especially relating to horses. The conception of the manager as devious was developed further when the job emerged as a distinct entity in the nineteenth century:

> At this point the concept of "manager" was a neutral one, even pejorative. Thus, Robert Owen, writing in 1811: "My intention was not to be a *mere* manager". "We rely not upon management or *trickery*, but upon our own hearts and heads" (Jowett, 1881). "Talent for *intrigue or management* usually counts for more than debating power" (Bryce, 1888). In the more refined employments — the colonial and civil services — there were no managers but "administrators".
>
> (Mant, 1979, pp. 21–22).

3.   THE INDUSTRIAL REVOLUTION

Slowly the patterns of human organisation began to evolve and the role of the leader was clarified, but then came the watershed of the Industrial Revolution which was to transform first Britain and then the rest of Europe and the United States into industrialised nations. Hitherto the practice of management had been confined to church, state and army; the job of prelate, prince or officer. Now the great institutions of commerce and industry were born, and the traditional leaders of society had no place in them — wanted no place in them — so we acquired a new occupation and a new class — the bourgeoisie:

> The bourgeoisie has created more massive and more colossal productive forces than have all preceding generations together. Subjection of nature's forces to man, machinery, application of chemistry to industry and agriculture, steam navigation, railways, electric telegraphs, clearing of whole continents for cultivation, canalization of rivers, whole populations conjured out of the ground — what earlier century had even a presentiment that such productive forces slumbered in the lap of social labour?'
>
> (Marx, 1848, p. 147)

The wealth of technological innovation at this time brought great economies of scale and the invention of power-driven machinery transformed the production process. The capital cost of the new equipment was beyond the individual worker so that he had to move out of his home and into the factory, where the machines could be economically located under one roof and efficiency could be enhanced by skilled co-ordination of employees' work.

Marglin (1971), using extensive examples from the weaving industry, argues that it was the discipline and supervision of the labour force in the factory that was most important in reducing costs as there was greater labour input, less embezzlement and patents were easier to monitor. Also by increasing the division of labour the entrepreneur had an essential role as integrator, controlling the process and quantity of output, as the worker was now selling his labour rather than a product.

In 1800 James Watt and Matthew Boulton built a new factory to make steam engines and introduced aspects of practice that were to form the basis of production organisation for more than 150 years:

Flow of Work.   Having estimated the demand for their engines, Watt and Boulton laid out their factory for a smooth flow of work between the various operations and equipped it with machines that were timed so that the expected output would match as closely as possible the anticipated demand. At the same time the jobs of individual employees were broken down and analysed to estimate their contribution — the beginning of time and motion study.

Wages.   Wage payment arrangements were developed to be consistent with the requirements of each job. As many jobs as possible were paid on a piece rate basis so that income was linked to output, and weekly rates were paid for those jobs where such measurement was not feasible.

Records.   Detailed records were developed for cost accounting, so that there was control of direct and indirect costs, enabling the managers to identify areas of inefficiency and high productivity. With this information the managers were able to control the operation by trying to raise the efficiency of those areas where it was defective and adjusting the payment system.

The flow of work had been one of the organisational problems of the early Egyptians, the keeping of records for control had been developed by the Sumerian priests, but the elaboration of wages as an impersonal means of motivating employees rather than the leadership ideas of, for instance, Machiavelli, was a new departure and a new breeding ground for the development of middle management expertise.

4. SCIENTIFIC MANAGEMENT

Perhaps the best-known name among management pioneers is that of the American Frederick Taylor, who was able to introduce considerable increases in productive efficiency by questioning traditional work practices and finding the one "best way" in which each job should be done. Having determined the best way the job should be done, Taylor selected appropriate employees, trained them in the method and required them to perform the job in the precise, described manner. Like Watt and Boulton, Taylor linked individual wages to individual output. So higher productivity brought higher wages and increased profitability.

Although much criticised, he introduced the concepts of management of work rather than simple custom and practice, and some of his key innovations — selection, training and job analysis — still form the basis of modern personnel management. Also his approach to problem-solving has served as a model for succeeding generations of managers. Although Taylor is the outstanding figure of scientific management, other contributors were Henry Gantt, who invented the planning and control tool known as the Gantt chart, which we look at in Chapter 18; and Frank and Lillian Gilbreth, who developed time and motion study with such effectiveness that they were able to increase the number of bricks a man could lay in an hour from 120 to 350.

5. ADMINISTRATIVE MANAGEMENT

Taylor analysed work from the perspective of the supervisor, but his contemporary, Fayol, evolved a top management theory. Henri Fayol is one of the few management pioneers who was neither British nor American. He was the French managing director of a mining company and enunciated five functions of management: planning, organising, commanding, co-ordinating and controlling. He also produced no fewer than fourteen different principles of management and made possible the teaching of management as an academic subject by producing a viable conceptual framework. A typical Fayol principle was his fourth — unit of command:

> For any action whatsoever, an employee should receive orders from one superior only.
>
> (Fayol, 1949, p. 24).

Reading Fayol today it is not easy to see the scale of his contribution as his assertions are mainly commonplace. Also his theories stemmed only from his own experience and observation, without any research data for further validation. The fourteen principles have been derided as 'proverbs' being so vague as to have no practical value to the practitioner. It has been argued that he was concerned only with the inner structure of organisation rather than its operating context, and — like Taylor — regarded the employee as a mindless robot to be manipulated only by financial incentives.

A contemporary of Fayol, Mary Parker Follet was the first to consider the organisation in its context and modified the universalism claimed by Fayol by her "law of the situation" that was a forerunner of contingency theory.

Although not an original thinker, Lyndall Urwick can be said to have summarised the whole of the work of the original theorists to produce a logical arrangement or general system of administration. As with the precision of Taylor, here too was to be seen the conviction that the employees have to be adaptable to the requirements of the organisation:

> In good engineering practice design must come first. Similarly, in good social practice design should come first. Logically it is inconceivable that any individual should be appointed to a position carrying a large salary, without a clear idea of the part which that position is meant to play in the general social pattern of which it is a component, the responsibilities and relationships attached to it and the standard of performance which is expected in return for the expenditure.
>
> (Urwick, 1943, p. 43).

Although no disciple of Fayol, the German sociologist, Weber, influenced this school of thought by his analysis of bureaucracy. He was not a practitioner but someone who had studied economics, religion and political science before turning his sociological insights to organisations. He argued that the market structure of western societies required business organisations to be highly structured, or *bureaucratic*, with the following qualities:

Role Definition. The duties and responsibilities of organisation members are clearly defined.

Hierarchy of Authority. There is a clear chain of relationships with all members knowing precisely to whom they are responsible and who is responsible to them.

Rules and Procedures. The organisation operates according to an elaborate system of rules determining the way in which each member should perform. Records should provide precedents to be followed so as to ensure consistency.

Qualification for Office. People are appointed to positions on the basis of merit that is formally attested and subject to systematic selection and training.

Impartiality. Members of the organisation discharge their duties without heat or partiality, motivated by the prospect of moving up the hierarchy, as well as by a sense of duty.

This has proved to be a very accurate account of how many organisations have functioned, especially the large and complex, but there is a tendency for rules to become an end in themselves and for personal initiative to be discouraged.

6. THE HUMAN RELATIONS MOVEMENT

A number of researchers set out to redress what they saw as an imbalance in the work of Taylor and Fayol, by taking greater account of the mind as well as the body of the employee.

The most famous member of what came to be known as the human relations school of management thought was Elton Mayo, who conducted an experiment at a Philadelphia textile mill in which rest periods were introduced with the result that productivity increased sharply, morale improved and labour turnover dropped. Mayo reasoned that the rest periods helped to lessen the effects of two key problems: fatigue and monotony.

The next step was a series of studies at the Hawthorne Works of the Western Electric Company, which were to continue for eight years and provide a seminal work for management researchers. The main conclusions were:

Work Pacing. The pace at which employees produce is one set informally by the work group.

Recognition. Acknowledgement of an employee's contribution by those in authority tends to increase output, as do other forms of social approval.

Social Interaction. The opportunities provided by the working situation for social interaction between fellow workers, especially if they could select for interaction those with whom they were compatible, enhanced job satisfaction and sometimes influenced output.

Grievances. Morale is improved by providing scope for employees to air their grievances.

The Hawthorne Effect. Changes in working arrangements often lead to an improvement simply because of the effect of their novelty and the workers concerned being at the centre of attention. This discovery was made because of the methodological confusion of the Hawthorne studies.

Here was a change in emphasis away from the precision of Taylorism. The worker was no longer the extension of the machine responsive only to the electric current of financial incentives; instead he was seen as an individual and a member of a social group, with attitudes and behaviours that were the key to his effectiveness. The focus, as with Taylor, was on the supervisory task, but another contribution from this period took up the strands of Fayol.

Chester Barnard was an executive of considerable, varied experience who was dissatisfied with earlier theoretical explanations and produced his own. He regarded the executive as having the task of maintaining co-operative effort, which was achieved through three functions. First he established and maintained a system of *communications*, largely by means of informal organisation and careful selection of organisation members. Second, *essential effort* was won from members by inducing them to identify with the business. Third, *purpose and objectives* had to be formulated, via a system of delegated authority so that each individual was responsible for some segment of the overall enterprise. Suffusing all that he said was the theme that authority could only be effective when accepted. This was not the image of managerial power and infallibility that had been in the minds of Taylor and Fayol, but Machiavelli had spoken of the need for mass consent and the manual workers of twentieth century America were not as compliant as the factory workers of nineteenth century Britain. Management was rediscovering some of the eternal verities about human organisation.

7. THE MANAGEMENT THEORY JUNGLE

The period following Mayo and Barnard has been one of uncertainty and conflicting views in developing management ideas often represented by the latest fashion rather than some systematic development of well-founded theories. With the increased status and academic respectability given to the use of scientific method, social scientists in the field of management have often divided problems into manageable units so they can carry out an academically viable study. For example, the comparison of two payment systems can be carried out empirically; whereas the general question of gaining the compliance of workers cannot. This division of problems is also reflected in the diversity of schools or approaches found in management literature. The *quantitative approach* was developed after the Second World War, during which mathematical modelling had been used to solve some of the operational problems of warfare. Techniques of operations research have been devised which have had great success in dealing with problems of production planning, warehousing and materials. The advent of the computer has boosted this field of work in defining objectives and constructing models for the solution of complex problems. The contribution to management effectiveness has been considerable, not only in the particular problems for which it has been able to provide optimal solutions, but also for its spin-off in management thinking generally by encouraging an orderly approach to problem-solving and measuring performance.

The *behavioural approach* has moved in so many directions that it is difficult to contain it under a single, general heading. The main thrust is obviously in studying how managers get things done through people, but some advocate an understanding of the individual as a means towards more effective management and others see management as a social system of interdependent groups:

> The recognition of the organised enterprise as a social organism — made up in turn of many social organisms within it, subject to all the attitudes, habits, pressures and conflicts of the cultural environment of people — has been helpful to both the theorist and the practical manager. Among other helpful aspects are the awareness of the institutional foundations of organization authority, the influence of informal organization and such social factors as those Wight Bakke has called "bonds of organization".
>
> (Koontz & O'Donnell, 1976, p.58).

The behavioural approach has produced invaluable insights relating to communication, motivation and leadership.

Continuing in the tradition of Fayol is what can be described as the *process approach*, in which management is viewed as a process of interrelated functions. It has the great appeal of providing a framework for systematic study and analysis, with variations of Fayol's five functions: planning, organising, commanding, co-ordinating and controlling. There follows the temptation to derive management principles from the functional process, and this is one of the main reasons for criticism of the approach. A typical principle is that managerial responsibility is absolute. He cannot escape from responsibility for the activities of this individual subordinates: he can delegate authority but not responsibility. To many commentators this is a statement of value rather than fact, is of little practical help, is not always feasible and attributes an unhealthy degree of social superiority to the manager.

Forty years after Mary Parker Follett had first spoken of the law of the situation, research studies were undertaken to demonstrate the situational nature of management, which became known as *contingency theory*:

> The basic idea of the contingency theorists is that the nature of the organization's technology, its size, its legal incorporation, the character of its markets, and other factors confront the organization with some opportunities as well as constraints and problems and therefore set the tone of the organization's adaptation as revealed by its structure. The idea is an elaboration of the biologist's functional view of the adaptation of living forms to their environment. For example, elephants have trunks to enable them to feed from their great height, and apes have prehensile fingers and toes to enable them to swing from trees. Contingency theory indicates the kinds of structure that may be appropriate responses to each of several different organizational contexts or situations.
>
> (Khandwalla, 1977, p.236).

Contingency thinking was earlier applied to studies of leadership and has demonstrated the impracticability of seeking universal principles. The best type of organisation structure, leadership style and method of control depends on the particular features of the situation. There are further references to this later in the book, especially in the section of Chapter 3 about differentiated structures and in the figure at the end of Chapter 4.

In the United Kingdom the development of *industrial relations* activity since the 1950s has had two main effects on the work of managers. First it has modified the view that the manager is the only focus for managerial activity and decision-making. The plurality of legitimate interests in the organisation has been recognised to the extent that management is now seen as a process through which managers and others seek to bring those varied interests into balance.

This has led to the second effect, the extended use of procedures: not simply administrative procedures as ways of obviating decision-making for situations where a formula has already been worked out, but also control procedures, like grievance and discipline, whereby management and employee delimit the scope of each other's activities by specifying the range of freedom of action each has.

M. Rose (1975) has argued that the various schools have continued to develop in an evolutionary manner. This has the attraction of integrating everything currently known and the latest product is the best. However, there seem to be fundamental differences in the basic assumptions of some schools that have not yet been reconciled or integrated. This has been well described by Burrell and Morgan (1979) who argue that some contrasting assumptions could never be reconciled.

8.   A BURST BUBBLE?

In some ways the development of management ideas now seems to have gone too far, in making of management something far more elaborate and mysterious than reality dictates, particularly in Britain and the United States where the management movement has flourished much more than in other industrialised nations. The fields of academic study that have expanded recently, and which have a direct bearing on management education, are organisation theory, organisation behaviour and — to a lesser extent — industrial relations and marketing. Those studying organisations have shifted the emphasis away from how managers manage organisations towards how people perform in organisations. As students from developing countries have flocked to the business schools of Britain and the United States, the relevance of Anglo-Saxon models to other situations has been shown to be small, especially with the rise as economic competitors of countries, like Japan and Western Germany, that do not seem to have a management movement at all:

The puzzle, then is to understand why we downgrade so many of the jobs that really matter whilst building around the idea of "management" a plethora of myths, shibboleths and incantations which our most successful competitors seem able to do without.   (Mant, 1979, p.3).

This is further developed in Fores and Glover (1978).

Review Topic 2.2

Why do we build around management a plethora of myths, shibboleths and incantations, while downgrading so many of the jobs that really matter?

The national wish for economic prosperity and the individual wish for employment offering status and material benefits have combined to impute great significance to the arts and sciences of management, so that the number of management jobs in the economy is increasing more than other types of job and the number of people seeking management training now exceeds the number pursuing training for the careers of, for example, teaching.

Perhaps we have become too much concerned with the grand design and lost a necessary emphasis on management-as-a-job-to-be-done. With that in mind, what are the lessons of the past? What are those aspects of management work that can be seen through a number of studies and pieces of experience that have been reviewed in this chapter?

First of all there are four central activities or methods of operation which form the core of all management operations:

Hierarchy.   Since the pyramid-building project, hierarchy has been used to distribute power, to centralise control and to provide the basic pattern of social organisation for those employed in the organisation.

Information.   The Sumerians established, and the industrial revolution pioneers developed, the storage and use of information as a means of making organisation work.

Specialisation.   As organisations grow in size the need for specialisation and economies of scale increase, and in turn that specialisation expands the need for management to co-ordinate the activity of specialists. The work of Taylor is the principal contribution to this type of practice.

Social Organisation.   The human relations movement demonstrated the importance of social organisation in the face-to-face group of working colleagues as an additional feature to traditional hierarchy.

Those four means to an end are fundamental and universal, although the emphasis will vary and the degree of development of the fourth much reduces the significance of the first.

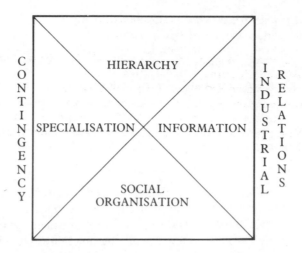

Figure 2.1   The Central Methods of Management and their Modifiers

There are then two important *modifiers* of those four central methods:

Contingency.   Management theory could be more precise if its fields of activity were more uniform, but the infinite variety of situations in which management is practised requires specific methods to be tailored to specific situations.

Industrial Relations.   There is a constant challenge from below in the hierarchy to the legitimacy of management actions, and this challenge can be channelled through formal organisation so that management decision-making cannot be unilateral but has to be the outcome of negotiation.

SUMMARY PROPOSITIONS

2.1. Management is but one aspect of human organisation, the development of which can be traced back to the earliest days of civilisation.

2.2. Some recent developments in management thought have confused rather than clarified our understanding of management, imputing to it an unjustified mystique.

2.3. There are four central activities or methods of operation forming the core of all management operations: hierarchy, information, specialisation and social organisation.

REFERENCES

Burrell, G. and Morgan, G., *Sociological Paradigms and Organisational Analysis*, Heinemann, London, 1979.

Cleverly, G., *Managers and Magic*, Longman, London, 1971.

Fayol, H., *General and Industrial Management*, Pitman, London, 1949.

Fores, M. & Glover, I., *Manufacturing and Management*, HMSO, London, 1978.

Jay A., *Management and Machiavelli*, Penguin Books, Harmondsworth, 1967.

Khandwalla P.N., *Design of Organizations*, Harcourt, Brace, Jovanovich, New York, 1977.

Koontz, H. & O'Donnell, C., *Management: a Systems and Contingency Analysis of Managerial Functions*, McGraw-Hill, New York, 1976.

Mant, A., *The Rise and Fall of the British Manager*, Pan Books, London, 1979.

Marglin, S., *What do Bosses Do? The Origins and Functions of Hierarchy in Capitalist Production*, Harvard University, Department of Economics, 1971.

Marx, K., Communist Manifesto, 1848, quoted in Bottomore, T. B. and Rubel, M., *Karl Marx: Selected Writings in Sociology and Social Philosophy*, Penguin Books, Harmondsworth, Middlesex, 1979.

Mendelssohn, K., *The Riddle of the Pyramids*, Thames & Hudson, London, 1974.

Rose, M., *Industrial Behaviour: Theoretical Developments since Taylor*, Allen Lane, London, 1975.

Taylor, F.W., *The Principles of Scientific Management*, Harper, New York, 1947.

Urwick, L.F., *The Elements of Administration*, Pitman, London, 1973.

Woolley, L., *Digging up the Past*, Penguin, London, 1963.

Chapter Three

TYPES OF ORGANISATION STRUCTURE

A popular misconception of organisation structure is of integrated precision in human action:

> What you may expect to see — but don't — is an animated organisation chart — a pyramid of little boxes, each sitting astride seven others, and seven more under each of those seven, and seven more, and so on. Perhaps too, you expect to see each of the top boxes occupied by a faceless figure in a gray flannel uniform and the lower boxes occupied by figures, also faceless, in overalls. Each figure is busily pushing levers to make other faceless figures turn and jump in unison until the whistle blows, when they all stop together.
>
> (Leavitt, Dill and Eyring, 1973, p.3).

For some this is a glimpse of nightmare, while for others it is a vision of perfection, taking the comfortable Victorian view of class structure — a place for everyone and everyone in his place — and adding to it the feature of specialised, interlocking tasks.

There are difficulties about this view. First, it is not true; no organisation operates with that degree of mechanical precision. Secondly, attempts to achieve precision of that type are ineffective as employees are not sufficiently uniform in their abilities and experience to fit neatly into boxes and are seldom willing to be constrained to that degree. Thirdly, the rigidity of the arrangements inhibits change and makes the organisation inappropriate for new challenges from the environment and the opportunities provided by technological change.

In the 1970s distaste for the formal structure became so great that there was a tendency to throw the baby out with the bathwater as enthusiasm for anti-structure developed. Face-to-face relationships were to replace formal reporting as the norm and the purpose of the organisation was no more than to service the freewheeling activities of its members. That vogue has altered but the feasibility of the rigid structure has been shown as dubious. A more common view is now of structure as being necessary but ideally sufficiently flexible as a system to enable bits of the structure to be altered or removed so that the remaining bits can adapt to change rather than having the entire edifice collapse. There is much more emphasis on communication between people and groups in the structure and an acknowledgement that it is the people in the structure, individually and collectively, who achieve results: procedures can do no more than enable people to achieve.

One outcome of this changing perspective is the growth in research and study of organisations, that was mentioned in the opening chapter. What used to be an area of interest only to managers for managerial purposes has become an area of interest to social scientists of varied disciplines studying the human condition in the organisational context. This has had some benefits for managers in producing new insights, but it has had the disadvantage of making the study of organisational life very diffuse. One of the most comprehensive reviews of the varied literature in organisations is provided by Clegg and Dunkerley (1980). An account that is likely to be of more interest to managers is by Mintzberg (1979). There are many echoes and references to this extensive literature throughout this book, but in this chapter we are limiting the discussion to aspects of organisation structure as a preliminary to considering management jobs and management work in the next two chapters.

1. THE ELEMENTS OF ORGANISATION STRUCTURE

The four essential building blocks for organisations are *job descriptions*, *the structure of working relationships*, *decision-making complexes* and *operating procedures*, all of which can be used to ensure the attainment of objectives.

Job descriptions are not popular among managers, especially when they are contained in lengthy typewritten documents lost in filing cabinets, and all too often the job description is the epitome of stifling, irrelevant bureaucracy. However, each member of an organisation has a job to do and some understanding is needed, by himself and his colleagues, of the content and boundaries of that job. Much is achieved by the job title. Titles like Managing Director, Electrician, Chef, Telephonist, Newsreader and Window Cleaner all describe what the job holder does in a way that will meet most organisational requirements. Other titles are less readily understood as descriptions of job content — Despatcher, Clerical Assistant, Organisation Development Adviser and Manager, External Relations, for instance. Also all jobs need some clarification at the boundary. What are the limits of responsibility held by this person? Do areas of influence overlap?

The job description is a problem for managers. It is a basic, essential requirement for allocating people to jobs and work to people in a way that can be understood and be used to avoid gaps and duplication, but there is always the risk that it becomes a restriction that people fight against or a defence behind which they hide when there is a need for change or when the unpredicted is encountered.

Review Topic 3.1

Why is the job description a problem for managers and how can the problem be overcome?

An excellent use of job descriptions is for a group of managers with interrelated jobs to write out their own, according to an agreed format, and then exchange copies with each other before meeting to discuss gaps and overlaps. This requires each one of them to work through the various parameters of his job and then explain aspects on which others ask for clarification. The draft documents will probably be thrown away after the discussion, but the process of which they have been the central part will have been invaluable in producing a mode of working that is more effective than any that could be achieved by other means.

The structure of *working relationships* is most commonly expressed in the organisation chart or "family tree", which sets out the membership of the various working groups or departments and how they interconnect. This describes the hierarchy and the system, expressed by that hierarchy, for distributing power through the organisation. As a tool of old-fashioned "classical" organisation theory it has been criticised as limiting the scope of individuals, emphasising subordination and rank and producing conformist, narrow thinking. It remains necessary to provide general guidance on where to find expertise and information, to legitimise the formal aspects of authority and to provide one of the means of resolving disagreements: the crossover point in the hierarchy. When two or more people cannot agree on a course of action, such as the interpretation of policy on an issue, one of the ways of resolving it is to "go upstairs". If the Head of Mathematics and the Head of English in a school meet a point of fundamental disagreement about the distribution of timetable hours between their respective subjects, they may well resolve that by seeking a judgement from the Head Teacher. It is not the only way of resolving such problems, but is one of the possibilities.

The hierarchical emphasis in organisation charts can be modified by the presentation device of drawing them laterally rather than vertically. They still describe the grouping of activities and the distribution of power.

Some decisions in organisations are made by individuals, others are made by groups. The scope of decisions to be made by an individual will be contained either in his job description or in his position on the organisation chart. Decisions to be made collectively are allocated to *decision-making complexes*. The obvious example is the board of directors who make certain decisions by majority vote, and those decisions cannot be made in any other way. Other decisions are reserved for particular committees or councils, sometimes as specified in collective agreements with employee representatives. These are called decision-making complexes rather than decision-making groups because the process of reaching decisions goes beyond the face-to-face discussion to include the collection and presentation of data. This is a significant feature of jobs done by people outside the decision-making group and sometimes is the sole activity of committee secretariats.

Just as the organisation chart is the main expression of power distribution, the composition and operation of the decision-making complexes can be another basis on which organisation members channel their interests in obtaining access to power.

Operating procedures are ways in which decisions are implemented and the standardised means whereby the everyday activities of organisation life are conducted. The sundry administrative routines range from the drill that is followed in determining who has time off with pay to attend funerals, to the elaborate routine of consultation that is required in authorising a purchase order for a new piece of equipment. John Child (1977, p. 8) includes in this grouping two further aspects, first the specification of working routines for how tasks are to be performed and secondly the determination of performance standards, such as level of output or quality of performance, when the methods of doing the job cannot be precisely tied down.

In this book we have some material on job descriptions in the next chapter, there is a full chapter on the working of committees and one on developing procedures as well as a number of outline drills. The remainder of this chapter is devoted to the organisation chart and what it describes. We first describe the three main forms of organisation structure: entrepreneurial, bureaucratic and matrix, and then consider situations in which different structural forms are combined and integrated. We conclude with a consideration of the span of control.

2. THE ENTREPRENEURIAL STRUCTURE

Most organisations start life as an *entrepreneurial* structure in that they are brought into existence to extend the capability and capacity of an individual, who has discovered a way of meeting potential customer- or client need, but cannot achieve results without assistance. The two essential components of any dictionary definition of the word 'entrepreneur' are risk and initiative. The fact of having had the initiative and taken the risk gives the entrepreneur such dominance in the evolving organisation that everything depends on him and most activities of other members are either replicating or mirroring what the entrepreneur is doing. The initiative shown usually includes a powerful ingredient of expertise or specialised knowledge that nobody else can supply, and which is the secret of success. Erle Stanley Gardner was a writer of crime novels that were so successful that he was able to employ a team of writers who wrote large parts of later novels according to his outline or formula, while Mr. Gardner provided the vital ingredients of the formula, the characters and his own name. The popular singer has a small entourage of acolytes (interestingly they are usually called managers) whose duties are to enable the performer to do well: they have no function or purpose apart from that. Eddie Land invented the Polaroid lens and later the Polaroid camera, so that all the members of his organisation centred their activities on his inventive genius.

The questions about entrepreneurial structures are to decide where such structures are appropriate and how practicable it is to maintain that form with increasing organisational size. Most people are employed in organisations that do not depend absolutely on the continuing, irreplaceable contribution of a single entrepreneur. The large oil companies, most public sector undertakings like the National Health Service or the Civil Service, High Street banks, schools, colleges, airline companies, insurance companies have a quite different type of drive to their activities. Other types of organisation appear to need, however, the strong centralisation of the entrepreneurial form to be effective. Where there is the need to move fast and take major decisions requiring flair and skilled judgement rather than a measured weighing of alternatives, then the entrepreneurial form is maintained.

There are many examples of entrepreneurial structure at the micro-level in larger organisations. The passenger aircraft in flight has a pattern of routine organisation that is decentralised: all members of the crew are trained and self-confident in discharging their specialised tasks, but at any hint of danger the crew members look to the captain for precise instructions which they will obey without discussion or argument. The routine of the hospital operating theatre is similar. There is not time for all those involved to confer about the most appropriate course of action while the patient bleeds to death. There is common consent to the need for someone to make decisions quickly, even if they turn out to be wrong. Larger scale activities that have this same need are the printing of daily newspapers, running a fashion house, much of merchant banking and some marketing operations. It is interesting that some other types of operation that are in many ways similar to journalism actually operate on a different, highly consultative basis. Advertising campaigns and magazine editing have been complex activities drawing upon and merging the expertise and insights of a team rather than imposing the ideas of a single person. These situations require strong leadership to avoid the pitfalls of "groupthink" that can come from trying to satisfy all participants, but the lack of immediacy provides the opportunity to work at getting the best possible formula.

The entrepreneurial form is attractive to many managers because of its emphasis on individual power and risky competition.

> This organization works on precedent, on anticipating the wishes and decisions of the central power sources. There are few rules and procedures, little bureaucracy. Control is exercised by the centre, largely through the selection of key individuals, by occasional forays from the centre or summonses to the centre. It is a political organization in that decisions are taken very largely on the outcome of a balance of influence rather than on procedural or purely logical grounds.
>
> (Handy, 1981, p. 178).

3.   THE BUREAUCRATIC STRUCTURE

Bureaucracy is the most common form of organisation and has been used, as we saw in the second chapter, in various forms for most of human history. It is only recently that the word has taken on the unattractive overtones that turn "bureaucrat" into a term of abuse.

The principle of bureaucratic organisation is that jobs are grouped according to some common feature and then ranked in a conventional hierarchy of responsibility to distribute power between organisation members. The most common grouping is *function*, with a marketing hierarchy, a production hierarchy and so on. An alternative is the *geographical* grouping, whereby there is a factory hierarchy and another for the London office and a third for the warehousing and distribution centre. In bureaucracy the employee focuses on his role in the organisation rather than on the relative power of individuals:

> Bureaucratic structures are characterized by an advanced degree of specialization between jobs and departments, by a reliance on formal procedures and paperwork, and by extended managerial hierarchies with clearly marked status distinctions. In bureaucracies there tends to be a strictly delimited system of delegation down these hierarchies whereby an employee is expected to use his discretion only within what the rules allow.
>
> (Child, 1977, p.12).

In its extreme form bureaucracy gives rise to the sort of picture mentioned at the opening of this chapter, but is is more usually a necessary and agreeable environment for people to work in, providing that the nature of the organisation's task is appropriate to this organisational form. The working routine is predictable and understood, jobs are defined so that individuals know what they are to do and how to do it, and efficiency derives from rational allocation of work and responsibility rather than individual flair and judgement. Standardised performances are required and it is a form of organisation that is reasonably equitable and proof against corruption.

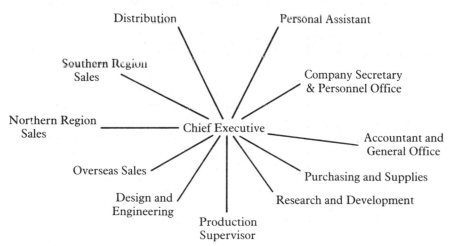

Figure 3.1 Entrepreneurial Organisation Structure

A useful example is retail banking or the work of building societies. Here the operations have to be standardised, not only in all branches of the same bank but also between competing banks, so that customers find the system easy to deal with. The work of bank clerks and, in a different way, bank managers requires knowledge, skill and accuracy, but it must be carried out strictly in accordance with the rules and there is little scope for individuality apart from one's manner in talking with customers and manual dexterity in counting banknotes. Bureaucracy provides scope for economies of scale and extensive specialisation at the expense of flexibility and product innovation. Their predictability provides a secure environment for the employee and a clear line of safe career progression.

Bureaucracy has recently acquired a bad name for a variety of reasons. It has been pointed out that it is not always efficient, especially in times of rapid change and with increasing complexity of organisational tasks. It is also criticised as pushing people to clone-like uniformity instead of developing individual ability and potential. The inflexible and immutable procedures of bureaucracy can become means of avoiding rather than discharging responsibility. If the secure, predictable environment changes, especially if it changes suddenly, the bureaucratic system is likely to collapse and the bureaucrats find their skills in running that system to be obsolete, while their capacity to acquire new skills for a new situation has not been developed.

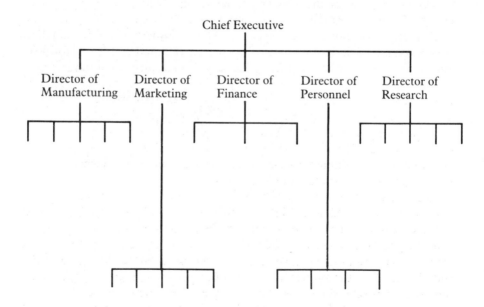

Figure 3.2   Typical Bureaucratic Organisation Structure

4. THE MATRIX STRUCTURE

As the entrepreneurial and bureaucratic structures have such obvious drawbacks, a third general mode has been evolved and used in some situations: the matrix. The method is simply to overlay a second set of hierarchical connections over a first, but at right-angles to it. This was first developed in the American aerospace industry because of government demands for a single project manager who would be responsible for the progress of each government contract and to whom government officials could channel all their queries and instructions. Companies soon found big advantages in this arrangement and expanded it so that the project manager was not only a communications link but also a direct superior of employees in different functional groups, although these employees would also still report to their functional superiors. This was directly flouting Fayol's dictum about unity of command that we saw in the second chapter, to say nothing of the New Testament observation that a man cannot serve two masters. Despite this, the form has proved popular because it provides a measure of individual autonomy and formalises the necessary, informal lateral lines of communication that are developed by people coping with interrelated problems.

An example could be the making of a television programme, which will require a range of specialist skills, such as set-building, make-up, special effects, design and engineering. The necessary specialists are a part of their functional area and have a place in that hierarchy, but they will mainly work on attachment to a particular programme. The attachment may be for a few weeks, like preparing for a Royal Wedding; a few months like a cricket season; or several years on a magazine programme. Whilst attached they are part of that programme team and thus have a dual link. For technical expertise they refer to their functional grouping, but for regular direction and control they are responsible to the producer of the programme. In this way the individual has full scope to use his expertise and judgement and to organise his contribution, the project team leader has "his own man" as a full-time team member, and yet there is the back-up of the functional organisation if additional resources are required and as somewhere for the team member to return to and identify with.

For the matrix to succeed there has to be depth of skilled personnel, so that a person can be allocated full-time to a project, and the operating context of the organisation has to be appropriate to the mode of working. There are still likely to be problems in dealing with resource allocation, as the project manager may want more people than the functional manager deems necessary and all too often the project manager wants a particular person whom the functional manager wants to deploy elsewhere. A further difficulty is with the specialist personnel themselves who have the benefit of independence but lack opportunities to develop specialised expertise, as they have to work on a variety of tasks. They will develop flexibility and experience but may not deepen their specialist skills. This can also lead to uncertainty about career progression and occupational identity. Do you stay with the functional career path or do you try and become a project manager? The administrative costs can be high due to a multiplication of hierarchies that tends to increase overheads as more and more people establish the inescapable need for private secretaries, personal assistants, larger offices, more telephones and computer facilities. The level of conflict requires managerial time for its resolution and an increased amount of political behaviour can lead to excessive paperwork as people make out their case in seventeen copies.

The matrix organisation does, therefore, need time and care in its creation, balancing the power of the two axes and working out a basis of trust and understanding among the key participants. It is not something to work out on the back of an envelope during a train journey; it requires extensive consultation and discussion, progressive implementation over several months and attention for several years as it settles down and moves towards effectiveness. Davis and Lawrence (1979) suggest three stages of matrix evolution. First *temporary overlay*, during which project teams are created only for special and immediate needs; secondly *permanent overlay* in which project teams are established as a continuing form of organisation working across the functional hierarchy; and thirdly the *mature matrix*, at which point the project lines of authority and influence are brought into balance with the functional lines.

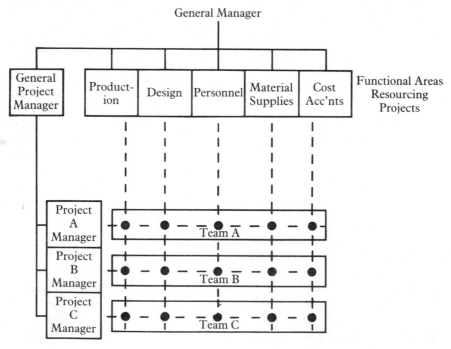

Figure 3.3   Typical Matrix Organisation Structure

Useful guidance on matrix management is in Galbraith (1977) and in Kingdon (1973).

Mintzberg (1979, chapter 21) uses the term *adhocracy* to describe a variant of the matrix organisation, where the work is complex and innovative, such as theatre companies and some computing specialists. Such an organisation is one in which there are many highly trained specialists with an organic structure that always remains flexible, and which tends to be very big in the middle. Organisations of this type have problems in balancing work loads between individuals and groups and in managing the conflict that such a diverse group of people generates.

5. DIFFERENTIATED STRUCTURES

It should not be assumed from the foregoing that an entire organisation must follow the same organisational pattern. The structure of organisation follows the requirements of the environment and the needs of organisation members rather than the whim of highly placed individuals seeking control, so that appropriate structures will vary from one part of the undertaking to another.

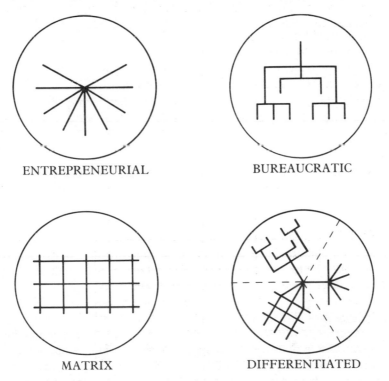

ENTREPRENEURIAL   BUREAUCRATIC

MATRIX   DIFFERENTIATED

Figure 3.4   Main Types of Organisational Structure

The sales manager will be properly concerned about satisfying customers' demands today while the R. & D. manager will be more interested in the development of products for the future. It is unlikely that the same form of organisation structure would suit both situations. A hospital will have within it an operating theatre in which surgeons conduct their high dramas in a way that has to be centralised and autocratic to cope with the crises on the operating table, but the same hospital will have a psychiatric unit requiring a different approach.

The pattern of the organisation could, therefore, have a tightknit entrepreneurial structure at the centre and bureaucratised functions or a matrix elsewhere. Bureaucracies can have within them small entrepreneurial organisations, as some large companies have set up such small groups to develop new business ventures. What is crucial in organisation differentiation is that the different structures are independent of each other in their operations. The entrepreneurs must be relatively free of set procedures and the bureaucrats must be able to escape the power-play needed by the entrepreneurs.

The seminal work on this aspect of organisation is by Paul Lawrence and Jay Lorsch (1967) working in the United States. They demonstrated that companies operating in an unstable, unpredictable environment had the greatest variations in organisational structure and style and those in the predictable environments had little differentiation. They also established that the high-performing companies in both situations had a higher degree of *integration* than low-performers. Whilst it is essential for subunits of organisation to be independent in their operations if their styles are different, it is also essential that their operations are integrated.

Part of the enthusiasm for matrix structures has been that it is a form of organisation that builds in its own integration. Other integrating methods are:

A planning device.   All units of the organisation contribute to, and have their activity monitored by, a form of corporate plan which sets out targets for different departments. The integrative value of this is the effort that has to be made centrally to understand the problems and opportunities of the various units and the extent to which these then have to be explained to others. It is a method which can only succeed as an integrator if the process is accompanied by full information and consultation, although it may succeed in meeting other objectives without consultation.

Getting people together.   This can be done in at least three ways, with varying degrees of formality. Among the most effective is arranging for people with different interests to meet informally. This is the logic of the company conference or convention, which enables bureaucrat and entrepreneur to have breakfast together or to meet in the bar and incidentally to find out each other's concerns and priorities. "Putting a face on the guy at the other end of the telephone" makes it easier to converse constructively in the next telephone conversation, to say nothing of identifying more people with whom to connect on the network of informal communication. Committees are a formalised way of getting people to talk to each other and consultative committees are opportunities for people to exchange views and information. The task force is matrix management in miniature as a small group of people with varying interests are asked to meet and work up a solution, or alternative solutions, to an operating problem.

Co-ordinators. These are individuals who ease or solve problems by direct intervention in intractable situations. To be effective they need genuine expertise to make their intervention acceptable and so that they can "authorise" the implementation of any decisions reached. They have to manage disagreement in such a way that the argument between two managers or departments is used to solve the problem confronting them.

The hierarchy. The method used most often to solve problems by simply referring the query to the crossover point, as was mentioned earlier in this chapter. It is used when "a ruling" is needed from higher authority. This is in contrast to intervention by co-ordinators who are used when people with differing perceptions need to hammer out their own accommodation, or where the problem requires the deployment of additional expertise to understand it.

6. THE SPAN OF CONTROL

One idea that has fascinated management analysts for decades is the span of control — what is the optimum number of subordinates for a manager? The idea of an optimum number has been so ridiculed in recent years that interest in it has waned, but we resurrect it here because it includes some of the detailed decisions that have to be taken by managers about how work should be organised and how bits of the organisation fit into the overall structure. Decisions about job descriptions and working relationships, for example, will affect the number of subordinates and will determine the number of posts in the organisation and the relative steepness of the hierarchy, with all the implications of cost, communication problems, potential overmanning and inefficiency.

The span of control has been seen as the standard method of integrating the work of individuals and maintaining balance, and there has been the assumption that there is a limit to the number of subordinates that a manager can have without impairing his effectiveness and theirs. It is felt that if you get the span of control right the rest of the structure will also be right.

No executive should attempt to supervise directly the work of more than five, or at the most six, direct subordinates whose work interlocks.

(L.F. Urwick, 1974).

To Urwick the feature of the work interlocking was important, as that required the executive to resolve problems more often. Such a pattern of 1:5 or 1:6 may be appropriate when looking at the question from the point of view of how the individual performs, and it is the pattern found in most

---

Review Topic 3.2

How useful is the idea that there is an optimum span of control for an individual manager?

---

hierarchies, but another aspect of the question is the amount of management and managers that such a norm builds into an organisation and the degree to which it introduces the inefficiencies of over-management. Figure 3.5 compares two actual organisations, one manufacturing and one retailing, but both part of large conglomerates. At first glance the disparity is enormous, even though both have ratios of managers to others that exceed the 1:5/6 suggested by Urwick, but there are a number of factors to explain the differences. The manufacturing operation is technically sophisticated, requiring a range of technical expertise, it is physically more widely distributed and shifts are worked over twenty-four hours for five and a half

Rank and Grade		Manufacturing	Retailing
SENIOR MANAGEMENT	1	4	4
	2	9	
MIDDLE MANAGEMENT	3	16	8
	4	40	–
SUPERVISORY MANAGEMENT	5	55	12
TOTAL MANAGERS		114	24
TOTAL OTHER EMPLOYEES		1500	600

Figure 3.5　A Comparison of Management Structures

days a week. The retailing unit does not have to buy or advertise and has a relatively simple operation, even though it is carried out with great skill.

However necessary the larger number and proportion of managers in the manufacturing organisation, there is both extra cost and administrative burden caused by the number of managers and levels: more secretaries, more memoranda, more necessary communication, more problems with role definition and boundary, less scope for subordinates to exercise responsibility, and a larger salary bill. There is obviously a potential benefit in *increasing* the average span of managerial control if this has the knock-on effect of reducing the number of levels in the hierarchy, which Child (1977, p. 52) claims to be typically four in the organisation employing up to one hundred people, rising to six when one thousand people are employed and seven or eight in the organisation with ten thousand people. Among the factors that can be examined to enable a widening of control spans to flatten the hierarchy are:

Standardising the work to be done.   If the work to be done by the managed can be standardised, then the need for supervision will decline as the individual employee is working to a standard, clearly understood procedure for which he will require little instruction and guidance. There is a narrow line separating the constraining standardisation of the many mindless tasks that are to be found in mass production and the liberating standardisation that can be found in skilled jobs, like that of the craftsman or travel agency booking clerk, where the standard is set for the output rather than the details of method.

Autonomy.   Closely related to the methods of standardisation are the methods of providing autonomy, whereby supervision is virtually removed from the work of a person who is sufficiently skilled and experienced to be able to do his own management. One version of this is the converse of Urwick's point about work that interlocks. Where there is close interaction between the work of people or departments, that interaction needs careful management to keep the varied activities in balance. Whether that is done by managers or by the people themselves, it is still a time-consuming activity. If the interlocks can be removed, then the management requirement can reduce.

Specialist advisers.   Theoretically the use of specialist advisers or departments eases the management burden in the line, by taking over responsibilities for activities such as safety, personnel or quality control. The introduction of these services should allow spans of control in the middle of the hierarchy to widen, although it means more departments for senior managers to co-ordinate. Such specialists can also develop standard procedures to simplify general administration. Specialists are, however, a dangerous drug as they are always likely to increase rather than reduce the managerial burden: the tail wags the dog. Information is called for, forms are required to be filled in and the specialist becomes aloof and didactic rather than genuinely easing managerial loads in the line. This is often because the detachment of the specialist enables him to be disinterested in everyday problems, but also it can be because the position of the specialist adviser is always precarious and he feels a need to make himself necessary by becoming a part of the administrative system of the undertaking and thus being "indispensable".

Quite apart from the possibility of increasing the span of control and the number of levels in the hierarchy, managers have to guard against the strongest pressure of all in the organisation towards increasing the number of levels, namely the managers themselves. When a hierarchy is established the members of the hierarchy want to go up it, so they are always looking for openings higher up and can often make out the most convincing case for a new opening that does not already exist.

In a medium-sized chemical plant there was a plant manager, four production superintendents reporting to him and twenty-two supervisors: a clear three-level hierarchy. Safety was the responsibility of the personnel manager, but the plant manager was anxious to be in charge of his own safety arrangements and eventually won a battle with the personnel manager to appoint his "own" safety officer. This involved not only a flurry of administrative activity in redefining the limits of responsibility between the personnel manager and the plant manager, it also required redefinition in the three-level hierarchy of the plant. The safety officer reported to the plant manager, so the four superintendents wanted to know whether he ranked above or below them (which was partly a coded question meaning, "Does he get paid more than we do?"). It was confirmed that he "ranked" below superintendent but above supervisor, which produced a problem in the personnel department, where the safety officer was on a supervisory scale. It also introduced a new level and within two years six of the supervisors had been promoted to the new position of senior supervisor, ranking equal with the safety officer.

This same tendency has been seen as groups of people have sought "improved career propects". Nurses in the National Health Service used to have vague career prospects beyond the clear and well understood posts of ward sister or charge nurse. After that there was Deputy Matron and Matron. When the case for career advancement was made, those two vaguely defined and amorphous levels became four: Nursing Officer, Senior Nursing Officer, Principal Nursing Officer and Divisional Nursing Officer.

Concern about the span of control led the Lockheed Corporation to devise a means of evaluating managerial posts in order to decide the number of subordinates for whom the job holder could be held responsible. This was used in 1961 to reduce the number of management levels in several sections of the undertaking. It has not proved to be a popular method in other organisations and is thus little more than a footnote to the development of management ideas, but some readers might be interested in the account of the method provided by Barkdull (1963). Child (1973) accounts for the growth of specialists' numbers in organisations as being related to the size, dispersion, technical complexity and number of divisions in the organisation. Howells (1981) made a comparative study of the Marks and Spencer chain store and the Civil Service. He found distinctive styles of decision-making with Marks and Spencer putting very little on paper and emphasising decision-making by individuals, whereas the Civil Service put a lot on paper and used committees to make decisions. Howells considers that the Civil Service operates in this apparently laborious way because of the complex decisions that have to be made with less clear criteria and operating with external accountability. This demonstrates how both environment and product influence formal organisation structures.

SUMMARY PROPOSITIONS

3.1. The four elements of organisation are job descriptions, the structure of working relationships, decision-making complexes and operating procedures.

3.2. The most common forms of organisation structure are entrepreneurial, bureaucratic and matrix.

3.3. Although undertakings may adopt more than one form of organisational structure, integration will be an element of their operations that will influence the success of their business.

3.4. Tendencies in organisations to being over-managed can be partly mitigated by increasing the managerial span of control and reducing the number of managerial levels.

APPENDIX A

Drill for tackling problems of organisation

This is a preliminary drill for deciding how to approach problems of organisation and similar issues, with the advantages and disadvantages of each.

Approach	Advantage	Disadvantage
1. Use one's own judgement	Reinforces one's role as the person in charge	No testing for the accuracy of diagnosis.
2. Ask for guidance from one's hierarchical superior.	Tests own judgement against that of person with wider view, who shares responsibility.	Might make superior's view of own judgement questionable; advice from superior difficult to ignore.
3. Consult with key subordinates.	Several views expressed and those consulted become partly committed to eventual solution.	Spreads uncertainty about existing arrangements, which then *have* to be changed.
4. Survey attitudes of all subordinates.	Comprehensive expression of opinion from all those most directly concerned, with anonymity of survey method ensuring reasonable frankness of views.	Some subordinates will feel that they are being asked to solve problems that are the proper domain of the manager, who is showing incompetence by asking subordinates.
5. Consult peers	Co-ordinating views with those from other units and perspectives in the organisation.	Some peers may regard consultation as sign of weakness and indecision. May influence competition for resources.
6. Seek external advice.	Tests own judgement against that of person with experience in a variety of organisation settings, who is detached from one's own.	Advice could be expensive and adviser does not carry responsibility to temper his advice.

APPENDIX B

Identifying problems of organisation

To identify problems of organisation one must have some criteria against which to judge the various features of the organisation being studied. There is a dearth of absolute standards in this field, but the following is a list of statements that are *generally valid* on the basis of the extensive research about organisations that has been carried out. They are useful as broad criteria, but should not be taken to have any more reliability than that.

1.   Size of Organisation Unit.

a)   As organisations grow they tend to become more bureaucratic, with a taller hierarchy;
b)   Large units tend to have problems of morale among members low in the hierarchy or remote from the centre;
c)   Increasing organisational size provides career progression moves (mainly for middle and senior managers) and the facilities of specialist departments;
d)   Small working units tend to have high morale among members.

2.   Age of the Organisation Unit.

a)   As a unit grows older it will become more stable (otherwise it would not have survived) and the conventions of custom and practice will become strong;
b)   As units grow older their structures become less flexible but their goals more flexible.

3.   The Setting of the Organisation Unit.

a)   A unit cannot operate independently of its setting and many of the norms, procedures and practice will be dictated by the setting;
b)   The unit will be able to make its strategic objectives more ambitious if the setting is buoyant or competitive or both;
c)   The unit will tend to be innovative, and its members creative, if the setting is changing and being challenged.

4.   Job Descriptions.

a)   All organisation members need some definition of their role and tasks especially where their activities interlock with, or overlap, those of other organisation members;
b)   Job descriptions written for them by others can cause members to ignore the descriptions or to use them as a means of limiting their contribution;
c)   Job descriptions written by members themselves can stimulate creative thinking about the members' roles and working relationships.

5.   *The Structure of Working Relationships.*

a)   Different forms of organisation structure are most appropriate for different settings;

b)   Entrepreneurial structure is most appropriate in situations of rapid change or constant crisis, or where the unit is not performing well in comparison with competing units;

c)   Bureaucratic structure is most appropriate in situations of relative stability with readily-measurable performance standards and/or public accountability;

d)   Matrix structure is most appropriate when responsibility for action has to be devolved to individual specialists so that they can work on their own account with peers having different qualifications of a comparable standard;

e)   Differentiation of structure is most appropriate when an organisation has diversity of objectives and methods of operating in the subunits, which can operate with reasonable independence of each other providing that there are co-ordinating mechanisms;

f)   Diversified organisations need co-ordination. This can be achieved by using various forms of face-to-face meeting to develop trust and understanding; by using the crossover point in the hierarchy when a "ruling" is needed; and by using co-ordinators to assist in finding solutions to major disagreements.

6.   *The Span of Control.*

a)   There is no universal, optimum number of subordinates for a manager;

b)   Increasing the number of subordinates reporting to an individual manager can reduce the risks of over-management;

c)   The hierarchy may be flattened by standardising the work to be done, increasing the autonomy of individual employees and providing specialist advisers or departments to support managers in the line;

d)   Managers may seek to steepen the hierarchy and narrow the span of control in order to improve their own career prospects.

7.   *Pitfalls of Organisational Change.*

a)   It is not possible to predict precisely the outcome of any particular organisational change: there are always unintended consequences;

b)   Individual organisation members sometimes seek changes which would satisfy their personal needs but which would not necessarily satisfy the needs of the organisation;

c)   The presenting symptoms may not necessarily be due to problems of organisational structure.

More detailed suggestions about identifying problems of organisation can be found in Khandwalla P.N. *Design of Organizations*, Harcourt, Brace Jovanovich, New York, 1977.

An alternative approach is that developed by Roger Harrison, who looks at the culture of the organisation. His scheme for finding how compatible an individual is with a particular type of organisation structure can be found in Handy C. B. *Understanding Organisations*, Penguin Books, Harmondsworth, Middlesex, 1981, pp. 205–11.

REFERENCES

Barkdull C.W. "Span of Control: a Method of Evaluation" in *Michigan Business Review*, vol. 15, 1963, pp. 25–32.

Child J. "Parkinson's Progress: Accounting for the Number of Specialists in Organisations", in *Administrative Science Quarterly*, September 1973, pp. 328–48.

Child J., *Organization: a Guide to Problems and Practice*, Harper & Row, London, 1977.

Clegg S. and Dunkerley D., *Organisation, Class and Control*, Routledge & Kegan Paul, London, 1980.

Davis S.M. and Lawrence, P.R., *Matrix*, Addison-Wesley, Reading, Mass., 1977.

Galbraith J.R., *Organization Design*, Addison-Wesley, Reading Massachussetts, 1977.

Handy C.B., *Understanding Organizations*, Penguin Books, Harmondsworth, Middlesex, (2nd edition) 1981.

Howells D., "Marks & Spencer and the Civil Service: A Comparison of Culture and Methods", in *Public Administration*, Autumn 1981, pp. 337–52.

Kingdon D.R., *Matrix Organisation*, Tavistock, London, 1973.

Lawrence P.R. and Lorsch J.W., *Organization and Environment*, Harvard University Press, 1967.

Leavitt H.J., Dill W.R. and Eyring H.B., *The Organizational World*, Harcourt, Brace and Jovanovich, New York, 1973.

Mintzberg H., *The Structuring of Organizations*, Prentice Hall, Englewood Cliffs, New Jersey, 1979.

Urwick L.F., "V.A. Graicunas and the Span of Control", in *Academy of Management Journal*, June 1974, pp. 349–54.

Chapter Four

TYPES OF MANAGEMENT JOB

Management covers a range of jobs more diverse than many other general occupational titles. The title "doctor" or "teacher" describes a job where all job holders have a common core of activity that is substantial and generally acknowledged, no matter how varied the specialisation. Managers have a common core to their activities that is more vague: a general concern with directing and controlling affairs, lacking a clear knowledge base the mastery of which enables the job holder to produce acceptable performance. The uncertainty is increased by the range of activities in which management is undertaken. The combination of an imprecise core of activity and knowledge and such a diversity of applications make categorisation difficult. The most familiar methods of differentiating between management jobs are to classify them according to *function* or *level*, and a consideration of those methods forms the bulk of this chapter. There is also an account of the research carried out by Rosemary Stewart in the United Kingdom and Henry Mintzberg in North America that have advanced the understanding of management work substantially in recent years.

1. DIFFERENTIATION BY FUNCTION

One of the most familiar ways of organising management jobs is to specialise them according to function, so that the pre-fixed label indicates the area of the organisation's activities in which the manager specialises, like this:

General Manager
Production Manager
Marketing Manager
Personnel Manager
Accounting Manager

There are many other specialisations; we find managers of purchasing, research, management development, distribution, data processing, public relations, warehousing and so on. This method is extensively used, even in situations where the fundamental activities of production and marketing do not exist. The different units of the British National Health Service, for instance, have been in the charge of management teams with the following membership:

Medical Officer
Nursing Officer
Finance Officer
Administrator
Works Officer

This method is designed to fit the classic methods of functional organisation that we considered in the last chapter, but functional labels are also used in matrix and other types of organisation, although the emphasis will differ.

This method of labelling assumes that a job holder is a specialist first and a manager second, so that a Nursing Officer qualifies as a nurse and works in that specialism before becoming a director and controller of nursing affairs. Management is represented as an aspect, or potential aspect, of a wide variety of jobs which have their main substance and justification in an area of specialised knowledge or skill that is deployed within the employing organisation. It also links the activities of the manager with those other employees who share his specialised knowledge. The Marketing Manager is a linking pin between all marketing personnel and other organisational members: he is the voice of marketing and responsible for its people. It is this sort of classification that makes sense of management education, in which students typically study functional areas, and is sustained by professional bodies. In the United Kingdom there are institutes that act as qualifying associations for specialists in accounting, marketing, production, personnel, purchasing and other functions. The degree of control these bodies exercise over their professions or quasi-professions varies, but they all represent a vested interest in functional affiliation by individual managers.

In the first example we gave of functional management, the General Manager was the odd man out: his specialisation was in co-ordinating affairs in general, acting as a mediator between the specialisms. Some methods of organisation have a number of general managers who act as the only manager in relatively small units, sometimes as a result of geographical distribution of activities. The picture of functional management is therefore only complete when we include the *non-functional* manager. The retail bank has a single manager, as do many shops, distribution depots and small factories. The product manager in a matrix organisation is a form of non-functional manager.

2. DIFFERENTIATION BY LEVEL

A more significant form of management differentiation is that of the level at which the manager operates, because we now see the effect of the *hierarchy*.

There may be any number of levels in a hierarchy, but we can identify four levels at which the nature of the management job differs: top, senior, middle and supervisory. Some readers may feel that this labelling is no more than attributing different amounts of status to people, but we will see that there are substantive differences in the type of jobs done by incumbents.

Top Managers

Many top managers are senior managers as well, so our account in this section only includes part of the work of such executives; the other part being set out in the next section. Top managers have few, but enormous, responsibilities, such as occasional major changes in direction: to introduce a new product, or not; to export to Chile, or not; to close a factory, or not; to dismiss the Chief Executive, or not. These activities are usually undertaken by the Board of Directors or comparable body with a broad legal responsibility to safeguard the shareholders' interests and the long-term interests of the company. The principal top manager is the Chairman, and his most important task is likely to be the appointment, with directorial colleagues, of the Managing Director or Chief Executive and other key senior appointments. When *The Times* and *Sunday Times* newspapers were bought in 1981 by the Australian entrepreneur Rupert Murdoch quite elaborate arrangements were made to vest the authority of appointing the editor in the hands of external, independent directors. The editor could not be dismissed without their concurrence, although they could not stop him from resigning. A director is not, as such, an employee or servant of the company. His accountability is to the shareholders or owners. He is not, however, precluded from holding employment in the company by his directorship and many board members are also full-time employees, discharging duties of senior managers, which we come to shortly. Also a very small proportion of directors are employees holding more humble positions in the hierarchy, usually termed worker directors.

The value of the top manager lies in his relative detachment from the organisation and its employees. He will probably be involved with several companies, giving him a range of current operating experience that full-time employees in a single undertaking will lack. His relative detachment and independence will also enable him to handle more easily some of the difficult decisions that have to be made. If a project has to be discontinued because it is no longer viable, many senior managers will be so committed to that project, for sentimental, career or status reasons that they will be committed to protecting it. But an independent director could view it more dispassionately. Many organisational changes involve making employees redundant. Senior managers frequently know the employees personally and have great difficulty in facing up to this operational necessity, so that the detachment of the top manager can be an invaluable element in the discussions that have to take place.

Top managers spend most of their time with outsiders and with peers; very little with subordinates.

Senior Managers

Senior managers are those who head up *functions*, such as marketing or personnel, as we saw at the beginning of the chapter; or they head up *operations*, factories, branches, depots or other units that are relatively self-contained with a number of functions being co-ordinated. While it is important to distinguish between top managers and senior managers, any neat distinction is made difficult by the fact that so many top managers are also senior managers. A way of clarifying the distinction is to say that senior managers are concerned with both *policy formulation*, in conjunction with top managers; and *policy implementation*, in conjunction with subordinates.

Hugh Parker (1970) gives the following list of functions concerned with policy formulation:

1. To establish the longer term objectives of the company, and the basic strategies for their attainment.

2. To define the specific policies (finance, personnel, marketing and the like) to be followed in implementing the company's strategies.

3. To decide the organizational structure of the company's management, and to appoint individuals to fill key positions in it.

4. To develop management planning, information, and control systems appropriate to the organizational structure of the company, and to use these systems effectively to ensure control by the board at all times over the results produced by the executive management.

5. To take decisions on such matters as the Articles of Association may reserve to the Board (e.g. payment of dividends, disposal of corporate assets, appointments to the board), or that the board in its own discretion decides not to delegate (e.g. capital projects above a certain amount, diversification into a new business).

Defined like this policy formulation is a collective activity where senior managers with specialist responsibilities and interests meet with each other, and with top managers who do not hold specific portfolios, to decide matters that can best or only be satisfactorily determined by consensus between them. A policy to resist trade union recognition on behalf of white-collar employees, for instance, might be an aspiration of the personnel manager, but he could not make that effective unless he could obtain the understanding and consent of his senior management colleagues to make it work. A plan to change advertising policy away from national newspapers to television would be for the marketing manager to devise, but he too would need to convince his colleagues of its wisdom.

Policy formulation has the predominant emphasis on *decision-making* but includes the element of control, mentioned by Parker, to ensure that decisions are being put into operation.

In policy implementation the senior manager changes his activity away from deciding what should be done towards putting the decisions into practice: he becomes an *executive* working with those who share his specialist concerns, knowledge and skills, whether that specialist interest be in a function or an operation. Implementation also involves constant activity in a boundary role on behalf of members in the specialist group, as the senior manager enlists the help of people elsewhere in the organisation or outside it, seeks clarification from other specialists, and mediates demands on his specialist area from outside.

Studies of the work of senior managers (for instance, Carlson, 1951; Mintzberg, 1975; Copeman *et al.*, 1963) all confirm that the senior manager's job tends to be a very hectic one, dealing with peers, outsiders and subordinates. Many of the matters he has to deal with are urgent and there are frequent interruptions: Copeman and his colleagues found an average of three visitors and four telephone calls each hour. Senior managers are frequently out of the office and spend the majority of their working time talking to people.

Middle Managers

Middle managers are creatures of medium to large organisations, as only in those situations are there enough people to generate hierarchical layers between senior managers and supervisors. It tends to be a difficult role because of its potential artificiality. It is not sufficiently senior to have a broad task of co-ordination nor significant decision-making powers and it is not closely in touch with the urgencies of the organisation's main activity, like making machine tools in a factory or caring for patients in a hospital.

The basic artificiality of their *management* work provides the main problem, not only for many middle managers, but also for their organisations. It is the organisation and its bureaucracy that "feed" the middle managers. Too few of them can enjoy the satisfaction of bringing off a sale, or manufacturing an excellent item, or acquiring a useful subsidiary, even though they may help towards such achievements. Many middle managers find their satisfactions within the organisation and its operating complexities.

In 1956 William H. Whyte coined the term "organisation man" to describe people who became over-preoccupied with, and dependent on, the organisation of which they were part. The following year Parkinson (1957) produced his devastating critique of administration, with particular reference to the British civil service. Both pointed to the way in which those holding middle management roles live in a world which takes on a life and purpose of its own, quite distinct from the purposes of the undertaking in which they are supposed to be engaged. Some discussion in the United States even reached the point of regarding organisational growth as a denial of individual freedom. The worst predictions of the organisation man syndrome have not been realised, but middle managers remain more concerned about organisational mechanics and process than products. This makes them vulnerable when the foundations shake.

Dickson (1977) found middle managers in a nationalised industry displaying low morale and lack of commitment as they steadily lost decision-making duties, and Marshall and Cooper (1979) found middle managers to be under greater pressure than their superiors and having less satisfaction. If an organisation goes out of business or sheds personnel, the displaced middle manager frequently finds that his chances in the labour market are poor because all his expertise has lain in making one organisational system work and knowing how to get through the administrative jungle that he, and others like him, have created. Out of the jungle he is helpless.

Middle managers' jobs can be either line or staff. *Line* jobs are those where subordinates are directly involved with the main product of the organisation, such as section manager in a margarine plant or editor of a television programme. *Staff* jobs are those in parts of the organisation providing supporting services for others, like management services, personnel or the company secretary. There has been a trend to an increasing number of staff rather than line jobs in middle management. Child (1978, p. 52) studied the employment records of the tyre company Dunlop between 1948 and 1977 and concluded that resources were moving from the productive to the non-productive sector within organisations as well as across them, suggesting an increase in middle management staff jobs. He went on to argue that, instead of dividing economic activities into manufacturing and non-manufacturing, we should distinguish between activities which produce marketable outputs and those that do not. For example, some public services, such as eduction, medicine and road tolls, are potentially marketable, and within manufacturing there are staff functions that are not directly productive.

Middle managers have a wide variety of jobs and roles. Some have large numbers of subordinates, while others have none. In one research investigation we spoke to an army major with 130 subordinates, but we also spoke to a management services consultant, a project manager and a senior nursing officer who did not have any subordinates. Some will share the same work as their subordinates, but have additional administrative duties, such as deputy heads and heads of departments in schools. Others will do quite different work, like the project manager mentioned above, who co-ordinates the work of engineers, designers, suppliers and customers. Middle managers of all types spend a great deal of their time operating procedures and responding to the requests, queries, demands and initiatives of others rather than generating their own work.

Horne and Lupton (1965) analysed the working lives of 66 middle managers and found that they spent most of their time exchanging information: (p. 26).

Activity	Percentage of time
Giving, seeking information	42
Giving, seeking advice	6
Giving, confirming, reviewing decisions	8
Giving, receiving, confirming instructions	9
Co-ordinating, reviewing plans	11
Seeking, preparing explanations	15
Other activities	9

Hunt (1979) and Kay (1974) argue that the dependency and lack of autonomy among middle managers is producing greater dissatisfaction in recent years as they are now experiencing two new problems: those lower in the hierarchy are being more extensively represented in dealings with senior managers, and some senior managers now use specialist advisers or outside agencies for advice and information rather than the middle managers in their own organisations.

The promotion to middle management often leads to people allowing their previous, technical expertise to wither. The salesman gives up seeing customers, nurses no longer give bedside care and engineers leave technical problems to others. This is because they are "too busy" with meetings, paperwork and other administrative tasks; learning the way of life that Mant sceptically calls "clean and gentlemanly". There are problems in abandoning previous expertise or involvement with the main task of the organisation; problems for the individual managers, for their subordinates and for the organisation.

Early in his career each middle manager acquires a body of knowledge and technical skill to qualify and practise as a pharmacist, engineer, teacher or whatever specialist career was followed. The jobs could not be done without that knowledge and more, specific information could always be obtained to solve an unexpected problem so that an answer could always be found.

When they cross over to the better paid, higher ranking (and logically more skilful) activity of managing, they expect the new activity to have a similar body of expertise: reliable, explicit and accessible. All they find is a ramshackle collection of humdrum tasks that any literate school-leaver could easily accomplish, but their earlier training makes it almost impossible for them to believe that there is not more to management than this, so they look for the solution to a non-existent mystery. To some extent they find what they are looking for in management development. The constant stream of books, lectures, seminars and symposia from the behavioural science entrepreneurs offer neat packages of answers, rapidly replacing one management myth with another, and the clientèle for such placebos is almost exclusively middle management.

As few middle managers are lazy they often set up activities to justify their position, producing administrative controls and requests for information that are not needed other than to build the individual middle manager more securely into the administrative system of the undertaking. Thus begins the political activity of the middle manager, that is discussed more fully in Chapter 6.

The problems for the subordinates of these middle managers are expressed in the complaint heard frequently in organisations that the manager has lost touch with the task and is making unrealistic demands and unreasonable decisions because he is out of date with current problems. Although much of this grumbling will be no more than the jaundiced view of those who resent the greater privilege of those immediately "above" them, the loss of technical skills by a middle manager does not help and leads to a situation in which subordinates are expected to comply with managerial requests on the basis of the manager's *position* of authority, whereas compliance based on experience and expertise is both easier to comply with and does not need the support of power and control of resources. This question of authority is explored more fully in Chapter 14.

One of the main problems for the organisation of middle managers abandoning their technical expertise is the loss of that experience. All too often they are promoted out of work connected with the main task of the organisation at the very stage where they have sufficient experience to work confidently and at their most effective. Our own study (Torrington and Weightman, 1982) found British organisations encouraging middle managers with proven expertise in a technical specialism to abandon this in favour of very general, and usually straightforward, managerial and administrative duties. Jones *et al.*, (1981) found similar difficulties in their extensive study of the nursing profession. The conclusion is that middle managers should maintain as much contact with, and practise in, their technical specialism as they can, even though this might appear to increase their workload. This will increase the respect of their peers and subordinates and will make them less vulnerable at times of redundancy, more marketable and less dependent on organisation-specific skills.

Senior managers might consider changing the balance in the demands they make of middle managers, giving greater weight to current performance rather than an assessment of nebulous and imprecise personal qualities. At present middle managers are often caught in a trap:

i)   They need to justify their *performance* in achieving results to their
       superiors in order to keep their jobs and meet current
       organisational requirements;

ii)   They need to justify their *personal qualities* as socially acceptable
      members of management to their superiors to gain promotion;

iii) They need to justify their *performance* to their subordinates and
      peers to obtain their support and collaboration; but

iv)   If they justify their *personal qualities* ("I have a way with the
      chaps',) to their subordinates, they are seen to adopt a personal
      superiority and aloofness that inhibits the support and compliance
      of subordinates.

Logically we can expect the number of middle management posts in
organisations to decrease in the future with the growing sophistication of
information technology that is available to senior managers and the increasing
complexity of operational tasks that are making necessary more regular
contact directly between senior managers and those at the operational level.
Whether the number of middle managers increases or contracts, Nancy Foy
sounds a word of warning:

> Many middle managers have stopped thinking of themselves as
> developable. Turning them back on may be one of the most
> important steps towards revitalising organisations . . . their power
> is immense, based on deep knowledge of how the organisation
> really works; thus, while they may not be able to bring about
> change themselves, they nonetheless have tremendous capacity to
> block changes other people want, to paralyze an organisation,
> consciously or unconsciously.   (Foy, 1981, p. 28/29)

Supervisory Managers

The largest number of managers are supervisors or first-line managers, with
a range of titles like foreman, office manager, ward sister, sergeant, chief
clerk, superintendent, charge hand, leading seaman, head steward, floor
manager, leading chef. In any organisation most employees report to a
supervisor, who is responsible for assigning tasks to them, overlooking their
work, making sure it is done satisfactorily and dealing with all complaints
and queries. It is a job that has suffered much recently:

> For half a century or more first-line supervisors, especially those in
> manufacturing and clerical work, have seen their roles shrinking in
> status, in importance and in esteem. Where a supervisor was
> "management" to the employee only half a century ago, he or she has
> now, by and large, become a buffer between management, union and
> workers. And like all buffers, the supervisor's main function is to take
> the blows.   (Drucker, 1977)

Unionisation of the workforce has led to shop stewards and other
employee representatives steadily bypassing the first line of management in
order to raise with middle and senior managers issues that lie beyond the
competence of the supervisor to deal with ("we want to see the organ grinder;

not the monkey"). There is also a widespread feeling among supervisors, that senior managers are reluctant to confirm that supervisors are used as expendable front-line troops in skirmishes with organised employees. Either they can be used to test out an initiative that senior managers can then repudiate if it does not work, or they are used to delay things while their senior managers try to decide on a plan of campaign.

Most top managers have previously been senior managers and nearly all senior managers have been middle managers, but few top, senior or middle managers have ever been supervisors. The supervisory post is often the career culmination for people who start in an operative post, so that in many organisations the management hierarchy starts in the lower reaches of middle management. There are exceptions: nursing, teaching and the police service are all occupations in which the only feasible starting point for a career is at the bottom. Marks and Spencer provides one of the best known examples of a career progression style that involves the potential manager starting at the bottom and working up from there. In most employment, however, it is rare for people to work their way up from supervisory positions. This has some interesting effects:

a) There is a clear gap between the management hierarchy or pyramid and the supervisory grades.

b) Supervisors come to rest in their supervisory position. It is the end of the road, so that their main objective soon becomes the maintenance of the status quo; they are seldom bidding for promotion.

c) Those in middle and senior positions frequently lack the ability to judge the fine detail of the actual job that the organisation exists to carry out. In the earlier section of this chapter about middle managers we saw the tendency for their technical skills to become outdated; here we are referring to the problem of them not being able to make a judgement because of never having had "coalface" experience. This has led to such problems as production engineers specifying equipment that is technically appropriate, but inappropriate to the skills and expertise of production employees. Many industrial relations disputes and difficulties with technological innovation begin for just this reason.

d) The supervisory role has been largely neglected in the whole management development circus. Management courses seldom have relevance to supervisory, first-line duties, although there are some separate courses for supervisors.

There is a dearth of recent studies of supervisors, but some of long standing (Guest, 1956 and Mahoney, 1965) show that the supervisor's life is remarkably similar to that of the senior manager in that he is likely to be busy, frequently interrupted and constantly switching between jobs, as he too is dealing with the immediate and the urgent. Unlike the senior manager, he spends most time with subordinates, some with peers and little with superiors or outsiders.

Level	Main Characteristics
Top managers	Relatively detached from the organisation; few, but very important, responsibilities; spend most of their time with outsiders and with peers, very little with subordinates.
Senior managers	Head up functions or operations; concerned with policy formulation and implementation; work tends to be hectic and frequently interrupted; often out of the office; spend time dealing with outsiders, peers and subordinates.
Middle managers	Work mainly within the organisation and are concerned with making the organisation work; can be line or staff; work mainly with peers and senior managers; calmer situation than that of senior or supervisory managers.
Supervisory managers	Relatively detached from the management hierarchy, but vitally concerned with the main activities of the organisation; busy, frequently interrupted and constantly switching between jobs; spend most time with subordinates, some with peers and little with superiors or outsiders.

Figure 4.1   Management Jobs Classified by Level

3. AN ALTERNATIVE APPROACH TO CATEGORISING MANAGEMENT JOBS

In organisations where the differentiation of top, senior, middle and supervisory does not fit neatly — such as matrix, differentiated and ad hoc structures (see Chapter 3) methods that might be more appropriate and helpful have been devised by Mintzberg (1973) and Stewart (1976). Here we give an account of Mintzberg's method and the alternative method of Rosemary Stewart is described in an appendix to this chapter.

Mintzberg studied management job holders in North America and subsequently listed ten management roles (see Fig. 4.2) that were present in the jobs of all managers, although the proportion varied with different jobs. He argues that managers derive status from the formal authority they have over the units, departments or activities with which they are identified. Because of this position they are involved in interpersonal relations with subordinates, peers and superiors, who provide the manager with the information he needs to make decisions.

Review Topic 4.1

If salary, conditions of employment and security were all equal, would you rather be a top manager, a senior manager, a middle manager or a supervisory manager? What are the reasons for your choice?

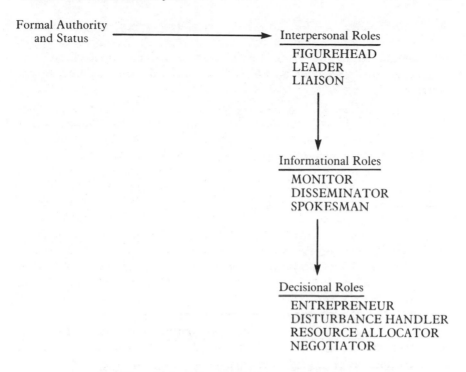

Figure 4.2   Mintzberg's Managerial Roles

Interpersonal Roles. These help keep the organisation running smoothly. The *figurehead* role is where the manager has certain ceremonial duties to perform, like taking a customer to lunch or greeting a visitor, where he is representing the unit or activity for which he is responsible. As a *leader* the manager is dealing with subordinates and enabling them to perform well and meet objectives, while his role as *liaison* requires him to deal with people outside his unit, either peers within the organisation or customers, suppliers and others outside.

Informational Roles. Mintzberg regards as the most important aspects of the manager's job those activities which are concerned with giving and receiving information. As *monitor* the manager seeks to be well informed about events relating to his section of the organisation. He gathers and stores information that will be useful, by questioning subordinates, tapping a personal network of contacts and scanning unsolicited information that comes in. As *disseminator* the manager distributes information to subordinates that would otherwise not be available to them. This, of course, is a crucial aspect of the manager/subordinate relationship and the main source of the trust or mistrust existing in that relationship. As *spokesperson* the manager passes on information he has collected to people outside his unit or outside his organisation. A large part of this role is keeping the boss informed, but other aspects might be advice to a customer about a product or information to a supplier about modifications that are required before delivery.

Decisional Roles. In these cases the manager makes use of the information he receives to make his decisions. In the role of *entrepreneur* he is trying to make changes because he thinks that a new idea is worth pursuing, that it will develop his area of activity and responsibility. As *disturbance handler* he is not initiating change but coping with the result of situations that he cannot control: a customer goes bankrupt, the warehouse is burned down, someone is away sick or any one of the thousand situations that have to be managed to prevent the disturbance reducing the effectiveness of his unit. The role of *resource allocator* is when the manager decides where and how the resources of his unit, including his own time, will be deployed. The final decisional role is that of *negotiator*, where the manager is doing deals with those people and interests whose consent or co-operation are needed by the manager's organisation but where there is no formal authority *over* them: union representatives, suppliers wanting to change their pricing, local authority officials seeking better employment opportunities, and so forth. Negotiating is an important activity for managers as only they have the information that negotiating requires and only they have the necessary scope of authority to make realistic decisions about progress in negotiations as the information available to the two parties separately is gradually exchanged and organised. As the proportions of the roles varied from job to job, Mintzberg (1973, pp. 126–129) concluded that there were eight types of managerial job:

The Contact Man, who is a figurehead and liaises with outside agencies.

The Political Manager, who spends a lot of time outside the organisation trying to reconcile conflicting forces that affect it.

The Entrepreneur, who seeks opportunities and implements change in the organisation.

The Insider, who tries to build up and maintain internal expectations by fire-fighting.

The Real Time Manager, who tries to build up and maintain a stable system over time.

The Team Manager, who is preoccupied with the creation of a team which will operate effectively as a cohesive whole.

The Expert Manager, who advises other managers and is consulted on specialised problems.

The New Manager, who so far lacks the contacts and information to be any of the other seven.

Review Topic 4.2

Of the eight types of managerial job listed by Mintzberg, which is most like the one you have now? Which would you like to be? What are your reasons?

SUMMARY PROPOSITIONS

4.1 Management jobs are of such variety that precise definition is impracticable.

4.2 The most familiar methods of classifying management jobs are according to function and organisational level.

4.3 The research of Rosemary Stewart and Henry Mintzberg has provided novel ways of classifying management jobs that enlarge our understanding of the variety that is comprehended by the term "management".

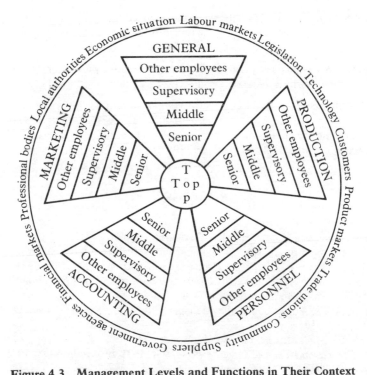

Figure 4.3   Management Levels and Functions in Their Context

APPENDIX

The Stewart method of classifying management jobs

Rosemary Stewart is a British research worker who has spent 20 years studying management work and who produced a quite original classification method in 1976. She regarded the main weaknesses of the function/level mode of classification as being the assumption of similarities rather than a search for differences. She studied the behavioural rather than the technical content of managers' jobs and asked questions about the demands that the job made on the manager's behaviour. After detailed examination of the demands made by 252 jobs she produced a novel typology, the bare outline of which we reproduce here as it enables the readers to think about their jobs in a fresh way and to understand better the constraints and opportunities available to them. (pp. 15, 16).

> HUB jobs have necessary contact with subordinates, superiors, peers and others above and below them in the hierarchy. This was the most common type of job among the managers studied and had a dominant man-management component. (*116 jobs*).

> PEER DEPENDENT jobs were those where there was less "vertical" demand and much dependence on winning the co-operation of peers. They were much found at the boundaries of the organisation. (*63 jobs*).

> MAN-MANAGEMENT jobs were those concerned primarily with the vertical type of working relationship, having contact mainly with superiors and subordinates. (*52 jobs*).

> SOLO jobs were those of managers who spent a large proportion of their time working alone on assignments. (*22 jobs*).

The full account of Dr. Stewart's work and results of her investigation are to be found in Stewart R. *Contrasts in Management*, McGraw-Hill, Maidenhead, 1976. Further development of both methods and ideas are to be found in Stewart R. *Choices for Managers*, McGraw-Hill, Maidenhead, 1982.

REFERENCES

Carlson S., *Executive Behaviour*, Strömbergs, Stockholm, 1951.

Child J., "The Non-productive Component within the Productive Sector", in Fores M. and Glover I. (eds.), *Manufacturing and Management* (HMSO) 1978.

Copeman G., Luijk H., Haneka F., *How the Executive Spends his Time*, Business Publications, London 1963.

Dickson J., "The Plight of Middle Managers" in *Management Today*, December 1977.

Drucker P.F., *Management*, Pan Books, London 1977, p. 243.

Foy N., *The Yin and Yang of Organizations*, (Grant McIntyre) London, 1981.

Guest R., "Of Time and the Foreman", in *Personnel*, May 1956, pp. 478–486.

Horne J.H. and Lupton T. "The Work Activities of Middle Managers", in *Journal of Management Studies*, February 1965, pp. 14–33.

Hunt   J., "The Plight of the Manager", in *Work and People*, Vol. 5, pp. 27–32.

Jones D. *et al.*, *The Role of the Nursing Officer*, Department of Health and Social Security, London 1981.

Mahoney T. "The Jobs of Management" in *Industrial Relations*, February 1965, pp. 97–110.

Marshall J. and Cooper C.L., "Work Experience of Middle and Senior Managers", in *Management International Review*, vol. 19, 1979, pp. 81–96.

Mintzberg H., *The Nature of Managerial Work*, Harper & Row, London 1973.

Mintzberg H. "The Manager's Job: Folklore and Fact", in *Harvard Business Review*, July–August 1975, pp. 49–61.

Parker H., "Managing the Managers: the Role of the Board", in *The Arts of Top Management* (Mann R. ed.), McGraw-Hill, London 1970, p. 31.

Parkinson C.N., *Parkinson's Law*, John Murray, London 1957.

Porter L. and Ghiselli E., "The Self Perceptions of Top and Middle Management Personnel", in *Personnel Psychology*, vol. 10, 1957, pp. 397–406.

Stewart R., *Contrasts in Management*, McGraw Hill, Maidenhead, 1976.

Stewart R., *Choices for Managers*, McGraw Hill, Maidenhead, 1982.

Torrington D.P. and Weightman J.B., "Technical Atrophy in Middle Management", in *Journal of General Management*, Summer 1982.

Whyte W.H., *The Organisation Man*, Simon & Schuster, New York, 1956.

Chapter Five

MANAGERIAL WORK

Having, in the last chapter, distinguished between different types of management job, we now examine what managers do, and especially what different types of manager have in common.

The work of management has to be assumed from the activities of managers, which are mainly talking, reading, writing, telephoning, using electronic hardware, driving cars, waiting for aircraft, attending meetings and so on. We have to infer the nature of management work from these activities, as well as distinguishing it from the work of people not called managers; and distinguishing it from the other work done by managers that is technical, such as selling, budget preparation, design engineering or whatever their specialist area happens to be.

There are five main ways of trying to understand management work. First one can study the behaviour of managers by asking them to fill in detailed *diaries* of how they spend their time or by observing their behaviour over a period. Classic examples of this type of study are Carlson (1951), Stewart (1967) and Mintzberg (1971). Secondly, one can read the *autobiographies* of successful managers and leaders who try to pass on what they found worked in their experience, their prescriptions of how others can replicate the success that they have enjoyed. Statesmen and generals are the best known providers of this type of material, but examples of successful managers' writing are Sloan (1967) and Falk (1961).

A slightly different version of this is where a person with a successful business career attempts an explicitly management book. Examples are Barnard (1938), Brown (1971) and Townsend (1970). A third method is to *interview* managers about what they do. Examples of this approach are Marshall and Stewart (1981), Kotter (1982) and Torrington and Weightman (1982).

Fourthly one can look at *management textbooks*. These make implicit assumptions about the nature of management work by choosing to include some subjects but not others, partly because some aspects of management are more suitable for written treatment than others, as was mentioned in Chapter One. Most textbooks employ the conventional categories of management work suggested by Fayol: planning, organising, controlling, commanding and co-ordinating. The fifth method is a detailed, *empirical study* of a particular area of management, which can provide a great deal of information about specific aspects such as motivation or leadership.

None of these is sufficient alone. Diaries are very revealing, but many managers are reluctant to compile them and to reveal themselves in what they regard as an unfavourable light. The problem of objectivity is also present with autobiographies, together with the fact that the very successful usually have the benefit of some exceptional personal qualities or good luck that were the main determinants of their success, and enabled them to operate in an idiosyncratic way that others would find hard to emulate. Interviewing managers introduces the detachment of the interviewer to achieve a more objective account than simple self-reporting, but the manager being interviewed is the sole source of information. Textbooks have the drawback that their purpose is to provide appropriate material for study, so there will always be a selection for emphasis of that which it is easiest to handle in written form. This is one reason why textbooks have always had such a large proportion devoted to decision-making. Empirical study is always partial and tends to isolate the subject being examined from the context in which it was undertaken.

The most fruitful way of trying to understand management work is to blend insights from all these sources.

1. HOW MANAGERS SPEND THEIR TIME

In 1981 Roger Mansfield and his colleagues reported on a detailed survey carried out in the previous year among 1,058 British managers, widely spread geographically and between different types of organisation. One question to the respondents was the amount of time spent on work each week. Remembering the problem of self-reported information that has already been mentioned, the figures suggest that managers spend about the same amount of time working as manual workers on overtime: see Figure 5.1.

Hours per week	Percentage of sample
less than 30	0.7
31–40	14.1
41–50	44.3
51–60	27.7
61–70	10.5
more than 70	2.7

(Mansfield et al., 1981)

Figure 5.1   Weekly Hours Spent Working by British Managers in 1980

Other evidence suggests that managers at middle and lower levels spend less time on work (Horne & Lupton, 1965) and chief executives seldom stop thinking of their jobs (Carlson, 1951). This can, however, give no more than a very general picture as these replies are affected by some uncertainty in the minds of the respondents regarding what does and does not constitute management work. Is reading *The Financial Times* work or pleasure?

Undoubtedly the activities of most managers are characterised by brevity, variety and fragmentation. For example, Mintzberg (1973) found that the chief executives he studied made contact, on average, with 52 people each day. Only 10 per cent of tasks took an hour or more and more than 50 per cent of tasks took less than nine minutes. This differs sharply from the specialisation and extended periods of application to a single task that characterise most non-managerial jobs.

Managers spend much of their time, between 50 per cent and 80 per cent, in conversation with others (Guest 1955, Stewart 1967 and Mintzberg 1973). Stewart found that they spent an average of 41 per cent of their time with subordinates, 12 per cent with superiors and 47 per cent with others. Mintzberg has similar results and suggests a preference among managers for spoken rather than written material and for current information and live action rather than considered reports.

Review Topic 5.1

With how many people do you make contact in each working day?
What percentage of your daily tasks take more than one hour?
What percentage of your daily tasks take less than nine minutes?

How much of your time do you spend with subordinates?
How much of your time do you spend with superiors?
How much of your time do you spend with others?

Are there any of those numbers or percentages you would like to change?
If so, why?

Mintzberg (1975) uses this sort of evidence to argue that managers are not in fact devoting their time to planning, decision-making and the other types of reflective activity which the textbooks suggest. If, however, we take account of what is being said in all these face-to-face encounters and telephone conversations, very often decisions are being taken and plans being laid, although the independent observer may regard the process as lacking system and thoroughness. Similarly the business lunch has considerable potential content in terms of information exchanged, discussion and agreement on actions to follow, even though some may consider it a wasteful and self-indulgent method for managers to conduct their affairs by.

These studies tell us that managers spend much of their time in conversation with a variety of people and they are frequently interrupted, but why do managers work in this way?

2. DIFFERENT TYPES OF MANAGEMENT WORK

There are three distinct strands in the work that managers do: *technical*, *administrative* and *managerial*. In Chapter Four we introduced the importance of technical skills for managers especially at the middle levels. The technical work of a manager is that work he does, not because he is a manager, but almost in spite of that fact; work concerned with the main task of the organisation, section or department, and it is probably the work of at least some subordinates as well. It is the head teacher teaching children in the classroom, the chief designer working at his drawing board, or the garage proprietor tuning the engine on a customer's car.

This technical work involves the manager using the skills and knowledge he acquired through qualifications, training and experience. Many of these technical skills could be transferred to all other organisations where they are used, like the examples quoted in the last paragraph, or they may be specific to the particular organisation in which the manager works, such as understanding precisely how Shell's polymer functions in practice, or how Coca-Cola is made. We suggested in Chapter Four that a manager abandons these skills at his peril, as he can then lose touch with the main task of the department or organisation, although the management development process in many British organisations appears to encourage managers to let their technical skills atrophy.

Administrative work is concerned with organisational maintenance, while managerial work is taking initiatives. The one is carrying out official, often regular, duties authorised by others, such as the organisational superior or a committee; the other is conducting and controlling organisational affairs with the freedom to create precedents. Much of "management" literature is about administrative activities with its emphasis on administering the stable state rather than the unstable, uncertain world faced by many managers.

One aspect of the managerial/administrative distinction is intuitively described by many managers when they talk about the scope that a person has to make mistakes or exercise discretion. The greater the discretion, the greater the managerial content of the job and the more one is setting rather than following precedents. This is reflected in the timespan theory of discretion advanced by Elliott Jaques (1970), who postulated that all jobs had a prescribed content and a discretionary content. The first were those elements of work over which the job holder has no authorised choice, while the second was that area of work where the job holder chose how to do his work. Jaques used this to describe *all* work, not just managerial work, and devised the concept of the timespan of discretion:

> The maximum period of time during which the use of discretion is authorised and expected, without review of that discretion by a superior.

(Jaques, 1970, p. 21).

It is the greater range of discretion open to managers, and especially the greater length of time that will elapse before the effect of mistakes is known, that is one of the distinctive characteristics of management work.

This administrative/managerial distinction can also be expressed in terms of novelty and comfort. Like many human activities, managerial work is active, extrovert and novelty seeking, concerned with initiating and taking risks by setting precedents. Administrative work is a quieter activity, introvert and providing the comfort of familiarity and dealing with what is known. It keeps the system going by maintaining things in working order. Scitovsky (1976) discusses how a number of psychologists have offered the opinion that the novelty/comfort balance in human beings is always in a state of change, according to the situation in which they find themselves. The behaviour of those facing bereavement is often characterised by actions that are so prosaic as to seem bizarre, like women needing to go to the hairdresser or to go shopping, and men deciding to decorate the back bedroom or work on the car. This is not callousness but seeking the comfort of the familiar at a time when the crises are too great to bear.

When a manager is faced with too many difficult problems and is uncertain about what to do, he may take great comfort in filling in timesheets, record cards or other routine administrative tasks. The executive briefcase is partly a badge of office ("I am important") but also contains a supply of administrative comforters to go with the indigestion tablets. The first-class compartments of intercity trains are full of managers travelling to meetings and passing the time by "catching up on their reading" or "checking through the figures". On the other hand, when the routine paperwork becomes too oppressive a manager may seek some stimulus to get the adrenaline flowing: he goes looking for novelty or excitement. Much of the by-play of organisational politics described in the next chapter comes from this need for challenge.

The career development circus has been one of the means whereby a manager's need to initiate has been met. Young men and women identified as having high potential have taken the opportunity to change jobs fairly often, perhaps seven or eight times by their early thirties. When they reach their peak the number of job changes drops sharply; and if that coincides with the time of life when the heyday in the blood is tame, humble and waiting upon the judgement, then the manager may welcome a shift in emphasis towards more administration of the stable state and less hectic excitement. Not all managers, however, age at the same rate or at the same time. Furthermore the career development move has become harder to accomplish with the contraction of the managerial labour market and this presents a new problem for aspiring managers and for the organisations in which their careers get bogged down. It is difficult to keep initiating new solutions to old problems and there is the danger that the creative drive of the enthusiastic young manager may be redirected into the more destructive aspects of organisational politics or away from organisational concerns altogether, so that the manager's working life is one of lack-lustre organisational maintenance during the day while his creative energies are channelled into selling life insurance in the evenings, writing crime novels or running the local operatic society.

Review Topic 5.2

In your job have you got the balance right between technical, administrative and managerial work?

---

3. THE DISTINCTION BETWEEN MANAGEMENT AND OTHER WORK

Most other jobs have an immediate inbuilt purpose and logic. The schoolteacher faces the classroom of children waiting to be occupied, the machinist has a pile of cloth waiting to be made into shirts, the chef has customers waiting for food to be cooked and the postman has a satchel full of letters to deliver. The job is clear in its logic, which is to translate a demand from the system of the organisation into activities or tasks to be undertaken by the job holder.

Managers have some aspects of their jobs that are like this: the in-tray full of papers, the incoming mail to be dealt with, the outgoing letters to sign, the telephone to be answered. These are responses, mainly administrative, to demands from the system of the organisation. An activity of a manager is to read letters that arrive in much the same way as the activity of a postman is to deliver the letters in the first place. *How* the manager responds to the letter will be one aspect of how management work differs from other work, as it is likely to involve some aspects of problem solving and decision taking with features of co-ordination and command. He is still, however, reacting to a situation and responding to the initiatives of others. Managers we have studied usually describe these activities — mail, paperwork, answering the telephone, dealing with enquiries — as time consuming and unsatisfying. They prefer those activities where they impose their own logic on a task rather than the task having its own logic which is imposed on the manager. They prefer "making things happen" or being proactive instead of reactive.

Managers enjoy the degree of autonomy which they have in being able to control the details of their working programme by the use of their personal diary. Every Christmas one of the favourite "executive presents" is the desk diary in hand-tooled leather, which is a status symbol because it declares the flexibility that managers have. Not for them the precisely controlled and timetabled day: they organise their own daily and weekly programme. Although many demands are made on their time, the individual manager usually reserves the right to agree that something can be "fitted in" to his schedule, which he spends much time reviewing, re-ordering and projecting. Most other workers have a daily schedule or just do what they are asked to do as it occurs, but managers have a greater range of discretion, so that they exercise choice (*pace* Rosemary Stewart) not only in *what* they do and *how* they do it, but also *when* they do it.

Another aspect of this range of choice is the degree of responsibility which managers carry. "That is my decision . . ." is a typical statement by a manager asserting and taking pleasure in his power. "That is my responsibility . . ." is the statement of a manager asserting his duty, but also declaring his status by setting himself apart from the ordinary people who merely hew wood and draw water, leading simple lives unburdened by any sense of duty. The responsibility may be for the results achieved by subordinates, for the decisions reached by the manager himself or for other aspects of the quality of his work, like the satisfaction of his colleagues with his performance and contribution. He certainly has more scope than others for organising his own work and changing the nature and direction of his activities, either through delegation or through initiating changes in his role *vis à vis* other members of the hierarchy. This contrasts with non-managers, who have virtually no choice, despite the programmes of job enrichment and job enlargement that have been popular.

In different ways managers assert and cherish their independence and autonomy, being free from close supervision, having duties that are not repetitive and not too specialised.

4. THE CORE BEHAVIOUR OF MANAGEMENT

Can we now produce a list of job dimensions that can characterise a job as managerial, no matter what title it carries?

Several systems have been developed to trade jobs within organisations. One that is highly regarded is the Hay-MSL system of job evaluation, which is based on an assessment of three elements in a job: knowhow, problem solving and accountability, each with subdivisions, as can be seen in Figure 5.2.

The purpose of this and similar systems is obviously to determine which jobs are the more valuable to the organisation and therefore which merit a higher level of pay. This approach has the value that it indicates some of the areas of work that are widely accepted in organisational circles as being managerial. The system defines what management is and then makes possible the assessment of individual jobs to determine how they compare with the model.

An attractively simple approach to defining the core behaviour of managers has been provided by Kotter (1982). In a study of general managers in the United States he concluded that they all had two activities in common: setting agendas for action, and setting up networks to implement those agendas.

He used the word *agenda* in the sense of a list of items to be dealt with, so that it becomes a way of putting into practice all the range of decisions that

1. *Know How*
   a) Technical, professional
   b) Managerial
   c) Human relations

2. *Problem Solving*
   a) Environment in which the thinking takes place; from routine to completely unstructured
   b) Challenge; from repetitive to creative

3. *Accountability*
   a) Degree of discretion; freedom to act
   b) Value of the areas affected by the job
   c) The directness of the impact of the job

Figure 5.2   The Hay-MSL System for Assessing the Content of Management Jobs

are made, such as policy, plans, strategies and agreements. Each of those is an occasional, cerebral act. Setting agendas is the constant activity of managers as plans and ideas are put into operation. "Increase sales turnover by 25 per cent over the next twelve months" is a splendid general statement of policy, but the manager responsible will set up a series of agendas to bring out the desired result. Some hard bargaining with union officials may produce an agreement "to introduce a new scheme of job evaluation", but that will be no more than a general declaration of intent until a manager puts together an agenda of what to do, what to do first, what to check, who to deploy, who to ask, when to aim for as a completion date, and so on. The organisation may have a corporate plan, but the individual managers responsible for achieving the results of the plan will each have a series of agendas, evolving, developing and extending, as the plan becomes a reality.

Review Topic 5.3

What agendas and networks are you currently operating? Is there any way in which you could extend and improve any of your networks?

These variegated frameworks for action are created by a process of thinking out possibilities, constant questioning and aggressively gathering information, with the questioning aided by a shrewd knowledge of the business. Choices are made both analytically and intuitively as careful calculation is combined with skilled guessing to move into action. The agendas are seldom written, although many lists are jotted down on the backs of envelopes, and may be either vague or specific, according to the subject matter.

Agenda setting is one way in which managers impose their will on the situation around them; the other is by setting up and maintaining *networks* through which the agendas are implemented. These are quite different from the formal structure, although no substitute for it. Networks are a reflection of the need for political activity that is discussed in the next chapter. The individual manager identifies a large number of people, both inside the organisation and outside, who will help in implementing agendas, as well as being sources of information to go into agendas. The popular picture of the manager constantly making telephone calls is an expression of the network process of "having a word with" his contacts: the people who help him get things done by speeding something up, providing information, jumping a queue, endorsing a proposal in committee, checking data, arranging for the manager to meet someone and — of course — doing jobs. Networks are peopled partly by subordinates, but by a large variety of others, including those who have some respect for the manager, those who are dependent on him or obliged to him. Position in the hierarchy is crucial to having a good network, but so is expertise and social skilfulness. Methods used to set up networks include using disarming candour, doing small favours for others, being a "nice guy", building a team of willing subordinates and generally shaping the relationships among the people in the network.

Enterprises often begin life as a partnership between two people, one of whom is better at agendas and another who is better at networks. Henry Royce was a brilliant engineer who could see clearly the "agenda" of what was needed to create high-quality motor cars, but it was Charles Rolls who was able to set up and sustain the "network" of business contacts that was to make Rolls Royce a long-running success story. One activity emphasises analysis, imagination and planning; the other emphasises social skill and political judgement. All managers do both, but the most effective are those with equal skill in both areas.

5. THE MANAGEMENT JOB

In Part I of this book we have been describing various ways of classifying managerial work as a means of understanding the range and variety of the managerial role. We have carefully avoided a definition of management or of manager because any definition tends to exclude as many jobs as it includes. Perhaps the most realistic approach is that of Rosemary Stewart in starting her research:

> We used the word "manager" very broadly to include anyone above a certain level, roughly above foreman, whether they were in control of staff or not. There was no need to be more precise because we were interested in studying the jobs that our companies called managerial, and which formed part of the management hierarchy for selection, training and promotion. (1976, p. 2)

Her investigation included jobs with titles like Mill Accountant, Assistant Treasurer, Chief Draughtsman, Nutritionist, Deputy Chief Architect,

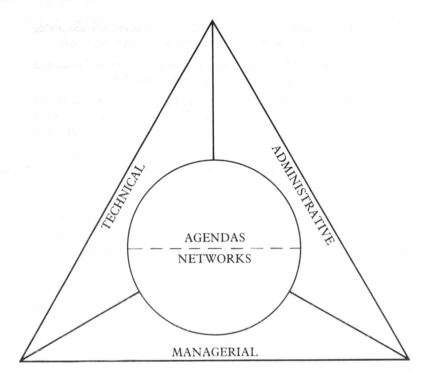

Figure 5.3   Managerial Work and the Core of Managerial Behaviour

Veterinary Officer, and Buyer. This is not because some jobs were included incorrectly, but because the essence of management appears in so many different jobs.

Some jobs have all the elements of management that have been considered in the last few chapters, yet the job holders are never described by that term and would probably not welcome its use about what they do. Only recently have head teachers begun to describe themselves, on occasions, as managers and the use of management ideas is quite widespread in nursing, but town clerks, solicitors, estate agents, orchestral conductors, film directors and choreographers are just a few of the job titles that carry a large management element; so there are some managers who are not called managers.

We have seen so far that managers, whether with that title or not, have a subtle and varied job, although the core behaviours of making agendas and operating networks is so simple that the detractor is inclined to say that the manager's job has been inflated out of all proportion and that any subtlety and complexity is around the job rather than in what managers actually do. In the remainder of this work we set out the details of what makes the management job so much more demanding and rewarding than it first appears, as those with the flair, common sense and experience to be in

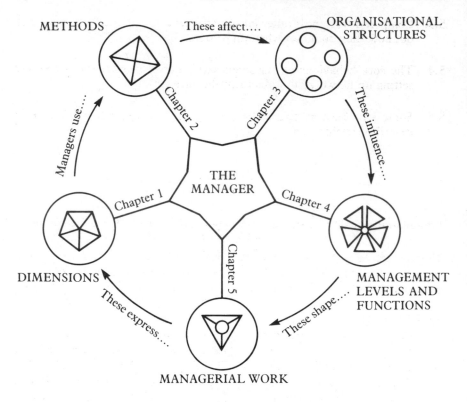

Figure 5.4   The Dynamics of Management

management positions combine the elements we have described to achieve equilibrium by getting all the components in a degree of balance. This is summarised in Fig. 5.4, The Dynamics of Management.

In understanding management work, however, we must always remember:

> Management is a much less tidy, less organised, and less easily defined activity than that traditionally presented by management writers or in job descriptions.   (Stewart, 1976, p. 125)

SUMMARY PROPOSITIONS

5.1. Management work differs from most other types of work in being more varied and staccato, involving extensive interaction with others and responsibility for initiating change.

5.2. The work managers do has three distinctive strands: technical (which is non-management), administrative (which is maintaining the system) and managerial (which is being able to change the system).

5.3. Compared with most other jobs, managers exercise choice in what they do, how they do it and when they do it.

5.4. The core behaviour of management is setting agendas for action and setting up networks to implement the agendas.

5.5. Some jobs have all the hallmarks of being managerial, but are never described in that way.

APPENDIX

Administrative drill to determine management content of one's own job

This is a simple method to analyse the management elements of one's job and the frequency with which they occur. This can help with understanding the demands of the post and modifying those aspects that can be improved.

Account for Time Spent.
1. Keep a diary for at least one week of exactly how time at work is spent.
2. The form is a basis that could be modified to your personal situation. Fill it in as events take place, rather than by recalling what has happened. Every time you switch attention from one subject to another, or from one person to another, that is a *change of activity*, requiring a new sheet. A meeting counts as one activity.
3. Read through the notes about how to analyse the results before starting to record.

Analysis of Diary. This record of exactly what you have done can be used in a number of ways. Here are some suggestions:

1. How many hours did you spend working each day and in the whole week?
2. What percentage of your time is spent with people?
3. How much of this time is spent with superiors, subordinates, others inside the organisation, people outside the organisation?
4. What is the average length of time you spend on an activity and, on average, how many activities do you have in a day? To what extent is your work characterised by brevity, variety and fragmentation, as suggested by Mintzberg?
5. What percentage of your activities is initiated by yourself, your boss, subordinates, others in the organisation, outsiders or by standard procedures? What proportion of your activities are you initiating?
6. Compare the top (giving/making) boxes in the type of activity section with the bottom (seeking/receiving) boxes, in order to see the balance of your activities between initiating and responding.
7. What do you do most and least?

Outcome of Analysis.   By looking at the descriptions can you sort the sheets into categories, viz:

a)   Mainly technical;
b)   Mainly administrative, e.g. routine paperwork, getting typing done;
c)   Mainly managerial, e.g. influencing others, resolving conflict;
d)   Others, e.g. personal, don't knows, mixture.

How satisfied are you with the distribution? What can you do to improve it?

Sample Diary Sheet.

	Change of Activity to (brief description)		
Time	*Start:*	*Finish:*	*Date:*
Who with	*Number:* Boss/subordinate/other in organisation/outsider/none		
How	Face-to-face/'phone/paper/computer terminal/travelling/thinking		
Initiative by	Self/other/boss/subordinate/standard procedure		
Type of Activity	Giving Information	Giving Advice	Giving Explanation
	Seeking Information	Seeking Advice	Seeking Explanation
	Exchanging Information	Giving Instructions	Giving Agreement
	Receiving Information	Receiving Instructions	Seeking Agreement
	Making Plans	Making Decisions	Making Inspections
	Receiving Plans	Receiving Decisions	Receiving Inspections
	Organising self – timetable, diary, packing up. Organising information. Filing. Social. Other (specify).		
Sort of work	Technical/administrative/managerial		
Outcome	Satisfactory/successful/neutral/disappointing/frustrating		

REFERENCES

Barnard, C.I., *The Functions of the Executive*, Harvard University Press, Cambridge, Mass., 1938.

Brown, W., *Organization*, Heinemann, London, 1971.

Carlson, S., *Executive Behaviour*, Strömbergs, Stockholm, 1951.

Falk, R., *The Business of Management*, Penguin Books, Harmondsworth, Middlesex, 1961.

Guest, R., "On Time and the Foreman", in *Personnel*, No. 32, pp. 478–468, 1955.

Horne, J. and Lupton, T., "The Work Activities of Middle Managers", in *Journal of Management Studies*, Vol. 2, pp. 14–33, 1965.

Jaques, E., *Equitable Payment*, Heinemann, London, 1970.

Kotter, J., *The General Managers*, Free Press, New York, 1982.

Mansfield, R., Poole, M., Blyton, P., Frost, P., "The British Manager in Profile", *BIM Survey 51*, British Institute of Management, London, 1981.

Marshall, J. and Stewart, R., "Managers' Job Perceptions", in *Journal of Management Studies*, Vol. 18, Nos. 2 and 3, pp. 177–190 and 263–275.

Mintzberg, H., "Managerial Work: Analysis from Observation", in *Management Science*, 1971, Vol. 18, p. 97–110.

Mintzberg, H., *The Nature of Managerial Work*, Harper and Row, London, 1973.

Mintzberg, H., "The Manager's Job: Folklore and Fact", in *Harvard Business Review*, July/August, 1975, p. 49.

Sloan, A.P., *My Years with General Motors*, (edited J. MacDonald), Pan Books, London, 1967.

Scitovsky, T., *The Joyless Economy*, Oxford University Press, 1976.

Stewart, R., *Managers and their Jobs*, Macmillan, London, 1967.

Stewart, R., *Contrasts in Management*, McGraw-Hill, Maidenhead, 1976.

Torrington, D.P., and Weightman, J.B., "Technical Atrophy in Middle Management", in *Journal of General Management*, 1982.

Townsend, R., *Up the Organization*, Michael Joseph, London, 1970.

Part II

WORKING IN THE ORGANISATION

The first collection of skills and knowledge that the manager needs are those concerned with being effective within the overall organisation framework, working with peers, superiors and outsiders.

This part of the book opens with a discussion of organisational politics, the flux of relationships involving authority and power. This is followed by an analysis of how organisation communication works, although organisational communication is only as good as the interpersonal communication forming its basis. For communication between people to be effective we have to understand something of human behaviour, both why those around us behave in the way they do and how they respond to us. When working with those outside their particular department or section, managers have to gain co-operation and collaboration, so we have one chapter about winning consent without having authority and another on the workings of committees, which are a relatively formal way in which such dealings frequently take place. The final chapter is on ways of developing administrative procedures and drills for action.

Figure 11.3, Working in the organisation, relates the activities discussed in this part of the book against the background of the Chapter 5 analysis of management work.

Chapter Six

ORGANISATIONAL POLITICS

The idea of behaving politically is one that managers do not readily accept for themselves. This is partly because of the immediate association of the word "political" with national and local government, but also because the word carries connotations of insincerity and deviousness and managers disparage these qualities in their colleagues (not themselves being guilty of such behaviour) and deplore the extent to which they detract from the main tasks of the organisation in which they are employed.

When Shepherd Mead wrote his book *How to Succeed in Business Without Really Trying*, he described the activities of his central character who achieved power and influence through *appearing* to do the right things whilst actually doing very little: image without reality. This idea was so unthinkable in the context of American business that it could only be expressed by making the whole thing a joke. It is a very funny book, but it became a best-seller because it also had the qualities of the good horror story, near enough to reality for the reader to thank his lucky stars that he was not such an unprincipled person; at the same time as working out how close each of his colleagues came to the model.

Much of management development activity in recent years and the underlying emphasis of organisation behaviour punditry is that openness in one's behaviour brings results as relationships with colleagues become more candid and constructive through stripping away the veneer of posturing and guile that otherwise masks integrity. The attractiveness of candour and integrity are so obvious that it may seem strange to bring discussion of politics into a book about management. Why should managers understand politics?

1. POWER IN ORGANISATIONS

The formal structure of the organisation, as described in Chapter 3, is a map of working relationships that are official and is the main device for distributing power among organisation members. The formal distribution is not the only determinant of the power held by individuals: it is the main

BM–D

factor in providing people with resource power, but not power from other sources. Dalton (1959) conducted a detailed study of the power structure in a large American manufacturing plant and included a grading of the relative influence wielded by different members of the management. In many instances this did not correspond with their position in the hierarchy. An example was the relative influence of a plant manager, Stevens, and his assistant, Hardy:

> In executive meetings Stevens was clearly less forceful than Hardy. Appearing nervous and worried, Stevens usually opened meetings with a few remarks and then silently gave way to Hardy, who dominated thereafter. During the meeting most questions were directed to Hardy. While courteous, Hardy's statements usually were made without request for confirmation from Stevens. Hardy and Stevens and other high officers daily lunched together. There, too, Hardy dominated the conversations and was usually the target for questions. This was not just an indication that he carried the greater burden of minor duties often assigned to assistants . . . for he had a hand in most issues, including major ones.
>
> (p. 23)

Hardy apparently was more strongly motivated than Stevens towards acquiring power and probably had more skill.

The amount of power can also vary according to the problems that are paramount for an organisation at a particular time, so that power accrues to those organisation members or sections who are coping with critical organisation problems.

Harry Denton was an order clerk in a company that supplied portable, battery-operated equipment for use in coal mines. Harry's job was to deal with all the orders that came in for the batteries, ensuring that the goods were despatched and invoiced. He was so quietly efficient that he got on with his job year by year and was left alone. Then there was a nationwide selective strike by a union that sought to bring industrial action to support its case by calling out on strike its members in some companies where the interruption of supply could be particularly effective. Harry's company was one of those where strike action was called because of the importance of the batteries that Harry despatched. Suddenly Harry was a man of great influence in his company, taking part in meetings with directors and senior managers much concerned about how many batteries were in stock, how many were in depots, how many in transit, how many orders pending; all questions to which Harry, and only Harry, knew the answers. He was an unassuming man, not seeking promotion or other personal advantage, but he had been trying for years to get a small change made in the warehouse administrative routines, and had been asking for months if he could have a direct telephone connection to the vehicle loading bay. Both requests were now agreed and dealt with in a few hours. Harry Denton had suddenly acquired power because of the critical organisational problem with which he was dealing.

Another factor in governing the political activity of managers is the degree of their dependency on others. A Management Development Officer, for instance, is more dependent on his colleagues than the Chief Accountant, as he has to convince them of the value of his activities and persuade them to participate in his training activities and co-operate in identifying training needs. Managers in dependent positions have to spend more time in building relationships with their colleagues and worrying about breakdowns in communication and understanding.

Kotter (1978) examined the situation of two managers. X was a plant manager whose main dealings were with only four groups: the company president, plant employees, customers and suppliers. He had high dependency on the president and the customers, but only medium dependency on employees and suppliers. Y was a hospital administrator with six high dependencies and seven medium dependencies. Kotter found that Y spent 80 per cent of her day in activities relating to power and influence over others, but X spent only 30 per cent of his time on that sort of activity (*ibid.* p. 30). This matches some of Rosemary Stewart's conclusions, reported in Chapter 4, about the different types of management job, one of which is peer dependent.

Having reviewed these aspects of the importance of organisational politics it is useful to take note of the following definition of Pfeffer (1981):

> Organizational politics involves those activities undertaken within an organization to acquire, develop, and use power and other resources to obtain one's preferred outcomes in a situation in which there is uncertainty or dissensus about choices.
>
> (p. 7)

Power is a property that exists in any organisation or system; politics is the way in which that power is put into action.

2. THE PLACE OF POLITICS IN MANAGEMENT

Dahl is one of the political theorists who helps us to an understanding of organisational politics, as he points out that political behaviour stems from conflicting aims:

> If everyone were perfectly agreed on ends and means, no-one would ever need to change the way of another. Hence no relations of influence or power would arise. Hence no political system would exist. Let one person frustrate another in the pursuit of his goals and you already have the germ of a political system; conflict and politics are born inseparable twins.
>
> (Dahl, 1970, p. 59)

Any organisation has within it limited resources for its members. Organisation members compete with each other for promotion in developing their careers. On an everyday basis they will be competing for resources in material terms: a bigger departmental budget, more space, newer equipment, more staff, and greater influence over the direction of the general organisational policy. This competition causes the nature of political activity to vary according to the state of growth or decline that the organisation is in. With growth there is the oportunity for all members to "win" the above sort of competitions. If the organisation is stagnant, then the person who gets a bigger amount of resources can only do this at the expense of someone else, so the arguments may be more bitter. If the organisation is declining, the political activity will often be less sparkling because of the demoralising effect of decline and possibly the greater anxiety to stick together in adversity. In the stable situation politics cause some to win while others lose, but the dynamics of that situation and the range of external considerations should cause the winners to be those who have a stronger substantive case. Only in growth is there likely to be a situation in which all are winners.

It may be that political behaviour often involves being devious and cunning, but the substance of political activity is the manipulation of *power*. Those who understand the subtleties of power in relationships are better able to get things done than those who ignore them:

> ...the graveyards of history are strewn with the corpses of reformers who failed utterly to reform anything, of revolutionaries who failed to win power . . . of anti-revolutionaries who failed to prevent a revolution – men and women who failed not only because of the forces arrayed against them but because the pictures in their minds about power and influence were simplistic and inaccurate.
>
> (Dahl, 1970, p.15)

Organisations have power as one their crucial dimensions, and only by understanding how power is distributed and deployed can members of organisations get things done. The innovative idea or the accurate diagnosis is insufficient without the means for their implementation. This is considered further in chapter 23.

Here are some of the ways in which organisational politics are important:

Competition.   Members of organisations compete with each other. They compete for more attractive posts further up the hierarchy and for opportunities to develop their careers and express their individual interests. The most important aspect of competition is for resources, which are always scarce in relation to the needs of organisation members and where one man gets his extra budget only at the expense of someone else who does not.

Performance measurement.   There are few objective means of measuring performance of those holding managerial and administrative posts because of the interdependence of their activities. An author writes books, the sales of which are a measure of his worth; a batsman scores a certain number of runs; a tennis player wins or loses a match; a research scientist can discover a new cure for a crippling disease; but the manager embedded in the complex web of relationships of a contemporary organisation is bereft of such objective criteria for determining his success and failure. He therefore has to win friends and influence people by impressing his superiors with his personal qualities and loyalty, by building an empire of subordinates or by making alliances with colleagues.

Job mobility. Political behaviour is encouraged by job mobility. In many large organisations job mobility is a requirement for all those with career aspirations, who are moved from post to post and often from location to location for most of their working lives. Geographical mobility has become less attractive with the tightening of the labour market and the development of career expectations among women, who may be very reluctant to abandon a satisfying and well-paid job in Birmingham to follow a husband to Aberdeen, where she may find her employment prospects to be poor and her husband to be even more preoccupied than before with his own career. Although less attractive, geographical mobility still features strongly in the organisational life of many high-flying young managers and movement within the organisation structure is very common. This means that it is even more difficult for the mobile manager to show depth of accomplishment in any one position, and he feels the need to impress and manipulate the perceptions of those around him. After moving from Birmingham to Aberdeen his wife will be left even more to her own devices because he has to spend so much time winning friends and influencing people in the strange, new business context to make sure that he is eventually promoted away from Aberdeen.

Style of Leadership. There has been a gradual change in leadership style in recent years which has changed the nature of politics in many organisations. The entrepreneurial form which was described in Chapter 3 is an overtly political situation as there is high concentration of power in the centre. Modern management thinking in bureaucratic and matrix structures has become more democratic than autocratic, and much of this book is devoted to winning consent rather than simply telling people what to do. Going along with this has been the increasing impracticality of an individual manager being able to get approval for a programme of action simply by selling the idea to his boss: there is more dependence on committees, task groups and alliances. Not only does this require the deployment of what could be called the skills of diplomacy (tact, skill and cunning in dealing with people to win their support for your aims) it also tends to produce underhand, Watergate-type behaviour among managers who are uneasy with a democratic style.

Political context.   All organisations operate in a political context. They are concerned with national political movements, international events that could close an export market or jeopardise the supply of a raw material, and with the volatility of the stock market. The salesman trying to land an order has to establish where in his customer's organisation the authority to purchase lies. Is he dealing with the right person? Some companies depend on changes in government policy for an improvement in their business, and those in public sector organisations are closely concerned with national political thinking.

Review Topic 6.1

The English philosopher and essayist Francis Bacon (1561–1626) made the comment "...it is a strange desire to seek power and to lose liberty...". Are the two necessarily connected in organisational life?

There are four main sources of power for the individual or group to garner in order to exercise political influence: resources, skill, motivation and obligations. The most obvious is the control of *resources*. He who controls what others need is in the position of relative power. We have seen this in the early historical developments, where it was the granaries of the Pharaoh that gave him the power to weld together the nation state of Egypt. The power of a contemporary government resides largely in the system of taxation and state spending, and the power of the British crown lies largely in the accolades of social esteem which only the monarch can bestow, whether it be an earldom or a telegram for your diamond wedding. The resources which managers control are similar. They may not be able to ennoble their subjects, but they do offer or withhold promotions. This is why most public sector employment has rules and procedures to ensure that at least the appearance of the process whereby people are appointed to posts is "democratic", so as to prevent any individual wielding too much power. Equally managers influence the level of earnings which people can receive, and employees have worked hard in their collective organisations to reduce managerial power over the pay-packet. Incremental pay scales are a further device for prising power away from managers and unions invariably resist "merit" payments for individuals with as much resolution as managers display in trying to introduce them. For a decade employment legislators struggled with the question of information disclosure by management to employees. Here was another resource over which managers sought to retain control while their collective bargaining

Most of the comments in the previous paragraph relate only to the power of superiors over subordinates, but another battle over resources takes place between peers, and that is the share of the budget, the staff, the time of the committees that make decisions, and all those other ways in which the relative power of functions or departments is mediated and altered. It would be quite inadequate to regard power through control of resources as being solely the exercise of power *over* subordinates. It is also power *vis-à-vis* peers and power *against* superiors.

Whatever resources you have you still need *skill* to deploy them. The best-loved aspects of patriotic folklore are those in which one's countrymen won battles against the odds. The Battle of Britian retains pride of place in the annals of World War II, partly because of the turning point it marked, but mainly because it seemed as if skill and courage outwitted an enemy with more planes and pilots. Control of resources is not sufficient to be powerful, because the political system is only brought into being as a result of competitive bids for power. Neustadt (1960) has compared the effective use of power by three consecutive American Presidents, Roosevelt, Truman and Eisenhower. All held the same office with the same resource control, yet achieved different degrees of success because of the varying skill with which they exercised their control.

Motivation can also explain why one manager has more power than another, even though they both possess the same resources and skills. Some seek power much more enthusiastically than others and use their resources to try and get it; others use their resources and skills for different purposes. This can be either due to varying degrees of personal need for power or the feeling that only by obtaining more power can the manager's function be effective. Personnel managers have long tended to be politically active (whilst often deploring "political behaviour" in others) because of the belief that they could only be effective by achieving influence over their colleagues through having power to deploy. Accountants seldom have this worry.

Another reason for individuals having varying amounts of power is the *obligations* owed by "dependants". The dependant may be a subordinate hoping for a favourable report at the next annual performance appraisal; it may be someone on an equal footing who is under an obligation to the manager for past favours; or it may be a superior who requires the particular skill of the manager with no satisfactory alternatives being available. The more of these debts a manager has to call in, the more powerful he will be.

3. TECHNIQUES USED TO OBTAIN POWER

There are further aspects of power and authority to be discussed in Chapters 9 and 15; so we conclude this chapter by reviewing some of the methods that can be used by individuals seeking to achieve power in organisations.

Alliances. Individuals collaborate in their power search with those who have interests sufficiently similar for an alliance to be mutually beneficial. The managers of manufacturing and personnel may form an alliance to block moves by a marketing manager to scale down production and buy in more ready-made materials, for instance. The benefits of an alliance are the obvious ones of having someone else on your side, together with his resources, skills and motivation; the drawbacks are the degree of commitment which you have to contribute. Also alliances cannot be readily discarded; in discarding an ally you probably make an enemy.

Lobbying.   Falling short of the alliance is the process of drumming up support on a particular issue — "I hope I can rely on your support for this . . .". This is much used in getting one's way with committees, as is described in Chapter 10, but is also appropriate for all the minor dealings that take place throughout the working day.

Doing favours.   There are various ways in which people with some power use that to provide services for others and therefore extend their power with the person they have helped. This is a time honoured way of ensuring the loyalty of subordinates, who feel grateful to the superior who has been benevolent and whose benevolence may be used again. It is also a method to be used with peers and superiors, who are put in the debt of the person providing the favour. There is a need to be cautious when using one's own power to elevate another, as the person elevated may then be wary of his erstwhile helper:

> ...whoever is responsible for another's becoming powerful ruins himself, because this power is brought into being either by ingenuity or by force, and both of these are suspect to the one who has become powerful.
>
> (Machiavelli, 1981, p. 44)

Being present.   It is the powerful man who can affort to be away. At one extreme post holders may find that they do not have a job to come back to; it is so much easier to dispossess someone who is absent. More common than that is the need to be present when significant decisions are made. Such decisions usually involve the balancing of conflicting interests in competing for resources or advantage. Each interest will have its spokesman and the interest that is absent will not be heard, so that the decision will seldom be favourable to that interest, unless there is some other aspect of power — like a veto — which can be exercised afterwards to nullify the decision that has been reached.

Cornering Resources.   The empire builder reasons that his importance to the organisation is in direct proportion to the number of subordinates in his section. That conclusion may be very dubious, but at least the number of subordinates can be measured, whereas contributions to organisational objectives cannot be.

Being indispensable.   A variant on cornering resources is to make oneself indispensable. This is done either by being a lone, but essential, expert or by being an essential part of administrative, decision-making procedures. Safety officers often have political influence as a result of their familiarity with health and safety legislation, which no one else except shop stewards finds very interesting, but the expertise is essential to the organisation. Personnel officers trying to establish a personnel function usually aim to break in on well established procedures. A typical initiative is to get a ruling that in future recruitment advertisements will have to be placed by the personnel officer, and not by anyone else, or that all management dealings with full-time union officials will be made only by the personnel officer.

Reciprocal support for a patron. Peter (1969) pointed out that it is much better to be pulled up in an organisation than to push yourself up. Political power can be enhanced by having a powerful patron. Those appointed to newly created posts nearly always define their influence by confirming to whom they report: "I am directly accountable to the Chief Executive . . ." or "I am part of the Manufacturing Division but have direct access to the M.D.". Some people have difficulty in finding such a patron and Jennings (1967) has coined the odd word *visiposure* to describe the need first to be in a position to see enough potential patrons to pick one but secondly to be in a position where a potential patron can see you. The first is visibility, the second is exposure; visiposure is both. Once the patron is found he will only support the acolyte if the acolyte helps him achieve his own objectives. Patrons enhance one's power but also exact fealty.

The remorseless logic of Machiavelli described the nature of the relationship between the patron and the patronised:

> To keep his minister up to the mark the prince, on his side, must be considerate towards him, must pay him honour, enrich him, put him in his debt, share with him both honours and responsibilities. Thus the minister will see how dependent he is on the prince; and then having riches and honours to the point of surfeit he will desire no more; holding so many offices, he cannot but fear changes.
>
> (Machiavelli, 1981, p. 125)

Being able to cope with uncertainty. The customary routines of formal authority structures, centralised control and circulating memoranda shelter people inside the organisation from the outside world, which is not controlled in the same convenient way. The outside is, however, a hard and urgent reality for the organisation, so that those who can cope with the demands of the environment in which the organisation operates are those towards whom political power tends to flow (Salancik and Pfeffer, 1977). It is the uncertainty of the demands from outside that gives political influence to those who confront them, and anyone dealing with organisational affairs that are uncertain acquires some power.

Michel Crozier (1964, p. 154) studied the work of plants in France where tobacco was processed and commented on the extraordinary power that was wielded by the maintenance engineers. The entire process was highly mechanised and predictable, so that the activities of every member were in a smooth routine. The only thing that could go wrong was for a machine to break down, yet that caused a complete disruption to the system. Because of this the only people who could put the machinery right (the maintenance engineers) wielded power out of proportion to their formal status.

This sort of power fluctuates. When the office photocopier breaks down the service engineer is much reviled, because he is not there. When he arrives he is greeted with warm smiles and cups of tea for his brief time of glory. When the photocopier works once more he is quickly forgotten or asked to move his car as it is blocking the car park. Small wonder that he seems to move so slowly in actually conducting the repair. The greatest worry for those who specialise in being able to cope with uncertainty is the fear of not being able to do it. The service engineer who has brought the wrong tools or cannot diagnose the fault suffers all the horrors of the fallen idol.

Review Topic 6.2

We have listed eight techniques to obtain power. Which have you used and which others do you think you will use in the future?

---

4. MAINTAINING BALANCE

In closing this chapter we revert to the problem that was posed at the beginning: how can we advocate behaviours that are so obviously devious and unattractive? Also, how can we set discussion about political behaviour alongside the widely canvassed behaviours of openness that are the basis of much contemporary management development?

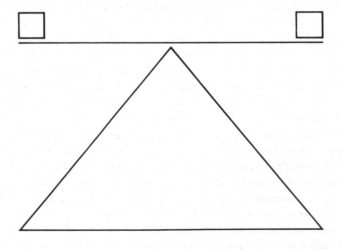

Figure 6.1   The Problem of Balance

The answer is that neither politics not openness are the total solution. An appreciation of organisational politics is an essential part of managerial effectiveness and some political behaviour is required of every manager. When the Polaris missile system was developed in the United States it was hailed as a remarkable achievement for rational management techniques. PERT (described in Chapter 18) was devised and has subsequently been used in many other applications. Harvey Sapolsky (1972) studied the project as a case history of success and came to the conclusion that PERT was as effective *technically* as rain dancing (p. 246) but that it was effective *politically* because of the reputation it gave the special projects office for efficiency, and that overall Polaris was a political rather than technical achievement in management terms:

> The success of the Polaris program depended on the ability of its proponents to promote and protect Polaris. Competitors had to be eliminated; reviewing agencies had to be outmanoeuvred; congressmen, admirals, newspapermen and academicians had to be co-opted. Politics is a system requirement. What distinguishes programs in government is not that some play politics and others do not, but rather, that some are better at it than others. (Sapolsky, 1972, p. 244)

Extremes of "politicking" are destructive as well as distasteful, and openness can mitigate such extremes. We must not overlook, however, that power is what the French political scientist Maurice Duverger has called "Janus-faced". Janus was the Roman god of doorways and passages, who was always depicted as facing both ways. Power is essential to the process of social integration, yet it divides people and produces conflict. For an organisation to work at all there has to be a distribution of power within the structure to get things done. Yet that very distribution is divisive and produces stress on the structure and members of the organisation. It is when that stress becomes too great that effectiveness declines.

Finally, how can one judge whether an individual manager is going too far in his political behaviour? A useful test is to think back to the distinction mentioned in the previous chapter between setting agendas for action and using networks to implement the agendas. Political behaviour is potentially useful when it is deployed to put agendas into action. It is counterproductive when it is deployed only to build and maintain networks.

Too much network and not enough agenda is associated with the type of person who is more concerned with *being* a manager rather than getting on with the job. The manager who underemphasises networks and concentrates on agendas can be inward looking and fail to take politics seriously, but we have found more examples of managers who spend so much of their time "networking" that they forget to do the job. We recently found an example in a very large multinational company where a manager dealing with a major customer relied on a gentleman's agreement rather than on a contract with serious results.

SUMMARY PROPOSITIONS

6.1   Power is an inescapable part of management in organisations.

6.2   Four aspects of power are resources, skill, motivation and costs.

6.3   Techniques used by individuals and groups to obtain power include alliances, lobbying, doing favours, being present, cornering resources, being indispensable, reciprocal support for a patron, and being able to cope with uncertainty.

6.4   Openness, as advocated in most management development programmes, can mitigate the extremes of political behaviour which would otherwise become destructive.

6.5   Political behaviour which helps the implementation of agendas is useful: political behaviour which only builds networks is counterproductive.

REFERENCES

Crozier M., *The Bureaucratic Phenomenon*, Tavistock, London, 1964.
Dahl R., *Modern Political Analysis*, 2nd edition, Prentice Hall, New Jersey, 1970.
Dalton M., *Men who Manage*, John Wiley, New York, 1959.
Duverger M., *The Study of Politics*, Thos. Nelson, London, 1972.
Hickson D. J. *et al.*, "A Strategic Contingencies Theory of Intraorganizational Power", in *Administrative Science Quarterly*, June 1971, pp. 216–229.
Jennings E.C., *The Mobile Manager*, University of Michigan Press, 1967.
Kotter J.P., "Power, Success and Organization Effectiveness", in *Organization Dynamics*, Winter 1978.
Machiavelli N., *The Prince*, Penguin Books, Harmondsworth, Middlesex, 1981.
Neustadt R.E., *Presidential Power: the Politics of Leadership*, John Wiley, New York, 1960.
Peter L.J., *The Peter Principle*, Morrow, New York, 1969.
Pfeffer J., *Power in Organizations*, Pitman, Marshfield Massachussetts, 1981.
Salancik G.R. and Pfeffer J., "Who gets Power, and how they hold on to it", in *Organizational Dynamics*, Winter, 1977.
Sapolsky H.M., *The Polaris System Development*, Harvard University Press, 1972.

Chapter Seven

COMMUNICATION STRUCTURES

The evangelist Billy Graham was due to address a meeting in an American city, but was prevented by a dense bank of fog that lay between his circling aircraft and the airport near to the stadium in which his audience had assembled. The thousands who had gathered to listen to his message could hear the noise of the aircraft engines and Billy Graham lacked nothing in conviction or material for the message he wished to convey, but the bank of fog prevented the message from being conveyed and the response elicited. Those working in contemporary employing organisations often feel a sense of frustration similar to that experienced by the evangelist and his expectant audience.

Most people feel reassured by contact with those making decisions about their destiny. Airline passengers convinced that the aircraft is about to disintegrate and drop them 40,000 feet into the sea will pay close attention to the message relayed over the public address system prefaced by the words ". . . this is your captain speaking . . .". Being in touch with those who decide gives one a sense of control over one's affairs, no matter how slight this may be. One of the effects of organisation is to distance people from the centre of actions which affect their lives. The rank and file employee, concerned about whether or not his factory is to close, will see that the yes/no decision is to be taken by — say — the board of directors, from whom he is separated by a "fog" of people and lines of communication that emphasise both his detachment from the decision and his helplessness to influence it.

The irony of the present situation is that the "fog" has been made denser by brave attempts to penetrate it and to compensate for it: more committees, handbooks, procedures and representatives. For the people waiting in the stadium to hear Billy Graham's message, books, pamphlets, gramophone records and addresses by close associates of the evangelist were not a satisfactory alternative to hearing the message in person. They were merely an incentive to hear the words direct.

In organisational life there is often no satisfactory alternative to face to face conversation, and the substitutes may simply dissatisfy both the senders and the receivers. Managers can feel that dealing with employee representatives makes it harder rather than easier for them to get their messages through to employees, while employees often regard the carefully-minuted proceedings of the works committee as a poor substitute for getting an engineer with a kit of tools to come into the workshop and mend the leaking radiator about which they have been complaining for months.

A further contradiction of the present is that we have problems of communication while having a surfeit of information, which turns the fog into smog! Drucker (1977), as usual, has a trenchant comment:

> The communications gap within institutions and between groups in society has been widening steadily — to the point where it threatens to become an unbridgeable gulf of total misunderstanding.
>
> In the meantime there is an information explosion . . . the abundance of information changes the communication problem and makes it both more urgent and more difficult.
>
> (p. 390)

Increasing the amount of information can impair rather than improve communication, as information only becomes communication where there is exchange, with the receiver signalling understanding of the correct meaning by his feedback to the sender. Information output that is not attuned to the needs of the receiver will obscure rather than clarify the receiver's understanding. People in organisations show a general preference for word-of-mouth communication. Mintzberg (1975) found that chief executives spent 78 per cent of their time in verbal communication (p. 52). It might be assumed that this was a feature of a very specialised job in the hierarchy, but another study was made among research chemists and engineers, a group of people who, one would assume, spend less time talking to others than chief executives. The findings were that they spent, on average, 61 per cent of their day interchanging facts, information, ideas, attitudes and opinions.

Review Topic 7.1
How do you understand the comment of Peter Drucker quoted here?

If there is preference for communicating by direct conversation rather than in other ways, it is at least debatable whether it is productive to push information into other channels, such as memoranda or announcements on the notice board, unless these are supplementary to the preferred mode of face to face and not a substitute. Equally there are some communications for which a channel such as a formal letter is preferred to word of mouth, like the offer of employment or notice of terms for early retirement.

1. ORGANISATIONAL COMMUNICATION AND MEDIA

Several chapters in this book deal with specific aspects of communication. Discussion here is therefore limited to one major form, *organisational communication*, which is best defined by distinguishing it from interpersonal communication:

> *Interpersonal communication* is face-to-face. It is person-to-person exhange of information that conveys meaning. *Organizational communication* is the deliberate establishment and use of a system to transmit information conveying meaning to large numbers of people both within and outside the organization.
>
> (Carlisle, 1982, p. 421)

Organisational communication is not, therefore, all the communicating that takes place in the organisation, but simply that which is a product of deliberate attempts by managers to communicate or enable specific communications within the organisational structure and to the outside environment. In a study to which we refer again shortly, Greenbaum (1974) has suggested that there are four main objectives that managers have for organisational communication:

Regulation, seeking conformity of employee behaviour with organisational objectives;

Innovation, seeking to change aspects of organisational functioning in specific directions;

Integration, maintaining the morale of the work force and developing a feeling of identity with the organisation and its members;

Information, passing out the mainly factual information that people need in their everyday duties: what has to be done, quality standards, customers' requests, and so on.

The value of this distinction is, of course, that the method of communication will vary according to its objective.

Organisational communication takes place in a variety of ways, using different *media*, and there are some messages that are conveyed unintentionally.

The Formal Organisational Structure

The organisation chart or formal arrangement of working relationships is itself a communication as it tells organisation members important things about their "place": how distant they are from the centre and what their official status is. The structure is also a prime communications media, as there is an assumption that information will travel up and down it, enshrined in doctrines of responsibility, accountability and reporting, to say nothing of grievance and disciplinary procedures, which invariably nominate stages in the procedure by identifying them with office holders in the structure. Katz and Kahn (1978, pp. 440–8) list the main types of up and down communication:

Down	*Up*
Job instructions;	Information about selves,
Job rationale;	performance and problems;
Procedures and practices;	Organisational practice and policy;
Feedback on performance;	What needs to be done;
Indoctrination about goals.	What should not be done.

The formal structure also has lateral as well as vertical connections, which are used to provide communication relating to co-ordination, mutual support and advice.

The Informal Organisational Structure

Behind and between the formal lines is the informal structure or grapevine, through which information passes that has not been officially sanctioned. Although this is not deliberately created, no organisational communication is complete without it.

The grapevine has the advantage of being a spontaneous form of expression, providing the satisfaction of talking face to face, and it can often be both more rapid and informative than official communications. Its operation does not follow the same pattern as the spread of rumours, where the amount of rumoured information increases as the amount of official communication decreases. Davis (1953) and Hage (1974) both found a positive correlation between official and unofficial communication. As the level of official communication goes up there is a fuelling of informal discussion and interpretation of it. Only in extreme cases of information suppression is there a sufficient stimulus to speculation for rumour to grow in order to fill the gaps that the official processes leave.

Davis was also able to identify aspects of how the grapevine works, so that the most common was what he called a *cluster chain*, which is shown in Figure 7.1. The person with the information (1) tells several others (2, 3, 4 and 5). Only some of them (4 and 5) pass on the information, so that the flow of information gradually peters out. Of any group who hear information, there will only be a proportion willing to pass it on. Some will feel constrained, some will forget and others will not bother. Davis found that 81 per cent of the executives in his study had been told the information he was tracking, but only eleven per cent communicated it to others. A later study by Knippen (1974) found that although managers accounted for only a small proportion of the 1970 employees in a grocery store, they were the source of half the grapevine information and told an average of eight people each; other employees only told four people each.

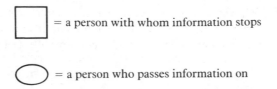

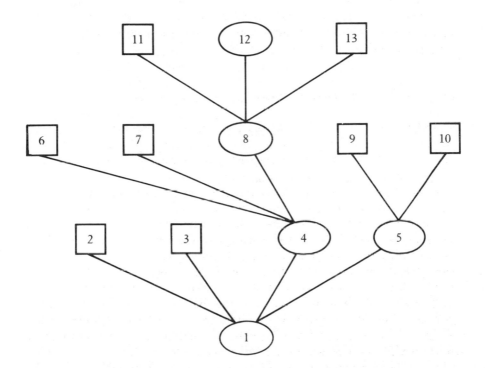

Figure 7.1 The Cluster Chain in the Informal Organisational Structure

Word of Mouth

Most of the messages passing through the formal and informal organisation structure will be by word of mouth, and we have already seen the preference for this mode of communication demonstrated by research. It is not, of course, only one speaking with one other. It includes interchange face to face in small groups and committees, as well as the rarer address to a large meeting.

Written Messages

Written material sometimes stands on its own as a message, so that the monthly statement of pay and statutory deductions is seldom a basis for discussion, unless it is incorrect. Other written material is an adjunct to discussion: the agenda for a meeting, the notice of a claim prior to negotiations, the draft report, the letter confirming an order of material from a supplier '. . . as discussed with your representative . . .'

It is a form of communication which is used often not to convey information for the first and final time, but as a preliminary to, or confirmation of, some action being discussed. The form can vary from letter to memorandum, from a notice on the notice board to the house journal, from job specification to sales order to instruction manual and many more. It is important that it should be used in circumstances for which it is appropriate. Changes in behaviour are seldom likely to follow from written instructions or particulars only. Pirani and Reynolds (1976) studied aspects of safety training in a Merseyside factory and demonstrated, *inter alia*, the relative ineffectiveness of posters and warning notices in persuading employees to adopt safer working practices.

Review Topic 7.2

Envisage an important decision that you have to make in your organisation that needs to be extensively communicated. What aspects would you communicate formally in writing, what formally by word of mouth, and what would you use informal methods for?

Electronic Means

A relatively new and rapidly developing means of communication is that provided by the advances in microtechnology. In some ways these merely expand the amount of written material, as photocopiers and word processors make it possible to generate an almost infinite number of copies of items. This adds considerably to the volume of information in circulation without necessarily improving communication, and with the possibility of making it worse by overload. This is a problem we consider later in this chapter.

The computer terminal and visual display unit introduce a fundamentally new method of communicating in organisations, with a variety of exciting potentials like the paperless office with the visual display unit replacing the memorandum, but it is difficult to see that the amount of word of mouth communication will decline.

Systems and Management Objectives

Greenbaum (1974) provides a technique for looking at the variety of systems, or structures, necessary to meet managers' objectives. If, for example, one

		REGULATION	INNOVATION	INTEGRATION	INFORMATION
Face to Face (2)	ORAL	directions & requests	superior/ subordinate ideas meet	selection interview	induction of new recruits
	WRITTEN	job descr. & performance standards	reports on visits, courses	letter of welcome to new recruit	memoranda
	NON-VERBAL	gesture		gesture	demonstration of task to be performed
Small Groups (3–10)	ORAL	dept'l meetings	problem-solving meetings	coffee break	training groups
	WRITTEN	agenda	suggestions after meeting	invitation to lunch	works handbook
	NON-VERBAL	pauses, silences	seating arrangements	meeting area conditions	demonstration
Organisation Wide	ORAL	meetings of dept. heads		address to members of organisation	mass meeting
	WRITTEN	organisation chart	suggestion scheme	house journals	notice board
	NON-VERBAL	style of office for org. member		house style in stationery etc.	

Figure 7.2   Media for communication

considers the number of people one wishes to reach and the appropriate media, one can summarise it as in Figure 7.2. This type of analysis could also be used to consider other structures, such as formal–informal.

2. OVERCOMING PROBLEMS OF ORGANISATIONAL COMMUNICATION

In the view of the variety of means whereby information can be passed around, it is of limited use to speak of *designing* a system of communications, but it is helpful to identify some of the problems and review methods of alleviating them.

Formal Structure

The flow of information and the effectiveness of communication is affected by the type of formal structure that exists. The first problem is of *size*. In an organisation with a strong central focus, like the entrepreneurial form mentioned in Chapter 3, satisfaction with communication is likely to decrease as numbers of organisation members increase. Structural alteration to split the overall organisation into a number of relatively autonomous units will be more successful than trying to generate more information for dissemination through a monolithic structure.

The problem of *hierarchical levels* has been discussed earlier in this book in examining the idea of an optimum span of control. In the last quarter of a century numerous experiments have demonstrated the validity of the simple hypothesis advanced by Robert Dubin in 1959, that the smaller the number of communication links in a system, the greater the efficiency of the members of the system in task performance. Every communicator is selective in what he passes on, even if he is only selective in emphasis or inference. One method that reduces this problem is to operate briefing groups, whereby a superior briefs not one but a group of subordinates simultaneously. Through question, answer and discussion the message understood by each subordinate will take on greater similarity and reinforcement than if they had been briefed separately. In turn they brief groups of their own subordinates, and so on. This improves the accuracy of the conveyed message, but eliminating a level in the hierarchy is much more effective.

Many difficulties surround the official *lines of authority and communication* in the organisation. First there is the problem of uncertainty amongst employees about means of access to information or decision. This difficulty was so widespread that legislation was introduced whereby the individual contract of employment now has to specify a person to whom an employee can apply to seek redress of any grievance relating to his employment, but there remain many other matters on which organisation members remain unsure of where to obtain informaticn. A second problem arises when a point of access becomes congested. In the 1960s it could take twelve months for a matter to proceed through the engineering industry disputes procedure, with the result that the procedure was eventually abandoned. Similarly management action may be reserved to too few people, so that decisions are held up because of the non-availability of a key manager to agree or disagree.

Michael Winston was the production manager of a furniture making plant who had to adjourn a meeting with shop stewards for 15 minutes in order to sign a handful of release notes for material from stores. A production line of 32 people had been idle for an hour and a half because the storekeeper was not allowed to release the material (which was of particular interest to DIY enthusiasts) without Winston's authority. Eventually the foreman persuaded Winston's secretary that the matter was sufficiently important to justify interrupting the meeting with stewards. At home that same evening

Winston received a telephone call from his production superintendent, who had been trying to see him for four days about two design draughtsmen who had been offered employment by a competitor but who would stay if there were small adjustments to their pay, which only Winston could authorise.

These problems become less severe when those with centralised authority in their own hands are able and willing to let some of it go, remembering that delegation does not mean giving people jobs to do. It means giving people authority and responsibility. The problem is, however, just as likely to be one of horizontal rather than vertical lines, emphasising the importance of the integrating devices described in Chapter 3.

Social Distance

Social distance is the problem that people may limit communication when dealing with someone holding greater prestige or on a higher hierarchical level in the organisation. To some extent the opposite applies also, with those in senior positions feeling inhibited about being candid with those holding more humble posts. Mainly this applies to adverse comments about company affairs. Two salesmen may readily discuss with each other the incompetence of the sales manager and the ineptitude of the marketing policy being followed by the company, but both will feel inhibited about expressing those same views to the sales manager. They feel dependent on his goodwill, which would be jeopardised if they disagreed with him. The much cherished concept of tenure in British universities has evolved for precisely the purpose of providing lecturers with sufficient security for them to be able to disagree with their professors. The anxiety to propitiate the person with more power than you have also extends to bad news for which the messenger cannot be held responsible. Cleopatra and her contemporaries were hampered in their military campaigns by their practice of tossing bags of gold to the bringers of good tidings and beheading the bearers of bad, so that the reliability of their intelligence reports was low. Hitler is described as making serious strategic blunders because none of his close advisers dared to tell him bad news for fear of his rage. These are extreme examples, but in every organisation subordinates seek the favour of superiors and are thus inclined to tell them what they like to hear.

Superiors can be restrained from candour with subordinates for fear that the subordinate will lose confidence in the superior. A senior manager will not readily say to a subordinate, "I have no idea how to deal with this situation" because of a feeling that the subordinate will regard this as a sign of weakness or incompetence.

In our interviews with managers we have frequently heard them comment on how to handle situations where they don't know something. To appear fallible is obviously a minor nightmare for many people. Arthur Tweedle is the manager of a city centre building society and has to know how far to go when lending money. One client may ask for much more than is actually needed, while another may underestimate his requirements. In uncertainty about the right course of action he prevaricates and steps away from the decision itself, by saying: "Well, *we* will obviously have to think about that and let you know". "Yes, *I* will be glad to arrange that for you". In uncertainty it becomes something that *we* will have to think about.

Social distance is desired by superiors and subordinates for certain reasons (wait until we look at authority, for instance) but at the extreme it can seriously impair communication. So some moves to its reduction are needed. One method is to tinker with status symbols, so that they become less inhibiting to those who have not got them. Segregated dining facilities, for instance, not only provide more agreeable and opulent catering for senior members of the organisation, but also cut off those people socially from everyone else by setting them apart at times of relaxation and communion. Another aspect of social distance is territory. People will often communicate more openly if they are in familiar surroundings. One of the authors was interested to observe this aspect of behaviour in a large food processing plant. The foremen and superintendents all wore white overalls and white straw hats, while the plant manager also wore a white overall but not a hat. The manager used to monitor affairs in the plant by calling each foreman and superintendent in turn into his office to talk in a very informal way about what was going on. He also made frequent tours of inspection of the plant. When entering the manager's office the foremen took off their hats and sat upright in a chair, often on the edge, and said very little that was not called for by the questions that were put to them. The manager changed his routine by incorporating the informal chats with his tours of inspection, so that he called in on the offices of the foremen and superintendents while going around the plant. The foremen did not now take off their hats and were much more relaxed and informative. They were on their own territory.

Intergroup Hostility

The contrasted aims and norms of groups in organisations often generate hostility, both between groups and individuals, which can seriously impair the quality of trust and communication between them. It is almost a commonplace that those involved with production are not always in sympathy with those concerned with sales and marketing; and technical personnel typically blame administrators for every misfortune that befalls them. This is a basic problem of organisation and some of the remedies have been examined in Chapter Three. It is necessary to accept the differences and to attempt co-ordination and integration by devices such as committees, co-ordinating departments or individuals. In many cases the difference grows worse through being suppressed. Those in Department A have a minor criticism about those in Department B, which they talk about among themselves but not to those in Department B, to whom they become slightly cool. Those in Department B discuss among themselves the odd behaviour of Department A. Uncertainty and suspicion harden into hostility, even though the substantive cause may be trivial and, if talked about, the suspicion would collapse like a burst balloon. It may therefore be helpful to bring about a confrontation between the two parties to discuss what causes the hostility between them.

Physical Setting

Increasing organisational complexity can increase the number of contacts that organisation members need to have with each other, while an increasing number of people in the organisation can make that contact less likely. When a department is set up, it is an elementary move to group those people near to each other, on the assumption that the interaction of their duties and responsibilities make such a juxtaposition necessary, but is it more important than some alternative juxtaposition? Should quality assurance personnel be located in some central corral from which they are sent out into the factory to assure the quality of production, or should they be based in production departments and only occasionally called together with other quality assurers to ensure appropriate standards and incorruptibility? Should typists and word processor operators work together for the benefits of flexibility and variety or should they be located in the same place as those who generate the words they process?

Often the answer is whichever alternative some individual person regards as preferable, but another method is to prepare a relationship chart, plotting the frequency of communications between individuals.

A similar question is whether people should be segregated in single or double offices, or whether they should share large open plan offices. Where there is frequent communication there is a good case for opening offices up, but office planners and organisation and methods experts have to remember that the social requirements of personnel will triumph over office landscaping plans, if the two conflict.

John Charles was a gifted chief designer of underground locomotives and he worked in a small office adjoining a large drawing office containing twelve draughtsmen. When he wanted something from the drawing office Charles would throw a paper clip against the frosted glass window separating him from the drawing office and his assistant Charlie Johnson would come bustling in saying, "Yes, Chief". If Charlie did not hear or see the paper clip signal one of the draughtsmen would say, "Chop chop Charlie, big chief Charles throw clip". Inevitably a newly appointed organisation and methods officer heard of the practice and arranged for a small hatch to be placed in the frosted glass so that John Charles could speak to Charlie Johnson direct to attract his attention. In everyday use the hatch would never quite work; it may have been poorly fitted or covered with too much paint, or it may have been that the draughtsmen and Charlie Johnson and John Charles preferred time-honoured methods. Two years later Charlie was still responding to paper clips.

In open plan offices it is amazing how carefully placed filing cabinets are gradually shifted, rubber plants appear, desks move to a different angle and hatstands are mobilised to provide a series of mini-offices in an open plan layout.

Overload

A common reason for managers not communicating with others is that they lack the time. Although this may be partly due to indolence or a failure to acknowledge the importance of communication, the amount of information to be handled is certainly increasing, as has been mentioned earlier. One way of dealing with the problem is to develop specialised scanning skills in reading, that are described at the end of this book, and another is to develop delegation, as has already been described as a means of dealing with problems about lines of authority. Few managers, however, can avoid having large amounts of paperwork to deal with, so they have to work out ways of coping with it, such as setting aside a particular period each day — usually at the beginning or the end — for reading, writing and dictating. General Douglas MacArthur never left his office in the evening until all the day's paperwork had been cleared.

3. ORGANISATIONAL COMMUNICATION IS ONLY AS GOOD AS INTERPERSONAL COMMUNICATION

Whatever initiatives are taken by managers in organisations to manipulate and "improve" organisational communications, they will only be as good as the quality of the interpersonal communication that is taking place:

> The line-and-box drawings we call organization charts are not the structure of the organization they describe. Structure is the development of relatively consistent patterns of interaction among the members of an organization. These patterns begin to develop when a group of individuals, in response to certain characteristics and needs of the environment, create a system of patterned activities for the accomplishment of a specific task. The process by which these relationships are formed and maintained is interpersonal communication.
>
> (Baskin and Aronoff, 1980, p. 97)

It is not practicable for employees to develop confidence in a series of procedures or routines. They can only acquire confidence in what those systems produce and in those other members of the organisation with whom they interact. That confidence is built by the substance of what people say and do, but it is also built by a climate in which people feel encouraged to express ideas, make suggestions and question the validity of decisions. Communication and behaviour are so closely connected and interwoven that everything which influences behaviour also influences communication. In the next chapter we consider how one understands the behaviour of others.

SUMMARY PROPOSITIONS

7.1. Communication is the most time consuming activity in which managers engage. Improving management usually requires an improvement in communication.

7.2. The fewer the number of communication links in a system, the greater the efficiency of members of the organisation in task performance.

7.3. Managers generally prefer word of mouth communication to other methods.

7.4. The growth of electronic methods of handling information will affect the amount of written communication in organisations, but will have little influence on the amount of word of mouth communicating.

7.5. Only in extreme cases of censorship is the grapevine a substitute for the formal system of communication: normally formal and informal systems complement each other.

7.6. Problems of organisational communication which can be at least partially overcome include those of the formal structure, social distance, intergroup hostility, the physical setting and overload on individual communicators.

7.7. Organisational communication is only as good as the interpersonal communication taking place in the organisation

APPENDIX

Administrative drill to study patterns of contact with other orgainsation members

Stage 1.   Draw a personal organisation chart, with yourself at the centre, using ▭ to indicate job positions and showing the names of those currently holding those posts. The chart should include *formal* relations you have inside and outside the organisation. The circle represents the organisation boundary and your drawing might look something like this:

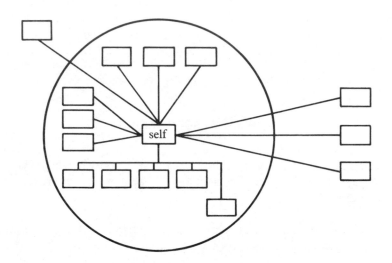

Stage 2.   On a second chart list all the individuals or groups who can affect how effective you are in your job, but with whom you do not have a formal working relationship included in the first chart. Give both names and positions. The drawing, which may look something like the one below, will describe your informal network.

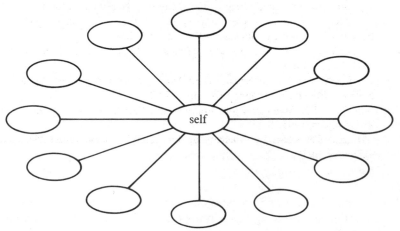

Stage 3. (a) Rank order the contacts, formal and informal, in their importance to you in getting your job done effectively. (b) Rate each contact on a scale between -3 and $+3$, according to how helpful the person is to you. (c) What can be done to improve communication with those you have rated between -1 and -3?

rank	contact	-3	-2	-1	0	1	2	3	improvement by....
1									
2									
3									
4									
5									
6									
7									
8									
9									

Stage 4. Is there anyone who should be in your network but is not yet?

REFERENCES

Baskin, O.W. and Aronoff, C.E., *Interpersonal Communication in Organizations*, Goodyear Publishing, Santa Monica, California, 1980.

Carlisle, H.M., *Management: Concepts, Methods and Applications*, 2nd ed., Science Research Associates Ltd., Chicago, 1982.

Davis, K., "Management Communication and the Grapevine", in *Harvard Business Review*, September-October, 1953, pp. 43–9.

Drucker, P.F., *Management*, Pan Books, London, 1979.

Dubin, R., "Stability of Human Organizations" in Haire, M. (ed.), *Modern Organization Theory*, John Wiley, New York, 1959.

Greenbaum, H.W., "The Audit of Organizational Communications", *Academy of Management Journal*, 1974, pp. 739–54.

Hage, J., *Communication and Organizational Control*, John Wiley, New York, 1974.

Hinrichs, J.R., "Communications Activity of Industrial Research Personnel", in *Personnel Psychology*, Summer 1964, pp. 193–204.

Katz, D. and Kahn, R.L., *The Social Psychology of Organizations*, John Wiley, New York, (2nd edition) 1978.

Knippen, J., "Grapevine Communication: Management Employees", in *Journal of Business Research*, January 1974, pp. 47–58.

Mintzberg, H., "The Manager's Job: Folklore and Fact", *Harvard Business Review*, July-August, 1975.

Pirani, M. and Reynolds, J., "Gearing up for Safety", in *Personnel Management*, February, 1976.

Chapter Eight

UNDERSTANDING OTHER PEOPLE

Other people do not necessarily see things in the same way that we do. Few comments can be more obviously true. Yet the behaviour and conversation of most individuals suggest that it is a truth we do not readily follow in our everyday lives. We find it difficult to understand how anyone can vote for a political party whose policies are opposed to those of the party we voted for. In industrial relations negotiations it is unusual for the protagonists to see, let alone appreciate, the opposing point of view. Those conducting selection interviews need constantly to remind themselves of the difference in perspective and understanding between themselves and those they interview.

The reason why we find it so difficult to adopt a different perspective is that we all need a set of operating assumptions to conduct our daily affairs and the one we find most comforting is that others see the world around them in the same way as we see the world around us. Recruiting for large organisations, especially recruiting for the management ranks, often follows a routine that selects those who are similar to those already employed. The operating assumption of a common view of the world is then safe. It is further consolidated by induction and training. Those entering the police force have attitudes about authority that are similar and which are reinforced by the process of training in the service. Not everyone outside the police force shares those views. In the electronics company Hewlett Packard there is constant reference to "The Hewlett Packard Way". This is known, felt and understood by those in the company, without being made explicit. IBM used to have a company song:

> Ever onward, ever onward.
>> We're bound for the top never to fall.
> Right here and now we thankfully
>> Pledge sincerest loyalty
> To the corporation that's best for all.
>> Our leaders we revere, and while we're here
> Let's show the world just what we think of them....

There are still many examples of organisations that seek to employ only those who conform to a particular set of values and behaviour, with that conformity being assessed in recruitment, emphasised in induction and confirmed in promotion. Managers in such organisations need to understand individual differences sufficiently for them to identify those who fit the pattern and to avoid those who do not.

A much stronger reason for understanding how individuals differ is the impracticability of any manager seeking to work only with the like-minded. If a manager could surround himself with clones he would get standardised, sycophantic responses to all his initiatives. Fellow managers may have surrounded themselves with clones of a different type and it is not feasible to man an entire organisation with carbon copies of the model organisation man. Organisations deal with a clientèle and the only thing the clients will have in common will be an interest in the organisation's products. As people they will vary enormously. Furthermore the remaking of organisations in their own image is a practice that can lead to criticism of unreasonable discrimination against other, worthy applicants who do not fit neatly into the mould.

Managers spend a large part of their time talking to others and trying to get others to do things. The more they can understand the nature of individual differences, the more effectively they can work with a variety of people.

1. SOURCES OF INDIVIDUAL DIFFERENCE

At birth each of us has a unique combination of genetical information that informs our physical processes for the rest of our lives, so that we are all physically different. Sometimes we make judgements about people on the basis of their physique: thin people are highly strung, red-headed people have hot tempers, small people are assertive. These are common assumptions, and Shakespeare put a very famous comment into the mouth of Caesar:

> Let me have men about me that are fat;
>> Sleek-headed men and such as sleep o' nights;
> Yond Casius has a lean and hungry look;
>> He thinks too much: such men are dangerous.

Sheldon (1954) carried out research at Harvard and produced a threefold classification of adult males. The short and plump (endomorphs) were said to be sociable, relaxed and pleasure loving; those who were tall and thin (ectomorphs) were described as restrained, self-conscious and solitary, while those with hard, muscular bodies (mesomorphs) were likely to be callous, aggressive, athletic and dominating. The difficulty of using this as a way of understanding people is shown by one or two very obvious exceptions. The mesomorphic Pablo Picasso should have been an ectomorph and the endomorphic Benito Mussolini should have been a mesomorph. It is clear that our physical differences influence the differences in our attitudes and behaviour, and classifications like Sheldon's have some general validity, but there are so many exceptions that we cannot yet produce a reliable code to link physical difference with behaviour pattern.

Gestures are a major part of our interpersonal communication and help us to understand some differences in behaviour. Often there can be no doubt about their meaning, especially when it is a form of emphasis to what is being said. Anger, for instance, is displayed much more by the gestures and facial expressions accompanying the words than by the words themselves, and in all expressions of emotion the words used are subordinate to the non-verbal behaviours that occur simultaneously. If someone were to smile warmly at you while saying "I hate you", you would believe the message of the smile rather than the message of the words.

It is very tempting to interpret the intentions and real feelings of others from their involuntary gestures, but there are many dangers in this practice, which have been well described by Desmond Morris (1977 and 1979).

All of us differ as a result of our *different experiences*. Being the eldest in a family is different from being the second child. We have different experiences going through school because of the people we befriend and the teachers who work with us. When approaching employment, some will experience discrimination against them, constant rejection and opportunity only to do work offering limited scope; while others will experience discrimination in their favour, encouragement and varied work challenges. In middle life those who have experienced success and achievement in their working lives will behave quite differently from those who have had fewer opportunities for achievement and perhaps regard their careers as failures. Differences of this type produce profoundly different attitudes to, for instance, the employing organisation and to more senior managers within it.

The differences in our physical makeup and our experiences combine to produce the sum of our individual differences — *personality*: the characteristics of behaviour and thinking that make the individual unique. Understanding personality is the business of many psychologists and there are various models that have been advanced. One school of thought is to look for basic traits (e.g. Eysenk and Eysenk, 1969) and there is some consistency among trait theorists in identifying two basic dimensions of introversion/extraversion and stability/instability. In contrast psychoanalysis assumes that personality consists of three systems: the id, which is irrational and impulsive and a mass of primitive instincts; the ego, which is realistic and the superego, which acts as a conscience, imposing a moral code on the ego.

All Freudian analysis is rooted in the unconscious, giving rise to the famous "Freudian slip", which describes how someone reveals his true feelings inadvertently by a word or phrase that "slips" into his conversation at the bidding of his subconscious. When polytechnics were first established in Britain, they were to be institutions enjoying parity of esteem with universities. A government minister was present at the opening ceremony of one polytechnic and was embarrassed to hear himself use the phrase "parody of esteem" in his speech.

Behaviourist psychologists (after Skinner, 1953) emphasise the external controls on an individual's behaviour. If an action is rewarded, or reinforced, it is more likely to recur than if it were not reinforced. Our current behaviour therefore reflects our reinforcement history. Those who seek to change the behaviour of others have to change the environment of the others as the environment can be observed and controlled. The art lies in finding the most suitable rewards for a particular individual. One clear conclusion from this school of thought and research is that people work most effectively *for* rewards rather than to *avoid* punishment.

The humanistic approach is one that has proved popular in management circles, as it holds that the individual is growth oriented, rational and capable of complex problem solving (after Rogers, 1942). Those holding this view look forward to what can be and how it can be achieved.

There is no agreement among psychologists about which of these explanations is correct. Each has its attractions, but general thinking in management seems to be to favour the humanistic view with overtones of the others. In simple practical terms managers usually have to assume that people are rational, but they also have to understand that logic can seldom alter internal drives. If a person is shy, it is unlikely that rational argument will persuade that person otherwise. Managers trying to deal with a poor performer may try to talk him out of it by explaining the error of his ways when a small change in the reward structure of the organisation would be more effective.

2. MANAGEMENT MODELS OF MAN

As mentioned at the beginning of this chapter, we all work with a model of man in our heads when we seek to understand others. We behave towards them in line with our beliefs and expect their behaviour to be predictable. The problem is that their model of man may not be the same as ours.

Those who know what their model is are more likely to recognise the occasion when someone else is using a different model. Such recognition not only reduces the likelihood of talking at cross purposes but also increases the likelihood of being able to understand the reasoning behind whatever the other is saying.

Schein (1970) and McGregor (1960) have looked at the models used by managers. Schein (pp. 55–76) describes four models that managers use to explain the behaviour of subordinates. Managers holding the *rational–economic* model of man assume that people are primarily motivated by rational appraisal of personal economic needs. The *social* model assumes that people are motivated by social needs, wanting rewarding on-the-job relationships and that they are more responsive to work group pressures than to management control. The *self-actualising* model sees people as both wanting to be, and able to be, mature independent people responsible for their own work. *Complex* man assumes that people cannot be slotted into any of the above categories but have various and complex desires that include all the above and some other needs, not all of which can be met at work.

As usual management thinkers want the best of all possible worlds and advocate the adoption of the fourth model as it includes the other three and rules out any one of them as being taken as the single explanation. Managers believing in rational–economic man can be baffled when they put up wages only to find that labour turnover rises or output falls. Other managers, who adhere to social man thinking, are aggrieved when an employee applies for a better paid job elsewhere, despite the manager's efforts to be nice to him.

Review Topic 8.1

Which are you....
  (a) Rational-economic man,
  (b) Social man,
  (c) Self-actualising man, or
  (d) Complex man?
Now ask a friend which *you* are.

Theory *X*:

1. The average human being has an inherent dislike of work and will avoid it if he can.
2. Because of the human characteristic dislike of work, most people must be coerced, controlled, directed, threatened with punishment, to get them to put forth adequate effort towards the achievement of organizational objectives.
3. The average human being prefers to be directed, wishes to avoid responsibility, has relatively little ambition, wants security above all.

Theory *Y*:

1. The expenditure of physical and mental effort is as natural as play or rest.
2. External control and the threat of punishment are not the only means of bringing about effort towards organizational objectives. People will exercise self-direction and self-control in the service of objectives to which they are committed.
3. Commitment to objectives is a function of the rewards associated with their achievement.
4. The average human being learns, under proper conditions, not only to accept but to seek responsibility.
5. The capacity to exercise a relatively high degree of imagination, ingenuity, and creativity in the solution of organizational problems is widely, not narrowly, distributed in the population.
6. Under the conditions of modern industrial life, the intellectual potentialities of the average human being are only partially utilized.

From: D. McGregor, *The Human Side of Enterprise*, McGraw Hill, New York, 1960, pp. 47–48.

Figure 8.1   Theory *X* and Theory *Y*

McGregor produced what is probably the best known theory about management attitudes to subordinates when he propounded his profoundly simple idea of the theory x manager and the theory y manager. He believed that prevailing assumptions among managers about the typical worker were outdated as they did not take account of the education level and psychological maturity of the workforce. What McGregor saw as the prevailing assumption was summed up by theory x, which emphasised direction and control in organisations with rigid structures and management styles. In contrast a theory y manager will give people greater freedom, will consult about methods and objectives and will delegate more authority. These theories are summarised in Figure 8.1.

McGregor was widely misconstrued as people, seeking the one right answer to all their problems, interpreted his analysis as replacing an "old" model with a "new" one. Theory x was wrong: therefore theory y was right. They fell into the trap of believing that there could be only one model of man, whereas McGregor was demonstrating the range of models that could be appropriate and freeing management from the narrow-minded orthodoxy that he found all around him in the 1950s.

3. MOTIVATION THEORIES

To some extent employees are in control of their behaviour; as are customers, suppliers, shareholders and other managers. Much of their behaviour will thus be *motivated* as they consciously seek to attain certain goals. Internal motives cause people to seek specific outcomes that will satisfy their needs. Just as separate models of man are all partially accurate, so theories of motivation at the moment can only partly explain the mysteries and complexity of motivation.

Needs or motives can be divided into two general categories. *Primary* needs are those relating to basic animal drives such as hunger, thirst, sleep, sex, pain avoidance, recovery from fatigue and safety. Their influence on behaviour is obvious and easy to identify. *Secondary* needs are acquired through experience and vary greatly according to culture as well as the particular experiences of the individual. They are the desires for power, achievement, social affiliation, status and a feeling of personal competence. Satisfying a primary need diminishes or temporarily extinguishes the drive. A hungry person does not feel hungry immediately after a large meal. Secondary needs are not satisfied in quite the same way as meeting a need for, say, recognition is likely to produce a desire for further recognition.

Maslow (1943) grouped needs into a five-step hierarchy, illustrated in Figure 8.2. The primary needs were physiological and safety. Secondary needs, dealing with the psychological aspects of man, were in three categories: social needs, esteem needs and self-actualisation needs. Maslow

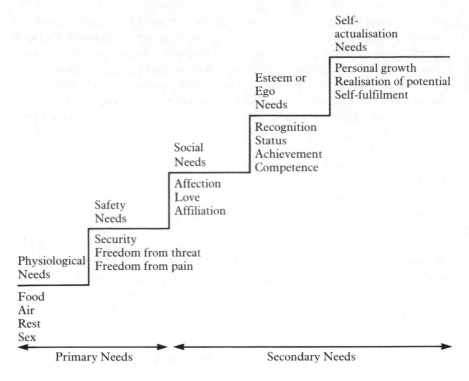

Figure 8.2   Maslow's Hierarchy of Human Needs

contended that individuals tended to move up the hierarchy of needs, and would occasionally move down for brief periods. More significant was that sets of needs came into consideration in sequence, so that until the lowest order needs were satisfied, others were relatively unimportant, but once the lower order needs are satisfied, they lose their potency. A severe headache needs to be relieved before the desire for friendship and affection becomes strong, but once the pain is relieved, then friendship may become important.

Employees in western societies generally have their primary needs met (although those unemployed may not) so managers are interested in the secondary needs. Some managers try to eliminate chatting between employees at work on the grounds that it distracts their attention from what they are doing. This can, however, cause output to go down rather than up because this type of social contact is a means of coping with tedious work.

The esteem or ego needs can be met at work because of the opportunities that are provided for doing relatively well when compared with others. Ego needs are interpreted in relative rather than absolute terms. The need can be satisfied by the employee feeling a degree of recognition or status that others have not achieved, or that he has now achieved so that he can compare himself with others who have already reached that level.

The sportsman raising his arms triumphantly above his head is asserting his achievement in the feat which he has accomplished. In organisational life there are innumerable ways in which status is marked. Some people have secretaries, while others do not; some wear white coats, while others wear grey; some carry skilled status union cards, while others do not. Management strategy in relation to these indicators varies. In some organisations much effort goes in to eliminating such status dividers, by ensuring that all eat in the same cafeteria, wear the same uniform and address each other only by their christian names. In other organisations the status indicators are cultivated to recognise the way employees are making progress. The Macdonald chain of fast-food shops provide their staff with name badges carrying space for four stars according to the range of tasks the person can undertake, so that this recognition is not only given to the individual to compare with the position of other employees, but it also seen by the customer.

Self-actualisation is the highest order of needs in Maslow's hierarchy as it represents the restless urge to self-fulfilment that the humanist psychologist believes we all have. This is not seeking after doing better — or as well as — someone else, but satisfying oneself that one is doing all one can. Recognition and status needs are met by someone else saying, "Well done!" Self-actualisation needs are met when one can say "Well done!" to oneself. Organisations provide potential satisfaction of these needs in the demanding and challenging work that can be found in most management and scientific positions. Employees may, however, be deprived of this sort of potential need satisfaction in jobs which are routine and thus give no scope for initiative. Other jobs may not be routine, but can still lack this type of need satisfaction because of limits that are placed on the scope of the job and the denial of creativity. This is often a problem of over-specialisation in management ranks: jobs are chopped up so small that few people are able to complete an assignment and have to pass it on for completion by someone else.

The ranking of these five sets of needs in a hierarchy is based on two important assumptions. First that a satisfied need is not a motivator and second that as one set of needs become satisfied, then the next set of needs become dominant. The implications of this for managers are obvious. It is not worth trying to provide means for employees to satisfy self-actualisation needs if lower level needs have not yet been met. Also it is pointless trying to "motivate" employees by considering their lower order needs if these are already satisfied. A further dimension is that the level of need satisfaction can vary. A group of managers who assemble for a two-day course, never having met each other before, will initially be much more concerned about the accommodation and catering arrangements than they will be later in the course, when social needs will become dominant, rapidly followed by esteem needs.

Herzberg (1968) developed the Maslow idea of the hierarchy by making a stronger distinction between lower and higher order needs. He described the lower order needs as potential *dissatisfiers*, or hygiene factors, and only the higher order needs were potential *satisfiers* or motivators. He contended that those managing organisations had to get the hygiene factors right, just as an operating theatre has to be clean and a kitchen well-scrubbed. Without those basic satisfactory conditions employees would be dissatisfied. Once the organisation was "clean", further attention to lower order needs would not enhance employee performance. They can hamper when they are not properly met, but they cannot motivate beyond the level of basic satisfaction. Herzberg listed specific hygiene factors for life in organisations as including:

> Company policy and administration
> Supervision
> Working conditions
> Salary
> Relationship with peers
> Personal life
> Relationship with subordinates
> Status
> Security

Most of these have in common the fact that they are *extrinsic*, coming from outside the person. Herzberg's list of satisfiers or motivators was shorter:

> Achievement
> Recognition
> Work itself
> Responsibility
> Advancement
> Growth

These are generally *intrinsic*, coming from the inside of the person, and are not so easily satisfied. The person who achieves something then wants more achievement; the person who has challenging, interesting work wants more of it to do. This has proved a most popular theory with managers, as it has provided a practical basis for management action: give people scope for achievement, recognition, enriched jobs etc., and they will work harder, be more content and appreciate the goodness of the manager who made it all happen.

Despite the popularity of Herzberg, based on Maslow, there are some words of caution. Herzberg's research was mainly among engineers and accountants — well educated, middle-class Americans, and other people may have quite different needs and attitudes. Contemporary with Herzberg, a study in a British car manufacturing plant described the *instrumental orientation* of those whose attitudes were examined:

> The workers were particularly motivated to increase their power as consumers and their domestic standard of living, rather than their satisfaction as producers and the degree of self-fulfilment in their work.
> (Goldthorpe *et al*, 1968, p. 38)

In other words, work for these workers was mainly a means towards another end rather than having intrinsic merit. The attempts by some enthusiasts to revolutionise the quality of working life by introducing motivators to jobs where they have been traditionally absent have usually failed after a brief honeymoon period. Maslow can be criticised for the precision of his stratified hierarchy of secondary needs, as human beings are not as consistent as that, and Herzberg made extravagant claims for the universal applicability of his theory, which have not been borne out in practice for all groups of workers. Despite these reservations, a careful consideration of what both Maslow and Herzberg say provides a very helpful framework for understanding general aspects of motivation.

Those wanting to delve further into this area are recommended to see the work of Salancik and Pfeffer (1979) for a detailed assessment of the relevance of this research and theorising to organisations.

4. MORALE

Close to motivation is morale: the degree of confidence people have in their situation and the way in which that influences their attitudes to their employment. It is not clear that this state of mind necessarily has an effect on work performance, although common sense tells us it should. Some researchers have claimed to demonstrate that high morale leads to high performance (for example, Herzberg et al, 1959) while others have argued exactly the opposite — that satisfaction results from high performance. Vroom (1964) examined 22 different pieces of empirical investigation and concluded that there was a significant relationship between morale and performance in only five of them.

If we are looking for incontrovertible evidence we do not find it, but common sense tells us that improved morale *can* lead to improved performance and seldom will it worsen performance. At least one research study (Mirvis and Lawler, 1977) showed a correlation between morale and both attendance at work and staff turnover, as well as the financial impact of employee attitudes.

Review Topic 8.2

The French writer and hostess Madame de Staël (1766 - 1817) is alleged to have written "To be totally understanding makes one very indulgent..." (*Tout comprendre, c'est tout pardonner*).

As managers try to understand their subordinates are they likely to become indulgent?

For managers there is often an initiative to be taken to build up the morale of employees, to build confidence in situations where it is absent. This is done by all manner of strategies under the general heading of leadership, which we consider in Chapter 15. Some other strategies we have come across in our researches have included, for instance, a sales manager altering the sales figures that were distributed to his salesmen in order to convince them that sales could be achieved at a time when the salesmen had lost faith in their product. A newly-appointed head teacher found the staff in her school dispirited because of apprehension about plans for reorganisation and reducing staff numbers. She adopted the simple tactic of describing the school as "good" or "very good" in all conversations: with staff, parents, children and local authority officials. The initial reaction varied from rage to amused disbelief but gradually one or two people began to think that perhaps there were less fortunate schools. A few months more and some members of staff were suggesting practical ideas for change; the parents' association realised that they had raised more money in six months than in the previous two years. The head teacher no longer described the school as "good"; it was now "very good" or "first class". The simple fact of persistently giving people one piece of basic good news gradually made it true: performance began to reach the standard of the description.

High morale can be associated with the product or process with which employees are engaged, especially in high technology or social service. Concorde was a commercial failure as a passenger carrier, but the technical achievement of its design and construction produced very high morale among those who built it.

A factor in morale is the *age* of the employee. Early enthusiasm and optimism tend to produce high morale at the beginning of a career, which will give way to a more glum view in many people by the late twenties or early thirties, as their aspirations remain high but their level of achievement fails to match it. This is the time of some self doubt ("Am I as good as I thought I was?") and some resentment ("Why am I not appreciated?") about the lack of opportunity provided by the situation. Gradually the career aspirations are adjusted so that they become more realistic and morale rises, even though it is unlikely to reach the soaring enthusiasm of youth. The period of forty plus in employment is one that has only recently attracted any attention by researchers (Torrington and Cooper, 1981).

> ...we can offer general comments about ways in which older employees have signal virtues. Absence from work due to short spells of sickness, lateness and absenteeism declines with age, so that the older employee is likely to be more reliable than his younger colleagues, but his most important feature may be the enhanced capacity for sound judgement. Francis Bacon produced the aphorism that young men are fitter to invent than to judge; fitter for execution than for counsel; and fitter for new projects than for settled business.
>
> (p. 7)

Morale is also affected by *education* and *occupational level*. The more extensive a person's education, the higher he can aspire and the more self-conscious he can feel about relative failure as he has one excuse less. Positions at the top of the hierarchy offer more scope than those in the middle and at the bottom, as we have already discussed, so that morale is often higher as you move up. Those with manual craft skills usually have higher morale than those without.

The final main influence on morale is the least tangible, that is the *character of the employing organisation*. The IBM song, quoted at the opening of this chapter, was an attempt to secure from employees a sense of identity with a cause that was worthwhile and important. Fighting troops in battle rally to their flag and one of the greatest problems for the Americans fighting in Vietnam was that the troops suffered from very low morale through not believing in their cause. Employee morale will be affected by the extent to which they regard their employer's business to be wholesome. This has caused some difficulties in tobacco companies, breweries, armaments manufacturers and other undertakings where some employees had reservations about the ethical acceptability of the operation. More common is the problem of organisational success. It is unlikely that morale will remain buoyant in a business that is failing, but expansion and rising turnover lead to high confidence.

5. STEREOTYPING

In trying to understand other people we all, instinctively use a short-cut method known as *stereotyping*. This is an essential aspect of dealing with others but can also be a straitjacket if we do not use it carefully. If you have lost your way in a foreign city and decide to ask someone for directions, you do not stop the first person you see: you pick out someone from the surrounding crowd who looks to you a potential source of good information. You probably look for someone who is not in a hurry, neither too young nor too old, appearing intelligent and sympathetic. You have a working stereotype of who would be an appropriate person to ask. At work we carry round in our heads a series of stereotypes which influence all our dealings with other people. Some of these are carried over from our general experiences and prejudices, for example:

> "Scotsmen are careful with money".
> "Small women are assertive".
> "Men with long hair are unreliable".

Others are linked to working experience and values:

> "Shop stewards are bloody-minded".
> "All engineers think clearly".
> "Accounts are dull".
> "Women make good secretaries".

Figure 8.3   Understanding Other People

There is seldom time in all working situations to abandon stereotyping as a way of approaching matters, especially in emergencies, where some sort of working hypothesis is needed immediately. The danger of stereotyping is, of course, that people are not treated and understood as individuals but as categories. This is unreasonable to them (and can be unlawful) and it limits the ability of the person who is over-dependent on stereotypes to work with others to the full extent of his abilities and theirs. A special form of this is the *halo effect*, where individuals are judged according to an imaginary halo above their heads. Someone, for instance, who is never late may be pointed out as an admirable employee even though the quality of his work is poor.

Stereotyping often occurs between departments in organisations, so that marketing people are often regarded by others as superficial, flashily dressed and not really doing anything, while production people are seen as earnest, harrassed and socially ill at ease.

In concluding this chapter here is a brief summary of suggestions made by Zalkind and Costello (1962) for improving one's ability to perceive others accurately:

a)   the better we know ourselves, the easier it is to see others accurately.
b)   one's own character affects what one sees in others.
c)   the accuracy of our own perceptions depends on our sensitivity to the differences between people.

SUMMARY PROPOSITIONS

8.1.   Individuals differ from each other physically, in experience and in personality.

8.2   Man has primary needs and secondary needs. Secondary needs are those which have the greatest influence on working behaviour.

8.3.   Morale is influenced mainly by an employee's age, education, occupational level and the character of the employing organisation.

8.4.   Stereotyping is a necessary mode of behaviour to cope with novel situations but limits a manager's scope for getting the best from himself and others working together.

REFERENCES

Eysenk H.J. & Eysenk S.B.G., *Personality Structure and Measurement*, Routledge & Kegan Paul, London, 1969.

Freud S., *Outline of Psychoanalysis, Vol. 23*, Hogarth Press, London, 1964.

Goldthorpe J.H., Lockwood D., Bechhofer H. and Platt J., *The Affluent Worker: Industrial Attitudes and Behaviour*, Cambridge University Press, 1968.

Herzberg F. "One More Time: How Do You Motivate Employees?" in *Harvard Business Review*, January–February, 1968.

Herzberg F., Mausner B., Snyderman D.B., *The Motivation to Work*, John Wiley, New York, 1959.

Maslow A.H., *Motivation and Personality*, Harper & Row, New York, 1954.

McGregor D., *The Human Side of Enterprise*, McGraw Hill, New York, 1960.

Mirvis P. & Lawler, "Measuring the Financial Impact of Employee Attitudes", in *Journal of Applied Psychology*, Vol. 62, 1977, pp. 1–8.

Morris D., *Manwatching*, Thames and Hudson, London, 1977.

Morris D., *Gestures*, Stein and Day, London, 1979.

Rogers C.R., *Counselling and Psychotherapy*, Houghton Mifflin, Boston, 1942.

Salancik G.R. & Pfeffer J., "An Examination of Need-Satisfaction Models of Job Attitudes" in Steers R.M. and Porter L.W., *Motivation and Work Behaviour*, 2nd edition, McGraw-Hill Book Co., New York, 1979, pp. 66–89.

Schein E.H., *Organizational Psychology*, 2nd ed., Prentice Hall, New Jersey, 1970.

Sheldon W.H. *Atlas of Men: Guide to Somatyping the Adult Male at All Ages*, Harper and Row, New York, 1954.

Skinner B.F., *Science and Human Behaviour*, Macmillan Free Press, New York, 1953.

Torrington D.P. and Cooper C.L., *After Forty*, John Wiley, Chichester, Sussex, 1981.

Vroom V.H., *Work and Motivation*, John Wiley, New York, 1964.

Zalkind S.S. and Costello T.W., "Perception: Some Recent Research and Implications for Administrators", in *Administrative Science Quarterly*, No. 7, 1962, pp. 218–235.

Chapter Nine

WINNING CONSENT WITHOUT HAVING AUTHORITY

Much managerial time is spent in winning people round. This is not the same as using power, as was discussed in our chapter on organisational politics, nor is it the exercise of authority in "the line" as we come to in Chapter 15. It is the ability to persuade and to influence, very similar to the art of selling. It is not the manipulation of resources and setting up situations which gives others little choice but to agree, and it is not the working relationship between superior and subordinate behind which there is the implicit assumption that the superior can command the obedience of the subordinate. It is a separate, specialised aspect of managerial work that enables him to get things done; an extension of his understanding of other people and how they are motivated.

Winning consent without having formal authority is becoming more important to managers for several reasons. First, the complexity of organisations increases the number of contacts managers make in which they have *no authority*. In the 1976 study by Rosemary Stewart (described in Chapter 4), 7 per cent of the managers interviewed were in solo jobs, spending a low proportion of time in contact with other people. In our own recent research we have found an increasing number of people in this type of lone, specialist role. Such a person not only has to be constantly persuading and influencing to get things done, but has continually to justify his position. Secondly managers find their *formal authority curbed*. It is a long time since any but a few managers had the straightforward, unchallenged right to dismiss people, but legislation has gradually reduced that type of authority further, so that the power to dismiss is seldom held by an individual manager in an organisation. Also the power to determine pay rates and pay rises has been gradually impersonalised so that individual managers have only a marginal influence on pay and other financial benefits received by their subordinates. (After extensive consultation we decided, for instance, that there was no place in this book for a section on payment methods.) The development of procedures in organisation has tended to remove the opportunity for managers to act as arbiters and judges in relation to subordinates.

As technology advances and companies diversify, managers find they have *limited expertise* in technical matters and therefore have to depend increasingly on the autonomous competence of others, whether in a subordinate position or not. Nobel Prize winner, H.A. Simon, distinguished between authority and other types of influence:

> The characterstic which distinguishes authority from other kinds of influence is . . . that a subordinate holds in abeyance his own critical faculties for choosing between alternatives and uses the formal criterion of the receipt of a command or signal as his basis for choice.
>
> (Simon, 1974, p. 330)

Winning consent without having authority is a process that assumes the other person will *not* hold his own critical faculties in abeyance and will use his own judgement, accepting responsibility for the outcome.

There are at least three common barriers to this type of interpersonal influence. One is the differences between individuals. The person you want to influence may not like you or trust you. Secondly the climate of the organisation may be inappropriate. If intensive competition between individuals is encouraged or unavoidable, then political means are more likely to achieve compliance than the more personal methods discussed in this chapter. The third reason is the number of mechanical barriers that can exist. It is difficult to influence the person you never meet and it can be suspect when you try to influence someone where there is a formal organisational barrier between you and that person.

1. THE APPROACH TO WINNING CONSENT

Leavitt (1978, p. 127) suggests that we need to consider three factors if we wish to influence another: ourself, the other person and the interaction that is to take place. Handy (1981, p. 126) adds to those a need to consider the environment in which the attempts to influence take place.

We need to understand ourself, so that we can consider the reaction of others and their expectations of us individually in our role. In considering the other person we take account of their experience, personality and position. Then we can think of how to approach the interaction between self and other. The environmental points vary. Seating arrangements, for instance, can affect the outcome of conversations. In counselling, career advice and similar discussions it is helpful to have relatively informal seating arrangements without a direct, head-on orientation between self and other. In arguments where there is a direct conflict of opinion, it can help to face each other across a table. Another aspect of the environment is the degree to which influence is achieved in group situations. Most people find it easier to participate in the discussion of a small group (say ten people or fewer) than a large group. It is easier to have a turn to speak and it is easier to win round half a dozen people with different views and expectations than it is to cope with twice that number of varied positions. Large committees struggling with a difficult issue may delegate it to a subcommittee or working party to make suggestions. Unless opinions are strongly polarised on the committee, the small working party should be able to produce recommendations with which all members agree, so that the consequent meeting of the full committee will be faced with a caucus of its members who are committed to the working party proposals, and that degree of commitment will be hard to counter.

There are a number of different strategies that can be used to achieve influence. In this chapter we review assertiveness, bargaining, collaborative influence, manipulation, persuasion and transactional analysis. At the close of the chapter there are notes on certain aspects of technique: reinforcement, reward, participation by the other and taking the view of the other.

2. ASSERTIVENESS

Assertiveness training is currently popular with women's groups and is designed to develop people's confidence to control their own affairs and involves breaking minor "rules" of polite behaviour.

Assertiveness training was initially developed in psychotherapy to help people who feel inadequate in their dealings with other people because they are afraid to speak up for what they believe and are not willing to resist when others appear to take advantage of them. Managers are not likely to suffer that degree of social handicap, but the techniques can be useful to develop self-confidence to deal with unfamiliar situations. The method is to work, with a friend or colleague, to identify the type of situations in which one is passive or diffident and then to think out some assertive responses for such a situation, which are practised with a friend and then gradually tried out in real life. This type of role playing has been a familiar part of many management training courses without ever being dignified with the term assertiveness training. Trainee salesmen often role-play with trainers playing the part of difficult customers, and personnel specialists frequently carry out dummy negotiations with tough shop stewards.

There are many situations which few people enjoy dealing with, for example:

People talking on the row behind you in the theatre,
People who jump the queue in front of you,
Complaining in a shop about the quality of something you have bought,
Going to a party where you do not know anyone.

In organisational life some of the worries experienced are:

Being criticised by a superior,
Criticising a subordinate,
Advocating an unpopular point of view at a meeting,
Being asked to do something you do not feel capable of doing,

Asking subordinates to do something that you think they will resent.

The reluctance to criticise underlies the widespread ineffectiveness of performance appraisal, which has been described as "a good idea gone wrong". Managers chafe at the chore of filling in forms, but they also resist having to be specific in explaining to subordinates the extent to which their performance is not satisfactory. Apprehension about giving unpopular instructions is probably the most common managerial nightmare and is why managers so often dread situations in which their authority is not clear-cut. What would happen if the subordinate would not comply? In practice the confidence to say "no" is much more difficult to find and hold to than the confidence to say "do as I say".

Review Topic 9.1.

Identify one or two situations at work in which you typically feel diffident and think out some assertive responses or initiatives to use in them.

---

3. BARGAINING AND EXCHANGE

Call it bargaining, negotiating — even cajoling or bribing in some situations. A agrees with B to give him something in return for desired behaviour. Sweets to a child, tips to the dustman, promotion to the executive are obvious examples. Less obvious, but perhaps more common, are friendship and favour, inclusion in a group, approval and status. Exchange methods can follow from any power source, depending on what is offered, but resource and position are the most frequent bases.

(Handy, 1981, p. 123)

Bargaining covers the explicit as well as the implicit. Occasionally there is an explicit deal, with offer and consideration: "If you can get the machine repaired by Friday, I'll put your departmental budget higher on the agenda for next week's meeting". But these are infrequent in transactions within the organisation, as they put on an informal and unofficial basis that which should not require any extra arrangement beyond straightforward request.

More common is the implicit offering of friendship, approval or gratitude if something can be done:

"I really have a problem, can you possibly help me...?"
"Be a pal and... ."
"You are the only person who could possibly do this... ."
"I always believe in asking the experts... ."

A similar version of this is to do favours to others, so that there is a scattering of IOUs that can be called in, the bread upon the waters of the

Bible. The problems with this type of dealing are first that the "rewards" offered may have to increase to maintain their value, but also that the exchanges depend on *both* parties being able to reward the other. Offering approval loses its value if your approval is not wanted, so that bargaining works best when the parties to the bargain are roughly equal in their power to reward each other:

> Perceptions of power inequality undermine trust, inhibit dialogue and decrease the likelihood of a constructive outcome. . . . Inequality tends to undermine trust on both ends of the imbalanced relationship, directly affecting both the person with the perceived power inferiority and the one with the perceived superiority.
>
> (Walton, 1969, p. 98)

The process of reciprocal reward takes a slightly different form when it becomes social exchange in a continuing working relationship between people. Homans (1958) studied the 'traffic patterns' of interaction in groups and concluded:

a)   the more often people interact with each other, the more favourable will be their mutual feelings,
b)   people who interact with each other frequently are more likely to adopt similar practices than people who interact less frequently.

4. COLLABORATIVE INFLUENCE

When it is important to people to believe in what they have to do, that belief will probably only be reached by participating in the process of deciding what should be done: they will support that which they have helped to create. There is a series of ways to do this, varying in the degree of participation. *Full participation* is the process whereby there is free and spontaneous discussion among members of a group, with the minimum of agenda, so that a collective will emerges from the discussion that will be supported by all members because of the full and frank exchange of views that produced the consensus view. This is not a denial of leadership, as there is a need for summarising, clarification and — ultimately — action, which has to be focused. It is, however, a process which makes the leader answerable to the group.

Consultation is a process in which the leader or manager retains the responsibility for deciding what should be done, but seeks a strategy that the responding individual or group will accept. Not always do the respondents have full commitment to such decisions, because they are accepting strategy but they do not have responsibility for the decision that is reached.

A different form is *elite corps involvement*, where members of the organisation are involved in making a decision, but their involvement is based on them being members of an elite group, called in for consultation. As they are specially selected they are flattered and may commit themselves fully to a course of action whether their involvement is by full participation, consultation or simply by being told before other people.

Collaborative influence is often achieved in the most informal ways without any calculation:

"What do you think...?"
"Any ideas?"
"I'd like to have a word with you about... ."
"I'm thinking of . . . but I'm not at all sure that it's right."

It is also not the sole preserve of those high in the hierarchy winning round those who are lower: it is just as frequently used by those seeking the backing of their organisational superiors.

5. MANIPULATION

The idea of manipulating other people is generally offensive, with its overtones of puppets and strings. It is, however, an ancient art and does not always arouse disapproval. For most of recorded history the young have indulged in courtship, the result of which is sometimes tears, sometimes frustration, but often a reasonable degree of mutual satisfaction, yet the process of courtship is one of manipulating emotions and cajoling a person to change his or her mind. This is all done against a background of uncertainty about motives. Are the intentions honourable or not?

In the everyday life of organisations consent is often won by manipulation. Leavitt (1978, pp. 157–60) summarises the process like this:

1. A is the manipulator; B the person to be manipulated.
2. A's motives are not fully known to B.
3. The relationship between A and B is either established or developed by A to provide a basis of influence; getting B to do what A wants.
4. A exploits dependency of B in the relationship.
5. Dependency of B increased by using emotions such as approval, support, recognition.
6. Influence develops incrementally, by adding bits and pieces as dependency increases.

Described thus, manipulation sounds no more than a confidence trick, but there are many circumstances in which it can be necessary or appropriate. One of the main bases of training is reinforcement through praising the faltering attempts of the trainee in the early stages. This is manipulative in that the trainer is trying to influence the behaviour of the trainee by exploiting the trainee's dependence, using the trainee's need for reassurance. Part of any manager's responsibility is to get others to do things. So a manager will often use manipulation to obtain compliance from someone else towards organisational objectives. The manager who manipulates others simply to advance his personal objectives is much more reprehensible.

One form of manipulation is propaganda, which is attempting to build a favourable image by appealing to a large number of people. The methods of public relations are too specialised to have a place in this book, but we can include some comments about public-speaking that is designed to win people round to a particular point of view. To be persuasive the public speaker has to be seen as having some expert knowledge and good intentions. His effectiveness will be enhanced by enthusiasm or conviction, and will connect a state of emotional preparedness — engendered at the beginning of the address — with some course of action advocated towards the end of the address. It is important that members of the audience should easily see the connection between the emotional feeling and the prescribed action. This can be helped by graphic illustration and examples.

Argyle and Trower (1979, p. 101) suggest that a propagandist should present his case in a certain order:

a) he makes amiable remarks to establish rapport with the audience.
b) he arouses guilt, concern or anxiety.
c) he presents a strong, positive case, showing how the feeling aroused can be resolved by the recommended behaviour.
d) he deals with any obvious objections.
e) he draws explicit conclusions and makes recommendations for action.

6. PERSUASION

Persuasion is talking someone round to your point of view, using the force of argument and the logic of evidence that is deployed to support the argument. This is straighforward and dignified without the worrying suggestions of being devious, as with manipulation, or aggressive, as with assertiveness. It also has the attraction that the outcome will be "right" as it will depend on the cogency of the argument and people will not comply if not convinced. Personal factors none the less make some people more persuasive than others. Persuaders are likely to be successful only when they are regarded as *credible*, having some track record of effectiveness. Employees find it hard to see a company management as credible if it is not successful in running the business. The persuader must also be *expert*, which is a more precise quality than credibility. It can be attested by qualifications, position or experience, but is a sign of having special knowledge that is seen as relevant and greater than that of the person being persuaded. *Trustworthiness* is important because of the feeling of helplessness that can come from dealing with an expert. The wisdom of the expert makes the person being persuaded conscious of his own ignorance and the need to place himself "in the hands" of the expert. So the expert must by trustworthy. The persuader who is *objective* adds strength to his case by being able to see both sides of a question, so that the person being persuaded is able to weigh both and decide. The opposite case has at least been set out, even if it is peremptorily dismissed.

7. TRANSACTIONAL ANALYSIS

Transactional analysis was developed as a form of group therapy for treating the mentally ill, but has been applied in management development for a number of organisations. It is a theory of personality as well as a form of therapy, but here we are using only a part of the whole concept: the means whereby transactions or communications between people can be understood.

The theory propounded by Eric Berne (1966) as the basis for transactional analysis is that there are three ego states of the individual, similar to the ego, id and superego that were mentioned in the last chapter. The *parent* ego state is one of authority and superiority, and a person acting in this state is typically dominant and scolding. It is the state in which all our value judgements are stored and the state of a person every time he acts in a way learned from his parents. The *child* ego state contains all the impulses that are natural to an infant. There is all the unpredictability of tantrum and charm, obedience and defiance, tears and laughter, sulks and joy. The parent acts in a way he was taught; the child acts in the way he feels, impulsive and uncensored. The *adult* ego state is objective and rational. No matter what prejudices or emotions were communicated by parents, someone in the adult state deals objectively with reality, analysing situations as realistically as possible; processing data, estimating probabilities and making decisions. It is not prejudiced by the values of the parent nor by the natural urges of the child.

These labels have nothing to do with age, nor do individuals fit into only one of the three categories. All of us have all three states and spend each day moving from one to another. The manager trying to win people round will discern the ego state of the other person and respond appropriately. Choosing the appropriate response requires an understanding of the three basic types of transaction: complementary, crossed and ulterior.

Complementary transactions. One that is:

...appropriate and expected and follows the natural order of healthy human relationship.

(*Berne*, op. cit., p. 29)

They take place between any two ego states, where the transactors are in the ego state appropriate to the transaction. Figure 9.1 shows first a diagram of a transaction where both parties are in the adult state and secondly a transaction where one is in parent and the other in child. Both are complementary, with the lines of transaction running in parallel, understanding and appropriate action being achieved.

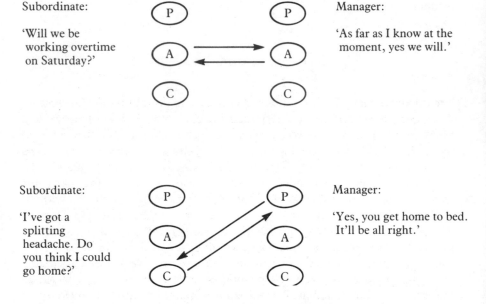

Subordinate:

'Will we be working overtime on Saturday?'

Manager:

'As far as I know at the moment, yes we will.'

Subordinate:

'I've got a splitting headache. Do you think I could go home?'

Manager:

'Yes, you get home to bed. It'll be all right.'

Figure 9.1   Complementary Transactions

Crossed transactions. Those in which the opening statement elicits an inappropriate response. Complementary transactions can continue indefinitely with communication and understanding being sustained. Crossed transactions cause an interruption. Either there is no communication or the subject is changed. Figure 9.2 shows two crossed transactions, first one in which the manager produces an inappropriate response and secondly an inappropriate response from the subordinate.

Ulterior transactions. These are more complex as they always involve more than two ego states. The most common form is where a real message is disguised under an explicit, but socially more acceptable, transaction. The communication is not straightforward as there is always an ulterior motive: a game is being played. In figure 9.3 we see an opening statement by a manager who wants a member of his staff to accept a move out of marketing into public relations because he feels it will be a good career move, but he also believes that the member of staff will not be keen to make the change.

Subordinate:

'I haven't had
my copy of the
new works handbook.
Have you got a
spare?'

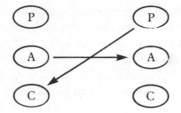

Manager:

'Surely you can see
I'm busy. Can't you
pick one up at the
office on your way home?'

Manager:

'According to the
rota, it's your
turn to stay behind
and clean up.'

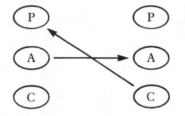

Subordinate:

'Oh no. I'm going out
tonight. Can't you
get someone else to
do it?'

Figure 9.2   Crossed Transactions

Manager:

'They have an
interesting vacancy
in PR, but I'm not
sure you're ready
for it.'

('Go on. Pick up
the challenge.')

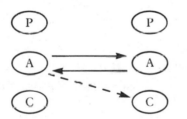

Subordinate:

'No, I suppose I had
better get a bit more
experience before I
try for a move.'

Outcome: the manager loses the game.

Manager:

'They have an
interesting vacancy
in PR, but I'm not
sure you're ready
for it.'

('Go on. Pick up
the challenge.')

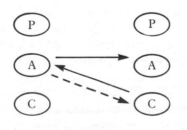

Subordinate:

'Why not? I think
I stand as good a
chance as anybody
else, and I'd
certainly like to
give it a try.'

Outcome: the manager wins the game.

Figure 9.3   Ulterior Transactions

The solid arrow in the drawing shows the explicit adult– adult message and the dotted line shows the implicit adult–child message. The response is either what the manager wanted (child–adult) so that the game has been won by the manager, or it is a simple response to the adult–adult explicit message and the manager has lost.

In most situations the ideal transaction is adult–adult, but any complementary transaction is better than any crossed transaction. If two people are both in the child state and start shouting at each other, they will not resolve their problems, but they will cope with the situation better than if one were in a different ego state.

Central to transactional analysis is the concept of *stroking*, the idea that we all need attention, recognition and approval. This influences much of our early life and influences our dominant ego state throughout later life:

> ...infants require physical strokes for survival: unless babies are touched, they will die. As we grow older, our need for physical touching diminishes, though it never disappears. We learn to survive on non-physical strokes, to substitute any kind of attention for the physical strokes we still want and need. Negative attention will do if we can not get positive attention.
>
> (Wagner, 1981, p. 35)

Stroking can therefore be either positive or negative. There are three kinds. *Positive conditional* strokes are those bestowed on behaviour that is approved, with the assumption that the stroking will continue as long as the behaviour continues. "That programme was just what we needed", "I am very pleased with your progress". *Positive unconditional* strokes are bestowed for some aspect of what you are rather than what you have done: "I like you", or "What do you think?" Perhaps the most common is the smile.

A *negative conditional* stroke is given to behaviour that is disapproved, with the implication that the disapproval would be lifted if the behaviour were to change: "You are still making too many mistakes", or "This is the third time you have arrived late this week". All of these have a useful place in transactions. A fourth has no useful place at all. The *negative unconditional stroke* is a bleak disapproval of the other person: "I don't like you", or "You make me sick". There are also certain dimissive behaviours under this heading, such as taking no notice when someone speaks or interrupting them in the middle of a sentence.

As long as managers realise the nature of the three ego states and work within them, they are able to analyse what is being said and how they should respond. The manager who can build a strong adult ego state, and encourage others to do the same, is able to conduct transactions in a forthright and objective manner. He will concentrate on complementary transactions, use ulterior transactions sparingly and avoid negative conditional strokes at the same time as developing his use of the other three.

8. MISCELLANEOUS ASPECTS OF TECHNIQUE

There are one or two aspects of social technique that everybody uses in conversation that can be identified and practised. The practitioner can then become more adept in social exchanges and more successful in winning people round.

Reinforcement. Similar to the stroking of transactional analysis. In our relationships with others we reward some behaviours that they produce; smiling, nodding, making agreeing noises or saying things that convey agreement, pleasure or wonder at the wisdom that is being offered. The effect of this is to reinforce the behaviour that is being rewarded. Equally the withdrawal of rewards prevents behaviours being reinforced. Frowning, not paying attention, yawning, shaking the head or saying things that express disagreement, annoyance or dismay tend to inhibit the behaviour with which they are associated.

The general effect of reinforcement is to increase the amount of the behaviour that is being reinforced, so that a man rewarded by his wife for taking an interest in the children will continue taking an interest in them and a trainee rewarded by the instructor for producing good work will produce more good work. Despite the general usefulness of this technique, there are two reservations. First those who are insecure, or anxious may be so keen on rewards that they will suspend judgement to obtain them, so that the reinforcer is rewarding sycophancy. Secondly reinforcement is most effective when provided by someone whose acceptance is worth having, so that its effect will not be great unless the personality of the reinforcer or the relationship between the reinforcer and the rewarded person is appropriate.

Reward. An aspect of manipulative style that is more pervasive than simple reinforcement. It is described by Argyle (1972, p. 74) as rewardingness and deals with the way in which a person becomes relatively popular and influential on the opinions of others. The manager rewards others by being responsive to their needs and interests, responding quickly to requests for information, return telephone calls and assistance. Explanations of why certain things are needed can be a reward, as can suggestions of how problems could be overcome and inviting comments on proposals that are being put forward. This is not quite the same as being permissive or *laissez-faire*, as some core of direction is usually needed. In deciding policy directions, for instance, the manager working with a group of others will not want to direct at the beginning of a discussion as it is important to generate as many ideas and alternatives as possible. So he will do no more than start the conversational ball rolling. Later, however, there will be a need to pull strands of argument together, find a small number of choices for further discussion and focus thinking on those. Later still it will be necessary to adopt a stricter style when discussion moves through decision-making to action.

The essence of being rewarding in one's behaviour is being warm and friendly towards other people, but the way in which the rewards are offered will vary between individuals, as will the way in which they are received. Cheerful exuberance may be interpreted as overbearing; congratulation may be construed as being unctuous; an attempt not to embarrass may be regarded as coldness. The manager also has to exercise control, as he cannot always respond in the rewarding way that the other would like.

In these situations he should look for an alternative. The young man in the policy discussion who is advocating a line of action that others regard as haywire will not get his proposal discussed further, but he has to be kept "in play" to redirect his attention constructively towards the other ideas that are being considered. He therefore has to be rewarded by some alternative such as an agreement to look at his proposal again in three months' time, or a frank acknowledgement that his proposal is very well regarded but too risky for his over-cautious colleagues.

Participation by the other.   A cumbersome phrase to encompass a range of ways in which one sees a matter from the point of view of the other person and so both rewards that person and participates with him in deciding what to do. The main aspect of this is the understanding of a different frame of reference, which is a sociological term to describe a set of basic assumptions that determines behaviour and attitude. This is most relevant on a large scale, and there is the regular example of managers and politicians failing to understand the bloody-mindedness of people who take industrial action at a time when that action will clearly imperil the jobs that the action is intended to protect. The reason is that the people taking the action have a quite different frame of reference, leading to different expectations, priorities and objectives. To them their action is logical and only the management are bloody-minded. Similar differences of view affect what is called "cashless pay".

Ray Hughes has worked in a clothing factory for 37 years. On Thursday evenings he receives his weekly wages, paid in cash, approximately £80 after deduction of income tax and national insurance. On the way home he deposits £5 in his Post Office savings account and puts £25 in his back pocket to cover his personal expenditure for the week. He then gives £50 to his wife, who deals with all the household expenditure. He and his working colleagues are resisting a proposal by the management of their factory that they should be paid by cheque. Not only does this involve the inconvenience of cashing the cheque, but it brings nearer the day when a major principle would be lost. Mrs. Hughes might find out exactly how much her husband gets paid, and in many families that is a jealously preserved confidence. The management persist in wanting to pay by cheque to overcome the time and expense of handling large amounts of cash, which pose a serious security risk. They point out all the advantages of having a bank account to Ray Hughes and his friends, but the fundamental difference in their frames of reference makes their exchanges a dialogue of the deaf.

On a one-to-one level managers need to think themselves into the position of the person with whom they are talking, to see the topic as clearly as possible from the other point of view in order to make the most of the exchange.

In this chapter we have reviewed some of the ways in which individual managers can get their own way and get things done without having the dubious benefit of formal authority to issue orders. All the comments centre round two aspects of style. First the confidence of the manager in setting out what he wants, being sure, clear and precise. Secondly is the ability of that manager to work with the responses and needs of the other person, rewarding, "stroking" and understanding the other point of view. To be effective, the manager needs not only to understand but also to practise. What we have described here are things that all of us do to some extent every day of our lives, as part of being a member of the human race interacting with others of our species. If we can understand that interactive process better, we can then practise our behaviours and improve our performance.

Review Topic 9.2.

Peter, the Distribution Manager of a food factory, wanted to pack cartons in lots of 10, as this would ease handling problems. David, the Marketing Manager, said this would be difficult for small customers. How might Peter try to influence David?

SUMMARY PROPOSITIONS

9.1. Winning consent without having authority is becoming more important to managers because of the increasing number of situations in which they have no authority; their formal authority is curbed or they have limited expertise.

9.2. To win consent managers need to understand themselves, the other person in the interaction and the interaction itself.

9.3. Methods of approaching particular situations include assertiveness, manipulation, persuasion and transactional analysis.

9.4. Aspects of style leading to influence include reinforcement, reward, and participation by the other.

APPENDIX

Self-Assertion in Everyday Life

The following sequence is given as an example of self-assertion in *Person to Person* by Michael Argyle and Peter Trower, pp. 95–96:

John is queuing up in a shop and someone apparently pushes in front of him. John feels angry, grabs the woman by the shoulder, and shouts: "Hey, just a minute, where do you think you're going? You've got a damned cheek...". This can be highly embarrassing, since the woman may have good reasons for her actions thus putting John totally in the wrong. On the other hand, John could react with resignation, accepting the situation and quietly fuming to himself....

There is however a more effective and widely used form of self-assertion, which we will describe below in a series of steps:

First step.   John should size up the situation. It may be that the other person has a good excuse. She doesn't realise she has queue-jumped, she may be an assistant taking stock on the other side of the shop, or a customer who has already paid and is making for the nearest exit.

Second step.   John should act cautiously to avoid the chance of putting himself in the wrong. A metaphorical or literal nudge to say "Did you mean to do that?" may be all that is required to draw the woman's attention to the situation. If she is reasonable, she will apologise or explain what she's doing and move out of the way. If she doesn't John has to go to the third step

Third step.   John can now be more explicit and say, politely but firmly, "Excuse me, I was here before you". This step is clearly more assertive and more clearly a demand, but still leaves open the possibility for the woman to explain herself without putting John in the wrong. If she doesn't excuse herself or refuses to move, John should resort to the fourth step.

Fourth step.   John can now demand his rights. He should square up to her, speak in a loud voice and use other signals of threat display. He can tell her bluntly what she has done, insist on keeping his position, moving himself physically into that position if necessary. But he should never use outright aggression and this includes verbal abuse.

REFERENCES

Argyle M., *The Psychology of Interpersonal Behaviour*, Penguin Books, Harmondsworth, Middlesex, 1972.

Argyle M. & Trower P., *Person to Person*, Harper & Row, London, 1979.

Berne E., *Games People Play*, Andre Deutsch, London, 1966.

Handy C.B., *Understanding Organizations*, 2nd edition, Penguin Books, Harmondsworth, Middlesex, 1981.

Homans G.C., "Social Behaviour as Exchange", in *American Journal of Sociology*, vol. 62, May 1958, pp. 597–606.

Leavitt H.J., *Managerial Psychology*, 4th edition, University of Chicago Press, 1978.

Simon H.A., "Authority" in Dubin R., *Human Relations in Administration*, 4th edition, Prentice Hall, New Jersey, 1974.

Wagner A., *The Transactional Manager*, Prentice Hall Inc., Englewood Cliffs, New Jersey, 1981.

Walton R.E., *Interpersonal Peacemaking: Third Party Consultations*, Addison-Wesley, Chicago, 1969.

Chapter Ten

COMMITTEES

As soon as he was installed as President of the United States in January 1961, John F. Kennedy was caught up in the plans for an American-backed invasion of Cuba in order to replace Fidel Castro with a right-wing government more sympathetic to the United States. The attempt was a fiasco and Kennedy took the chair at a meeting to discuss what went wrong. As the committee members departed after blaming everyone else for the failure Kennedy is alleged to have said that everyone is the father of success, but failure is an orphan.

The use of committees in organisational life is often viewed with cynicism. They are regarded as cumbersome methods of decision-making, ways whereby individuals avoid responsibility, and activities which consume far too much time, begrudged by everyone. In order to understand the use and abuse of committees we shall review in this chapter what their *purposes* are, the features of behaviour in committees and aspects of their *operation*. The chapter closes with notes on how to handle the activity of chairing and how to be a member, as well as a drill for producing the agenda. As a preliminary we consider some more general aspects of meetings and group working.

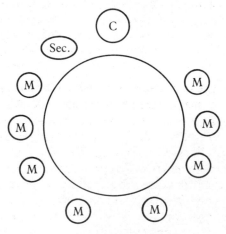

Figure 10.1   Committees: Chairman, Secretary and Members

1. MEETINGS AND GROUP WORKING IN ORGANISATIONS

Meetings are an integral part of any human community, serving an underlying need of our species to confer, draw support from each other and assert our role and membership in the group, even though this need is not always acknowledged. Housebound housewives often deliver their children to the school gate earlier than is needed and linger, swapping conversation, knitting patterns, recipes and the telephone numbers of piano teachers until after all the children have vanished to their lessons. The operational purpose is taking the children to school, but there is an underlying need to meet with others. In adolescence young people meet at tennis clubs, youth clubs and discotheques. The operational purpose is to play tennis or to dance, but the underlying need is to meet and appraise each other. This can be done fairly comfortably while playing tennis, or — better still — waiting to play tennis, because there is a decent distance which can be maintained. In the discotheque there is the excitment and the awe of physical proximity, which can only be tolerated when the senses are partially anaesthetised by pitch darkness and deafening noise.

Review Topic 10.1

How can decision-making by committee avoid the risk of everyone being the father of success, while failure remains an orphan?

In his highly original analysis of modern organisations as jungles in which corporate man struggles for survival, Anthony Jay (1972, p. 217) discusses the need for committees in organisations:

> ...the species we belong to, and from which we have descended, survived by keeping together, and irrespective of the demands of the job, Corporation Man needs to come together regularly with other members of the species — operational objectives can always be found to justify this deeper need. I suspect that meetings are most frequent and most enjoyed by men whose work keeps them solitary or in very small groups for most of the week. . . . There is a need to feel the security of the group around you, even if you do not belong to a real or effective one.

Here there is the same theme as with the housebound housewives at the school, needing to make contact. Coping with this need for physical proximity is demonstrated by the importance which is attached to the place in which meetings are to be held. In any organisation there is only one type of room which rivals in splendour and comfort the office of the Chief Executive and that is the board room, used only on *very* special occasions. In universities lecture theatres have benches or tip-up seats and tiles on the floor, as they are only for people to spend long hours listening and taking notes. If those same people go to a seminar, for a *meeting*, they will have much more comfortable chairs and probably a carpeted floor. Before the meeting of some important national or international conference newspapers often carry reverent photographs of the room in which it will take place, with the notepads, pencils and flasks of water all marshalled neatly. Reporting on the progress of such meetings, television journalists try to be filmed speaking from the very place in which the momentous decisions were made.

There are many types of meeting and group working in employing organisations that do not constitute committees, all of them operating on the assumption that some tasks are better undertaken by groups than by individuals. Uris (1960) has suggested that this is because the problems of organisations are complex and involve large sums of money and that the decisions are too risky, or too demanding, for one person to make. They also fit in with the democratic idea, implicit in our culture, of consulting with others. Blau and Scott (1963) list the main reasons:

a)   The sifting of suggestions in social interaction serves as an error-correction mechanism.

b)   The social support furnished in interaction facilitates thinking.

c)   The competition among members for respect mobilizes their energies for contributing to the task.

One type of informal group is *brainstorming*. (Smith, 1973, p. 69):

> ...groups attempt to create a freewheeling atmosphere where any ideas, however absurd, are recorded. Evaluation of the quality of ideas is strictly excluded and is carried out after the idea-generation phase is complete. . . . (The) view is that the flow of ideas in the group will trigger off further ideas, whereas the usual evaluative framework will tend to stifle imagination. This may be because group members are concerned not to appear ridiculous in the eyes of others.

Variations of this method have been used in many areas of organisational life, where fresh ideas have to be developed and creativity is required. This method is not always successful as individuals can often produce better ideas working alone, but it can be useful if group members are provided with working information and when the ultimate acceptability of the decision is important. A summary of recent research is in Summers and White (1976).

A further variant is the *task force*, which comes into existence for a limited period to undertake a single task before being disbanded. Group members are chosen for their particular expertise rather than their rank and they have specific tasks, such as how to reduce costs in a department, improve the quality of a product or plan the introduction of a new product. This is a specialised activity, quite different from the committee. Drought (1967) describes how a small group was set up to reduce the cycle time in a factory. It was so successful that it was made permanent, but its permanent state made it ineffective as more people joined, many of them inappropriate to the sort of work the group had discharged but attracted to it because of its success and able, through rank, to ensure their membership. It ceased to operate cohesively and lacked adequate goals.

2. PURPOSES AND PROBLEMS OF COMMITTEES

Committees are more formal bodies than those we have considered in the past few pages. There are usually explicit responsibilities and they are semi-permanent bodies, performing a range of functions.

The Plural Executive

The most obvious reason for a committee is to make decisions. Matters that are complex, unfamiliar or frightening may best be settled by discussion between a group of people who all carry a share of the problem individually and who can contribute to a collective decision because they all have a stake in the issue under discussion and can all provide some relevant expertise and be committed to the implementation of whatever decision is made. The Health Authority Management Team described briefly at the opening of Chapter 3 is just such a plural executive. Another way in which such bodies come into existence is as substitutes for key individuals. Louis XV of France acceded to the throne as a child and therefore was judged unable to govern, so a plural executive was established under Philip Duke of Orleans to act as a regency council during his minority. If the founding-father Chief Executive of a company is absent negotiating big deals in Japan, then a plural executive may be able to keep decision-making going while he is away.

The Linking Pin

The committee can perform another function in the complex organisation: to keep people informed of what is going on, a feature of the communications network we looked at in Chapter 6. Organisation members with varied responsibilities come together to be briefed, to brief each other, and then to carry information away with them to be passed on to others. The personal messages which the individual member conveys can never be replaced by the official communiqué. The company, for instance, that has lost a major contract will need to get a lot of quick, widely dispersed information to all its members. The written communication can do no more than convey the bare facts. If the chief executive explains the situation to the members of the joint production committee, those members will then convey a wider range of messages to the work groups from which they come, whether they be managers or employee representatives. They will carry away with them beliefs about the seriousness of the situation, the degree of alarm being expressed, fresh resolution, renewed common purpose, hope, confidence; all those aspects of communication that can rarely be achieved in writing:

> We set up part-time groups whose members, though primarily identified with subgroups, come together periodically to relate their problems to one another, to resolve common problems. This is a crude mechanism — time-consuming and frustrating. And yet it is one of the most effective mechanisms we know. Even companies that have tried consciously to kill the committee system have ended up resorting to it in one form or another. Face-to-face interaction between members of different groups, formal or informal, is still the best available means of binding a loose set of subgroups together.
>
> (Leavitt, Dill & Eyring, 1973, p. 184)

Making Recommendations

Some committees serve an advisory purpose by working out strategies and rough-cut decisions for others to accept, reject or modify before taking action. Factory safety committees are of this type:

> '...it shall be the duty of every employer, if requested to do so by the safety representatives...to establish, in accordance with regulations made by the Secretary of State, a safety committee having the function of keeping under review the measures taken to ensure the health and safety at work of his employees'.
>
> (Health & Safety at Work Act, 1974)

Similar are those committees that recommend appointments for others to make or weight the advantages and disadvantages of a particular course of action. Heads of state are advised by many such committees.

Blooding

A small, but useful, purpose of committees is the blooding of young or inexperienced members of the organisation. They can attend meetings either as observers or in company with some more established member to gain understanding and experience before having to assume full responsibility.

Problems with Committees

One of the main criticisms of committees is the time they consume, which makes them very expensive to operate, especially if one considers time to travel as well as the time of participating. If one person can solve a problem or reach an appropriate decision in eight hours of solitary ratiocination, that will be more cost effective than five people together reaching the same decision in two hours. This reservation, however, takes no account of the need for speed and the problems of implementation. If a decision has to be taken quickly, it may be better to use five people to make the decision in two hours rather than wait for one person to do it in eight. Also, making the right decision may be less problematic than getting it put into practice. Discussion between five people may take time, but they will disperse with a commitment to the action agreed and a full understanding of what is to be done. The solo decision-maker would have to win consent for his decision when he had made it.

Another problem can relate to the quality of decisions made by committees, due to a need to settle for the lowest amount of conflict and a tendency to compromise. Although this is a strong common sense argument, it is not supported by psychologists' experimentation with groups and individuals on risk-taking. A number of studies have shown that group decisions on the level of risk are more daring than those of individuals (see, for example, Kogan and Wallach, 1967; Teger and Pruitt, 1967).

3. FEATURES OF BEHAVIOUR IN COMMITTEES

The thrust of behaviour by committee members will be divided betwen *competition* and *co-operation*. Although they share some common purpose, they will also have differing personal interests and aspirations in their committee work and will often be competing for limited resources that the committee has at its disposal. These resources range from the tangible, such as proportions of the budget, to the intangible benefits of esteem and status or outperforming a rival.

Members of managing committees are usually competing for a slice of the budget. When the marketing director introduces proposals for a new advertising campaign to boost sales by x per cent, the production director will think defensively about the agreement he won at the previous meeting to spend an extra £y,000 on repairs to plant. Will this new venture imperil that expenditure? Will production facilities and personnel be sufficient to meet the new sales level that is forecast? Will the new campaign boost sales of new products now being introduced but depress sales of other lines that are languishing but of which there are large stocks due to inaccurate market forecasts last year? Other members of the committee will also be thinking from their own point of view and there is an accompanying tendency to grouping and coalition between members, often involving behind-the-scenes deals, ("If you support me on this, I will support you on that"). Committee members are inevitably in this sort of situation and competitiveness among committee members can raise the level of achievement of the group of individuals by social facilitation (Cartwright and Zander, 1968).

Committee members also co-operate; not only in factions, as was suggested above, but also as a whole. Usually any competition is resolved by a consensus in which individual objections or reservations are withdrawn in favour of a co-operative strategy after the competing views have been aired. There is obviously a need for balance and the main art of chairing a meeting is in ensuring that there is the stimulus of competition so that committee members are on their mettle, but in a reasonably secure and open atmosphere so that competition does not become destructive of the appropriate degree of co-operation in reaching agreement and making progress.

Bales (1950 and 1953) studied the interaction process in groups of small committee size and was able to categorise the behaviours of participants under twelve headings:

1.   Shows solidarity
2.   Shows tension release
3.   Agrees
4.   Gives suggestion
5.   Gives opinion
6.   Gives orientation
7.   Asks for orientation
8.   Asks for opinion
9.   Asks for suggestion
10. Disagrees
11. Shows tension
12. Shows antagonism.

This shows that some of the behaviours in the middle of the list are task-oriented while those at the beginning and end are oriented to the group and the person's membership of the group. By identifying these categories a member of the group, not necessarily the chairman, can influence the direction of discussion by producing a behaviour to match his objective, so that if he sees A showing tension because B and C are disagreeing with the opinion he is giving, an intervention could be to ask for an opinion from D, who is known to support A, but be diffident in declaring his position.

Tuckman (1965) produced the alliterative jingle "forming, storming, norming and performing" to describe the way in which a group works out a means of collaborative activity. His analysis is that in the early stages of *forming* members of the group are unsure of each other and likely to restrain extremes of view or opinion while testing each other out. *Storming* is the next stage in development, when members have developed enough knowledge of each other to put forward their views forcefully, including strong disagreement and hostility. The third stage of *norming* is when members produce norms of behaviour for themselves as they accept the need to collaborate and control their disagreements in order to produce results. The final stage is *performing* at which point the members have set up their rules and concentrate on achieving results, while sharing positive feelings of need satisfaction.

The very simple model is helpful to committee members to understand the stage of development that their committee has reached. With committees that meet seldom, or have a changing membership, the process can be seen to some extent at every meeting. Chapter 14 deals in more detail with the behaviour of people in working groups.

4. COMMITTEE OPERATIONS

Committees operate in a relatively formal way. There is invariably a chairman and usually minutes are kept. These may be drafted by a secretary during and after the meeting, with the draft then modified by the chairman, but eventually they have to be accepted by all members at the next meeting. The chairman has considerable scope for determining the way in which proceedings are recorded and emphasised, but there is less scope for determining decisions, unless the committee is remarkably compliant. Before a decision is reached it will be framed with some precision, even though it may not be put as a formal motion. Either the chairman will frame it in a leading way — "Are we all agreed then, that we offer the post to Smith?" — or it will be put to the meeting as a motion from committee members. The wording is likely to be clarified and tidied up before the committee as a whole votes on it.

Other aspects of formality are that there are usually an agenda, some rules of procedure about who speaks and how voting is conducted and the convention of conducting all debate through the chair so that remarks are directed to him rather than to other committee members.

There will be a predetermined frequency of meetings and some terms of reference about what the committee is intended to do, what range of authority it has, how it is to operate, and how the membership is to be made up.

One determinant of effectiveness will be the *size* of the committee. What is appropriate depends on the committee's main purpose. Hare (1981) produces evidence that a membership between six and ten is preferred for problem-solving and making decisions. Fewer members means that there may be insufficient input of information and ideas. More people leads to unwieldly discussion, diverse information input and the inhibiting of the less confident members of the committee. Schwartz (1980, p. 342) makes the following suggestions:

Relatively large committees are desired when:

A principal purpose of the committee is to inform the members who comprise it.

Widely differing talents and experience are needed to make the recommendation or decision.

The scope of the committee's activities is very broad. In these cases, however, it may be wise to divide the work into sub-committees.

Relatively small committees are desired when:

Speedy action is needed.

The matter assigned to the committee must be kept confidential. Obviously, the more persons serving on a committee, the greater the chance of information leaks.

Committee effectiveness is also influenced by the nature of the *membership*. There are nearly always some ineffective members who hold their place for political reasons or even as a form of punishment. They are likely to delay, confuse or demoralise the committee as a whole. Driver (1980) argues that the main matter to be resolved is whether an individual is essential or "possibly useful": only the essential should be recruited. The ideal committee member should be interested in its purpose, so that he would not concur with nonsensical proposals, and he should also have knowledge and experience that is also relevant, with sufficient time to attend and prepare for meetings. Finally the ideal member should be psychologically equipped for the committee process: able to compromise after reasoned argument, listening as well as talking, but sufficiently resolute to persist in trying to persuade other members to his point of view. In this way his contribution is made and used by the group as a whole in the search for consensus.

The *method* of committee discussion is basically the exchange of information followed by working on hypotheses. On each issue or item on the agenda members first seek out the facts, even if those facts do not necessarily support their personal cause. This search for information may be aided by information being provided by the chairman or secretary for study beforehand. Nearly all committees have some preliminary documentation of this type, but it will be expanded by verbal contributions from committee members. This will add to what is written or provide interpretation. A committee deciding whether to install gas- or oil-fired central heating will be provided with the comparative cost estimates, but individual members will have a myriad of questions to put to the various interested members, which could not all be anticipated beforehand. As more and more information is exchanged the committee members build up a shared information base that makes ultimate consensus possible.

Once committee members find answers to all their questions they are reaching a point where decisions could be made, and this decision-making is expedited by exploring hypotheses. The nature of contributions changes. In information exchange the contributions are mainly question and answer, with questions like:

"Do we know how long it would take?"
"Could Fred tell us...?"
"Will the suppliers provide...?"

When discussion on a topic moves to hypotheses, the questions become leading:

"It seems to me that we have only one course to follow".
"Does this mean that we have to...?"
"Would anyone agree with me that...?"

Review Topic 10.2

The Roman poet Ovid (43 b.c. – 17 a.d.) made the comment "You will go most safely in the middle..." (*medio tutissimus ibis*).

Does decision-making by committee increase or decrease the desire for safety?

As working on competing hypotheses develops, the chairman will be looking for the most acceptable hypothesis in order to single it out for the committee's consent. When topics are extremely complex, the committee may divide up the work between subgroups of themselves, so that a series of working hypotheses are developed and the committee reconvenes to find a viable amalgam of the contributed part-decisions.

SUMMARY PROPOSITIONS

10.1. Committees formalise the act of groupworking. This is fundamental to the working of any organisation.

10.2. Committees are semi-permanent bodies of which the main purposes are to make decisions and diffuse information.

10.3. Although decisions by committee may be less cost-effective than those made by individuals, they may be bolder, and a committee decision starts life with all the members committed to its success.

10.4. Members of committees compete with each other as well as co-operating. When controlled by the chairman, this improves the quality of the committee's work.

10.5. The main operating method of committees is the exchange of information, working on hypotheses and achieving consensus.

APPENDIX A

Interaction guide for committee chairman

I   Before the Meeting

Decide

a) What the purpose is — decision-making, briefing, problem solving, generating ideas, or something else.

b) Whether the meeting is needed, or whether the purpose could be achieved better by other means or at a different time.

c) What should have been achieved by the end of the meeting.

d) What your role should be in the meeting — leader, sage, synthesiser, statesman, spokesman, or something else.

Review

a) Minutes of previous meeting, papers for present meeting.

b) Expected attendance and opening positions likely to be adopted by members.

c) (with secretary) arrangements for the meeting and the distribution of information to members about time, place, etc.

d) (with individual members) who will introduce different agenda items, perhaps making suggestions about data to be included or aspects to be developed.

e) The agenda to consider timing and pacing of discussion.

II   During the Meeting

Introduce

a) Any new members.

b) A brief overview of the business to be considered.

c) The secretary, for apologies and the minutes of the last meeting.

d) (progressively through the meeting) each agenda item with a summary statement about the reasons for the topic and general background for the discussion.

Recognise

a) Members to develop your introduction by inviting them to "speak to" the agenda item.

b) Members who want to speak by selecting between those trying to "catch your eye", so that there is a balance between varying points of view.

c) Members whose contribution could be important but is not being offered, by asking them to comment.

d) Members whose *style* of contribution could be timely, such as the member known for his calmness, invited for comment at a time of heated exchanges.

e) Members whose *authority* of contribution would be useful to move discussion forward, such as the person who initially "spoke to" an item, asked to offer a hypothesis or propose a motion.

Control and Facilitate

a) By expediting decision through picking the time when you can use your authority with a phrase like, "I take it that we agree that..." without your authority being challenged.

b) By focusing on disagreements and finding a resolution.

c) By summarising the state of the discussion and pointing a new direction.

d) By curbing contributions from members that are irrelevant or too long.
e) By asking for clarification from a group member of a point that is signalled by the non-verbal behaviour of other members as being puzzling or unacceptable.
f) By being interested and alert throughout.
g) By finishing on time.

III   After the Meeting

Check   a) (with the secretary) that the minutes or notes of the meeting are compiled, agreed with you and circulated.
            b) That those who are to take action know what to do, and do it.

Assess   a) How you could have conducted the meeting better and build that assessment into your preparation for the next.
            b) The appropriate time for the next meeting, material to be prepared for it, and any review of membership to be considered.

Studies and suggestions on chairmanship include Hoffman (1965), Maier and Solem (1952), Anstey (1965) and Cammallari (1973).

APPENDIX B

Interaction guide for committee member

I   Before the Meeting

Decide   a) What the purpose of the meeting is (see Chairman's list).
            b) What you want to have achieved by the end of the meeting — as a member and as a representative of an interest.
            c) What should your role be in the meeting — sage, synthesiser, statesperson, delegate, adviser, brake, stimulus, or something else.
            d) Decide whether you could/should be replaced by someone else for this meeting — subordinate, superior, colleague.

Review   a) Minutes of previous meeting, papers for present meeting.
            b) Action you were asked to take at the previous meeting.
            c) (with other individual committee members) their tentative views on agenda items in which you have a particular interest, possibly eliciting support for your own position.
            d) Notes you plan to use, papers you are to table, or visual aids to support your contribution.

II   During the Meeting

Signal   a) A wish to speak, by using non-verbal signals to "catch the eye" of the chair.

        b) Reactions to the contributions of others by non-verbal signals —
            such as nods and frowns.

Ask   a) For direction from the chair about points of order or terms of
            reference.
        b) For clarification, from the chair or another member, on
            information presented.
        c) For opinion, suggestion or hypothesis, from chair or from another
            member.

Offer   a) Information for exchange, including prepared presentations asked
            for by chair before meeting.
        b) Opinion, suggestion or hypothesis; either when called for or when
            mood of the meeting judged to be appropriate.
        c) Support for, or criticism of, opinions etc. offered by others.

Seek   a) By using social skills to persuade others.
Influence b) By using objectivity and seeking solutions that will be acceptable to
            others.
        c) By avoiding rancorous personal attacks on other committee
            members that will isolate you from the sympathy of other
            members.
        d) Support and develop the contributions of other members which
            you regard as constructive and likely to be generally acceptable
            after modification.
        e) By displaying expertise, both on your specialist area and on the
            general committee documentation and precedents.

III   After the Meeting

Consult a) With those you represent to advise them of committee decisions
            and required action.
        b) With those you represent about the position you have taken on
            agenda items and any ways in which this should be modified.

Assess a) How you could have participated in the meeting more effectively
            and build that assessment into your preparation for the next.
        b) The minutes, when they are circulated, and any suggestions you
            may have for future agenda items. Note corrections needed to the
            minutes.

        On those items which require action from you.

APPENDIX C

Administrative drill for committee secretary

(To make this illustration concrete we are assuming a meeting once a month, lasting
between two and three hours each time, on Wednesday, Day 28).

Day	**Phase One: MINUTES AND PRELIMINARIES**
1, 2.	Write draft of minutes, including notes of action items.
5.	Clear minutes with chairman and confirm date of next meeting.
6, 7.	Type, copy and distribute minutes.
7.	Book room for next meeting.

Phase Two: AGENDA

12.	Ask committee members for items to be included on next agenda.
16.	Discuss order of agenda and inclusion/deferment of items with chairman. Suggested sequence:

    a)   Announcements (apologies, introduction of new members, chairman's points).

    b)   Minutes of previous meeting and matters arising, where matter involves brief report. Matters arising for further discussion to be separate agenda items.

    c)   Items requiring decision but involving little controversy.

    d)   Most difficult item.
        (possible break)

    e)   Next most difficult item.

    f)   Items requiring discussion but not decision.

    g)   Easy items.

    h)   Any other business.

    i)   Provisional date of next meeting.

Phase Three: RUN-UP

19.	Circulate agenda and other papers to members, with note of date, time and venue.
23.	Check seating, catering, visual aids.
27.	Collate all papers, past minutes, apologies.
28.	Attend meeting and take notes for minutes.

REFERENCES

Anstey E., *Committees: How They Work and How to Work Them*, George Allen and Unwin, London, 1965.

Bales R.F., *Interaction Process Analysis*, Addison-Wesley, Cambridge, Mass., 1950.

Bales R.F., "The Equilibrium Problems in Small Groups", in *Social Encounters*, Penguin Books, Harmondsworth, Middlsex, 1976.

Blau P.M. and Scott W.R., "Processes of Communication in Formal Organizations" in Argyle M. (ed)., *Social Encounters, op. cit.*.

Cammallari J.A., "Effects of Different Leadership Styles on Group Accuracy", *Journal of Applied Psychology*, 1973, pp. 32–7.

Cartwright D. and Zander A., *Group Dynamics: Research and Theory*, Harper and Row, New York, 1968.

Drought N.E., The Operations Committee: an Experience in Group Dynamics, *Personnel Psychology*, 1967, pp. 153–63.

Hare A.P. in Borgatta E.F. and Baker P.M., Symposia on Small Groups, *American Behavioural Scientist*, May/June, 1981.

Health and Safety at Work Act, 1974, HMSO, London Section 2 (7).

Hoffman L.R., "Group Problem Solving" in *Advances in Experimental Social Psychology*, 1965, pp. 110–32.

Jay A., *Corporation Man*, Jonathan Cape, London, 1972.

Kogan N. and Wallach M.A., "Risk Taking as a Function of the Person, the Situation and the Group", in *New Directions in Psychology*, Holt, Rinehart and Winston, New York, 1967.

Leavitt H.J., Dill W.R. and Eyring H.B., *The Organizational World*, Harcourt, Brace Jovanovich, New York, 1973.

Maier N.R.F. and Solem A.R., "The Contribution of a Discussion Leader to the Quality of Group Thinking" in *Human Relations*, 1952, pp. 277–88.

Schwartz D., *Introduction to Management: Principles, Practices and Processes*, Harcourt, Brace and Jovanovich, New York, 1980.

Smith P.B., *Groups Within Organisations*, Harper and Row, London, 1973.

Summers I. and White D.E., "Creativity Techniques: Towards Improvement in the Decision Process", *The Academy of Management Review*, April 1976, pp. 99–107.

Teger A.I. and Pruitt D.G., "Components of Group Risk Taking" in *Journal of Experimental Social Psychology*, 1967, pp. 189–205.

Tuckman B.W., "Developmental Sequence in Small Groups" in *Psychology Bulletin*, 1965, pp. 384–99.

Uris, A., *Seven Rules of Committeeship*, Textile World, October 1960, pp. 32–6.

Chapter Eleven

DEVELOPING PROCEDURES FOR ACTION

Procedures are the life blood of any organisation, yet are scarcely ever discussed. Many books on general management extend over more than 500 pages but the term "procedure" does not appear in the index. The reason why they are ignored is that they are dull. The reason why they are important is that it is by the use of procedures in organisations that things get done. Exciting decisions may be taken, creative ideas may be developed, new products may be conceived, but all of them depend on organisational procedures for things to get done.

In some organisations one major procedure is the key determinant of success or failure, like the procedure for booking seats in an airline, or order processing and despatch in a mail order company, but in all organisations procedures are essential to success; they get things done. Three universal examples are post, pay and minutes. When post is delivered to a company, a procedure is operated. There are two stages of sorting, as some letters and packages will be addressed to individuals, but others will be addressed simply to the company, or to the general manager, and will require opening so that a decision can be made about where they should be routed. Sometimes records are kept of the arrival of particular categories of mail and many companies stamp the date and time of arrival on the envelope so that any subsequent queries can be dealt with. After sorting there is distribution to the various departments and offices within the organisation where the mail is to be dealt with. Then there is a reverse procedure whereby outgoing mail can be collected, franked and taken to the post office.

When a new employee joins an organisation there is a procedure for getting him on the payroll: the right rate of pay, the right arrangements for routeing the pay, the correct deductions and so forth. After meetings there is a procedure, as was described in the last chapter, for disseminating the minutes and preparing for the next meeting.

Managers' lives are dominated by procedures and much of their creative energy is spent in trying to circumvent them or expedite processes through them. A popular managerial self-image is of the person who can "beat the system" or "get things done without waiting for procedures which always take such a hell of a long time". The idea of procedures is such anathema to most managers that many readers will have passed over this chapter entirely! There are obviously many occasions when procedure is not appropriate — like the apocryphal story of the man in the burning building who could not find the right requisition form for a fire extinguisher — but the impersonal, dead hand of administrative routine is the best way to put into practice the majority of the decisions taken within organisational structures. Managers need, therefore, to consider and design procedures with consummate care, so as to save money, so as to save time, and so as to run a successful operation.

Review Topic 11.1

What type of decisions in organisations are best implemented by the impersonal, dead hand of administrative routine?

---

1. THE PURPOSE OF PROCEDURES

Procedures...establish a customary method of handling future activities. They are truly guides to action, rather than to thinking, and they detail the exact manner in which a certain activity must be accomplished. Their essence is chronological sequence of required actions.

(Kootz, O'Donnel and Wehrich, 1980, p. 166)

The relationship to policy is one needing some elaboration. A *policy* is a general statement of intention, for example:

"Wherever possible we will purchase component parts from British rather than foreign suppliers... ."

"We are going to switch our advertising from television to national dailies... ."

"We are going to discontinue manufacture of... ."

"We are an equal opportunity employer".

Each of those statements requires to be "sold" to members of the organisation before it can become effective, not only for them to be advised, but also for them to be convinced that the policy is appropriate, so that they will put it into practice with enthusiasm and thoroughness. The policy statements also, however, need procedures to make them work. If British rather than foreign suppliers are to be used, there will need to be a modification of the administrative routines operating in research and design, development engineering, production engineering, purchasing and production scheduling.

Procedure is the link between policy and practice and policies that fail may be poor decisions or good decisions that people elsewhere in the organisation never understood, but most often they are good decisions that foundered because there was no procedural follow-through.

The reasons for using procedures are first *to reduce the need for future decisions*. This is like the cookery recipe. A chef does not say to himself, "How should I bake a cake?" and then work it out by trial and error or even from first principles: he uses a recipe, a routine that has worked before and will work again. The personnel manager needing to fill a vacancy for a clerical assistant will similarly use a "recipe" or standard operating procedure. This not only has the advantage of speed in implementation because the decision-making has been done before, it also provides the opportunities of efficiency through practice and a modest amount of de-skilling. The smooth procedure can be operated by those with less skill than the decision-maker and procedure inventor, just as a million cooks can use one of Mrs. Beeton's recipes.

The second value of procedure is *consistency*. Most operations that are to be repeated benefit from being repeated in the same way, particularly when they involve other people who have to respond to the operation. Customers gradually become familiar with an organisation's procedures and practices, so that they waste less of the organisation's time if all organisation members treat them consistently. Organisation members become accustomed to a routine of departmental practice and are able to develop smooth interaction and swift handling if the method remains the same. Herein lies one of the great problems, as well as an advantage, of procedures: they are very difficult to alter and those who use them will abandon them only under duress. This is well illustrated in the field of industrial relations, where not adhering to procedure is the most heinous of crimes.

Thirdly procedures provide *autonomy for organisational members*. Without procedure subordinates have to await decisions from others, and they have to be told how to do things as well as what to do, so that they are dependent and have little scope for individual action. Procedure authorises and informs. The individual member of the organisation knows what to do and how to do it and, providing that the procedure is well devised, he will have some scope for individual action and decision as the administrative rules will be simple so as to provide him with both the authority and information he needs but also the freedom of action to make judgements in interpreting the rules for particular situations.

A final main advantage is that procedure is a means towards *management control of operations*. The delegation that was implicit in providing the autonomy mentioned above means that a manager can turn his attention to other things, confident in the system that will keep things moving in the right general direction. There will be fewer requests for information and guidance, fewer complaints and errors, fewer worries about the minutiae of organisational life. At the same time as providing freedom from control for individual members of the organisation, procedure provides effective control of operations to the management generally.

2. TYPES OF PROCEDURES

There are four types of procedures generally found in contemporary organisations: task performance, planning and expenditure authorisation, information and co-ordination, and mutual control.

Task performance procedures. These are among the most common.

> How does the part get fabricated? How are the books kept? How are the products priced? In terms of quantity of words, probably most of any given recorded standard operating procedure consists of specifications of methods for accomplishing whatever task is assigned to an individual member or subgroup of the organization.
>
> (Cyert and March, 1963, p. 103)

The ability of the engineering craftsman to work to drawings is an ability to work to procedures. Other examples are the job description, which describes a job partly in order to explain to the job holder what he has to do and how to do it; the training manual, which is used by the new recruit to acquire a knowledge of the routine which his job involves; the list of operations that are run through in closing down a plant; fire drill for evacuating the premises in cases of emergency.

Some task performance procedures are brought to the organisation by trained, newly-recruited personnel. The typist arrives knowing the procedures involved in producing a page of accurate typescript, the electrician arrives knowing how to wire a plug. Many of the tasks to be done in the organisation depend on task performance drills that are learned elsewhere, but there is a further set — for all personnel — that are specific to the organisation in which they are carried out. The typist knows how to type, but does not know where to obtain supplies of paper and envelopes, where to put outgoing mail for despatch, nor a whole series of procedures relating to house-style, number and destination of copies and so on. The accountant charged with pricing a product to ensure a proper return needs to know not only good practice in the accountancy profession and a technique for making the calculation, but also the organisational practice on credit in order to establish the appropriate criteria for the calculation.

An important subset of task performance drills are those concerned with changing the rules and coping with new situations. An example is the introduction of legislation that presents new problems. Legislation on the payment by employers of statutory sick pay was a simple idea that spawned innumerable one-day seminars, training packages and computer programs to explain it to managers. However, what was being "explained" was not the law, but devices for changing organisational procedures in task performance so that organisational members did their routine operations in a different way. It was the daunting nature of *that* task that caused the managerial anxiety.

Planning and expenditure authorisation procedures. Mostly the domain of senior managers, but minor authorisations are replicated at all levels of the organisation. Although long range, corporate planning is not as comprehensive an activity as the writers of management books would have us believe, there is always some amount of planning which seeks to set goals and targets for achievement. The plan specifies not only the ultimate destination but also the intermediate steps to be reached on the way. A marketing plan would, for instance, specify not only a target market share of *x* by a stated date, but also steps of 25 per cent of *x* to be achieved by an earlier date, 50 per cent of *x* to be achieved six months later and 75 per cent to be reached six months after that.

Any such plan is based on untested assumptions and is therefore theoretical, so it is not as tight and specific as the task performance procedure, but provides a more general operating framework that is susceptible to change and updating as circumstances evolve. The way in which the plan is given influence over the behaviour of organisation members is by allocating resources and authorising expenditure. The retailing organisation that has a plan to double its number of outlets in three years will not see any action until resources are allocated and expenditure agreed, but once the personnel director is authorised to recruit 700 more staff in each of the next three years and the marketing director is allocated £*x* million in each of the years to acquire and convert premises, then the plan becomes more than a possibility: it become a requirement for those two executives to implement the proposals.

> The budget in a modern, large-scale corporation plays two basic roles. On the one hand it is used as a management control device to implement policies on which executives have decided and to check achievement against established criteria. On the other hand, a budget is a device to determine feasible programs. In either case it tends to define — in advance — a set of fixed commitments and (perhaps more important) fixed expectations. Although budgets can be flexible, they can not help but result in the specification of a framework within which the firm will operate, evaluate its success, and alter its program.
>
> (Cyert and March, *ibid*. p. 111)

We are concerned here with the procedures of planning and expenditure authorisation, rather than with planning methods, discussed in Chapter 18, and the procedures of planning are unusual in the participative nature of their generation. Agreeing on the budget and setting operating plans are nearly always collaborative acts in which a range of interests are reconciled to obtain consensus support for the programme. Key aspects of procedure are thus the meetings at which plans are agreed and any possible power of veto which an individual, or another committee, might deploy; the timing of such meetings and the source of initiatives for consideration. Procedures for expenditure authorisation are of two kinds. Setting the overall budgets is aligned with the planning agreements and probably follows the same procedures precisely, but authorising items of expenditure against budget is an activity delegated to officers who have task performance rules for this procedure. Spending the company's money is not just being allowed to do it because your proposal has been accepted by the senior management team, but following the drills which check that the expenditure is in accordance with another set of rules on proper organisational behaviour.

Information and co-ordination procedures. These have a less precise objective in that organisations can limp along without them, but performance is generally improved if people know what is going on and feel that they are kept in touch. Typically information flows in from the outside of the organisation to the apex of the organisation pyramid or to well-identified other places in the hierarchy as is suggested by Figure 4.3. The need for parts of that information then to be passed on to other members of the organisation was discussed in Chapter 7. The method of such passing on will lie in procedure, so that there is some semi-automatic means whereby dissemination takes place, rather than dependence on the individual recipient to take thought and decide on dissemination.

Review Topic 11.2

The procedure for salesmen claiming expenses in a large chemical company was elaborate. Four authorising signatures were needed plus two separate clerical checks. The time from claim to settlement was usually between 16 and 20 working days. An internal consultant devised a different procedure that needed only one signature and one clerical check. The time from claim to settlement would drop to 5–8 days. There were no objections to this new arrangement, but four months later it had not been implemented. Why do you think this was?

Among the procedures found for information and co-ordination are the use of minutes of meetings, which are often circulated to a wider group than just those who attended the meeting at which the minutes were taken. A common refinement is to include a note as to who is expected to take action on the decisions made at the meeting. Another procedure is the checklist of recipients of memoranda, so that a manager will have two or three standard routine lists for passing information onwards. Notice boards are a potentially useful means of distributing information, but a procedure is needed to make it an effective means: who is responsible for putting items on the board and removing them? What items are appropriate and inappropriate, bearing in mind that all have to be read and understood in a very brief timespan? How long should items be displayed? A procedure which deals with these questions can make good use of a notice board system.

Mutual control procedures. Those which enable the employing organisation and the individual employee to exercise a degree of control over each other. Grievance and discipline procedures are the main example, as the parties to the contract of employment have a series of procedural steps available to them so that they can limit the action of the other:

> Joint regulation seeks to reconcile the interests and viewpoints of management and employees by a process of negotiation but it begins with the recognition that there are such differences of interest and view point and that there is sufficient strength behind them to make the quest for agreement necessary and desirable. Agreed procedures establish a *modus vivendi* reflecting the interests and strength of the parties.
>
> (Singleton, 1975, p. 5)

These industrial relations creations should not only be seen as ways in which action is prevented or made more difficult, they also *authorise* certain actions by managers and others. Discipline procedures, for instance, specify who has the authority to make relevant decisions, the circumstances which would justify those decisions and the means whereby a decision would be implemented.

3. PROBLEMS AND SOLUTIONS

Procedures present problems as well as opportunities, the most difficult of which is their dullness:

> ...managers often fail to obtain the interest and support of top managers in the tedious and unromantic planning and control of procedures.
>
> (Koontz *et al*, *op cit.*, p. 769)

That is difficult to resolve, but has to be recognised. Another problem is that *they inhibit change*. When they eventually become operational and everyone is used to them, they provide a comfortable, secure routine, an aspect of organisational maintenance where people can feel at home with the familiar. This is much like the way in which managers move from management to administrative activity, when the management work gets too hectic, as was described in Chapter 5. There is always the risk that procedure becomes custom and practice and as immutable as the laws of the Medes and the Persians.

Overlapping and duplication cause problems when each section of the organisation has its own procedures that do not quite coincide with those of other sections. Purchasing have procedures that are not quite the same as Accounts and both are quite different from those in Engineering. The varying emphasis is necessary as accountants have different responsibilities from buyers. The problems come when the overlapping or duplication becomes too great.

A less obvious problem is when procedures are used to try and solve problems that require a *policy solution*. Just as procedures are needed to put policy into practice, policies are needed for procedures to be effective. The personnel manager in a small textile company was anxious to eradicate racial discrimination from personnel practice within the organisation and made a number of procedural adjustments to this end. Standardised forms of words to be used in job advertisements were devised, instructions were given to telephonists about handling telephone enquiries, short-listing arrangements in the personnel office were altered and various other methods of preventing unfair discrimination were introduced. He failed, however, to explain these moves to anyone outside the department and was accused of high-handedness and deviousness by his colleagues. He also found that the procedural devices did not work: checks on advertisement wording were overlooked, departmental managers disagreed with short lists and there was a formal complaint to the Commission for Racial Equality. All of this was due to a lack of policy decision and commitment. The policy decision was made only in the personnel manager's mind, being neither discussed with, nor communicated to, anyone else. The telephonists and personnel staff did not fully understand the reasons for the changes they had been asked to make and other managers did not understand what was being done. Once the policy was clear, sold and accepted, the procedure worked well. Procedure can only deal with organisational problems for which a procedural solution is appropriate.

Procedure has all the inherent risks of *rigidity*. In producing a standard way of doing things, there is the danger that it is regarded by some as the only way of doing things. Grievance procedures nearly always specify that the aggrieved employee should raise his dissatisfaction first with his immediate organisational superior. This is for a number of very good reasons, such as to prevent the immediate superior being by-passed and to ensure that the matter will be resolved as quickly as possible and by the people most closely involved. Carried to an extreme that could be interpreted as prohibiting an employee talking to a more senior manager about anything. When organisational change is needed, the rigidity of procedures can prove too much for the enthusiasm with which the change is sought.

A common problem is the *complexity* of procedures. This is where the procedural steps are intended to eliminate any discretion at all. Such procedures are difficult for people to remember and to understand, so that they may be used only by — literally — following the book. They are also a challenge to the ingenuity of people who resist the lack of scope for personal judgement and interpretation. An example is in safe working procedures, which are regularly ignored by skilled and experienced operators who have sufficient skill and knowledge to do, safely, what would be highly dangerous for others.

To overcome these difficulties those designing procedures should always aim for *simplicity*, so that they can be readily understood by those who operate them and those who are affected by them, allowing scope for interpretation to suit particular circumstances. Procedures should also be as *few* as possible, so that there is less to remember and so that the degree of overlapping and duplication is limited. Also a new procedure should not be introduced unless it is deemed as really necessary. To be necessary a series of future incidents has to be likely so as to require some thought out decisions in advance. Producing a procedure to deal with a situation that occurs seldom but with similar results is useful. Producing a procedure to deal with a situation which occurs seldom and with very varied results is pointless. A sombre example of the first is a procedure for dealing with attendance at funerals of those who die while in the employment of the organisation — who attends the funeral, how much time off, with or without pay, in company cars or not, etc. An unbelievable example of the second is "Procedure for the Golden Jubilee of the Monarch", found to be still available in the head office of an insurance company.

Procedures should be tested to see if they meet their *objectives*. A hospital was receiving a number of complaints from patients' relatives, so a complaints procedure was set up. This had the unfortunate effect of lengthening the time taken to deal with complaints and increasing their number. We have to make sure that procedures have not only an internal logic, but also that they do what they are set up to do.

Procedures must have the *before and after* stages of policy and communication. There must be a policy for the procedure to implement, even if it is only the implicit policy of established practice, and all affected must know what the procedure is. "Knowing" is not the same as "being told about".

Monitoring can prevent procedures becoming obsolete and inefficient. Not only must they be communicated, they must also be monitored in operation to make sure that they are being worked properly and that there are no unintended effects that should be smoothed out before too much damage is done.

4. PROCEDURAL METHOD

There are four methods of producing procedures: task logic, modelling, checklist and flowcharting.

Task logic. This is the method of work study and associated techniques, whereby the logic of the task to be accomplished dictates a sequence of actions or activities to be carried out in task performance. This method is not dealt with in this book, but a standard reference is Larkin, 1969.

Checklist. The checklist method is to set up a series of check questions as a basis of formulating the drill. Such a list could be derived from the sections of this chapter.

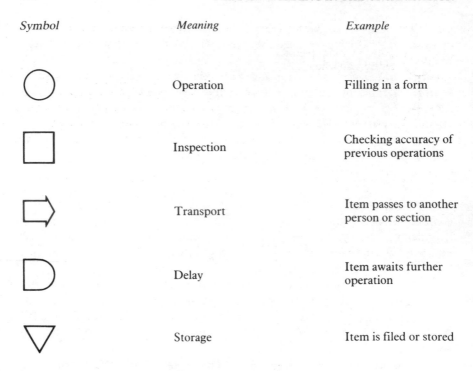

Symbol	Meaning	Example
Operation	Filling in a form
Inspection	Checking accuracy of previous operations
Transport	Item passes to another person or section
Delay	Item awaits further operation
Storage	Item is filed or stored

Figure 11.1   Symbols Used in Flowcharting

Modelling. A method much used with industrial relations procedures. A typical procedural system is devised as a model that could be used, with modification, for a wide variety of similar situations. In the Appendix to this chapter there is a model of a grievance procedure.

Flowcharting. The most sophisticated method is flowcharting, which is a simplified form of systems analysis. This is appropriate for those administrative drills that consist of a lengthy system of interrelated activities, possibly involving several different departments and certainly involving a number of different people. It can sometimes be elaborated from its basic linear form into a network analysis of the type described in Chapter 18. Figure 11.1 shows the symbols used in flowcharting and the Appendix to this chapter has a sample procedure produced by this method.

There is a danger in regarding procedures as dull and not requiring managerial time and attention. The organisation without satisfactory procedures can rarely operate effectively unless it is in an unusually favourable business situation. Any organisation can be hamstrung if its procedures get out of control. The need for swift action and consistent decision-making has to be balanced against the need for managerial initiative and employee creativity.

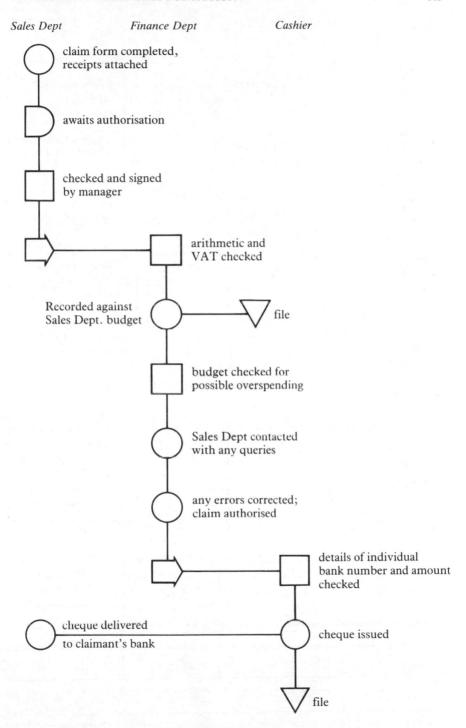

Figure 11.2 Flow Chart of Procedure for Settling Expense Claims

AGENDAS   NETWORKS

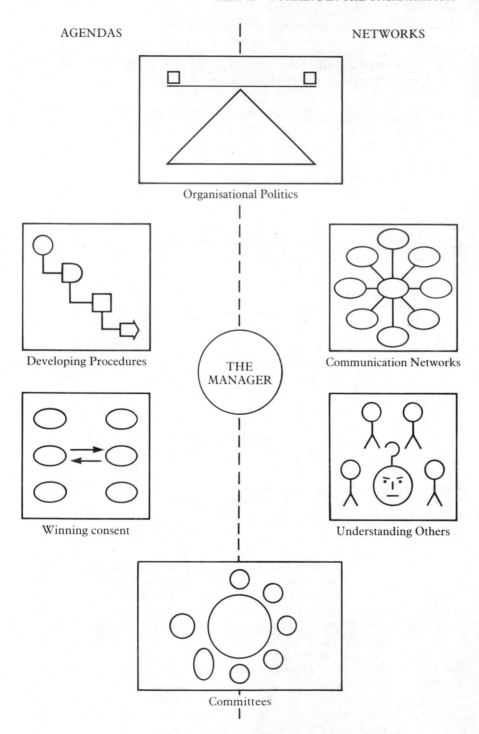

Figure 11.3   **Working in the Organisation**

SUMMARY PROPOSITIONS

11.1. Procedures are the link between policy ("what we would like to happen") and practice ("what is happening").

11.2. Reasons for using procedures are to reduce the need for decision-making in the future, to ensure consistency, to provide autonomy for members of the organisation and management control of operations.

11.3. Types of procedure are task performance, planning and expenditure authorisation, information and co-ordination, and mutual control.

11.4. Problems with procedures are that they can inhibit change, overlapping and duplication, providing the wrong solution to a problem requiring a policy solution, rigidity and complexity.

11.5. Problems can be overcome by having few, simple procedures, meeting objectives, with before and after phases and monitoring.

11.6. Methods of procedure are task logic, checklist, modelling and flowcharting.

APPENDIX

Outline model for grievance procedure

Statement of Intent
The purpose of this procedure is to enable individual employees of ... employed in ... to obtain satisfaction of grievances which they have about their employment. It provides a framework for the employee to voice his dissatisfaction and seek improvement. It is separate from the disputes procedure for resolving matters relating to employees collectively in their relationships with the management.

Step 1 (Preliminary)
The dissatisfied employee discusses his complaint with his immediate superior and serves notice that he would like his case heard at the next stage if he has not received a satisfactory reply within .... days.

Step 2 (Hearing)
The dissatisfied employee duly presents his case to a more senior manager (position to be specified). The reason for this being that this manager will be able to take a more dispassionate view of the matter than the immediate superior and will have the benefit of a broader range of responsibility to judge potential problems in meeting the employee's requirements.

Step 3   If still not satisfied the employee may take his case to appeal within
(Appeal)   .... days of the hearing. This will be with a more senior manager
                    or committee (position to be specified) or external arbiter, invoking
                    greater authority to examine the first two decisions.
                    If the employee is still not satisfied he has no further recourse within
                    this procedure.

REFERENCES

Carter R., *Business Administration*, Heinemann, London, 1982.

Cyert R.M. and March J.G., *A Behavioural Theory of the Firm*, Prentice Hall,
    Englewood Cliffs, New Jersey, 1963.

Koontz H., O'Donnell C., Weihrich H., *Management*, 7th ed., McGraw Hill,
    Kogakusha, Tokyo, 1980.

Larkin J.A., *Work Study, Theory and Practice*, McGraw Hill, London, 1969.

Singleton N., *Industrial Relations Procedures*, HMSO, London, 1975.

Part III

THE WORKING TEAM

Managers work with teams, usually groups of up to seven or eight people, whose integration and harmonious working is crucial to their collective success and the contribution that they make to the overall success of the organisation of which they are a part. The effectiveness of this team will be one of the main criteria for judging the manager's performance.

When given the opportunity to select the team members they want, instead of simply accepting whoever happens to be there, managers take great care in ensuring that the new arrival is the sort of person who will fit in with the other team members, even though he will undergo some training and coaching to make the fit as neat as possible. Effective team working depends largely on leadership and on understanding the social processes that working groups experience. The manager needs to understand not only those processes, but also how authority can be exercised without impairing the autonomy that individuals need in order to be effective. Performance appraisal is a way of monitoring and providing feedback to individual members of the team. The manager can also design individual jobs and the organisation of the department to maximise team performance.

A composite model of the manager's activities in working with his team is in Figure 17.3.

Chapter Twelve

SELECTING TEAM MEMBERS

Few managers are able to pick their own team. When a manager moves into a new post, he is the newcomer surrounded by people who are already established. Except in rare circumstances it is either unethical, unlawful, too expensive, impractical or simply foolish to discard those who are established and replace them with one's own nominees. Selecting team members is, therefore, a quite different activity for the individual manager than it is for the personnel specialist, who is recruiting people for the organisation as a whole. The individual manager is an occasional selector only, and is concerned much more with the internal dynamics of the group of people with whom he works than with the broader issues of promotion prospects, pension entitlement or union membership.

The manager selects a few members of his team either single-handed or in consultation with others, but tolerates the vagaries of many others. One could almost say that picking one's own people is an abdication of management, a part of the art being to organise and co-ordinate the contribution of different types of people, including those one does not get on

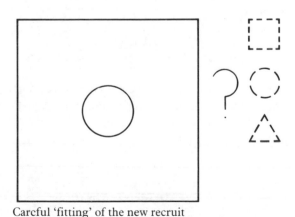

Careful 'fitting' of the new recruit
to the context of the working team is
needed to ensure effective co-ordination.

Figure 12.1   Selecting Team Members

with. This involves the manager adapting his style and approach to the varied expectations and needs of others, rather than being able to work only with kindred spirits, hand picked for their compatibility.

Daniel Greensmith had founded and developed a small printing business, working closely with three colleagues who helped him start the company and who "grew" with it. When the proprietor of a nearby, slightly larger printing company retired for health reasons, Daniel Greensmith bought the business. The move was welcomed by the managers and staff of the taken over company, as Greensmith was known and well regarded. To avoid any misunderstanding, a consultant was engaged to advise on the management structure of the combined business and how the senior positions should be filled. Greensmith told the consultant what he was looking for and the consultant advised him about which members of the two companies fitted his specifications. The three loyal lieutenants were appointed to three of the top four posts reporting to Greensmith. Within six months the business was in difficulty, and Greensmith had enough self-knowledge to see why. He explained it to one of the authors like this:

> I only knew one way to run a business and the three lads who had been with me from the beginning knew no more than I did: they were really just extensions of me. When the merger came along I hired a consultant because I wanted everything to be done fairly, without any feeling of favouritism, but I hired a personnel consultant instead of a business consultant. He was very good at finding out and describing what *I wanted*, but he was not the right person to tell me what *the business needed*. I appointed the people I knew and felt comfortable with, but we were ignorant of the subtleties of the company we had taken over. What I needed was strong, articulate opposition to my new ideas from people who knew what they were talking about, so that the good ideas would have been made better and the nonsense filtered out. What I got was a bunch of yes men.

Review Topic 12.1
In what sense is picking one's own people an abdication of management?

Picking one's own team is a luxury few managers are able to enjoy and it can be a dangerous privilege, leading to the appointment of sycophants instead of creating a robust, balanced group of individuals, working *with* rather than *for* the person in charge.

1. THE EMPLOYMENT CONTRACT

Notwithstanding the warning of the last paragraph, managers have some part to play in selecting those who join the working team, and this chapter deals with that selection activity.

The approach to selection is to appreciate that selecting people for jobs is a process of setting up an *employment contract* between the individual employee and the employing organisation. This is much more than the legally binding contract of employment which summarises the rights and obligations of the two parties; it is matching two sets of needs and expectations (Schein, 1979; Mumford, 1972: Torrington & Chapman, 1983). It is natural to think in terms of what contribution to organisational success will be made by the employee, although this is seldom thought out very clearly and often centres round narrow, personal preferences of the manager in charge of the section where the appointment is to be made. It is also accepted that individual employees expect certain satisfactions from their employment, but frequently these two sets of requirements are seen as being satisfied independently of each other: the employee gets a salary, some holiday and contributions to a pension scheme in exchange for which he sets aside personal interest and achievement in order to accommodate the routine requirements of the employer. Satisfactions for either party are likely to be mainly at the expense of the other.

In reaction against this there are some employment situations where too much is done to satisfy the employee, in such a way that the attempt is self-defeating. The conditions of work are enhanced — more money, longer holidays, free meals, flexible working hours — but nothing is done about the work, which remains an irksome necessity to be tolerated with as much restraint and dignity as possible. The result is often inefficiency, slackness and employees who not only are dissatisfied with their work, but also feel guilty about their dissatisfaction because of the paraphernalia of good conditions that surrounds them.

The essence of the employment contract idea is simply that the two sets of needs are not independent but complementary; the employee seeks satisfaction in the work done as well as from the circumstances in which it is done, and the employee satisfied with his work will be more secure, more creative, more responsive to customers, more reliable and more efficient. The personnel department can do no more than clear away some of the possible impediments to a good employment contract. It is the individual manager who clarifies the needs of the organisation and integrates those with the needs of the employee, so that both are satisfied by the same processes.

The importance of this approach is that the manager selecting team members has to think just as much about what the appointee is looking for as about what the job requirements are. Both selector and appointee are choosing and it is important to both that each makes a sound decision.

2. ATTRACTING TEAM MEMBERS

People, working groups and departments acquire reputations and one aspect of those reputations is to influence the number and type of people who want to join the group. All managers are interested in the reputation that they and their departments enjoy. "A really first-class, very enthusiastic bunch of people" is the sort of label that is likely to attract people seeking that sort of working environment whereas "It is very well run and the manager is scrupulously fair" conveys a different image that will appeal to different people.

Unfortunately reputations can be reliable indicators within an organisation, where the grapevine will do its work, but are much less useful as indicators to those outside the organisation, who may be influenced more by stereotypes. One local government official grumbled to us about the difficulty of recruiting people other than those who were looking for "a safe billet". She felt that local government had a popular image of being comfortable but dull and this image became a self-fulfilling prophecy as applicants came either because that was what they wanted or because they could not find anything else and thought themselves into the model they expected.

The reputation of the employing organisation in the labour markets is mainly a job for the personnel manager, but other managers can ensure that they are people worth working with and their departments worth working in. They can, however, do little to alter the truth. So they need to declare and embody what they *actually* are and how they really work, rather than generate some artificial picture of what they think will make them "attractive".

This process of establishing and sustaining a reputation is similar to the "visiposture" activity mentioned in chapter six. Managers are attracting potential team members in two ways. First they are attracting the person who is looking for an internal move or awaiting their new posting. In this context reputation can be vitally important. If there is a loosely structured method of career advance, wherein individuals apply for jobs that appeal to them, managers are traders on the internal labour market and will want to create a climate of opinion about who would fit into their department before specific vacancies occur. If movement is centrally controlled, so that individuals are moved between jobs, then the reputation of an individual manager and his department will affect the attitude and expectations of the new arrival.

Secondly managers are attracting potential members by creating recommendations. Existing employees ask if there may be a vacancy for their next-door neighbour, cousin, son, or someone with whom they have worked previously. This remains the dominant way in which new employees are recruited. In 1980 51 per cent of male job changers and 43 per cent of female job changers heard of their new job through friends or by direct approach to the employer (*Social Trends*, 1982).

3. INFORMATION SUPPORTING SELECTION DECISIONS

The reputation of candidates and of departments and organisations in which candidates seek openings spreads informally. There are other sources of information, some of which will be available in any selection process.

Application forms. These are nearly always available for scrutiny. Either the candidate is from outside and is completing one with the vacancy in view, or he is an insider who completed a form some time previously. The value of this document is that it sets out systematically the basic information about the person being considered. Because of this orderly display it is also the common basis for the selection interview.

Surveying application forms from candidates enables one quickly to pick up and compare a few key points about a number of applicants, such as age, qualifications, current post, salary and location. It is the easiest and most effective method of producing a short list. The way in which information about candidates is displayed in it provides a logical sequence for the selection, or employment, interview. The information is presented in biographical sequence so as to provide a pattern for questioning that is fruitful for the interviewer and coherent to the respondent. Some forms also provide space by each entry for the interviewer to make his own comments.

Job descriptions. May be available in detailed documents, or simply be a picture in the mind of the selector. Usually the written job description is preferred as it sets out what the candidate wants to know about the job for which he is applying, and summarises for the selector the points against which he is matching those interviewed. It is also argued that the process of producing the job description clarifies for the selector the details of the job to be done.

Candidate specifications. Profiles of the ideal candidate, prepared beforehand on the basis of the job description. This too may be just a picture in the mind of the selector, or it may be a written profile that specifies requirements in terms of qualifications, length and type of working experience, aptitudes, skills and intelligence. The advantage of this is mainly in the short-listing of candidates, comparing application form details with points in the specification. It then has a later role in the examination of the ways in which preferred candidates do not quite meet the specification and deciding which requirements are the most important.

Job descriptions and candidate specifications are the product of *job analysis*, extensively described in many books about organisational psychology and personnel management. Tyson and York (1982, pp. 81–94) provides a succinct summary.

Test scores. Sometimes available in larger organisations, or where external candidates are being put forward for consideration by consultants. Easiest to deal with a test of *skill or proficiency*, such as a typing or driving test, which indicates a level of competence by a generally acknowledged yardstick. Tests of *intelligence* are not so easy to use. They measure some of a person's abilities against a standardised indicator, such as intelligence quotient or quartiles of the general population, but there is often resistance from candidates to taking such tests, especially if they are well established in their careers and feel that undertaking such tests is like testing Giotto to see if he knows how to hold a paint brush. A test of this type that is widely used is the Graduate Management Admission Tests, which is administered by the University of Princeton and used by business schools in many countries to decide whether or not candidates will be able to cope with their master's programmes. More specialised are tests of *aptitude*, like those used to select prospective trainees for aircrew duties or recruits for engineering apprenticeships. They assess not skill but the potential to develop a skill that depends on some aspect of natural aptitude like manual dexterity or spatial judgement. The most controversial tests are those of *personality*, which claim to produce profiles of human traits and motivation, so that selectors can have a prediction about a candidate's potential for a post that goes beyond an assessment of existing skills, intelligence and aptitudes. A selection of contributions made by Ungerson (1983, pp. 96–160) summarises what is currently available.

References provided by previous employers, family friends and Justices of the Peace are notoriously unhelpful and often misleading. They are now used extensively in the public sector of employment and are almost unknown in the private sector. They are supposed to provide evidence of character, but the self-selecting nature of their nomination by candidates tends to bias their objectivity. Candidates choose reference writers because they think they will provide a "good" reference, and "bad" references are extremely rare.

4.   THE SELECTION INTERVIEW

Every time someone is selected to join a team, there will be an interview to precede the appointment. Mainly this is for the selector to decide whether the candidate is suitable, but the candidate will also be making up his mind whether the move is one that he wishes to make or not. Some selection processes seek to rule out the possibility of the candidate deciding against the job as a result of the interview, on the grounds that candidates should have made up their minds firmly and should not waste the time of the interviewers with interviews that may not be needed. Sometimes candidates are asked to declare at the beginning of the interview that they are firm applicants. In other situations travelling expenses are not paid to candidates who do not accept an offer of employment. This is part of the ritual of the selection interview, which is partly an initiation rite. The candidate always arrives in his best clothes and is expected to show deference to the interviewers and great keenness to be employed, whilst the selectors are unlikely to wear their best clothes, sometimes demonstrate their superiority by being late or preoccupied with other things, and will never show enthusiasm to employ the candidate — willingness maybe: enthusiasm never.

Review Topic 12.2

Write a reference for someone applying for your job, avoiding outright condemnation or unequivocal enthusiasm. Then show it to a friend and ask if they would be disposed to employ or not to employ the person on the basis of the reference, with their reasons.

Although these ritual elements are inevitable in the selection situation, and their importance should not be underestimated, the purpose of the interview goes much further and has as its main purpose the ability of the selector to decide whether the candidate is appropriate or inappropriate for the post under consideration. How can this be done effectively? The remaining pages of this chapter seek to offer general advice for the occasional interviewer. More detailed guidance is available in, for instance, Fraser (1978) or Torrington (1982).

The setting for the interview. This should be one that is appropriate for a private conversation, so that the exchanges will be frank and constructive. Many people also feel that the setting should reduce the status barriers between interviewer and respondent on the grounds that the interviewer is in the socially superior position of having a job to offer, or not, while the respondent is in the inferior position of wanting the job and being disposed to propitiate the interviewer in order to get it. If the seating arrangements underplay that distinction, then the respondent candidate will be more relaxed and more open in what he says. This status reduction can be done by avoiding direct, face-to-face interviewing across a desk and moving to a situation where both participants are sitting at the same height, not directly opposed and without any obvious advantage to the interviewer.

There is a danger in the setting becoming too informal and thus destroying rather than mitigating the ritual elements. The friendly chat over a drink in a local pub may be pleasantly relaxed and the candidate will probably (eventually) become very loquacious, but it is a difficult "interview" to structure and may disconcert the candidate, who is expecting something more businesslike.

The plan of the interview. This is most easily taken from the sequence of the application form particulars. The development of the questioning is then one that builds logically in the mind of the selector and can be followed constructively by the candidate, who can see how the interview is progressing, rather than feeling that there is some hidden agenda that he does not understand and which consequently worries him. There is one preliminary, setting up *rapport*. At the opening of the interview candidate and selector assess each other and tune in to each other. It is usually done by exchanging words about trivia (some people believe that it rains frequently in Britain simply to provide people with a topic of conversation at the opening of interviews), explaining procedure and plenty of nods and smiles. It also gives the selector an opportunity to sketch out what is to happen and where the interview fits in with the rest of the decision-making process.

After the pleasantries of rapport, there is a change of pace as the interview moves to *information exchange*, and we need to remember that the information is moving both ways, not only towards the selector. If the candidate is from the inside of the organisation, he will know most of the things he needs to make up his mind about the post and will probably have just one or two check questions as well as a keen interest in the type of person the selector is. Candidates do not have the benefit of application forms, test scores or candidate specifications of the people with whom they will be working, but they are still keenly interested and try to understand as much as they can during the brief encounter of the interview. The external candidate will have a wider range of uncertainty and more gaps in his understanding to fill in; again the interview is his opportunity. Convention says, however, that candidates do not ask selectors questions about their qualifications and ambitions, so they rely on clues and information conveyed unwittingly by interviewers.

The selector has the advantage of being able to structure the encounter as candidates expect to have to respond to initiatives, rather than take initiatives themselves. The first question is important in setting both the tone and direction of the exchange. Consider this very common opening question:

"Tell me, why have you applied for this job?"

Despite its extensive use, that is an ineffective way to begin, as it puts the candidate on the defensive, feeling that he has to say the right thing, whether it is true or not. It is also a very difficult question to answer as the reasons for seeking a move are probably varied and hard to summarise. Also some of the common reasons — more money, dislike of present boss, easier travel, more holidays, more security — are the sort of reasons that candidates often feel inappropriate to mention, especially at the beginning, so they speak vaguely about challenge and unfulfilled potential. The interview thus gets underway as a form of verbal fencing, with the candidate wary of the next question to trip him up.

Now consider this, alternative, opening question:

"Could you give me a general outline of your present responsibilities?"

This has a number of advantages. First, the candidate will know the answer and his answer will be full of relevant, valuable information as it relates to what he can do rather than to his subjective evaluation of his motives. Secondly, it is not likely to be regarded with suspicion by the candidate trying to guess what the question is "really after". Thirdly, it will provide an admirable starting point as there will be a number of aspects that could usefully be developed further. This is not to suggest that all selection interviews should start with this particular question, but to suggest that questions that are about real facts and events are more sensible and useful than questions that require candidates to speculate or make them uneasy.

A further development on the interview plan is to take a step back in time to an earlier point in the candidate's career and then move forward to the present, reviewing various developments on the way. This should be done with only one backwards move, if possible, as it is much easier to explain something and to understand something if it is examined as it developed rather than in reverse. Selectors get quite bewildered and candidates become incoherent when asked to explain their choice of degree, *then* their choice of "A" levels, and *then* their "O" level performance.

Selectors may find it useful to note key issues and check points. *Key issues* will be two or three features of information from the application form that stand out as needing clarification or elaboration. A particular episode of previous employment may need to be explored to see the range of responsibilities held, the difficulty of the circumstances or the number of subordinates. There may be key issues in the educational record, overseas experience or work in a specific industry that needs to be discussed. *Check points* are details that need to be confirmed, like grades in an examination or dates of appointment.

All of this has to be done in a framework and atmosphere that is not a sceptical cross examination of an evasive witness, but a meeting in which the candidate is *enabled* (not just allowed) to talk about himself fully, frankly and with relevance to the vacant post for which he is being considered. As long as the selector organises and leads the interview, that sort of information flow from the candidate will be much more useful and informative than if the candidate is required only to provide clipped replies to a list of predetermined questions.

5.   DECIDING THE APPOINTMENT

The job of deciding who should be offered the appointment is simple to describe, but less easy to accomplish. It involves deciding first whether there is a good match between the person being considered and the job that has to be done, and secondly whether there is a good match between the group of people among whom the work will be done and the person being considered.

The first of these decisions is the more straightforward and can be based on the self-interest of the candidate, who will not want to get into a job he cannot do, and on the systematic matching by the selector of the job description and candidate specification on the one hand and the information obtained about the candidate on the other. A systematic approach on the basis of good documentation should decide whether someone is appointable or not. The best known aids to this type of decision-making are those of Rodger (1952) and Fraser (1978).

Deciding whether or not the candidate would fit socially is more problematic as it raises all the risks of appointing only "clones", as was mentioned in Chapter 8, and also the risk of being unlawfully discriminatory. Seear and Pearn (1983) provide comments on keeping within the law. There may be helpful advice from the personnel department if they have run personality tests, but the likelihood of a good match between the prospective new recruit and the other members of the working team is mainly a matter for the selector's judgement. There are some comments on the complementary skills and abilities required of different team members in Chapter 14.

Consultation with team members can help. The more people who meet the candidate, the more opinions there will be about his suitability and the greater willingness to make the match effective, even if individual opinions have been overruled. Information to the candidates can also help. The more frankly they have had problems and opportunities discussed with them, the more prepared they are to make their contribution to a constructive working relationship. Finally, a group of people working together apathetically, poorly organised and critical of their leaders can undermine the effectiveness of even the most enthusiastic new recruit. A robust, well organised team of confident people who work well together with mutual respect will be able to assimilate some inappropriate appointees without serious trouble. Whereabouts in that spectrum does your team stand?

6. INDUCTION

Whether a new team member comes from outside the organisation or from within, the first few days and weeks are an important period of "reciprocal moulding" as he is fitted into the structure and into the informal framework of relationships. Wise selections are made to work by sensible induction and even unwise selections can be made tolerable by hard work in the early stages of the working relationship.

SUMMARY PROPOSITIONS

12.1.   Deciding the type of skills and experience required in a new appointment is more important than pondering the personal qualities of applicants.

12.2.   In selection processes both the selector and the appointee are making choices and decisions; it is important to *both* that the other gets what he is looking for.

12.3. The selection interview is partly an initiation rite and the importance of the ritual elements should not be underestimated.

12.4. The most logical and helpful sequence for the selection interview is to review the biography of the candidate.

APPENDIX A

Interaction guide for the selection interview

I   Before the Interview

Review   a.   Job description.
                b.   Candidate specification.
                c.   Application forms.

Note   a.   Key issues.
                b.   Check points.

Check   a.   Timetable.
                b.   Interview setting.

II   During the Interview

Begin with   a.   Welcome.
                b.   Rapport, through the discussion of trivia, explaining procedure and adopting a relaxed, friendly manner.

Exchange   a.   Questioning, e.g. "Could you give me an outline of your present
information   duties".
by   b.   Logical sequence, such as working chronologically through the application form.
                c.   Listening and observing.
                d.   Enabling the candidate to be frank and informative.
                e.   Remembering key issues and check points.

At all times a.   Maintain rapport.
                b.   Keep notes.
                c.   Control the interview.

III   After the Interview

Consider the a.   By reviewing the job information:
person/job   i.   Job description
match   ii.   Candidate specification.

                b.   By reviewing the candidate information:
                     i.   Application form
                     ii.   Interview notes
                     iii. Test scores (if any)
                     iv.   References (if any).

                c.   Deciding whether there is a good match or not, and the significance of any "poor fitting".

Consider the	a.	By reviewing results of personality tests (if any).
person/group	b.	By consulting with team members.
match	c.	Guard against unlawful discrimination.
Decide	a.	To whom the job offer should be made.
	b.	The terms of the offer.
Notify		(after job offer has been accepted) the unsuccessful candidates.

APPENDIX B

Drill for recruitment

(After extensive consultation, the Institute of Personnel Management published a Recruitment Code in 1980, listing obligations for both recruiters and applicants).

Recruiters	*Applicants*
1. Job advertisements will state clearly the form of reply desired (for example, curriculum vitae, completed application form) and any preference for handwritten applications.	1. Advertisements will be answered in the way requested (for example, telephone for application form, provide brief details, send curriculum vitae, etc.)
2. An acknowledgement or reply will be made promptly to each applicant by the employing organization or its agent.	2. Appointments and other arrangements will be kept, or the recruiter will be informed promptly if the candidate discovers an agreed meeting cannot take place.
3. Candidates will be informed of the progress of the selection procedure, what this will be, the time likely to be involved and the policy regarding expenses.	3. The recruiter will be informed as soon as a candidate decides not to proceed with the application.
4. Detailed personal information (for example, religion, medical history, place of birth, family background etc.) will not be asked for unless and until it is relevant to the selection process.	4. Only accurate information will be given in applications and in reply to recruiters' questions.
5. Before applying for references, potential employers will secure the permission of the applicant.	5. Information given by a prospective employer will be treated as confidential, if so requested.
6. Applications will be treated as confidential	

(Taken from *The IPM Recruitment Code*, Institute of Personnel Management, London, August 1980)

APPENDIX C

Drill for selection decisions

(based on Fraser J.M., *Employment Interviewing,* 5th ed., Macdonald & Evans, 1978)

	Names of candidates				
Categories of personal qualities	Adams	Brown	Clark	Davis	Evans
1. Impact on others, or the kind of response an individual's appearance, speech and manner calls out from others.					
2. Qualifications and experience, or the knowledge and skill different types of work require.					
3. Innate abilities, or how quickly and accurately an individual's mind works.					
4. Motivation, or the kind of work that appeals to an individual and how much effort he is prepared to apply to it.					
5. Emotional adjustment, or the amount of stress involved in living and working with other people.					

For each candidate score A, B, C, D or E in each box, with A indicating much above average and E indicating much below average for the category. The selector uses this as a way of organising his thinking about candidates and then weighs the significance of his scores for the particular vacancy.

This five-fold framework for selection decisions, devised by John Munro Fraser, is used extensively in companies as a basis for selecting between candidates.

REFERENCES

Fraser, J.M., *Employment Interviewing,* 5th edition, Macdonald & Evans, London, 1978.

Mumford, E., "Job Satisfaction: A Method of Analysis", in *Personnel Review,* Summer, 1972.

Rodger, A., *The Seven Point Plan,* Paper No. 1, National Institute of Industrial Psychology, London, 1952.

Schein, E.H., *Organisational Psychology,* 3rd edition, Prentice-Hall, Englewood Cliffs, New Jersey, 1979.

Seear, N. and Pearn, M., "Selection within the Law", in Ungerson, 1983, *op. cit.*
Social Trends 12, (HMSO), London, 1982.
Torrington, D.P., *Face to Face in Management,* Prentice-Hall, London, 1982.
Torrington, D.P., and Chapman, J.B., *Personnel Management,* 2nd edition, Prentice Hall International, London, 1983.
Tyson, S. and York, A., *Personnel Management Made Simple,* Heinemann, London, 1982.
Ungerson, B., *Recruitment Handbook,* 3rd edition, Gower Press, Aldershot, 1983.

Chapter Thirteen

COACHING AND TEACHING

Coaching and training are both intended to improve a persons's working performance, but each involves a different working relationship. The coach is trying to improve the performance of someone who is already competent, while the trainer is trying to bring someone to the level of competence. The most accomplished tennis player needs a coach from whom to receive guidance, criticism and analysis of performance, and that can come from someone who is a less accomplished performer. The child learning to play tennis for the first time has to be trained in the basic techniques and methods of the game, and the accomplishment of the trainer is fundamental to successful instruction.

Both activities are concerned with how people learn, but the nature of the authority required in the coach is not the same as is needed in the trainer. Because of that difference, the approach of the coach is different from that of the trainer and the dependence of the trainee is much greater than that of the person being coached. Although it has received scant attention in the management literature, coaching seems an important activity to discuss in a management book as it is so difficult to isolate what makes a good manager. Effectiveness lies much with individual style, confidence and personality, just as effectiveness in sport lies much with such qualities as touch, timing and a good eye. None of these can be taught *to* people, but coaching may be able to develop them *in* people.

There is a distinction to be drawn between coaching and counselling. Lopez (1968, p.112) points out the danger:

> The supervisor's function is to coach, not counsel. The proper object of *coaching* is to improve present job performance; the proper job of *counselling* is the realisation of potential. The former emphasises *doing,* the later, *becoming.* If the supervisor attempts to counsel rather than coach, he will indeed do exactly what some critics accuse him of doing: "play God".

The counselling relationship involves a great deal of trust and a concern in the counsellor for the wellbeing and personal growth of the client above all else. The manager acting as coach cannot claim that degree of altruism and the person being coached will not be likely to share with him *all* his concerns about the future. Coaching is centred on performance in the job now.

1. HOW PEOPLE LEARN

As learning is intrinsic to both coaching and training, we need to understand something of the process whereby people learn. It is a subject that has attracted much attention in the training field as well as in schoolteaching. The traditional distinction between cognitive learning, learning skills and developing attitudes was based on the proposition that these were not only three different types of objective but also three different types of process. This has recently been refined for practical application in adult learning by the CRAMP taxonomy (ITRU, 1976) based on the work of Eunice and Meredith Belbin (1972).

CRAMP divides learning into five basic types:

Comprehension. Where the learning involves theoretical subject matter, knowing how, why and when certain things happen. Examples would be most of mathematics, the elements of computer programming or the theories of economics. Learning of this type is best approached by methods that teach the whole subject as an entity, rather than splitting it up into pieces and taking one at a time. The lecture is the time-honoured method of doing this.

Reflex learning. Where the trainee is acquiring skilled movements or perceptual capacities. Effectiveness requires practice as well as knowing what to do and speed is usually important so that the learning process involves constant repetition to develop the necessary synchronisation and co-ordination. An obvious, but extreme, example is juggling, but there are many more common examples, like machining, inspection on an assembly line or computer input.

Attitude development. Concerned with enabling people to alter their attitudes and social skills. This has been very popular in management development and centres on the understanding trainees have of themselves. Group methods are typically used for this purpose as attitudes are very difficult to influence and change permanently through instruction although many — like politicians — find it difficult to believe that conversion cannot be achieved by exposition. Socialisation seems more effective.

Memory training. This obviously deals with people learning information, like the periodic table of chemical elements, and is usually done in the same way as reflex learning with trainees learning parts of the information at a time and then proceeding to the next stage.

Procedural learning. Very similar to memorisation except that the drill to be followed does not have to be memorised: it has to be located and understood. A lawyer does not have to learn all the statutes and cases, but he does need to know where to locate them. If a process plant is run down once a year for annual maintenance, the engineers do not have to memorise the rundown procedure, but they have to know where it is and be able to understand all its stages when it is required.

In practice most forms of training involve more than one type of learning, so that the trainee motor mechanic will need to understand how the car works (comprehension) as well as practising the skill of tuning an engine (reflex). The car driver needs to practise the skill of co-ordinating hands, feet and eyes in driving as well as knowing the procedure to follow it he breaks down, but the CRAMP analysis helps us to identify the type of learning that is predominating in any particular situation.

Gagne (1975) has examined all processes of learning and identified a chain of eight events which take place.

First, motivation. The learner has to want to learn, and that requires that he wants to achieve the product of his learning. A person will be motivated to practise five-finger exercises on the piano because of wanting to achieve the ability to play a Beethoven sonata, which would be the end-product of his learning.

Second, perception. The matter to be learned has to be identified and separated from other matters around it, so that it becomes a clear and specific objective.

Third, acquisition. The matter being learned is made sense of by being related to other things known by the trainee.

Fourth, retention. The material or skill acquired is retained in the long-term memory and/or the short-term memory. The two-stage process of human learning comprises first the short-term memory in which one holds, for instance, the name of a person to whom one has just been introduced. Secondly there is the long-term memory to which one transfers those names which one wishes to store permanently. This is an important distinction in learning as some material goes into short-term memory only to aid understanding at the time and then should *not* be transferred to long-term. An example is the joke in the lecture, which may be remembered at the expense of the point that the lecturer was using the joke to illustrate.

Fifth, recall. The learner has to be able to summon up items from his memory when they are needed.

Sixth, generalisation. This is the ability to apply what has been learned to a wide variety of situations other than the specific situation in which learning has taken place. The skilled motor mechanic will be able to apply the essence of what he has learned to the maintenance of a new model of car that was not produced at the time he was trained.

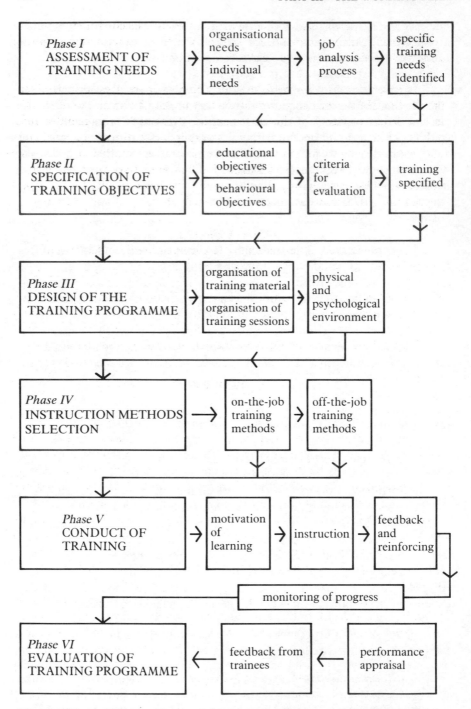

**Figure 13.1   ASDICE A Systematic Approach to Programme Development,
           based on a more detailed analysis in Torrington & Chapman (1983)
           pp. 480–481**

Seventh, performance. That which has been learned is now done: the trainee pianist plays the piano, the student writes his examination script, or the embryo salesman goes out and sells something.

Eighth, feedback on performance. The learner receives some feedback on whether the performance was satisfactory or not. To some extent this lies in the obvious quality of the performance. If the task is to mend a fuse, success or failure is clear, but with most learners some degree of approbation and comment is needed from the coach or trainer, as this can not only incorporate varying degrees of satisfaction and encouragement but also be analytical: what went wrong, how it could have been avoided, what aspect needs more practice, what to do next and so forth.

Review Topic 13.1

Throughout the book we have these boxed review topics. Which one of Gagne's eight events are they trying to help?

A failure in learning can be because of difficulties at any of these eight stages and this sequence applies to all learning, whether of the relatively formal type that is found in training for industrial skills or in an activity like coaching, where the learning may be incidental to some other activity.

2. TRAINING

We have already seen that training is the process of bringing someone to a level of competence. In most large organisations there is a training department or training officer who has the organisational responsibility for this sort of activity and most managers need no more than a passing understanding of the process that is involved. Figure 13.1 summarises the ASDICE model for training in organisations. This is one of a number that have been developed, and is a basis for the administration of training programmes and courses. The individual manager will not be involved in all of these elements, but may need to use the framework as a way of approaching an *ad hoc* piece of training he has to organise with a member of his team.

As a training objective, for instance, the manager will want the trainee to understand the task to be performed and what is required to reach a level of competence. So the manager has to decide how much understanding is needed at the outset in order to provide a satisfactory basis for the training.

In designing the training programme how much should the task to be performed be broken down into components or subroutines to aid learning? When Clive Sinclair introduced the personal computer for use in the home, arrangements had to be made for users to learn computer operation and programming at a distance. What had to be learned was divided up into small packets of information that could be both understand and practised in sequence. Each packet of information, set out in an instruction manual, could be understood by reference either to its own content or what had already been covered. The sequence was:

1. The computer and setting it up   2½ pages
2. The keyboard   3 pages
3. Numbers, letters and the computer as a calculator   3 pages
4. Some simple commands   2 pages
5. Simple programming   3½ pages
6. Using the cassette recorder   3½ pages
7. Colours   1½ pages
8. Sound   1 page
9. What's inside the case   1½ pages

(Vickers & Bradbeer, 1982)

Trainee typists learn subroutines for each hand before combining them into subroutines for both hands together as they use their hands in ways that are relatively independent of each other, with the left always typing "q" and the right always typing "p", so that co-ordination of the hands is needed only to sequence the actions. A further aspect of learning to type is to practise short letter sequences that occur frequently, such as "and", "the", "ing" and "ion". This sort of practice enables actions to become both automatic and reliable. The amateur typist will often transpose letters or hit the wrong key, writing "rwong" instead of "wrong" or "hte" instead of "the". The properly-trained typist will rarely do this because the repeated drills will have made the subroutines automatic and therefore usually correct.

Every person training others has to provide feedback, so that the trainee can compare his own performance with the required standard and can see the progress that he is making. The characteristics of good feedback are immediacy and precision. If it comes immediately after the action, then the trainee has the best chance of associating an error with that part of the performance that caused it, whereas delay will emphasise what was wrong, but the memory of what happened will have faded. Precision in feedback requires the information conveyed to be as accurate as possible and related to what the trainee has done, rather than the results of his action, so that he is able to pinpoint the action of his that needs to be remedied and how it can be altered. In teaching someone to drive a car, you may well have the alarming experience of the car lurching forward from a stationary position and then stopping dead. The comment to the trainee driver "not smooth enough" is unhelpful as it makes an obvious statement about what the car has done instead of a comment on what the driver did wrong. "Too quick on the clutch" focuses on what the driver did, but probably in language that will be imprecise to the listener. Something like "You brought the clutch pedal up too quickly with the left foot" would be precise feedback.

Fig. 13.1 links feedback and reinforcement, which is praising and underpinning satisfactory performance by encouraging trainees with plenty of positive comment and reward, like giving lumps of sugar to a well behaved horse. Although this is a useful general rule, it is not a complete explanation of how people learn:

> ...learning is *not* fundamentally a matter of gradually strengthening connections but rather an all-or-none event. Thus most modern theorists tend to favour the idea that the individual connection is acquired on a single occasion. ...The effects of repetition may be to recruit more and more single connections, but each one is learned or not learned.
>
> (Gagne, 1975, p.44)

3.   TRAINING METHODS

Recent preoccupation with training methods may have led some people to the conclusion that training would be effective providing that the correct method was selected for a given application. This chapter has already suggested that group methods, for instance, are the most appropriate way of developing attitudes, but that the lecture will be more appropriate for training which involves comprehension as its main purpose. There has, however, developed some reaction against too great a concern about method at the expense of substance. A study conducted among 64 students taught by different modes and tested both immediately after the teaching session and again one month later showed no difference in the results achieved by lecturing, case studies and role play or other experiential methods, with the conclusion:

> It appears trainees can learn effectively in a variety of modes, perhaps indeed finding as much or more satisfaction from *what* they are learning than the *way* in which they are trained.
>
> (Gale, Das and Miner, 1982, p. 16)

In the generally vague area of management development there is perhaps need for more attention to what it is appropriate for managers to learn.

Despite this cautionary note the method of training still has to be appropriate for the purpose to be served, so we have a review of some of the more common methods. Figure 13.2 summarises the methods most suitable for the five sections of the CRAMP listing.

Assignments. Used where a number of different types of learning are needed and where the trainee can work largely on his own initiative. It is the basis of research training in universities and other educational establishments, where it has been found to be the most appropriate means for the able and well-qualified student to further his education and develop a thorough understanding in an area. It is a method also found in management training schemes, which sometimes require a young manager to undertake an assignment to deal with an organisational problem. It is also the core method

Type of Learning	Typical Training Methods
Comprehension	Lecture Seminar or discussion Film, film strip or video
Reflex	Progressive part Cumulative part Simplification
Attitude	Experiential methods
Memory	Mnemonics Jingles
Procedural	Rules or routines
Varied	Assignments Distance learning

Figure 13.2   Types of Learning and Training Methods

used in *action learning,* developed by Revans and now extensively used in management education by setting up groups of eight to twelve trainees from different organisations — or from different parts of the same organisation — who then work together on a real problem, deploying their varied expertise. The prerequisites for success are a supply of genuine problems, a will and ability to implement the solutions that are proposed, and the availability of data and research findings for trainees to consult.

Lectures. These are for conveying information and understanding, on the basis that the lecturer has enlightenment in his head that can be coherently transferred to the heads of his listeners.

Discussion or seminar. When meetings take place to exchange information and to discuss problems of understanding of that information, the process is similar to the lecture except that the activity centres round what the trainee does not understand, rather than round what the lecturer wants to say. It is still concerned with data and not skill, but can be most effective as a way of reinforcing data and overcoming problems of understanding.

Films. These provide a useful variant of the lecture but cannot be used to achieve much else. Through its careful preparation and by adding a range of visual images to the words of explanation it can be an effective means of exposition. Some of the tape/slide and videotape forms of presentation can have the useful added feature of enabling the trainee to "participate" by rerunning particular parts of the exposition that he has difficulty in following.

Distance learning. A mode that puts the control of learning in the hands of the trainee. Long used by correspondence schools, it is a method that has become much more widely adopted as a result of the Open University. The trainee is provided with a mass of notes and assignments which he works through while the tutor guides his progress at long range by commenting on his written or taped assignments. It has many of the advantages of the seminar and enables each trainee to proceed at his own pace, but the solo nature of the study does not suit all trainees.

Part methods. Used in reflex learning of skills. It is particularly in this type of learning that the detailed behavioural analysis developed from Skinner's work is most useful. The task is split up into steps that are appropriate in difficulty for those who are to learn the task. In retraining a pilot, for instance, to fly a Boeing 757 instead of a 747 one would expect relatively large steps because of the substantial amount of relevant skill and understanding that is already known to the trainee. Training a novice to pilot a Boeing 757 would require more and smaller steps in the learning process. There is great emphasis on the precision with which instructions and prompting (help) is given.

Progressive part methods break down the task into a series of actions or subroutines. The trainee practises action 1 until competent, then action 2, and then $1 + 2$. He next practises action 3, $2 + 3$ and $1 + 2 + 3$. Each action is practised progressively and then attached to the full task, which is constantly being practised as a developing entity. This can also be done backwards so that completion of the task is always practised. In such a situation the sequence would be $7, 6, 6 + 7, 5, 5 + 6 + 7, 4, 4 + 5 + 6 + 7$, and so on. This is not always appropriate or possible, but is used in circumstances where the criteria for the finished task need to be carefully established. An example is the laying out of a surgeon's trolley. *Cumulative* part method is slightly different as the trainee begins by practising the irreducible minimum part of the whole task and then gradually adding extra components, but the extra components are not practised separately. So the sequence would be to practise action 1, then $1 + 2$, then $1 + 2 + 3$, and so on. This is necessary if actions 2 and 3 cannot be performed without 1 (like juggling, for example) and it can be useful in skills where the most difficult actions can be dealt with first, so that they get much more rehearsal than what comes later.

Simplification. Can be used where a job cannot be subdivided into separate elements, so the task to be performed is retained as a whole but reduced to its simplest form with skilled performance being reached by gradually increasing the complexity of the exercise. Learning a language sometimes follows this pattern.

Mnemonics or jingles. Aids to memorisation whereby a simple formula provides a clue to a more comprehensive set of data. If initial letters are difficult, a jingle can help. How many people could remember the sequence of colours in the spectrum without the clue of ROYGBIV, which is easier to remember as Richard Of York Gave Battle In Vain.

Routine. A helpful training device is the rule or routine, which reduces the volume of material to be remembered. *I* before *e* except after *c* is a simple rule to prevent a certain type of spelling mistake. Every maintenance engineer works to a set of fault-finding rules, as do doctors, who gradually eliminate possibilities by a series of questions about the location of pain, the experience of temperature and the frequency of bowel movements which progressively rule out possibilities and eventually reach a diagnosis.

Experiential methods. A term to embrace a range of methods used by management trainers whereby the experience of the trainee is the way to understanding. Role playing is probably the most widely used version of experiential training as people play out parts in contrived situations. Salesmen play the parts of buyers and thus come to understand the process of selling from a point of view opposed to their own. Industrial relations managers pretend to be shop stewards. Careers advisers try to imagine that they are sixteen years old, unemployed and without qualifications. Other experiential methods, of which sensitivity training is the most notorious, do not depend on a contrived structure for the interaction between people, but try to confront members of a group with how they really see and feel about each other.

In concluding the section of this chapter about training, we note the current fashion for *self-development methods* as described, for instance, by Pedler, Burgoyne and Boydell (1978). This has much in common with the action learning approach and distance learning, as the focus is on what the trainee knows he needs to do instead of on what someone else believes he should be told. This approach is particularly advocated for management training.

4.   COACHING

In the opening of this chapter we distinguished between coaching and training by describing coaching as improving the performance of someone who is already competent rather than establishing competence in the first place. Further aspects of coaching are that it is usually on a one-to-one basis, is set in the everyday working situation and is a continuing activity. It is gently nudging people to improve their performance, to develop their skills and to increase their self-confidence so that they can take more responsibility

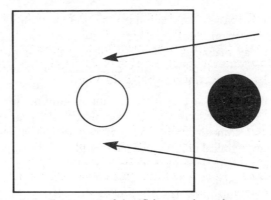

Detailed adjustments of the 'fit' come through
training and coaching of the new arrival

Figure 13.3   Coaching and Teaching Team Members

for their own work and develop their career prospects. Most coaching is done by people with their own subordinates, but the subordinate position of the person coached is by no means a prerequisite. What is essential is that the coach should have qualities of expertise, judgement and experience that make it possible for the person coached to follow the guidance.

Examples of coaching incidents are the head of a fashion section in a department store chatting about new lines while putting out the stock with a member of staff, or the foreman working alongside an engineer while changing a gearbox. The coaching process was implicit in the much maligned "sitting next to Nellie" method of industrial training, whereby a new recruit worked alongside an experienced hand in order to pick up the way of working. This is a valid criticism when used as a method of initial training, as the learner is not able to discriminate between what he can use and what he can disregard in the performance he is observing. It is only appropriate when the learner is in a position to make detailed and subtle changes in his own performance: he has the necessary basic skill and knowledge and is merely adding to his repertoire of skills.

Early moves in the United States to integrate black workers in previously all-white workshops used the buddy system of attaching the newly recruited black to an experienced, established white worker to act as his buddy during the early days of his employment.

Review Topic 13.2

How can a performer be coached by someone who is not as skilled as the performer himself?

It is what is said and how the discussion develops that can turn these pleasant exchanges into constructive coaching sessions. As with most aspects of managerial activity there is no standard method of coaching as the locus of the activity is the person being coached, whose needs and capacities will be so varied. One way managers differ has been described by Schein (1980) when he advanced his theory of the *career anchor*, arguing that every manager has some aspect of his attachment to his work that he will not abandon and which will act as the dominant guiding force in his life. Examples are autonomy, creativity, organisational security, managerial competence and technical competence. If a manager is anchored to the importance of his technical ability, a coach would need to emphasise that and support it while perhaps looking for some modification to another activity like becoming more managerially competent. The coach would never succeed in his approach if he were to denigrate the importance of the technical and emphasise the managerial instead.

One of the most difficult judgements in coaching a manager is to distinguish between those aspects of performance that are essential and those that are just a matter of style. Much management training has foundered on the belief of a manager training subordinates that his way of doing things was the only way they could be done.

Stewart and Marshall (1982) have found that managers often reject much of management training as they believe that their own situation is unique and does not fit the generalised analysis of behavioural research. If this applies, then it not only requires a developmental approach that is specific to the individual, but also makes coaching a particularly apt method.

The essence of coaching is in two activities, delegation and discussion, neither of which will work very well unless accompanied by the other.

Delegation. One of the least understood words in the management vocabulary. It is *not* giving people jobs to do; it is giving people scope, responsibility and authority. When the legendary James Bond says to a barman "A medium dry Vodka Martini — with a slice of lemon peel, no ice, shaken and not stirred; with either Polish or Russian Vodka", he is giving the barman a job to do with no scope for initiative, only the opportunity to perform a skilled task to a precise specification. When Bond's boss, M, says "Your assignment, Bond, is to stop Blofeld by any means you know how" he is delegating to James Bond considerable responsibility and authority.

The question we have to ask about delegation is how much scope it gives to the individual to test his own ideas, develop understanding and confidence, and flex his muscles. The more specific the instructions and terms of reference, the less learning will be managed as a result of that activity. With the assignment delegated the individual then starts work with the initiative also of seeking guidance and discussion on progress from the coaching manager, so that action is always in his own hands rather than in the hands of the coach, who will have to exercise a nice judgement on the degree of his intervention. Too many interventions and the person being coached leans on the coach and becomes dependent. Too few interventions and the person being coached makes mistakes and loses confidence.

An example of this is the "shadowing" of hospital consultants by qualified, but junior, hospital doctors and medical students. Initially the junior observes and discusses the case only, but later he takes the major role, with the consultant observing and discussing the case. Another example is "handover time" when a person about to leave a post and his successor are both in post together for a short time. This period is useful for discussing major issues, for introductions and for demonstrating procedures. It should not be too long a period or the person taking over is less likely to try new methods; he will have become too convinced of the unchallengeable correctness of what exists.

A systematic use of job exchange for training, an extension of the coaching idea, has been developed by Revans (1971) who argues that groups of about six senior managers from a variety of settings can learn a great deal by tackling a particular problem that is currently being faced by one member of the group. Each group member works in one of the other organisations to find a solution to the problem, while all group members meet regularly to discuss their progress — an example of coaching by peers.

Discussion. In the appendix to this chapter there is an interaction guide for the coaching discussion, which is the necessary adjunct to delegation. Effective coaching discussion depends on a sound working relationship with the coach, whose comments are welcomed rather than resented or mistrusted. The coach can assist by analysing problems and helping to work out alternatives from which choices are to be made. As far as possible criticism is based on facts and not on opinion, and aimed at positive, constructive improvement of the job, not denigration of the job holder. Even reinforcing by praise has to be specific, otherwise it produces a warm glow (and perhaps intensifies a feeling of adoration for the coach) but the warm glow will fade and the praised person is not left with anything on which to build.

The delegation that is involved in coaching involves taking risks:

> No man can be certain that his subordinates will perform well, but the act of giving responsibility should imply confidence that the task set will be achieved. It is unreasonable to expect a man to give of his best if he suspects that his boss, because of his behaviour, does not really expect him to succeed and is only waiting for him to fail before doing the job himself.
>
> (Singer, 1974 p. 63)

5. THE POOR PERFORMER

Often training or coaching is undertaken because a team member is not performing well, either not producing enough work or not reaching required standards of work quality. A first step in this situation is to check the facts against requirements in job descriptions, appraisal schemes, manuals and similar yardsticks. If a shortfall can be clearly seen, then the problem is relatively straightforward. Where it is not clearly demonstrable, it is often described in the extremely vague term of "the wrong attitude".

A preliminary to attempted corrective action is to consider why the performance is poor (Miner and Brewer, 1976). It may be a *personal quality,* such as physical or mental health, intelligence and ability, motivation, confidence and understanding of the job. Alternatively it could be some aspect of *domestic circumstances,* such as marital breakdown or bereavement. A third possibility is an aspect of the *work group,* such as cohesion, leadership, or personality clashes. Fourthly come *organisational factors,* such as lack of investment, the balance between planning and improvisation, the degree of discipline or permissiveness, poor management and the design of the individual job. There could be a conflict of moral or religious *values* between what the job requires and what the employee regards as right; or there could be *situational* stress because of where the job is located. Lastly there may be lack of *training.*

If one of these is identified as the cause of poor performance, then the obvious strategy is to deal with that specific cause, either by the manager dealing with the matter directly — as with organisational factors, for instance — or by seeking assistance — suggesting a visit to the local marriage guidance council to assist with a marital problem.

The most realistic tactics for a manager seem to be to concentrate on the facts of the performance, to focus on future performance and to set short term objectives for the employee's improvement. At the close of chapter 15 there is an appendix on the disciplinary interview. This, as well as chapter 16 on performance appraisal are relevant to the problem of the poor performer.

SUMMARY PROPOSITIONS

13.1. There are five basic types of learning: comprehension, reflex learning, attitude development, memory and procedural learning.

13.2. All learning has a chain of eight events: motivation, perception, acquisition, retention, recall, generalisation, performance and feedback.

13.3. The appropriateness of training method varies with the type of learning.

13.4. Training is the process of bringing someone to a level of competence; coaching is improving the performance of someone who is already competent.

13.5. Improving the performance of the poor performer requires analysis to determine the reason for the poor performance.

REFERENCES

Belbin E. and Belin R.M., *Problems in Adult Re-training,* Heinemann, London, 1972.

Gagne R.M., *Essentials of Learning for Instruction,* Holt, Rinehart & Wiston, New York, 1975.

Gale J., Das H. and Miner R., "Training Methods Compared" in *Leadership and Organisation Behaviour Journal,* vol. 3, No. 3, pp. 13–17.

ITRU (Industrial Training Research Unit), *Choose an Effective Style: a Self–Instructional Approach to the Teaching of Skills,* ITRU Publications, Cambridge, 1976.

Lopez F. M. jnr., *Evaluating Employee Performance,* Public Personnel Association, Chicago, 1968.

Miner J.B and Brewer J.F., "Management of Ineffective Performance" in M. D. Dunnette, 1976, *Handbook of Industrial and Organisational Psychology,* Rand McNally.

Pedler M., Burgoyne J. and Boydell T., *A Manager's Guide to Self-Development,* McGraw Hill, Maidenhead, 1978.

Revans R.W., *Developing Effective Managers,* Longmans, 1971.

Schein E.H., *Organizational Psychology,* 3rd ed., Prentice Hall Inc., Englewood Cliffs, New Jersey, 1980.

Singer E. J., *Effective Management Coaching,* IPM, London, 1974.

Stewart R. and Marshall J., "Managerial Beliefs about Managing", in *Personnel Review,* Vol. 11, No. 2, 1982, pp. 21–5.

Torrington D. P. and Chapman J. B., *Personnel Management,* 2nd ed., Prentice Hall International, London, 1983.

Vickers S. and Bradbeer R., *Sinclair Spectrum Introduction,* Sinclair Research Ltd., Cambridge, 1982.

Chapter Fourteen

TEAM WORKING

In a game of football the members of each team work very closely together, the ball is passed constantly from one to another and their success or failure depends completely on their mutual understanding and interdependent skills. In a game of cricket or baseball, the degree of interdependence is less although team members still work in concert. There is a greater range of specialist skills to be deployed and there is more scope for variety of individual performance. One player can bat both brilliantly and successfully while his team colleagues achieve little. In a national athletics team, the interdependence will be even less. The weight lifter and the sprinter have little of skill or training routine in common; their events take place at different times and in different places. Yet all are teams and all have captains.

The teams of people at work are at least as varied as that in the degree of involvement with each other that team members have. The members of a choir or a team of dancers have to work together with split-second precision, subordinating all aspects of their own personality to a tightly controlled, collective activity. Those working on machine paced production lines have equally specific and inflexible operations to perform, but with less skill and variety being offered in the routine they follow. A group of sales representatives introducing a new brand of photocopier all follow a similar selling routine and are selling an identical product, yet they spend most of their time alone and are physically dispersed from each other. The people running an hotel have duties that interrelate closely, but with very different skills and conventions. However varied the nature of working teams, the one thing they have in common is a desire by all members that the team should succeed. The desire of an individual to succeed personally at the expense of team success is dangerous.

It is unrealistic always to seek team spirit and commitment to management objectives. Some groups of working people may mistrust or not accept management objectives, yet will still be able to make the specific contribution that managers require of them. Although it is not the subject of any chapter in this book, studies of conflict demonstrate that groups whose interests diverge can still find an accommodation for those divergent interests that will satisfy both, just as the Russians are able to purchase large quantities of surplus North American grain to supplement the poor yield of their own harvests at the same time as vigorously opposing the economic system that produces the abundance.

An interesting footnote to British industrial relations is by Harvie Ramsay (1975), who explored how reasonable it was to regard firms as being like football teams, with managers and workers on the same side. This was a single element in wider ranging research, but the conclusions showed that a majority of employees agreed with that proposition, but mainly on the grounds that it was necessary for people to work together to get things done. Only eight per cent agreed because "managers and men have the same interests in everything that matters".

Although this chapter is mainly concerned with the working of tight knit groups in team situations, there are many other team-working styles in which members have a much looser interconnection.

1. THE REASONS FOR WORKING IN TEAMS

The group or team is a significant centre of organisational power. An organisation is not just an elaborate mass of interconnected individuals; there is the intermediate organising element of the group. Managers get things done by understanding the overall context in which they work, by understanding and dealing with individuals in that context, but also by understanding and dealing with working groups.

> The little community of people with whom one works closely and knowledgeably has a direct effect on the decisions made by individual members of the group. It also affects the decisions of the whole organization and the values, loyalties and attitudes of its members. Groups are sources of frustration for managers, but they can also make him or break him.
>
> (Leavitt et al. 1973, p. 148)

Working via a group of people rather than via individuals has many problems. Groups tend to work slowly and present the difficulty, already mentioned in our chapter about committees, of producing compromise solutions that may be too timid for the problem they are designed to tackle, but managers and administrators persist in convening new groups or working parties. Company reorganisation is a commonplace of industrial and commercial life, and the essence of this activity is regrouping of individuals and the re-allocation of managerial responsibilities. Whatever the reservations, the way in which groups operate, and the way in which group membership is set up, are both obviously regarded as crucial to management and organisational effectiveness. There are three reasons for this.

First, a group approach is usually best when the problem to be faced is unfamiliar and difficult or risky, without a clear procedural basis for action. Secondly a group approach is needed when a range of skills and understanding has to be deployed in concerted endeavour, individual skill being insufficient. Thirdly there is the shrewd view that "people will support that which they have helped to create". If action is to follow decision, then action will be taken more accurately and more willingly by those who have participated in shaping the decision.

Review Topic 14.1

Company reorganisation usually has the changing of working teams at its centre. What does this tell us about the importance to managers of these teams? What does it tell us about the importance to individuals of these teams?

An advertising campaign will be created largely by imaginative individuals having brainwaves, but underpinning those creative leaps are a series of meetings and conferences at which ideas are swapped, derided, developed and improved. A clever turn of phrase by a copy writer is turned into a sketch by an artist and sight of the sketch triggers off a further development of the initial idea. The operating theatre of a hospital has in it a group of people all of whom have varying levels and types of skill. The surgeon is at the centre, controlling the operation, but the surgeon cannot complete the operation without the effective and swift co-ordination of all the other skilled people present. When a company is to introduce a new product, the launch is usually preceded by a sales conference at which all those involved in sales promotion, marketing, face-to-face selling and (perhaps) distribution come together to learn what is involved and to generate enthusiasm about the new venture. Many of the traditional problems of tension and disagreement between production and marketing in companies can be traced to the fact that the production people (who were not invited to the sales conference in Majorca) see a new product as a series of headaches while marketing people see it as a golden opportunity. A time honoured way of overcoming this problem is reorganising employeees into product groups, so that the focus of selected marketing and production experts is made the product rather than the function. Taking *everyone* to Majorca is so expensive.

There may be advantages to management interest in team working, but why should individual employees want to work in this way? We saw in Chapter Two how the research of Mayo and his colleagues in the Hawthorne series of experiments demonstrated the importance of group membership as a means of improving productivity because the workers studied preferred participation in informal working groups. Although we vary in the degree of our willingness to work closely with others, we each have an inbuilt need to belong to groups with which we can identify and in which we can compare ourselves with other individuals. These needs are not met completely by family and out of work friendship groups, there is a need for work group attachment as well. This can operate at the level of attachment to the industry

("I am in engineering"), to an occupation ("I am an electrical engineer"), to an organisation ("I am with XYZ & Co."), to a small group ("I am on the design team"), or to a role ("I am the electronics specialist on the design team"). For some people all those attachments will be important, but for most one form will dominate the others, and a few people will have very low attachment. It is difficult, for instance, to imagine Beethoven wanting to identify with any working group, yet he was remarkably productive. Every organisation has its share of minor Beethovens.

Katz and Kahn (1978) advocate groups as being an important arena for individuals to find a sense of accomplishment and completion of a task; particularly in those work settings where this cannot be experienced individually, as in many manufacturing processes. This is the main argument behind the movement for autonomous work groups and for quality circles in factories.

> By being part of something beyond the physical self, the individual can achieve a sense of belongingness and can participate in accomplishments beyond individual powers.
>
> (Katz and Kahn, 1978, p.374)

2. TEAMS AT WORK

An initial distinction that has to be made about working in teams is between the *task* that the group has to achieve and the *processes* by which the team members operate. We are here concerned mainly with the processes but an important emphasis is that only by completing the task satisfactorily is there any justification for considering the process. There is always a danger that the activity of being in the team, with all those other nice people, can be emphasised at the expense of the task, but there is some evidence that a significant basis for the satisfaction of individual team members with their membership is the sense of achievement in producing results. At the same time it is necessary for the team to maintain cohesion while being unsuccessful. Most teams experience failure as well as success and the test of effectiveness may well be the ability to get through the bad times without disintegrating.

Teams differ according to their purpose. The working party, or task force, is a short-term grouping while the work group is fairly permanent and those who are members of the first will also be members of the second, although, maybe, not the other way round. Some teams, such as the board of directors in a company, have decision-making as their prime task; while others, such as autonomous work groups, have the objective of making things by co-operative effort.

Stage of Development	Process	Outcome
1. Forming	There is anxiety, dependence on leader, testing to find out the nature of the situation and what behaviour is acceptable	Members find out what the task is, what the rules are and what methods are appropriate
2. Storming	Conflict between sub-groups, rebellion against leader, opinions are polarised, resistance to control by group	Emotional resistance to demands of task
3. Norming	Development of group cohesion, norms emerge, resistance is overcome and conflicts patched up; mutual support and sense of group identity	Open exchange of views and feelings; co-operation develops
4. Performing	Interpersonal problems are resolved; interpersonal structure becomes the means of getting things done; roles are flexible and functional	Solutions to problems emerge; there are constructive attempts to complete tasks and energy is now available for effective work

Figure 14.1   Stages in the Growth of Group Cohesion and Performance (based on Tuckman B.W., 1965 pp. 384–399)

3.   CHARACTERISTICS OF TEAMS

As was mentioned in Chapter 10, Tuckman (1965) suggests that there are clear stages in the growth of relationships in groups of people working together, as shown in Figure 14.1., of *forming, storming, norming* and *performing.* People come together and conflict develops between members as they assess each other before they move to the third stage of finding a way of working together. Finally they work well and produce results.

The length of time required for this process varies. For a team that is to be together for a long time, it may take many months to work through these stages to a point of effective performance because the degree of investment required from each member is so high and the personal risks of failure so great. If the team is convening as a short-term, part-time activity — like the group that is arranging the office party at Christmas — then the individual investment is less, the risks fewer and the mutual tolerance much greater so that the process is easily truncated. Individual tolerance of the process varies, so that there is always at least one person who will quickly make a comment like "If we don't get something settled soon, we will be here all night". This poses a test for the group leader. Does he use that comment from someone else as a way of nudging the other members towards the next stage, or is the comment insufficiently representative of the general feeling? If the team leader pushes on more quickly than the other members are prepared for, then norming and performing may be further deferred as the early unresolved uncertainties will be raised again.

A helpful indicator of progress is the extent to which team members in discussion use the pronoun "I", when they are feeling apart from the rest of the group and "we" when their thinking and feeling is identified with that of their colleagues. This process of development does not only apply to people sitting around a table and talking things through. It can happen in slow motion among members of a geographically diverse team. One of the more weird and depressing aspects of life in organisations is "war by memorandum" as people "fire" off memoranda at each other, taking care to distribute plenty of copies to potential allies.

A number of experimental studies have attempted to establish which method of communication within a team is the most appropriate. The classic study was that of Leavitt (1951), which is summarised in Figure 14.2. For experimental purposes members of a small group were given tasks to do which involved communicating with each other, but they were required to communicate in differing, specific ways. The Wheel and Y networks had a central controlling person in the system, while the others were decentralised with varying degrees of limitation on the freedom with which group members exchanged information. Centralised networks were best for getting simple jobs done and decentralised networks produced better solutions to difficult problems. Centralisation was highly satisfying to person C at the centre, but frustrating for others.

The patterns illustrated each represent a typical situation found in working life. The Wheel is like a regional sales team with four members reporting to a regional manager. The chain is like a department with two executives, B and D, each reporting to a manager C and having personal assistants A and E. The Y is similar to an orthodox chain of command with one person B who is outside and who communicates only with C, as is the case of a key supplier or customer. The Circle and the Completely Connected Network are like discussion groups, with the Circle being an unusual form which is more important from the experimental point of view than because of the frequency with which it is found.

The most effective teams are those which can vary their mode of operation between, say, the Wheel and the Completely Connected Network in line with task requirements. Managers who try to centralise all communication will find resistance from team members, who will lack any sense of involvement in what is taking place. Managers who decentralise everything will miss opportunities through wasting time and team members will come to regard the process as one of all talk and no action. Managers who can achieve a shrewd balance and have thorough, decentralised consideration of matters which can only be dealt with in that way will then find that their

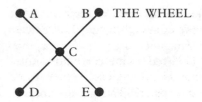

THE WHEEL

All communications have to go through person C at the centre. This network provides quick answers to simple questions, but A, B, D and E are likely to be dissatisfied with their roles.

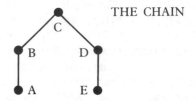

THE CHAIN

No one member is able to communicate with all the others. Members of the team are reasonably satisfied with this system of communication, but it can be inaccurate and slow.

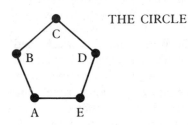

THE CIRCLE

By closing the chain each team member can communicate directly with two others. This provides the highest level of general satisfaction and can be effective for dealing with complex problems.

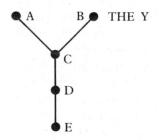

THE Y

This combines features of the Wheel and the Chain in a centralised network.

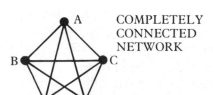

COMPLETELY CONNECTED NETWORK

Each team member can now communicate freely with every other member and all are satisfied with their role. It can be an effective method of dealing with complex problems, but is unsatisfactory for dealing with straightforward matters.

Figure 14.2   Types of Communication Network
Based on Leavitt, 1951

team members readily acknowledge the right and necessity of the managers operating in a centralised way for the majority of straightforward decisions and information.

Another classic study was that of Rice (1958). It is interesting that this was conducted in an Indian textile factory; not all our evidence comes from North America. Rice had four main conclusions (pp. 37–39).

1. The most productive group, and the one most satisfactory to its members, is the pair; then groups 6–12, with 8 as the optimum.
2. Group stability is more easily maintained when the range of skills is such that all members can comprehend each others' skills; that is they could aspire to acquire them.
3. The fewer differences in prestige and status within the group, the more stable it is.
4. When a member of a work group becomes disaffected and no longer fits in, he should be able to move elsewhere.

Group size is particularly important for teams who need to exchange ideas as too few people are not able to generate sufficient richness of ideas, but too many can lead either to a baffling excess of suggestions or to some more cautious members being inhibited.

4. TEAM ROLES

Working teams have two overriding functions. The first is to keep the team members moving towards the goal in a co-ordinated way and the second is to ensure that relationships remain sufficiently harmonious and the satisfactions of individuals good enough to prevent them quitting. Also there has to be a balance between these two functions. We need a brief comment on quitting. Some teams, like public advisory committees, have a membership that is completely voluntary so that people will only turn up if they are interested and if they can see some payoff for themselves from their participation. Teams of employees, particularly subordinates of the team leader, are not volunteers so their physical presence can probably be guaranteed. They may, however, not participate in more than a token way. Satisfying team members therefore remains important.

R. F. Bales (1950) developed a series of observation categories for studying the process of interaction in small groups. These are shown in Figure 14.3. He found that groups needed both members who were effective in the task area and those who were effective in the social and emotional area. Team members who were task oriented were the most influential and those who were social–emotional oriented were the best liked, but both were necessary for the continuing effectiveness of the group. Bales also differentiated between behaviour in the group that was emotionally positive and that which was emotionally negative. Although this investigation was

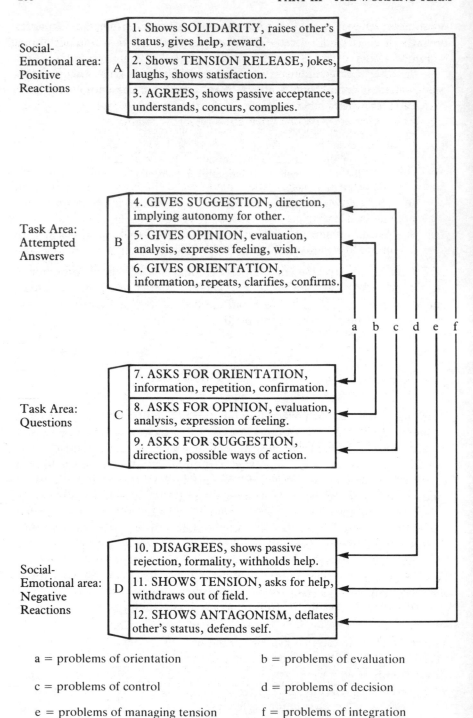

Figure 14.3   **Interaction Process Categories**
(from Bales R.F. 1950)

about the behaviour of face-to-face groups that came together for short periods, it is a useful indicator of behaviour in groups of people developing team working over a semi-permanent period. There are always the conciliators, the antagonists and the neurotics, working alongside the questioners, clarifiers and directors. Neither can succeed without the other and each group member will be partly task oriented and partly social–emotional oriented, with one orientation typically dominant.

This explanation remains the best explanation of such behaviour thirty years after the early studies that Bales conducted in Harvard. They are particularly helpful to managers in pointing out the need to balance both sets of group requirement: task orientation and social–emotional orientation, and the need to identify the type of contribution to be expected from each member and ensuring that both types are deployed to keep things moving.

Of the developments of Bales' work, Schein (1969) presents a slightly different framework, but Belbin *et al.* (1976) carried out a systematic study of management teams and concluded that six roles were needed in effective management teams apart from specialist and functional roles.

His six have now been expanded to eight roles (Belbin, 1981):

1. Company worker
2. Chairman
3. Shaper
4. Ideas man
5. Resource investigator
6. Monitor/evaluator
7. Team worker
8. Completer/finisher

Here again we see the importance of task orientation as well as the social–emotional area or team maintenance, but a related aspect of the roles which team members assume is the way in which conflict can develop. It was suggested at the opening of this chapter that the mode of team working is distinct from conflict accommodation as a management approach to action and decision-taking, but within the general mode of team working there is a degree of interpersonal conflict than can emerge. As with conflict between management and a collective of employees, this can be constructive or destructive. John Hunt (1979) summarises the possibilities:

> Conflict may:
> Introduce different solutions to the problem,
> Clearly define the power relationship within the group,
> Encourage creativity and brainstorming activity,
> Focus on individual contributions rather than group decisions,
> Bring emotive, non-rational arguments into the open,
> Provide for catharsis, release of interdepartmental or interpersonal conflicts of long-standing.

Conversely, if conflict is destructive, it may:
  Dislocate the entire group and produce polarisations,
  Subvert the objectives in favour of sub-goals,
  Lead people to use defensive and blocking behaviour in their
  group,
  Result in the disintegration of the entire group,
  Stimulate win–lose conflicts, where reason is secondary to
  emotion.

(Hunt, 1979, pp. 90–1)

The team leader is always vigilant for the level of conflict in his team. Although the comments of Hunt, above, are directed towards behaviour in face-to-face groups, there is a similar problem with the general, long-term working relationships between team members. They are all to some extent in competition with each other, all likely to feel that they are being left out of important meetings and all likely to mistrust the manoeuvres of their colleagues. This can keep people on their toes and ensure a keen level of contribution, but there is always the risk that the conflict can become destructive and the manager will need to confront the problem. This is not a favourite job for managers, as it can involve unpleasantness and the outcome is hard to predict. The best guide for dealing with such problems is a publication on interpersonal problem-solving by Richard Walton (1969).

Review Topic 14.2

Think of a group you were with within the last few days, for example:
  a business meeting,
  a lunch group,
  a sports team,
  a seminar, or
  a dinner party.
(a) Who spoke most?
(b) Who spoke least?
(c) Who gave most task-oriented conversation?
(d) Who gave most group-oriented conversation?
(e) Did you find it a satisfying experience? Why, or why not?

---

5.   TEAM DEVELOPMENT

Understanding the ways in which teams work is the best way to working effectively with and through them, as most people have to find a way of working with what there is rather than being able to make changes. For managers, however, who are able to take initiatives to improve their teams, some techniques have been evolved for assisting this process.

Sensitivity training. A controversial method of developing in people an awareness of their impact on others. It is potentially useful to develop an ability of individuals to work in teams and uses group methods to achieve its objectives. The idea is that all of us dissemble in our everyday dealings with others; we smile at people we dislike and restrain critical comments about others, either because we fear retaliation or because it is not accepted behaviour. Sensitivity training forces trainees to be more open in their behaviours towards others and, in the process, become more sensitive to the feelings and attitudes of others. The method is basically to put a group of 8–12 people in a room without any agenda or programme and leave them there for long periods. The lack of structure provides a void which group members try to fill and their comments gradually become more frank. As there is nothing to talk about, they inevitably talk about their relationship with each other. Those who are task oriented or social–emotionally oriented become apparent and everyone comes to a deeper understanding of how he relates to others. The value of this method can be considerable, but the risks are also great. It encourages people to be more open and honest with each other, but has the following drawbacks:

1. It forces many individuals to undergo a personality-humiliating and anxiety-provoking experience from which they might not recover.
2. It strips some people of defenses they badly need and provides them with nothing to replace those defenses.
3. It encourages behavioural modes that are acceptable in the laboratory but unacceptable in most organizational settings.
4. Any benefits accrued from the experience are so short-lived as to make the experience a waste of time and money.
5. It encourages and subtly coerces individuals into revealing aspects about themselves that constitute an invasion of privacy, thus harboring later resentment in participants.

(du Brin, 1974, p.424)

Against such a catalogue of drawbacks it is remarkable that the sensitivity training method was used so extensively. It is described here because elements of the method are to be found in many other training approaches.

Organisation development. A term that has been applied to many different approaches, but one of them is to use an Organisation Development (OD) consultant to work with a group of people to improve their collective performance. The group consists of people who *do* work together and the discussion is based on what they have to say rather than on any "instruction" from the consultant, who is often described as a change agent because this method has so often been used to make working teams more effective at innovation. There will be an agenda, with items such as:

1. Are we each clear about our duties and responsibilities?
2. Are there any areas of overlap? Anything missing?

3.   In what ways do we communicate well with each other? In
     what ways badly?
4.   How can we communicate with each other better?

The role of the consultant is to direct the discussion to the agenda and to
ensure that it is kept to the way the job is done rather than attacks on
individuals and their personal characteristics. This produces candour and
constructive discussion, but deflects the behaviours that could be
destructive.

This is not a speedy process and it will probably take a number of
meetings before all participants are convinced that there will be an
improvement. Ideally some everyday working experience is interspersed with
the training sessions to put into practice some of the proposals in order to
reexamine, in the everyday situation, some of what has been said in
discussion. One method is to start with a weekend of discussion and then
have two or three follow-up sessions after a few weeks back in the workplace.
The consultant should be phased out towards the end of the training period.

The Managerial Grid. This is probably the best known of all team
development methods. It lacks thorough validation for its effectiveness, but
most of those who take part in grid exercises feel that it is a very useful
method. The Managerial Grid was developed by Blake and Mouton (1969)
and identifies *concern for production* and *concern for people* as the two axes
of a grid, illustrated in Figure 14.4. At the lower left hand corner is a "1.1
management style" which is the style of managers who have a low concern for
both people and production, try to stay out of trouble and simply do as they
are told. In the upper left hand corner is the "1.9 style" of high concern for
people but low concern for production, and so on. The "9.9 style" of high
concern with both people and production is the obvious goal.

Grid training requires team members to identify their own management
style, as they perceive it themselves, and then as it is perceived by others, so
there is an element of sensitivity training thinking in the approach. It is
possible to identify the management style composition of any team and either
alter team membership to increase effectiveness or enable individual team
members to modify their personal style. This emphasis on style rather than
personal characteristics is probably the secret of the success that grid
methods have enjoyed, as it provides useful criticism of the type that most of
us can live with and can hope to modify.

A similar method of training has been devised by Reddin (1970). It is
based on an elaborate theory which adds the dimension of effectiveness to the
dimensions of concern for people and concern for production that Blake and
Mouton identified. It is much influenced by Fiedler's contingency emphasis
(discussed in Chapter 15), but has not found the same degree of popularity as
the Managerial Grid.

In the early nineteen seventies, there was a large team development
need in the British National Health Service as a result of a reorganisation that

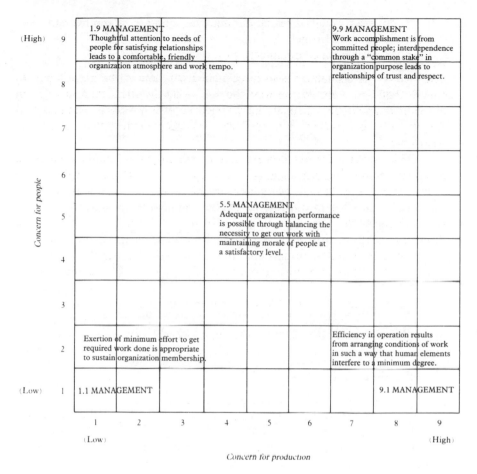

Figure 14.4   The Managerial Grid

brought into being 183 District Management Teams. This was a new form of management within the Health Service framework and provided an unusual training opportunity. A team development workshop was devised by Frada Eskin and Brian Nichol (1979). Their approach is an interesting example of this method.

6.   MANAGERS AND TEAMS

For managers the areas of team working and leadership merge together; so this chapter and the next are complementary. There can be no question of the importance of finding greater effectiveness in team working, especially as the range of technical skills and backgrounds becomes more diverse. A recent London conference on technical assistance to third world countries had at its centre the puzzle of co-ordinating the knowledge and the interests of the many people involved in such development work:

> That implies a form of creative dialogue between a wide range of intellectual disciplines — civil engineers, electrical engineers, agronomists, agricultural economists, pedologists, foresters, climatologists, community medical workers and fishery ecologists. The difficulty ... in practice is that the intellectual training of each of these disciplines ... actually makes such communication almost impossible.
>
> (Elliott, 1983, p. 429)

Review Topic 14.3

Recalling the material in Chapter 10, are committees just teams by another name?

SUMMARY PROPOSITIONS

14.1. The working team is the fundamental unit of organisation and many organisational tasks cannot be achieved by other means.

14.2. All employees can achieve a degree of satisfaction in team working that they cannot achieve by other means.

14.3. A distinction can be drawn between the task of a group and the processes whereby the group deals with the task. Teams need contributions that are both task oriented and social–emotionally oriented.

APPENDIX

Analysis of team roles in management groups

Team leaders can make their teams more effective by analysing the roles that team members fill, to see what contributions are being made and what are being left out. This can also provide the basis of developing the contributions and career prospects of individual team members.

Use the matrix below to record incidents of team members' behaviour that you observe in any aspect of team working. The types of activity will vary between teams and the situations in which they are working, but the most common are:

Face-to-face (informal)
Memorandum
Telephone
Formal meeting

The matrix is set out with the six roles identified by Belbin and referred to in this chapter. These are on the vertical axis with columns for each team member arranged horizontally. Each of the resulting boxes is divided into four sections, so that the behaviours can be tallied with strokes to record each incident. The sections are thus:

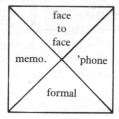

Incidents should be recorded over a week and at the end of the week you can see both the emphasis of the contributions being made by individual team members and the team roles which are being filled and those which are not. Most people make contributions in a variety of roles but you should also find some who consistently make more contributions in one particular area.

Are there any roles not being filled? Should they be? Who might be encouraged to fill them? (for example, someone who makes an occasional contribution in this area, or yourself?).

This method of analysis is the one we regard as most appropriate for management teams, although the methods of Bales and Blake and Mouton (both mentioned in the text) are extensively used.

Drill for role analysis in management teams

(based on Belbin R. M. *et al.* "Building Effective Management Teams" in *Journal of General Management*, 3, 1976, pp. 23–9)

| Category of contribution | Names of team members | | | | |
	Adams	Brown	Clark	Davis	Evans
IDEAS MAN					
MONITOR/EVALUATOR					
RESOURCE INVESTIGATOR					
COMPANY WORKER					
COMPLETER					
TEAM WORKER					

REFERENCES

Bales R. F., *Interaction Process Analysis*, Addison-Wesley, Reading, Massachussetts, 1950.

Belbin R.M., Aston B.R. and Mottram R.D., "Building Effective Management Teams", in *Journal of General Management*, 2, 1976, pp. 23–9.

Blake R.R. and Mouton J.S., *Building a Dynamic Organization through Grid Organization Development*, Addison-Wesley, Reading, Massachussetts, 1969.

Blake R. R. and Mouton J. S., *The New Managerial Grid*, Gulf Publishing, Houston, 1978.

du Brin, A.J., *Fundamentals of Organizational Behaviour*, Pergamon, New York, 1974.

Elliott C., "Making Excellence Useful", contribution to a conference, *Technical Assistance Overseas and the Environment*, reported in *Royal Society of Arts Journal*, no. 5324, vol. CXXI, July, 1983.

Eskin F. and Nichol B., "Team Development in the National Health Service", in Ottaway R. N. (ed.), *Change Agents at Work*, Associated Business Press, 1979.

Gahagan J., *Interpersonal and Group Behaviour*, Methuen, London, 1975.

Hunt J., *Managing People at Work*, Pan Books, London, 1979.

Katz D. and Kahn R.L. *The Social Psychology of Organisations*, 2nd ed., John Wiley, New York, 1978.

Leavitt H.J., "Some Aspects of Certain Communication Patterns on Group Performance", *Journal of Abnormal and Social Psychology*, 45, No. 1, 1951, pp. 38–50.

Leavitt H.J., Dill W.R. and Eyring H.B., *The Organizational World*, Harcourt Brace Jovanovich, New York, 1973.

Ramsay H., "Firms and Football Teams", in *British Journal of Industrial Relations*, vol. XII, no. 3, 1975, pp. 396–400.

Reddin W.J., *Managerial Effectiveness*, McGraw Hill, New York, 1970.

Rice A. K., *Productivity and Social Organisation*, Tavistock, London, 1958.

Schein E.H., *Process Consultation*, Addison-Wesley, Reading, Massachussetts, 1969.

Tuckman B. W., "Development Sequences in Small Groups", *Psychological Bulletin* 63, 1965, pp. 384–99.

Walton R.E., *Inter-personal Peacemaking*, Addison-Wesley, Reading, Massachussetts, 1969.

Chapter Fifteen

AUTHORITY, LEADERSHIP AND AUTONOMY

Recently an American book on management had the title *If I'm in Charge, Why Is Everybody Laughing?* This summarises the unspoken fear of many managers: how do they control the behaviour of employees in the organisation to produce co-ordinated, productive effort? Top managers hire and fire key personnel, while setting broad objectives and putting together the main components of the business structure; senior managers work out policy guidelines and staff the organisation; middle managers produce procedures to implement the policies and try to maintain a creaking organisational machine; supervisors assign jobs to individuals and groups while sorting out the day-to-day problems of materials, environment and employees. All of them fear that their personal authority will be ineffective, either because action they decree will be demonstrably ridiculous or because subordinates will reject it. These worries find focus in concern about shop stewards, bloody-mindedness, lack of co-operation, lack of enthusiasm, absenteeism, laziness, cheating the system and all the other ways whereby individual employees or groups fail to reproduce precisely the vision that the manager has in his head.

Chapter Six on organisational politics dealt with the nature of power in organisations and how managers can increase and manipulate the power available to them. This chapter deals with a specific aspect of how individuals deploy power in relation to direct subordinates: power made legitimate by expertise or hierarchical position. The three words in the chapter title describe the combination which managers need for effectiveness. Authority is a right to control and judge the actions of others. Leadership is the exercise of the power conferred by that right in such a way as to win a willing and positive, rather than grudging and negative, response from subordinates. Autonomy is that freedom of action which subordinates see as being necessary and reasonable if they are themselves to be effective in their roles.

1. AUTHORITY

One of the problems of managers being in authority is that their frame of reference is different from that of their subordinates. Partly this is a simple matter of individual difference and partly it is difference in role. After the Allied invasion of Normandy in 1944, there was widespread criticism among senior service officers and politicians of how Field Marshal Montgomery was conducting the fighting round the city of Caen. Supreme Commander Eisenhower came under pressure either to dismiss Montgomery or to issue direct instructions that would require Montgomery to act against his own better judgement. Eisenhower refused, because of his practice of always delegating authority to subordinates and giving them fullest support. Even in an operation that had such detailed planning and extensive information available, Eisenhower realised the importance of being on the spot:

> (Eisenhower) did not have Montgomery's feel of the battle as a two-sided encounter in which he kept the initiative by actions which put the enemy at a disadvantage and kept him at a disadvantage. Eisenhower did not see that by the fighting round Caen the enemy was placing himself in a position from which he would not be able to recover. ... Eisenhower had rightly delegated command of the land battle to Montgomery: he had wider tasks.
>
> (Sixsmith, 1973, p.158)

On a more general level there is a difference in objectives over much of employment. The manager is looking for efficiency, return on capital and trouble-free co-ordination of employee effort, while the subordinate is seeking an agreeable, dignified way of life within the confines of the employment contract. This perennial dissonance between the points of view has been pointed out in relation to the period in eighteenth century England, when workers could appeal to the local Justice of the Peace if they considered their rate of pay unfair:

> ... the buyers in the labour market operated on the principle of buying in the cheapest market and selling in the dearest. ... But the sellers were not normally asking for the maximum wage which the traffic would bear and offering in return the minimum quantity of labour they could get away with. They were trying to earn a decent living as human beings ... they were engaged in human life rather than in economic transaction.
>
> (Hobsbawm, 1975, p. 222)

Taylorism at the beginning of the twentieth century changed that general wage/employment relationship to a specific cash nexus with a concentration on what would be paid for each of a range of human actions. This was a shift of power as employees lost their control of discretionary knowledge in order to centralise control in the hands of the managers. The long-standing refusal of skilled craftsmen to accept time study and "the tyranny of the stop watch" has maintained for them a degree of autonomy that is jealously guarded.

As we saw in Chapter 2, the ideas of F. W. Taylor continue to suffuse much of management thinking but has had overlaid upon it the doctrine of human co-operation advanced by Elton Mayo over forty years. This depends on well knit human groups and the development of social as well as technical skills:

> Social skill shows itself as a capacity to receive communications from others, and to respond to the attitudes and ideas of others in such fashions as to promote congenial participation in a common task.
>
> (Mayo, 1975, p. 12)

In considering managerial authority, the juxtaposition of these two innovations is usually misunderstood. Taylor's scientific management is often regarded as the tough but fair way of the old days that was very good as control, but which has now become impracticable; while Mayo's human relations thinking is wishy-washy, undermines managerial authority and leads to dubious practices like underlings addressing managers by their Christian names. In fact scientific management and the cash nexus may well tie down employees to organisational demands as a whole, but can deprive individual managers of effective power over subordinates. The control lies not with the individual manager but with the payment system, so that the employee who has filled his daily quota or who is "ahead of the clock" may feel under little obligation to his supervisor. The dominance of the control *system* detracts from the legitimacy of the individual manager's authority. When the style changes to "congenial participation in a common task", that common task is assigned to the working group by an individual manager, and the need for collaboration with other groups in the organisation who are congenially participating in an over-arching common task makes individual group members dependent on a controlling figure to communicate, explain and protect. The manager may resent being called Fred (or, in other situations, have to tolerate being pushed away from the social group so that he is no longer called Fred) but he gains, rather than loses, authority in an organisation where social skills are demanded. There is again the problem about different frames of reference. Subordinates look to the manager for authority on which they can rely to act on their behalf, solve problems and correct guidance, while the manager may be looking for deference to him as a superior kind of person.

Review Topic 15.1

Some managers complain that they have responsibility without authority. Where this happens, what are the consequences?

The authority of managers is underpinned by a predilection to obedience that we all have. Stanley Milgram (1974) carried out a startling series of experiments in the United States, which showed this predilection in a way that many people found disconcerting. Volunteers were led to believe that they were taking part in a study of memory and learning. They had to administer electric shocks to learners when the learners made mistakes in answering simple questions. The electric shocks became progressively more severe with each incorrect answer. If the volunteer questioned the procedure with the experimenter, who was in charge, he was simply told that he should continue. The range of instructions began as "Please continue" and went up to "You have no other choice: you must go on".

Eighteen different experiments were conducted with over one thousand volunteers, but no matter how the variables were altered the volunteers did as they were told even when administering shocks of 450 volts to a victim begging for release. Some were unwilling to continue, but the majority continued all the way through to the end. It is not quite as bad as it sounds. The shocks were not really being given, the learner was an actor pretending to be on the point of collapse, but the volunteers thought the shocks were real and carried on "doing their job". Two samples:

> Mr Batta
> "The scene is brutal and depressing: his hard, impassive face shows total indifference as he subdues the screaming learner and gives him shocks. He seems to derive no pleasure from the act itself, only quiet satisfaction at doing his job properly."

> Mr Gino, speaking at the end of the experiment
> "Well, I faithfully believed the man was dead until we opened the door. When I saw him, I said 'Great, this is great.' But it didn't bother me even to find that he was dead. I did my job."
>
>   (Milgram, 1974, p. 46 and p. 88)

Readers of this book will probably not want their subordinates to electrocute their colleagues, but the importance of this study is that it demonstrates a remarkable readiness to obey. Milgram explains this by saying that when people enter a hierarchical system ("someone else is in charge"), those people then see themselves as agents carrying out the wishes of others and put themselves in what he calls an "agentic state". Others take the responsibility, so that compliance is not only easy, but also the criteria of satisfaction.

Milgram explains the willingness with which people adopt the agentic state by reference to a series of experiences which virtually everyone undergoes:

Parental regulation. The experience of almost everyone when young, as parents remorselessly issue instructions on a range of matters concerning every department of an infant's life — eating, sleeping, washing, keeping quiet and so on. The one common element in all of these is the implicit "obey me".

The institutional setting. The child emerges from the cocoon of the family into an institutional setting. At school he is always a subordinate, although he gradually acquires seniority in relation to other subordinates. At college and in the early years at work he always has to do things prescribed by others.

Rewards. Given to those who comply with authority and the disobedient are frequently punished.

Normative support. Authority is normatively supported as any group or institution is expected, by its members, to have a socially controlling figure. This was shown in the last chapter about team working and the process of small groups.

Justifying ideology. There is a justifying ideology that supports, or legitimates, the authority of the individual controlling figure. In Milgram's experiments the volunteers came to a university to take part in scientific investigations about learning. Science and education are two powerful sources of legitimacy. Other obvious sources are religious belief and patriotism. Others again are service to the customer, the general good of the organisation and the wellbeing of the employees.

The explanations above have been used to explain such things as the willingness of ordinary people to participate in the slaughter of Jews in Nazi Germany or the massacre of villagers in Vietnam, but political philosophers have long debated the idea that the majority of people *want* to be subservient to a dominant figure or group, who will look after them. This argument runs that people have a choice as humans between freedom and happiness. Freedom involves being responsible and making decisions and judgements. Happiness relieves a person of those "burdens" as others decide what is right and wrong, what should be done and what should not, so that the individual person enjoys the contentment of having his life organised for him.

Expressed so bluntly the argument sounds to be an extreme of cynicism, yet the history of human society can readily be interpreted in this way and it is a theme that occurs frequently in art and literature. A famous and vivid version of the argument is the fable of the Grand Inquisitor by the Russian Dostoevsky, in which he visualises an encounter between Jesus Christ and the Cardinal in charge of the Spanish Inquisition. The Cardinal orders the arrest of Jesus Christ and visits him in his cell to explain how his teaching about freedom was unsettling and disturbing to ordinary people who needed the reassurance of bondage rather than the anxiety of responsibility. A contemporary commentary is by D. H. Wrong (1979).

Whatever the reasons for obedience, the important lesson for managers is that there is a predilection for those in organisations to comply with instructions from those in authority within the organisational framework. That is the authority of those *in* authority. This can be immeasurably enhanced by those who are also *an* authority, who have some aspect of expertise to make their instructions convincing and welcome. French and Raven (1959) suggest that there are five main bases of power to influence others.

(i)   A (the person wishing to exercise power) has the ability to control the *rewards* of B (the person to be influenced). Managers control promotions, pay rises, some aspects of fringe benefits, and are important potential sources of praise.

(ii)   A has the ability to *coerce* B by providing punishments. Praise can be withheld, unattractive duties can be allotted to B, he may be rebuked and eventually dismissed.

(iii)   A may have *legitimate* influence because of his role. The quality assurance official has the right to examine the work done by others, just as customs officers have the right to open suitcases at national frontiers.

(iv)   *Referent* power is where B wishes to identify with A. An extreme form is seen in the clamorous followers of popular singers, but managers tend to attract a following in organisations, even though the followers may not express themselves with such exuberance.

(v)   Finally A has authority in relation to B when A has *expertise* which B acknowledges and wants to use. An example we used in the discussion on organisational politics was of the maintenance engineer who can work the miracle of restarting the machine that has stopped, but there are many such examples in every organisation, and this is an authority base that does not depend on hierarchical position. Another example is of the young legal advisor in a large international company, who told the members of the main board of his company that they could not go ahead with the planned sale of a subsidiary for legal reasons. In the hierarchy he ranked low, but his technical expertise was not queried.

From our discussion so far in this chapter it may seem that managers should have no problem in getting others to do things; if people generally are predisposed to obey, then presumably all that managers need to do is to issue instructions and wait for them to be carried out?

Life, of course, is not so easy. The general predisposition to compliance is something of which all managers have to be reminded, but it is not sufficient. Although the majority of Milgram's volunteers complied, 35 per cent did not; also they were being required to carry out a routine task rather than one depending on enthusiasm, imagination or some other quality that cannot be conjured up by simple command. How many managers could tolerate a situation in which they operated by simple decree? They fear that the result will be the corruption of themselves by the power they wield, although Wrong (*op. cit.* p. 107) points out that Lord Acton was only half right when he made his famous comment about power corrupting: power can also ennoble.

The manager seeks something more. He seeks the secret of leadership, a heady concept indeed.

2.   LEADERSHIP

The implication behind the notion of leadership is that there is a combination of personal qualities and skills that enables some people to elicit from their subordinates a response that is enthusiastic, cohesive and effective, while other people in the same situation cannot achieve such results. There are two problems about that type of view. First it is often bad for the leader, who grows an inflated view of his own importance, believing that his success lies in who he is rather than what he does. Secondly, it limits the number of people who can safely be put in charge of sections, departments and operations because it emphasises relatively rare qualities of social dominance. It is significant that qualities of leadership are a greater preoccupation among potential leaders than among potential followers. "I know how to get the best out of them" is heard more frequently than "He knows how to get the best out of us". The "great man" theory of leadership was summed up by the postwar American president Harry Truman:

> I wonder how far Moses would have gone if he had taken a poll in Egypt? What would Jesus Christ have preached if he had taken a poll in Israel? Where would the Reformation have gone if Martin Luther had taken a poll? It isn't polls or public opinion of the moment that counts. It is right and wrong and leadership — men with fortitude, honesty and a belief in the right that makes epochs in the history of the world.
>
> (*Wall Street Journal*, 16th December 1980, p. 2)

Studies of effective leaders in order to identify the *traits* of leadership have failed to provide clear cut results and it is now appreciated that there are other factors of comparable or greater significance in explaining leader effectiveness. A review by Davis (1972) shows there to be four general traits related to leadership success, although they do little more than confirm common sense:

Intelligence. Leaders usually have a slightly higher level of general intelligence than the average among their followers.

Social maturity. Having self-assurance and self-respect, leaders are mature and able to handle a wide variety of social situations.

Achievement drive. Leaders have a strong drive to get things done.

Human relations attitudes. Knowing that they rely on other people to get things done, leaders are interested in their subordinates and work at developing subordinate response.

A more comprehensive understanding requires a consideration of the needs that a particular group of people have of their leader, and of the situation in which the led task is performed.

In 1902 the Scottish dramatist J. M. Barrie wrote a play *The Admirable Crichton,* in which an English aristocratic family is shipwrecked on a desert island. The authority of the head of the family rapidly disintegrates in this situation and the role of leader is gradually assumed by the one person in the party who has the skills and experience necessary: Crichton, the family butler. Previously his ability and resourcefulness has been recognised with the patronising term "admirable"; suddenly they become essential. Not born great, Crichton has greatness thrust upon him. On the desert island, his leadership was unchallenged. When the party was rescued, the crew of the ship that found them immediately re-established the norms and values of Edwardian England, so Crichton resumed his tail coat and served his master an excellent breakfast in bed.

As with so many areas of social science investigation, much of the work on leadership over the last thirty years has been to present slightly different versions of explanatory model that are basically very similar but express differing emphasis according to the values of their proponents. So we shall describe just two of these explanations which are mutually consistent and the second depends partly on the explanations in the first.

Fiedler (1967) has developed *a contingency model of leadership effectiveness* in which he argues that any leadership style may be effective, depending on the situation, so that the leader has to be *adaptive*. We thus have a clear difference between this approach and that of the trait theorists, as we are talking of leaders adapting their *style* to the situation. He also appreciates that it is very difficult for individuals to change their style of leadership as these styles are relatively inflexible: the autocrat will remain autocratic and the freewheeling *laissez-faire* advocate will remain freewheeling. As no single style is appropriate for all situations, effectiveness can be achieved either by changing the manager to fit the situation or by altering the situation to suit the manager. Three factors will determine the leader's effectiveness:

1. *Leader–member relations*. How well is the leader accepted by the subordinates?
2. *Task structure*. Are the jobs of subordinates routine and precise or vague and undefined?
3. *Position power*. What formal authority does the leader's position confer?

Fiedler then devised a novel device for measuring leadership style. It was a scale that indicated *the degree to which a man described favourably or unfavourably his least-preferred co-worker (LPC).*

> a person who describes his least-preferred co-workers in a relatively favorable manner tends to be permissive, human relations oriented and considerate of the feelings of his men. But a person who describes his least preferred co-worker in an unfavourable manner — who has what we have come to call a low LPC rating — tends to be managing, task-controlling and less concerned with the human relations aspects of the job.
>
> (Fiedler, 1965)

Fiedler then argues that high LPC managers will want to have close ties with their subordinates and regard these as an important contributor to their effectiveness, while low LPC managers will be much more concerned with getting the job done and less interested in the reactions of subordinates. It is then possible to combine all these elements to show how the style of leadership that is effective varies with the situation in which it is exercised. Figure 15.1 shows the result of 800 studies which Fiedler carried out, using eight categories of leadership situations and two types of leaders.

High LPC leaders tend to be permissive, human relations oriented and considerate

Low LPC leaders tend to be concerned with getting the job done and less interested in the reactions of subordinates.

Condition	Leader–member Relations	Task Structure	Position Power	
1	GOOD	HIGH	STRONG	Low LPC leader more effective
2	GOOD	HIGH	WEAK	Low LPC leader more effective
3	GOOD	LOW	STRONG	Low LPC leader more effective
4	GOOD	LOW	WEAK	High LPC leader more effective
5	POOR	HIGH	STRONG	High LPC leader more effective
6	POOR	HIGH	WEAK	Similar effectiveness
7	POOR	LOW	STRONG	Low LPC leader more effective
8	POOR	LOW	WEAK	Low LPC leader more effective

Figure 15.1   Leadership Performance in Different Conditions (from Fiedler, 1976, p.11)

High LPC leaders were likely to be most effective in situations where relations with subordinates are good but task structure is low and position power weak. They do reasonably well when they have poor relationships with their subordinates but there is high task structure and strong position power. Both of these are moderately favourable combinations of circumstance. Low LPC leaders are more effective at the ends of the spectrum, when they have either a favourable combination or an unfavourable combination of factors in the situation.

The value of Fiedler's work is that it concentrates on *effectiveness* as its yardstick and demonstrates the fallacy of believing that there is a single best way to lead in all situations. It is interesting that the majority of situations he describes appear to call for a generally less attractive type of person as leader, but we should remember that he was examining a range of situations for the purpose of explanation, and that situations which are at the extremes of his continuum may not be very frequent in organisational life. Although this remains the most widely accepted analysis of the leadership process, some people have found rather depressing Fiedler's accompanying argument that individual leaders have little chance of adopting a style which is more appropriate to their situation, so that it is more important to match available managers to a situation than to try changing the individual manager's style. An alternative is to tinker with the situation: modifying the task structure, varying the formal authority or changing the subordinates. The last is the most drastic and is usually only possible to any significant extent in very few situations. It could, however, transform condition 8 to condition 4.

Some people, especially those concerned with training, cannot believe in the degree of inflexibility that Fiedler found. One person whose ideas on training have been widely influential in the United Kingdom (though not elsewhere) is John Adair.

Adair produces a synthetic picture of leadership by arguing that people in working groups have three sets of needs, two of which are shared with all group members, and one being related to each individual:

a.   the task to be accomplished together,
b.   maintaining the social cohesion of the group, and
c.   individual needs of team members.

These three sets of needs are interdependent:

> ... if a group fails in its task this will intensify the disintegrative tendencies present in the group and raise a diminished satisfaction for its individual members. If there is a lack of unity or harmonious relationships in the group this will effect performance on the job and also individual needs (cf. A. H. Maslow's *Social Needs*). And obviously an individual who feels frustrated and unhappy in a particular work environment will not make his maximum contribution to either the common task or the life of the group.
>
> (Adair, 1982 p. 9)

Review Topic 15.2

There is great interest among managers in leadership ideas. Is this solely to justify their idea of their own importance as men deserving larger salaries and bigger cars?

Figure 15.2 shows these three sets of needs, or leadership functions, are expressed as three overlapping circles. This emphasises the essential unity of leadership, so that a single action by a leader may have influence in all three areas.

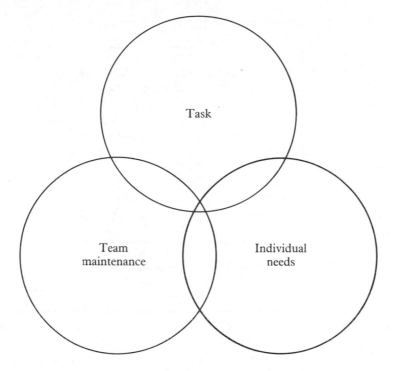

Figure 15.2   Adair's Three Circle Model of Leadership

This was used by Adair to develop leadership at the Royal Military Academy, Sandhurst, but the methods have been adopted in a wide variety of organisations. They are set out in detail in Adair, 1982.

3.   AUTONOMY

Research and discussion about authority and leadership tend to centre on the role and personality or, more recently, on the needs of groups to have a leadership function exercised on their behalf. These emphases tend to overlook the need of organisation members for autonomy, and the complementary need of organisations to have members who are autonomous. From the point of view of the individual employee, there is a life cycle theory of leadership (Hersey & Blanchard, 1969) which points out that people at work need lessening task structure as they mature in an organisation, as well as during their maturation as human beings. Most forty-year olds will find close supervision and direction as irksome as most sixteen-year olds will find it necessary. From the point of view of the employing organisation, close supervision is time consuming and expensive, as we saw in the discussion

Figure 15.3   Authority, Leadership and the Manager

about the optimum span of control in Chapter Three. Also many tasks in contemporary organisations cannot be done well without the job holder having full range for his imagination and responsibility. Bob Ramsey retired in 1981 from the position of Industrial Relations Director at Ford of Great Britain. This is not a company renowned for its weakness and inefficiency, yet Ramsey frequently spoke of employees looking for a better *service* from management. The main work of organisations is done by engineers and salesmen, by designers and analysts, and by many other people with some acquired skill that the organisation needs. Managers enable those employees to do well by the management service they provide in support of the autonomy that is needed for effective individual performance.

4.   AUTHORITY, LEADERSHIP AND THE MANAGER

The basic job of getting people to obey orders is not as problematical as many managers believe, and little skill or personal charm is needed. The reason, however, for the abiding interest of managers in ideas of leadership, motivation and influence is that managers usually seek to do more than bring about simple obedience — they are trying to win a performance. They are trying to enable the members of the group, team or department to produce a workaday contribution to the organisation in commitment, collaboration, imagination, persistence and forbearance. The type of leadership that is effective varies with the situation in which it is exercised, just as the behaviour of team members varies according to the scope which their jobs offer. As with so many other aspects of management, there is no single best way of being in charge of a group of people, but in an increasing range of working situations it seems as if the successful manager is the one who is most thorough in ensuring that the team members have the correct facilities and environment to work. Skilled individuals know what to do, and need appropriate autonomy and services to perform.

Review Topic 15.3

Recalling the material in Chapter 6, is the autonomy of individual workers incompatible with the power implicit in organisations?

SUMMARY PROPOSITIONS

15.1. The authority of managers is underpinned by a general human predilection to obey commands from those holding higher rank in the hierarchy of which they are members.

15.2. Tight control of employee performance by incentive payment schemes reduces rather than enhances the personal authority of individual managers in relation to employees.

15.3. Effective leadership depends on the situation in which it is exercised; the main variables being leader–member relations, task structure and position power of the leader.

15.4. A convenient way of understanding what is involved in the leadership of a group is to consider three overlapping needs: the needs of group members to accomplish a task together, the need to maintain the social cohesion of the group, and the needs of the individual group members.

15.5. Increasingly employees — especially those with skills or specialised knowledge — need a style of leadership that acknowledges their need for autonomy in order to make their optimum contribution.

APPENDIX

Interaction guide for the disciplinary interview

I   Before the Interview

Check   a. Facts as they are known and have been reported.
                 b. Position in relation to disciplinary procedure and employee's legal rights.
                 c. Check who will be present. The respondent may wish to be accompanied. You may want to have witnesses available.

II During the Interview

Begin with	An explanation of the management position, which is based on some unsatisfactory *facts* about the employee's behaviour, not on opinions about those facts.
Ask for	The employee's comment about the facts, reasons for them and his attitude towards them.
Ensure	That you understand his position and that he understands yours.
Examine	The shared problem to find a solution. Usually the matter will be resolved by this joint examination.
Persuade	If the matter is not resolved, first try to *persuade* the employee that his continued action is not in his own best interests.
Disapprove	If persuasion fails, use *disapproval* of what he has done.
Penalties	If all else fails, deploy *penalties,* either for what has been done or as the inevitable result of repetition in the future.

III After the Interview

Record	Problems and agreed action.
Take action	If any management action was agreed as necessary, e.g. moving the employee to a different department.
File	Interview notes for later review, especially if there is any possibility of dismissal.

REFERENCES

Adair J., *Action-Centred Leadership,* Gower Press, Aldershot, 1982.

Davies K., *Human Behaviour at Work,* 4th edition, McGraw Hill, New York, 1972.

Fiedler F.E., *A Theory of Leadership Effectiveness,* McGraw Hill, New York, 1967.

Fiedler F.E., "The Leadership Game: Matching the Man to the Situation", in *Organizational Dynamics,* Winter, 1976.

French W L. and Raven S., "The Bases of Social Power" in Cartwright D. (ed.) *Studies in Social Power.*

Hersey P. and Blanchard K.H., "Life Cycle Theory of Leadership", in *Training and Development Journal,* May 1969, pp. 26–34.

Hobsbawm E.J., *The Age of Capital,* Weidenfeld & Nicholson, London, 1975.

Mayo E., *The Social Problems of Industrial Civilisation,* Routledge and Kegan Paul, London, 1975.

Milgram S., *Obedience to Authority,* Tavistock, London, 1974.

Sixsmith E.K.G., *Eisenhower as Military Commander,* Batsford, London, 1973.

Wrong D.H., *Power: its Forms, Bases and Uses,* Basil Blackwell, Oxford, 1979. Particularly relevant is Chapter 5, pp. 84–123. Readers may also like to read Chapter 5 in Book V of *The Brothers Karamazov* by Fyodor Dostoevsky, which is available in many imprints, including that of the Everyman Library, J. M. Dent, London, 1947.

Chapter Sixteen

PERFORMANCE APPRAISAL

When children are at school their performance is monitored and reported upon. Week by week marks out of ten are written in the margins of exercise books, already sprinkled with ticks and crosses. Comments are made about the exercise which has been completed, pointing out any errors and emphasising what has been done well. At the end of each term or school year the general judgement of the teacher on the progress of the child is compressed into a few sentences on the school report. These regularly reported judgements are regarded as essential by the recipients as they give clues to the perennial question: "How am I getting on?"

When children start work, the reporting stops. It may continue in a different form during apprenticeship or similar initial training, but once the rudiments of the job are learned, feedback on the quality of performance is usually occasional, accidental and ill-considered, especially where there is not an obvious unit of production to be completed. Also there are not the same milestones through the year; life just goes on.

Although we are usually glad to leave school and school reports behind, we still hanker after feedback on our performance in order to feel secure, to have a sense of progress and to enjoy praise. It is only the fear of bad news that makes us uncertain.

In some jobs the "report" is easily available. The barrister wins or loses his case, the salesman gets his repeat order or sees new business moving to his competitors, waiters and waitresses experience the direct response of their customers, possibly reinforced by a tip. Others have a clear quota of work to do, and its completion indicates success. The coach driver finishes his journey, the chambermaid completes the designated number of bedrooms that have to be prepared, a magazine editor completes an edition. But satisfactory completion of the assignment does not answer such questions as "Could I do better?" "How?" "Can I look for promotion?" "What do I have to do to achieve it?" Also most of those in managerial, administrative and clerical jobs do not even have the satisfaction of regularly completing a quota of work. Many people in such positions provide substitute goals for themselves, so that when the goal is reached they can enjoy the satisfaction of achievement that the continuous nature of their duties denies them. An example is clearing the in-tray. This may provide satisfaction, but is it an appropriate yardstick of effectiveness?

Performance appraisal is intended to overcome the lack of all that is involved in the progress checking system of school examinations and reports: it is intended to provide milestones, feedback, guidance and monitoring. Unfortunately it nearly always fails, for reasons we shall see shortly. Most of our readers who have experience of performance appraisal will regard it as little more than an administrative burden placed upon them by the Personnel Department. Despite this the idea of performance appraisal remains attractive. Hilaire Belloc produced the aphorism "If a thing is worth doing, it is worth doing badly" and this is a helpful way of considering schemes designed to appraise working performance. The potential advantages are so great that it is worth always trying to make it work, no matter how often the scheme falls short of the thoroughness and fairness that advocates regard as essential. In this chapter we shall not prescribe a system, but will set out to explain the problems and opportunities, the methods that can be deployed and the part that individual managers can play.

The two essential elements of appraisal are *judgement* and *reporting*. The performance is not simply being measured, as in the completion of a work quota, it is being judged. This obviously involves discretion, worry about bias and the possibility of being quite wrong. This judgement is not, however, made in isolation. It has not only to be made, but also passed on to one or more other people in such a way that the other(s) understand what is intended and take action on it. Those devising performance appraisal schemes devote most of their energies to finding ways of making the judgements as systematic as possible and the reporting as consistent as possible between different appraisers.

Our working definition of performance appraisal is therefore: *The process of judging a person's performance and reporting that judgement.*

1.   ORGANISATIONAL PURPOSES AND PROBLEMS IN APPRAISING PERFORMANCE

Why do organisations seek to appraise the performance of organisation members?

Social Control. It is first a method of shoring up the hierarchy, confirming the authority of those supervising the activities of others, and sustaining the dependence of subordinates within the cohesive structure of the organisation. "Big brother is watching you."

Human resource considerations. The second consideration is that of maximising the use of human resources. The abilities and energies of employees are an input to the organisational processes, and there is a logical argument for monitoring the performance to see whether the resources are being efficiently deployed.

Training. If employees are to develop their skills and their contribution, they will require periodic training. Appraisal can identify the training that individuals need.

Promotion. Organisations need regularly to move employees up the hierarchy or across it, and occasionally down. Appraisal can aid the decision-making involved in determining who goes where as it can keep up to date knowledge that is held about employee's skills, experience and aspirations. In some large organisations, like the armed services and a number of multi-national corporations, career movements are frequent and involve a regular use of annual appraisals.

Planning. Associated with promotion considerations are those of preparing for future manpower requirements. Theoretically the regular appraisal process can feed into a manpower inventory, making it possible to pinpoint future skill shortages and to prepare succession plans.

Problems

The problems encountered in running schemes of appraisal are formidable, despite constant attempts to build bigger and better schemes that cannot possible fail.

Paperwork. Systems always involve a lot of paperwork and documentation which is disliked by the managers who have to carry out the appraisals. There is no escape from the documentation, as an essential feature of appraisal is reporting and schemes invariably include attempts to make both the judgements and the reporting consistent between different appraisers. This involves forms and detailed instructions.

Formality. The forms and the general paraphernalia introduce an inhibiting feature into the everyday working relationships between managers and their subordinates, who dislike the idea of formal evaluation and prefer a more relaxed, easy going basis to their working relationship. Reverting to the analogy of the schoolteacher which began this chapter, there is not the same social distance between managers and their subordinates as there is between teachers and their pupils, and managers do not so readily accept the idea of their own responsibility for developing the careers and performances of their subordinates. Performance appraisal thus becomes a burdensome extra to the manager. To the teacher it is burdensome, but central. Managers usually argue that they provide regular, informal performance feedback and evaluation hour-by-hour in the superior/subordinate relationship, so that form filling is irrelevant. This conveniently ignores the benefit of thinking out a considered view of the whole working performance rather than pointing out errors when they occur. It also does not take account of providing the counselling and training aspects of feedback to the person appraised, which are only likely to register when there is a serious discussion about performance.

Outcomes are ignored. Managers will not stick with their judgements, so if it is agreed that Mr A should have six months' training elsewhere, the manager may still not find time to send the person. Promotion decisions often are inconsistent with the results of the most recent appraisal, in that the most appropriate person, according to the appraisal forms, is not the one chosen for promotion. This may be due to the promotion decision being irrational, or a need to maintain a necessary political balance by advancing someone's protégé, or of experience and judgement overriding the dictates of the system.

Review Topic 16.1

Consider the five purposes of performance appraisal cited here: social control, human resource considerations, training, promotion and planning.

Are there alternative methods of achieving any of these that would be better than performance appraisal?

Performance is measured by proxy. Performance appraisal is used in situations where performance cannot be readily measured, so proxies for performance are often measured instead:

> It may be difficult for me to determine if you are effective at your job; however, I can tell if you are at work on time, if you look busy, if you are pleasant and agreeable, or if you respect authority. While these characteristics may or may not have a relationship to performance, they are frequently easier to measure than performance per se. So, what we often find in organizations is the use of one or more proxies for performance rather than actual measures of performance. The use of proxies by managers, especially inadequate ones, can produce considerable dysfunctional behavior among employees. However, this does not stop managers from using them.
>
> (Robbins, 1978, p. 209)

The "just above average" syndrome. The appraisal carries either an explicit or implicit statement about the general ability and acceptability of the person appraised. Designers of appraisal systems go to great lengths to force appraisers to provide a range of judgements, but there is great reluctance to tell anyone that they are not doing well enough, or to put "black marks" on paper. There is also a reluctance to tell people that they are outstanding, as this raises expectations that may not be satisfied. There is thus a tendency for most people appraised to be judged as comfortably above average. There is then no demand for remedial action by poor performers and no problem about high flyers asking for more money. The best that this achieves is to prevent the scheme causing too much trouble: the high flyers are frustrated through lack of recognition and the under-achievers leap enthusiastically to the conclusion that they are doing just the right thing.

The unwillingness of managers to face up to unpopular judgements is not because they lack moral fibre or powers of judgement. They are concerned that it will destroy the working relationship between them and the subordinate hearing the bad news, and this is compounded by the preference for informality. A formal structure enables you to be critical. Without that structure adverse criticism is likely to develop into recriminations and vituperation, especially when it is judgement that is being deployed rather than measurement.

Incomplete coverage. For appraisal schemes to be fair they have to be applied to all employees in a particular cadre, and for schemes to be effective they have to be seen as fair. In operation most schemes fail to achieve complete coverage. In schemes we have looked at, the completion rate has been between 50 and 75 per cent in many cases. This can produce strange side effects and reinforces some of the other problems mentioned so that the scheme is regarded as an administrative burden, dreamed up by the personnel people to give themselves something to do.

Ron Barnes is twenty-five, employed at the British headquarters of a multinational company based in New York. He has been with the company two years and is a marketing specialist. His main career objective in the short-term is to get "off reports"; that is he will no longer have an annual appraisal. This is an indication that one has risen above the everyday ranks of managers and administrative staff and been "noted" for the future. This is a completely unofficial move, but has become established as one of the ways in which senior managers assert their authority and control by undermining aspects of the system that keeps them in power.

Jean Whitehorn is a member of the same company and feels that she is not making progress, but cannot figure out why that should be. Last year all her immediate colleagues had appraisals completed, but she was left out. She asked her immediate manager who explained that "he had not got round to it" but would do it as soon as he could. He was then suddenly transferred to Rome, so Jean enquired of the Management Development Officer who told her that her erstwhile manager had declined to complete an appraisal on her because "she wasn't going anywhere".

Another aspect of complete coverage being lost is in the decay of schemes. An enthusiast with a career at stake may succeed in bullying all his colleagues to complete appraisals once or even twice, only to be succeeded by someone seeking to try appraisal in a different way and gaining the approval of his colleagues by leaving the existing scheme in abeyance for the time being. However, schemes only begin to pay off when they become an established part of the way the organisation functions. Altering them can be as damaging as digging up a plant to see if it is growing.

Ill-informed appraisers and context problems. A prerequisite for sound appraisal is knowledge by the appraiser of the performance that is being appraised. Without safeguards, managers may be asked, because of their rank, to appraise members of the organisation whose work they do not know. Alternatively they may be unduly influenced by recent events which are clear in their minds. A trainee health visitor was doing very well until she dropped a baby. The baby was not unduly concerned and passed the matter off with a cynical cough and a weary shake of the head, but all the members of the general public and the nursing profession in the vicinity had a topic of discussion that kept them going for days "Did you hear about the trainee who dropped the baby...?" Her end-of-training performance review took place just over one week later and she was asked to repeat the final phase of her training.

The problem of context is how one disentangles individual performance from its context, especially if the scheme is one based on setting objectives. Has the dishwasher salesman who exceeds his sales target handsomely because of a reduction in VAT and extended industrial action at a rival's factory done better than the refrigerator salesman who has not met target because of industrial action affecting output from *his* factory?

2.   PERFORMANCE APPRAISAL AND THE INDIVIDUAL EMPLOYEE

Although employees may often contemplate performance appraisal with misgivings, this is usually no more than the type of mixture of feelings that we contemplate on visiting the dentist: we desire the outcome of a "good report" and helpful guidance, but dread the possibility of bad news. Here are some of the benefits for the individual:

Ability is enhanced. The person appraised can become a more able performer by emphasising strengths and understanding what changes are needed.

Motivation. The reassurance and confirmation of encouraging appraisal can increase the level of enthusiasm about, and commitment to, the job that is done.

Career objectives. In considering career moves and job changes, individuals seek guidance and indicators in making decisions on what to do and where to aim. Performance appraisal can clarify intentions and underpin the confidence needed to take risks or to aim high. It can also temper aspiration to make career objectives more realistic.

Career development. There should be the advantage for the individual from performance appraisal that he will not only clarify his career objectives but also be assisted in reaching those objectives by the outcome of the appraisal process: training will be arranged, moves offered and counselling given.

Review Topic 16.2

(a) For an organisation that you know, write notes of a *management* argument against performance appraisal.
(b) For the same organisation write notes of a union or employee argument against performance appraisal.
(c) Write notes that seek to satisfy both sets of reservations.
(d) Repeat the exercise, but place it in a quite different organisational context.

Against these advantages, there are the problems that have been referred to already. Subordinates are as inhibited by formality as their managers, bad news is demoralising and will probably be fended off. Also trade unions tend to resist performance appraisal as it breaks down the collective interests of employees, by "dividing man from man".

3. METHODS OF APPRAISAL

Deirdre Gill (1973, 1977) has carried out two surveys of appraisal practice in the United Kingdom. Table 16.1 summarises her finding about the use of different systems.

Type of system	1973 per cent.	1977 per cent.
Result oriented/MBO	51.2	56.7
Alpha/numerical rating	35.9	10.6
Personality trait rating	17.9	33.9
Written report	10.2	6.7
Self-rating	7.6	28.3
Miscellaneous	18.6	13.1

(Based on Gill, 1973; and Gill 1977)

Table 16.1   Methods of Performance Appraisal

This table provides us with a useful summary of methods to consider.

Management by objectives. This, or some variant of appraising against results, is now the most popular form of appraisal used after being first advocated by two of the best-known publicists in American management; Drucker in 1955 and McGregor in 1960. The basis of the system is simply to agree, between appraiser and appraisee, a set of verifiable objectives to be achieved over a predetermined future period. By emphasising preset and jointly-agreed targets, the focus is on performance results rather than personality factors. It is less susceptible to appraiser bias or diffidence and less likely to outrage the appraisee. Glueck provides an example of an MBO evaluation report:

OBJECTIVES SET	Period objective	Accomplishments	Variance
1. Number of sales calls	100	104	+4%
2. Number of new customers contacted	20	18	−10%
3. Number of wholesalers stocking new product 117	30	30	0%
4. Sales of product 12	10,000	9,750	−2.5%
5. Sales of product 17	17,000	18,700	+10%
6. Customer complaints/service calls	35	11	−33⅓%
7. Number of sales correspondence courses successfully completed	4	2	−50%
8. Number of sales reports in home office within 1 day of end of month	12	10	−20%

(from Glueck, 1979, p. 217)

Table 16.2   MBO Evaluation Report for Salesperson

This has the appearance of precision and all is performance without any subjective assessment of personality, but to what extent are these achievements and failures absolute and unequivocal? Is the relative success of 5 more important than the apparent failure of 4? The figures only become significant in context, so that the method provides a basis for discussion, it does not provide a neat yardstick of success and failure. This method now is more widely used than all the others combined, but it can only centre on what can be made reasonably precise and takes no account of circumstances beyond the control of the person appraised.

Rating. There are various methods of rating, but the basis is that the appraiser is presented with a series of performance factors, such as job knowledge, versatility, analytical ability and so on. Each of these he is required to rate with a number or letter in a scale: 1 to 7 or A to E, with A being regarded as outstanding and E as unsatisfactory. In a way it is this sort of rating that has given performance appraisal a bad name and it is interesting to see that its use has declined so sharply. A survey for BIM in 1967 showed this as being the most popular method at that time.

Personality trait rating. This is similar to the above rating method except that it is the person rather than the performance that is judged. Schemes use such factors as drive, initiative, judgement and reliability.

Written reports. This is most similar to the school report and is still used extensively in the armed forces, although in decline elsewhere. The appraiser is asked to write a pen portrait of the person appraised. It has the main drawbacks of the great difficulty of comparing one pen portrait with another and the dependence on the rare skill of pen portrait writing.

Self-rating is a growing technique in which the person appraised evaluates his own performance and indicates how he would like to see his job and career develop. So far this is usually used as well as, and not as a substitute for, appraisal by an organisational superior.

Critical incidents and BARS. In an attempt to make appraisal more precise and discriminating, some schemes are based on critical incidents which the supervisor is asked to identify over the assessment period as indicating satisfactory or unsatisfactory performance. While being appraised the appraisee has a note kept of each time such a critical incident occurs and at the end of the period the appraiser bases his judgement on the number of satisfactory and unsatisfactory critical incidents. For example, a scheme developed in the public sector had the following critical incidents for relations with members of the public: "Always keeps clients waiting ten minutes, even when not busy"; "Often phones other departments for a client who has come to the wrong place."

This can then be developed into Behaviourally Anchored Rating Scales (BARS) by giving a grading to each critical incident. Although popular among some psychologists because of its potential for precision and accuracy, it has not yet been widely adopted. One great advantage is that in discussions between appraiser and appraisee exchanges can be based on what has actually happened instead of on value judgements. A practical account of the development and use of BARS is in Fogli *et al.* (1971). One development of the method departs from the use of behaviours specific to a job and uses ten standard dimensions: interpersonal relationships, organising and planning, reaction to problems, reliability, communicating, adaptability, growth, productivity, quality of work, and teaching (Goodale and Burke, 1975). This is not a simple reversion to rating, but a move in that direction with the discipline of critical incidents and rating scales.

4. CONDUCT OF THE APPRAISAL AND ACCESS TO THE OUTCOMES

Appraisals are usually carried out by managers about their immediate subordinates, but there are other possibilities. Appraisal could be done by *a group of superiors,* as is the practice in some parts of the Civil Service. It depersonalises the process, reduces the likelihood of bias and maintains the easy working relationship between the appraisee and the immediate superior ("... I did the best I could, old man, but X swayed the meeting that afternoon ..."). There may also be more information available about the performance.

Peer rating is a very rare practice and requires a high degree of trust and integration in the social group. *Rating by subordinates* is very logical but very rare, although it is often used informally as part of the appraisal process ("... one or two of the people in the Department have mentioned to me in passing — no names: no pack drill — that you can be a bit heavy-handed sometimes with the younger ones ...").

An example of formal rating by subordinates that we found was in a research department of a large chemical company. The graduate researchers reported on their section manager's annual assessment form about such matters as generation of ideas, resourcing of development work and encouragement of work. These comments were seen by the section manager's superior.

Outsiders can be used either by inviting in someone from outside the organisation completely as an unbiased third party, or by using an internal specialist without departmental affiliation, such as a management development advisor, who appraises everyone. There are obvious snags about this as the appraiser can only have limited knowledge about what performance has been achieved, and will therefore have to base his appraisal either on some form of personality trait assessment or on the grievances of the people appraised, or on both. He is not able to do anything other than report, and it is a report that is often not acted upon. It is the sort of strategy that could be used as a single event in an organisation where there had been serious dissatisfaction and there was a need to review the career situation with all individuals in a particular cadre as a preliminary to reorganisation or similar initiative. It is not common as a regular event, although the development of *assessment centres* (see Stewart and Stewart, 1981) is a specialised method of taking the whole process of career development out of the line.

A frequent addition to the usual appraisal of the immediate superior is a process of vetting or clearing the appraisal, which is passed to a more senior manager or notionally independent person before it is finalised. This helps to reduce inaccuracies and can help consistency, but it makes more difficult the involvement of the appraisee, and this is the most important feature of all appraisal schemes.

A closed system of appraisal is one where the appraisals are made and reported without the person appraised knowing what has been said. This removes some of the inhibitions which worry managers making appraisals, as they have not got to justify their comments to the person about whom they are made and do not jeopardise their comfortable working relationships. The obvious drawbacks are that those appraised are full of suspicion, possibly stooping to low tactics to ascertain the contents of their reports. More importantly, the person appraised is denied the advice that might improve the performance. This mode is now unusual, but disclosing the contents also has problems. It makes for "safe", bland appraisals or for simple avoidance — remember Jean Whitehorn. The approach can be to tell the appraisee what is said, to show him, or to discuss with him what the report should be and agree the wording with him.

What happens to the appraisals when they are complete? It is a pity if this is regarded as of overwhelming importance, as the most valuable aspect of the procedure is the process of appraisal itself. In that process the two people most concerned with the working performance — the performer and the person immediately responsible for the performance — think about, understand and review what has been happening. That can increase mutual understanding, help to set realistic future targets, develop ability, enhance motivation and meet most of the other payoffs that performance appraisal is supposed to deliver. The next destination of the report is still important for various reasons. Without a destination for the report, the report is less likely to be written and the appraisal unlikely to be carried out. Some organisations use appraisal for career progression organised from a central staffing section and in some there is a centralised training initiative where appraisal reports are used to suggest training and development strategies for employees.

5. APPRAISAL INTERVIEWING

So far the purpose of this chapter has been to work through the reasons why individual managers may decide to participate in a system of appraisal run in the organisation of which he is a part, together with an explanation of the appraisal techniques he may encounter and the operational problems. This final section deals with an aspect that is an integral part of most organisation-wide schemes, but which can also be used by managers individually when there is no scheme: appraisal interviewing.

This form of interview is not easy to conduct. Randell (1970) conducted a survey in a large pharmaceuticals company and found that managers had difficulty in interpreting the factors contributing to a person's overall performance, such as intelligence and life goals; they were not able to pursue these in interview and did not agree firm recommendations and actions towards improvement. Gill (1977) found that 67 per cent of her respondents regarded appraisal schemes as valueless unless accompanied by formal training in appraisal interviewing.

Norman Maier (1976) describes three alternative approaches that are used for this type of interview.

Tell and sell. The role of the interviewer is that of judge and he is using the interview to tell the appraisee the outcome of the appraisal and to persuade him of the need to improve. This method is seldom used in appraisals of managers but can be appropriate for appraisees who have high respect for the appraiser and are insufficiently experienced to have developed self-confidence and the capacity to analyse their own performance.

Tell and listen is a modification of tell and sell. The appraiser is still in the role of judge and he is passing on the outcome of an appraisal that has already been completed, but he then elicits the appraisee's reactions, including resentment and disappointment, and this may lead to a change in the evaluation as well as enabling the two to have a reasonably frank exchange.

Problem-solving. This is a quite different mode of interview. The focus is not the judgement of the appraiser but the growth and development of the person appraised, with the appraiser acting as helper rather than judge. The assumption is that discussing job problems leads to improved performance in that job, and the more skilful the appraiser, the greater the change and improvement that will take place. There is still the need for follow-up and there are problems if the appraisee lacks ideas or if his ideas do not fit in with what the appraiser regards as appropriate. It is important not to be over-optimistic about problem-solving, which sounds ideal. The appraiser will normally be in a hierarchically superior position to the appraisee and this could inhibit the type of candid exchanges that this style of interviewing requires. Also it requires the appraisee to be reasonably confident, secure and knowledgeable about possibilities. If all circumstances are favourable, it is the most appropriate for the appraisal of managers and an outline is given in an appendix to this chapter.

6.   PERFORMANCE APPRAISAL AND THE MANAGER

As an organisation-wide administrative system, performance appraisal has a bad name because of its extensive documentation, the time it takes and the way in which the system is seen to rule the participants. Despite the difficulties, the potential advantages are so great that attempts will continue to improve schemes and make them work. The individual manager can run his own, do-it-yourself appraisals of his team members if there is no over-

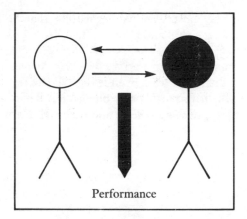

Figure 16.3   Performance Appraisal and the Manager

arching scheme in which to participate. He will centre it on a form of the appraisal interview, but there will still be a need for preparation, the development of interviewing skill, some record of what has happened and what is to be done, and a willingness to cope with some unwelcome or problematical outcomes. Appraisal interviews of the problem-solving kind are almost certain to produce some improvement, but appraisal of any sort only becomes really worthwhile when it is established and regular, so that those involved see it as a necessary part of their contract with the organisation.

SUMMARY PROPOSITIONS

16.1.   Performance appraisal is used in working situations where the achievement of satisfactory performance is not obvious from the nature of the task, and it is the process of judging a person's performance and reporting that judgement.

16.2.   Schemes of organisation-wide performance appraisal frequently break down in practice because appraisers dislike the discipline and the amount of work involved, and because appraisees may be apprehensive about the outcome.

16.3.   The most widely used schemes of appraisal now in use are those where the appraisal is related to results achieved. Methods incorporating an element of self-rating by the appraisee are gaining popularity.

16.4.   Interviewing is a central feature of appraisal and the problem-solving approach is the most effective, providing that both appraiser and appraisee have the skill and ability to handle this mode.

16.5. Individual managers can carry out performance appraisal among members of their own team even if there is not an organisation-wide scheme in which to participate, but lasting benefits will only come from making appraisals a regular and thorough feature of the working relationship.

APPENDIX A

Interaction guide for the appraisal interview

I   Before the Interview

Brief   Appraisee on purpose and form of interview, possibly asking him to complete a self-analysis questionnaire in readiness.

Review   Reports, records or other sources of memory-jogging regarding appraisee performance in the period under review.

Check   Previous appraisal and outcomes.

II   During the Interview

Begin with   a.   Rapport, to calm down the appraisee (and the appraiser) who may be nervous due to the significance of the interview.

               b.   Explain how interview is to be run, reiterating points made in pre-interview briefing.

Review   Main facts about performance, without expressing opinion about the facts, but merely summarising as mutual reminder.

Encourage   Single out aspects of performance that are clearly satisfactory, mention them and comment favourably.

Ask for   a.   Statement from appraisee about queries or problems he has experienced.

               b.   Statement from appraisee about any dissatisfactions he has with his own performance.

               (Talk these out fully with appraisee, adding the appraiser's perspective and opinion *on those points*. Some will be talked out as baseless, some will be seen as less drastic than they first seemed, and some will be confirmed as problems needing attention.)

Offer   Comments from appraiser about aspects of performance that he does not regard as satisfactory, but which have not already been mentioned.

Agree   Action to be taken — by appraiser and appraisee — to improve future performance and satisfaction.

III After the interview

Record   Problems and agreed action.
Take action   On points requiring appraiser action.
File   Interview notes for later review.

APPENDIX B

Drill for management by objectives

Pro-forma work sheet for setting and reviewing objectives

Prepared by ....(appraiser)................ and ....(appraisee)............						
Date of objective-setting .... Date of review						
Job Objectives	*Per Cent of Work Time*	*Measure of Results*	*Target*	*Date*	*Results*	*Date*

REFERENCES

Drucker P. F., *The Practice of Management*, Heinemann, London, 1955.

Fogli L., Hulin C.L., Blood M.R., "Development of First-level Behavioural Job Criteria" in *Journal of Applied Psychology*, Vol. 55, 1971, pp. 3–8.

Gill D., *Performance Appraisal in Perspective*, Institute of Personnel Management, London, 1973.

Gill D., *Appraising Performance*, Institute of Personnel Management, London, 1977.

Glueck W.F., *Foundations of Personnel*, Business Publications, Dallas, Texas, 1979.

Goodale J. and Burke R., "BARS Need Not be Job Specific" in *Journal of Applied Psychology*, Vol. 60, No. 3, 1975, pp. 389–91.

MacGregor D., "An Uneasy Look at Performance Appraisal", in *Harvard Business Review*, 1972.

Maier N.R.F., *The Appraisal Interview: Three Basic Approaches*, University Associates, La Jolla, California, 1976.

Randall G.A., Packard P.M.A., Shaw R.L., Slater A. J., *Staff Appraisal*, Institute of Personnel Management, London, 1972.

Robbins S.P., *Personnel: The Management of Human Resources*, Prentice-Hall Inc., Englewood Cliffs, New Jersey, 1978.

Stewart A. and Stewart V., *Tomorrow's Managers Today*, 2nd edition, Institute of Personnel Management, London, 1981.

Chapter Seventeen

THE DESIGN OF JOBS AND DEPARTMENTAL ORGANISATION

The two activities in the title of this chapter are fundamental to the process of management, yet they are not often undertaken deliberately. It is more common for jobs to develop or to be brought into being as a response to some aspect of organisational change, than it is for jobs to be designed in the sense of being thought out. It is more common for people to be grouped together in a rough-and-ready form of departmental structure than it is for departmental organisation to be thought out to find the best method.

The job of sales assistant in a department store, for instance, has certain characteristics that are dominant because of the demands of customer service and which override any possibility of designing the job in the way most satisfactory to the employee or most efficient in departmental co-ordination and organisation. With many jobs the operating context dictates the main job characteristics and job design can seldom do more than modify existing practice.

Departments in companies usually come into existence as a result of company expansion. At one stage there will be one or two safety officers in a company, each attached to a factory and reporting to the production manager. When there are eight or nine safety officers, they are likely to be grouped together with a safety manager in charge. The method of working in this new alignment will evolve gradually, probably following the forming-storming-norming-performing pattern that was mentioned in Chapter 14, so that initiatives in organising the members of the department will come in stages rather than being worked out in detail before operations begin.

This chapter contains material on both the design of jobs and the design of departmental organisation, but our opening comment is that most managers will find few opportunities for approaching either task from scratch. Redesign is a much more common activity than design.

1. THE NATURE OF JOB DESIGN

Job design is the process of putting together a range of tasks, duties and responsibilities to create a composite for an individual to undertake in his work and regard as his own. Some of the job dimensions begin with the reasons for people to be employed in a particular organisation. This can be illustrated by using the example of employees in a department store that was used earlier.

Shop assistants are employed for *product market* reasons. The customer expects some type of sales service, ranging from detailed advice and technical explanation to simple cash-and-wrap operations. This is why shop assistants have to be on view, standing, identifiable and willing to respond to customers' requirements. The *technology* of the product requires cosmetic saleswomen to wear what they sell and for those selling popular records and tapes to be able to tolerate sustained high-volume noise. Others are employed for *administrative* reasons and the administrative structure will be the main influence on their jobs, so that wages clerks spend most of their time sitting and doing solo manipulations with figures while buyers spend most of their time not buying at all but filling in forms to get the right balance between materials bought and materials sold.

Others are employed for *social system* reasons and a particular aspect of the social system determines the main dimensions of their jobs. The fire officer wears a special uniform so that people will respond in times of emergency. Catering staff have to fit in with a grossly inefficient timescale for their operations: intense activity around teabreaks and lunchtime.

Part of the management process is to mediate operational constraints and requirements like these in dividing work up between members of the organisation, so that there are a number of composites — or jobs — that employees will be motivated to undertake and are combined in such a way as to produce satisfactory working performance in the co-ordinated effort of the department and the organisation.

Much of the recent interest in job design has centred round attempts to improve employee satisfaction with the working situation. It is inappropriate however, to regard this type of initiative as only suitable for mass production jobs. Administrative and managerial jobs, especially in large organisations, can be crying out for job design initiatives. Creating opportunities for senior managers can all too often involve limiting the scope of middle and junior managers to such an extent that the initiatives of their seniors are jeopardised. An American study was carried out among forty large organisations that were chosen because they made particular efforts to use their managers effectively, yet:

> management in the typical organization was characterized by having rather narrow jobs and very tightly written job descriptions that almost seemed designed to take the newness, conflict and challenge out of the job

(Campbell et al. 1970)

Review Topic 17.1

(a) Reproduce the following elementary matrix on a piece of paper:

Job	Product Market Reasons	Technology Reasons	Administrative Reasons	Social System Reason
Film actor				
Fireman				
Nurse				
Teacher				
....				
....				

(b) Write in a job dimension in each column against each of the printed jobs and then add in three or four more jobs with which you are familiar, with the dimensions.

(c) Are there any of those job dimensions that could be altered to make the job more efficient *and* more satisfying?

Job design sets the individual to work and organisation design sets that work in a departmental, co-ordinated setting.

2. FACTORS IN JOB DESIGN

John Child (1977) points to three key aspects of the ways in which jobs can be shaped: specialisation, definition and discretion.

Specialisation. The extent to which a job is clearly identified and different from others, so that there is a clear justification for a person doing it, due to his skill, experience or some other distinguishing factor. The reason for this is obviously that it enables the greatest degree of expertise to be developed. The teacher who concentrates on teaching French, rather than on teaching French, Physics and Woodwork is likely to become more skilled at teaching French because of the specialised development that is then possible. But how specialised should a role be? If the French teacher were also to teach German or Latin, would that enable the development of complementary skills and understanding to produce a generally higher quality of work?

Specialisation develops expertise and expertise produces authority and autonomy, so that the right degree of specialisation enables the job holder to "own" his skills and knowledge in a way he is likely to find satisfying, but if jobs are made too narrow there is the risk of the problem identified by

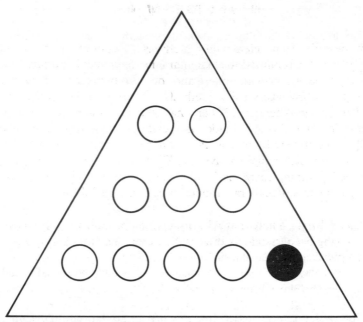

The individual job to which the employee has been 'fitted' may be
redesigned as activities are co-ordinated with those of other job holders.

Figure 17.1   The Design of Jobs and Departmental Organisation

Campbell and his colleagues that we have just seen. Specialisation is not
always based on skill, sometimes it is a simple administrative division of
duties. Child illustrates this most effectively by contrasting the practice in
two companies:

> In one organization... "Peter Jones from Quality or one of his team, and
> a chap from Engineering — quite often Phil Bond or Jim Dankworth
> usually get together on that one. They will sort it out, and call in anyone
> else, as they think best." In another organization, you might be referred
> to page 23 of the procedures manual where it states that "customer
> complaints are the responsibility of the Assistant Quality Control
> Manager — Warranty and Complaints." This man, you are told, "has a
> job description which lays down quite specifically the way he should deal
> with a complaint, including the maximum amount of expenditure he can
> incur. Should he wish to spend more, or involve anyone from another
> Department, he must first refer to the Quality Control Manager."
>
> (Child, 1977, pp. 26–7)

The first of those two organisations emphasises skill rather than
position and responsibility, with the specialisation not being too precise. It
appears more civilised and constructive as a way of running a business, as
long as one is looking at it from inside, where individuals can be deployed
and appreciated as individuals. Once the interface with the outside world

becomes important, then the emphasis on role becomes more logical. The customer telephoning from Land's End to John o'Groats with an urgent complaint would probably begin to foam at the mouth if he were told about Peter Jones and Phil Bond or Jim Dankworth.

Definition. The degree to which job boundaries are clearly marked. This is the area of job descriptions, procedures and drills, which have already been discussed in earlier chapters of this book. There will always be a degree of such definition, the managerial problem is again to decide how much. The process of definition has the great merit that the manager has to work out exactly what is required, how it can be done and what the contribution of each team member can be. Ambiguity is lessened and the mission of the individual becomes clearer. Organisational practices can be made identical so that swapping people about is easier.

The overwhelming danger of precise definition is its lack of flexibility and the risk that job holders regard the definitions as challenges to be defied rather than as guidelines for effectiveness. However precise or imprecise the definition the objective should be to define jobs in a way which makes them "whole", so that the scope is sufficient for job holders to see assignments through to a completion. They can seldom do all that they would like, but the work needs to have both the variety and integration for it to be a coherent, satisfactory whole. This was the direction of many of the job enlargement initiatives that became popular in the early 1970s. The satisfaction of seeing something through is not limited to the job holder; there is a greater satisfaction for the client, whether he be inside the organisation or outside. Most people have experienced the frustration of being a client in a large, bureaucratic system, like a hospital or an insurance company, where the client feels as if he is clinging by his fingertips to the side of the organisational machine as it grinds through its cycle. Individuals to whom he speaks can always answer only some of his questions and deal with only some of his requirements before he is passed on to someone else.

In considering job boundaries, the manager needs to think in terms of whole jobs, with a logic and coherence that meets the needs of clients as well as the needs of job holders. The manager must also think in terms of what he wants to have done, but here it helps if he can think of what Kellogg (1968) has called "long term missions", as these will give a sense of purpose and responsibility that is more complete than that of dealing only with the immediate, and it describes the duties of the job holder in a way that produces a clear contribution to organisational affairs.

Discretion. The degree of autonomy that the job holder enjoys. We saw in Chapter 15 that effective leadership requires the autonomy of the led, but again the vexing question is to decide how much discretion job holders should have. Discretion leads to responsibility and thoroughness as the blame for mistakes can less easily be transferred elsewhere. The job enrichment initiatives that have been widely documented (e.g., Wild, 1975) have the deepening of discretion at the heart of the strategy for "enriching" manual jobs.

Although specialisation, definition and discretion are the main issues in job design, there are one or two common sense points to add. Where people are employed at the same status in an organisation, doing jobs that are interdependent, it is sensible for them to be of roughly equal complexity, with critical matters also distributed between all posts. It is always useful to look for a combination of duties that fit the logic of the situation rather than a random collection. Some combinations are obvious, like one person doing all that is involved in servicing a motor car, but others are less clear. Consider your experience in eating out at a restaurant. Taking your order, serving your meal and taking your payment are three separate activities; you will have visited restaurants where they are all done by one person and others where they are divided between two, three or more people. It is difficult to say which is the most effective. Finally a manager has to take care that he does not specify a job dimension that is merely a reflection of his own personal style rather than something that is necessary for effective performance.

3.   THE NATURE OF DEPARTMENTAL ORGANISATION

Companywide organisation structures and processes, of the sort we considered in Chapter 3, provide an overall framework and philosophy for the integration of all the jobs in the undertaking. Between that and the ways in which individuals and small groups perform their everyday tasks lies the process of departmental organisation.

> "Department" designates a distinct area, division, or branch of an enterprise over which a manager has authority for the performance of specified activities.
>
> (Koontz et al. 1980, p. 334)

This is an aspect of organisational practice that has received little attention recently. Companywide organisation has been much studied and has been the focus of debates about industrial democracy, employee participation and rationalisation in the face of recession. In industrial relations the interest is always in getting to the top, speaking to "the decision-makers". In the analysis of company performance, profitability, merger and acquisition there is similarly a focus of interest in overall performance, with the assumption that a Rupert Murdoch, a Michael Edwardes or an Ian McGregor will produce a miraculous change single-handedly through the overall strategy that is pursued.

There is a different sort of close interest in the individual: the man on the shop floor, the apprentice, the trainee, the executive. We have a plethora of advice on how such people should be recruited, selected, trained, paid, developed, appraised, counselled and given enlarged or enriched jobs.

The importance of both these areas is obvious, but sometimes departmental organisation can be more important, even though it is a concept that fails to fire the imagination. It lacks the fascination of the power play of the boardroom and the attraction of the individual with his humble hopes and fears, yet the individual employee often finds his greatest frustration in minor aspects of departmental affairs and grand new company strategies can founder through inadequate co-ordination of individual activities, usually euphemised as "communication problems" or "the human factor".

The lack of interest in departmental organisation was demonstrated in an extensive review of research and organisational design by Kilman and his colleagues in 1976, when they found that the process of organising activities in a department was usually intuitive rather than analytical and was likely to express the personality and whims of the "designer". They also found that when the pattern of organisation had been designed it was put into operation in a relatively rigid way, allowing little flexibility in practice.

Review Topic 17.2

Think of some departments you know and categorise them as having their basis in function, territory, product or time period.

The basis for grouping or clustering activities can be one of several. Most common is *function*, like the safety officers mentioned earlier, who were grouped together because of that specialised interest and identity. Grouping on a basis of *territory* is logical when activities are dispersed, so that a fire station is a unit within the fire service and a ship is a unit of organisation in a shipping company. We also see departments based on common interest in a *product* and others, like night shifts, based on a *time period*.

Although most departmental organisation may be intuitive rather than analytical, it is easy to establish a logical sequence, shown in Figure 17.2. First a purpose for a department is decided and tested against such questions as: "Is it really necessary?", "Is there a better way of achieving the same objectives?", "What will be the knock-on effects of this elsewhere in the undertaking?" Secondly, the activities necessary to achieve the purpose are identified. Thirdly, the activities are grouped together (job design) in ways that make up jobs that can and will be done. Fourthly, the necessary formal authority for individual job holders is attached to them, and, finally, the jobs are connected through information systems and lines of reporting.

This assumes the ideal situation of organising a department from scratch, but the sequence is still useful when trying to identify problems of organisation in a long-standing department.

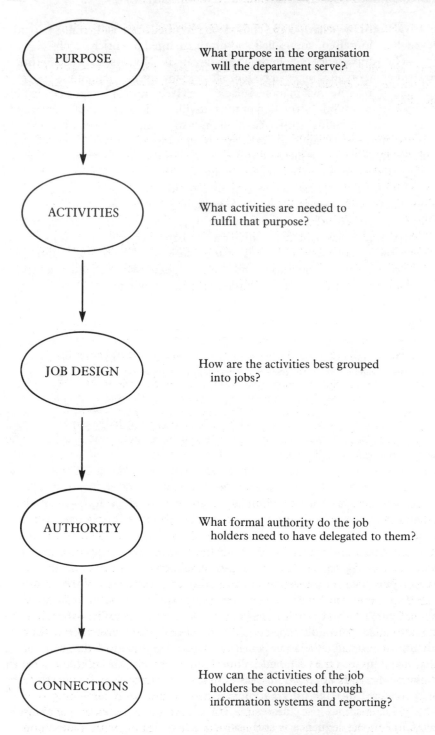

Figure 17.2   Five Steps in Departmental Organisation

4. THE NUTS AND BOLTS OF DEPARTMENTAL ORGANISATION

We can now consider in more detail four of the steps described in Figure 17.2 (the third step — job design — has already been dealt with at the beginning of the chapter).

Purpose. The purpose of creating a department may be a basic organisational objective, such as production, or sales, or maintenance, or it may be a purpose of hoping to make things run more smoothly. Much organisational tinkering is of the second rather than the first type: the creation of a new department for organisational rather than business objectives. The regrouping of safety officers, mentioned earlier, is such an example. Another very common creation has been the establishment of a systems department to intercede between the people in the organisation and the electronic monsters that process data. Those who understand the electronic gadgetry are grouped together because of a skill they have in common.

> The search for a basis of classifying activities that leads to the association of those which are similar eventually brings organizers to the skills of people. At first, they may be persuaded that the important element is the object to which labor is applied. But that which results from labor depends on the skills applied to it. After determining what needs to be done and what skills are required, the organizer can then group them under such heads as typing, chemical analysis, process engineering and accounting. In this way, people who perform similar activities can be grouped in one department, and the advantages of occupational specialization can be realized.
>
> (Koontz *et al.* 1980, p. 387–8)

There is always a countervailing argument against the grouping of skills together and in favour of their dispersion. Matrix patterns of organisation go part way towards this dispersion. Once a skill based department is established there are the risks of separation, aloofness and problems of communication. All the while that the personnel department has one or two of its members who are interested in computing and spend part of their time introducing computer based systems for the personnel function, they are personnel people working with computers. Once such specialists are taken into a systems department and merged with other systems specialists, they become systems people, the personnel department is bereft of that type of expertise and there is the risk that the developing systems will fall into disuse or that new methods developed by the systems department will be not quite what is required. Setting up a new department to deal with something that senior managers do not understand (like computers or new pensions legislation) or something they find unattractive (like dealing with trade union negotiations) may give them an easier time in the short term, but there will be headaches in the long term if there is not a well thought-out organisational purpose.

An alternative to organisation on the basis of skills in common is to group people in departments on the basis of frequent contact. The obvious example is the grouping of typists. If they are all together in a secretarial services department there are the benefits of flexibility, shared facilities — from dictionaries to duplicating machines — specialised supervision and general economies of scale. On the other hand, if they are located individually with the people for whom they type, there are the advantages of easy access for receiving what has to be typed, a wider range of duties etc.

Creating a new department always brings problems as other departments either resent losing some part of their role or eagerly off-load chores they have been trying to get rid of for years. There are also problems of more communication, more memoranda, more meetings and so on, so any such decision must answer the questions about whether there is a better way and what the knock-on effects will be.

Identification. Identifying the activities to meet the purpose is largely straightforward when the purpose is to bring together those who have a skill in common, although there will follow arguments about how many typists, errand boys and tea ladies are required.

Organising on the basis of frequent contact can be more difficult as the criteria are less precise, members of staff to be drafted in to the new department may wonder whether such a move is in their best interests or whether it represents a veiled demotion, and other managers will be resistant to losing their star team members and over-co-operative in offering the services of people they do not like.

Simon Petch was the son of the Chairman of a small printing company that was expanding quickly. He had just joined the company after university and a period of working experience in a larger organisation. He was put in charge of a newly created Marketing Department, to deal with marketing, sales promotion and advertising, although his father would continue to handle sales through agents and two company representatives. Those joining the new department had mixed feelings. Some welcomed the opportunity to be part of a new departure with fresh ideas and working with the man "who would be chairman one day", while others felt that they were being moved sideways and that their careers and livelihoods were being jeopardised by being used as a training ground for a tyro. The Chairman was about to see those who were uncertain and tell them that they would have to do as they were told, but Simon dissuaded him and offered to take a much smaller initial role, dealing only with marketing and leaving sales promotion and advertising to his father. Also he would start by having only two members of staff, both of whom were particularly interested in marketing and keen to work with him. He was very successful and his success brought him onto a number of informal communications networks that had previously been closed to him. Progressively he assumed control of advertising, sales promotion and then all sales, so that within two years he had a "department" of people readily working with him and smoothly co-ordinated.

Authority. Allocating authority in departmental organisation is the process of enabling an employee to trigger other processes in the organisation by delegating to him authority to act, so that others recognise him as being authorised to act. One familiar method is the job description and its definition of boundaries, but other methods can be simpler and more effective in some circumstances. Being authorised to sign documents is one way of giving power to subordinates. If material cannot be issued from stores until Mr Jones has initialled the docket, then Mr Jones is clearly and effectively given that authority. Knowledge of computer codes, possession of keys to the safe are similar allocations of authority and not to be confused with status symbols, like having a key to the executive washroom.

Communication. The department organisation is finally made to work by the means of communication between the members. Standard methods are multiple copies of memoranda, meetings and departmental drills specifying the routeing of paperwork or other material undergoing transformation. Less obvious is office landscaping, considering how closely people should work together and who should be next to whom. Those who are constantly swapping items between them, who share a skill and need regular interaction should probably sit together. A set of records to which four different people regularly refer should logically be equally accessible to each of them. There are many ways in which the layout of the working positions of people can aid the communication between them, but this is always limited by the social needs and expectations of employees. Very few people indeed really need an office to themselves and the private office is an impediment to communication, yet the interest in privacy and status is such that many people regard it as a basic requirement.

We can conclude this chapter with an example of the informal integration of a department that is so vital in any department. The pensions department of a large multinational business at one time had to send out 3,500 letters and the particulars on each letter had to be checked. It was not only a very boring job, but also one that took a lot of time. Often such work is "delegated" to the most humble member of the department, who takes too long to do it, makes mistakes, produces complaints and everybody gets cross. In this company all members of the department did it, working in the last half hour of the working day. It was completed in a week, so that the task was completed quickly. It was also done thoroughly and the members of the department were integrated not only socially through sharing a single task but also all of them thoroughly understood the letter and its implications, so that they were all able to deal with queries that came from recipients of the letter.

The sequence of main activities involved for managers in working with their teams.

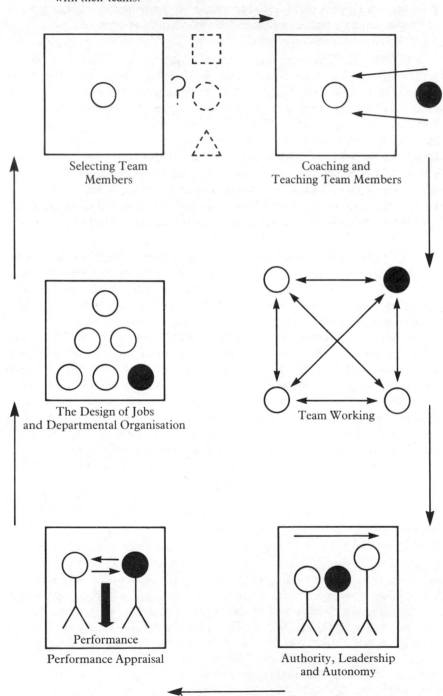

Selecting Team
Members

Coaching and
Teaching Team Members

The Design of Jobs
and Departmental Organisation

Team Working

Performance Appraisal

Authority, Leadership
and Autonomy

Figure 17.3   The Working Team

Review Topic 17.3

Recalling the material in Chapters 3 and 11, to what extent is the design of departments, jobs and procedures all part of the organisational design? Can an individual manager design his own, or do they all have to comply with overall designs?

SUMMARY PROPOSITIONS

17.1. There is more scope for redesigning jobs than for designing them; and more scope for modifying the organisation of departments than for setting up a complete department from scratch.

17.2. The three key aspects of job design are specialisation to ensure scope for expertise, definition to make clear the boundaries between jobs, and discretion to give job holders autonomy.

17.3. The most common bases for clustering activities to create departments are according to a functional role that job holders share, a territory where people are grouped, a common interest in a product, or the fact that a set of people come together to work at a particular time of day — like a shift.

17.4. The five steps in departmental organisation are deciding the purpose of the department, identifying the activities to achieve the purpose, grouping the activities into jobs to be done, attaching necessary authority to job holders, and connecting jobs together through lines of reporting and communication.

REFERENCES

Campbell J.P., Dunnette M.D., Lawler E.E. and Weick K.E., *Managerial Behaviour, Performance and Effectiveness,* McGraw Hill, New York, 1970.

Child J., *Organization,* Harper and Row, London, 1977.

Kellogg M.S., *Putting Management Theories to Work,* Gulf Publications, Houston, Texas, 1968.

Kilman R.H., Pondy L.R., Slevin D.P. (eds.), *The Management of Organization Development,* North Holland, New York, 1976.

Koontz H., O'Donnell C., Weihrich H., *Management,* 7th ed. McGraw-Hill, Kogakusha, Tokyo, 1980.

Wild R., *Work Organization,* John Wiley, London, 1975.

Part IV

PLANNING, DECISION-MAKING AND CONTROL

If a manager is to lead his working team, he must know where he is heading, so that he is constantly thinking ahead to the future and trying to determine what will happen as well as being ready to respond to future developments when they occur.

Planning requires the careful examination of various possibilities and the anticipation of events by weighing and deciding between alternatives. The process of decision-making is almost the same, although it follows after the plan has been decided and the implications are calculated. Budgets provide the financial facilitation — and the financial discipline — within which the plans proceed, and all of the activities rely on records of what has happened, so that future budgets can be based on realistic figures, so that plans have a factual basis for their development and decisions have evidence to support them and indicators for the decision process.

The "control cube" in Figure 20.4 shows the interdependence of planning, decision-making, budgets and record-keeping.

Chapter Eighteen

PLANNING

Planning is a management activity much lauded in principle, but not extensively used in practice. It is so obvious that managers should work with detailed schemes for attaining their objectives, that we need to see why what managers actually do sometimes falls short of this ideal.

An American on a package tour of Europe is once alleged to have said "If it is Tuesday, this must be Amsterdam," implying that his tour was dominated by the schedule rather than what he was visiting. Managers tend to have that sort of feeling about plans, especially when they are prepared by someone else. There is always the risk that adhering to the plan becomes the dominant activity, rather than satisfying customers, producing goods or some other more important objective. A similar worry is about the degree of planning. If there is too much planning, the manager feels hemmed in, lacking scope to use initiative and express individuality, with the status of the managerial role depressed. This is particularly when the plans are the creation of a planning group or a superior who has not consulted, but simply "handed down" the plan. Perhaps the main difficulty about plans is when they go wrong. If you have put your trust in a scheme which runs into difficulty there is a danger that action is paralysed because actions that are *unplanned* are *not legitimate*. Faced with a situation where things do not go "according to plan" some managers carry on, while their colleagues lose confidence and plot betrayal. If they are proved right by subsequent events they are heroes; if not, the knives are sharpened. Other managers do not carry on when faced with the unexpected, they adjust their strategy against a background of complaints about panicking and not allowing time for plans to work.

Against those reservations are the unassailable arguments that if one does not prepare for the future, it may not happen. Without planning one is reactive rather than proactive, and many opportunities are lost. We all seem to hanker after the secure framework that planned activity produces; but, to repeat a metaphor already used, it must be a framework and not a straitjacket.

1.   THE PLANNING APPROACH

Planning involves decision-making, but is distinct from it in the extent to which an unknown future is involved. From an operational point of view there is great similarity between plans and procedures. A procedure is a plan of action that is a standardised method of dealing with matters as they occur so that decisions do not have to be constantly worked out from first principles as the solutions to problems and the answers to questions are largely predetermined. Planning is an attempt to bring under control the variables of a future scenario that will probably only happen once. If repeated, the variables will be sufficiently different for the planned guidelines to be rethought, even though some elements will remain unchanged.

Strategic planning is the term used to describe the broad and long-range plans of an enterprise:

> 'Strategic planning is the process of selecting an organization's goals; determining the policies and strategic programs necessary to assure that the policies and strategic programs are implemented.'
>
> (Stoner, 1982, p. 101)

This is a top management activity, often undertaken with the assistance of aides who analyse large quantities of data in order to prepare the outline of possibilities for further analysis, discussion and judgement. This activity, sometimes known as corporate planning, deals with fundamental issues like the nature of the business and considers a relatively long time period in the future. Even if the answers are not right, the activity itself gives coherence to all other organisational activities and should provide a momentum and sense of direction for all organisation members.

Within that structure there is *operational planning*, which is putting into practice what strategic planning dictates or requires. The difference here is not simply one of hierarchical level, it is also a different activity. Drucker (1981, p. 44) has distinguished between efficiency ("doing things right") and effectiveness ("doing the right things"). Strategic planning is doing the right things; operational planning is doing things right. In 1980 there was a group of American hostages held in the United States Embassy in Tehran. Despite intense diplomatic pressure the Iranian authorities refused to release them so the American President, Jimmy Carter, took the advice of his staff and decided on a rescue mission. President Carter had to make the stragetic plan. What was the right thing to do? Who should be consulted? Who should be advised? What would be the risks? and so forth. Naval, army and air force officers then made the operational plan of how the rescue would be conducted, using aircraft, helicopters and marines. The factors to be weighed and assessed in the two planning processes were quite different, but they were interdependent. The operational plan failed dismally, leaving eight American servicemen dead amid a tangle of twisted metal and blazing equipment in the Iranian desert. There had been no rehearsal of the operation; lack of adequate arrangements about the command of the mission caused problems under pressure; pilots had not been briefed about the weather conditions; the possibilities of mechanical breakdown had not been fully calculated and the desert rendezvous had been badly chosen. That operational disaster had grave implications for the strategic planner, as well as wrecking the strategic plan. The hostages almost certainly remained in custody for longer than would otherwise have been necessary, international opinion was for some time less supportive of the American position and the President was blamed for the humiliation by an infuriated people.

With the growing complexity of the social and economic environment and the rate of technological advance, interest in strategic planning has increased and it has become a more common style for top managers to adopt. The ever-fertile brain of Henry Mintzberg (1973) has described three ways of top management operation:

The entrepreneurial mode. When an organisation is directed by a single strong leader, making decisions based on judgement, personal experience and flair and with the aim of constant growth.

The adaptive mode. The process of reacting to each situation as it arises, making erratic progress and operating defensively to moves by competitors.

The planning mode. This involves a systematic procedure, analysing the environment and the organisation to develop a plan for the future.

Because of its complexity and specialised nature strategic planning needs comprehensive treatment. We are therefore not dealing with it any further in this book. Readers looking for suitable reading on the topic are advised to look at Ansoff (1970), Chandler (1962) or Argenti (1976).

We now move to consider operational planning, the process of making plans to do things right, as this is potentially part of the job of everyone at work, especially middle managers:

> Middle management breaks down the big decisions into meaningful parts for divisions, departments and units. The plans developed by middle managers include policies, procedures, rules, intermediate-level budgets, and organizational changes.
>
> (Glueck, 1979 p. 177)

2. OPERATIONAL PLANNING

There are four logical, simple steps in operational planning.

Goals. What are you trying to do? What objectives are you trying to reach? What are the priorities? Without asking and answering this type of basic question there is a danger of trying to achieve too much and of uncertainty in execution. It is only if goals are brought into reasonable focus that managers can deploy resources effectively. This is particularly important where resources are scarce or time is short.

Sally Ann Nield was a social worker having great difficulty in coping with her workload, so that there were many complaints and she was suffering considerable strain. Her section leader asked her to sort out her priorities so that she could clear some of the backlog. Sally Ann could not acknowledge that any one activity took preference over any other. She was not willing to concentrate on the preparation of social enquiry reports for a day if that meant deferring something else. As a result her affairs became even more muddled and she eventually left the career for which she had trained.

Review Topic 18.1

(a) How would you have persuaded Sally Ann Nield to take advantage of a planning approach to her work?
(b) Think of a friend or colleague of your own, similar to Sally Ann. How would you get them to make use of planning?

The present position. How far are you now from reaching the goals you have identified? What resources are available? This definition of the starting position and state of readiness begins to eliminate those features of operations that are not a problem and to direct attention to those areas where action is needed.

Aids and Hindrances. What factors can help to achieve the goals and what might cause problems? This is scanning the future to see what is likely to change the present position for better or worse. When General Eisenhower was planning the D-Day landings in the Second World War, a crucial factor was the weather. He and his advisors had the most detailed and comprehensive weather reports they could obtain, but so did the Germans. The significance of judgement (and perhaps of luck) in the implementation of plans was shown by the fact that both sides knew the weather was expected to remain clear, but not for long. General Eisenhower decided that the landings must therefore proceed before the weather broke. His counterpart on the other side of the Channel, Field Marshal von Rundstedt decided that the allied landings would be postponed until the weather improved.

The plan. The final step is to work out alternative series or programmes of action and eventually choose the one that seems most appropriate as a way of reaching the objective, taking account of the opening situation and the way in which the future is expected to develop. This activity often has contributory elements for verification, like test marketing, design prototypes, computer simulations and other ways of trying out the plan to test the likelihood of it being successful.

3. AIDS TO PLANNING

We now describe some elementary methods of improving the quality of plans. The chapter is limited to elementary methods mainly because they are the only type the authors can understand, but also because we have found so few examples of managers using methods that are even as sophisticated as those we are going to describe. Where managers base their plans on forecasts and predictive data, this information is usually provided from elsewhere and is accepted uncritically by managers as if it had emerged from a black box, the contents of which remain a mystery. We have not found managers *using* sophisticated planning methods in the sense of determining and tinkering with the parameters of elaborate models of future possibilities.

Gantt Charts. These have been in use for much of the twentieth century, having been first devised by H.L. Gantt. A Gantt chart quite simply provides a plot of activities to be achieved over a period of time, but the visual display clarifies ways in which things can be speeded up and offers the opportunity of monitoring progress when the plan is put into operation. The method can be used to schedule all sorts of activities: jobs to be assigned to individual production employees, the routeing of freight and the use of machines being among the most common. The example in Figure 18.1 displays four items of information about two different employees in the same department:

- The number of units to be produced in the day.
- The number of units actually produced in the day.
- Cumulative actual production.
- Percentage of units planned for production actually produced daily.

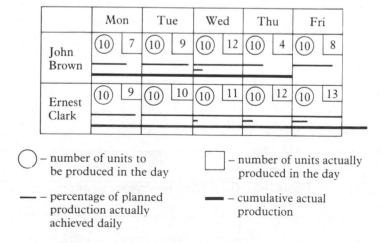

Figure 18.1   Simple Gantt Chart for Production Operations

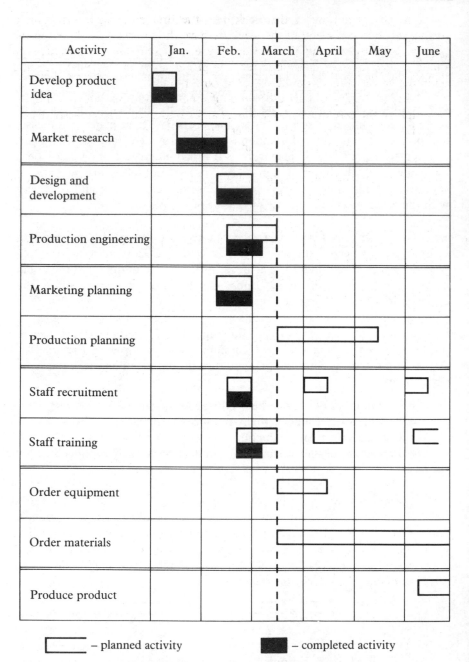

Figure 18.2   Gantt Chart for Product Launch

At the beginning of the week only the first piece of information is displayed, but at the end of the week we have the information shown in the figure. John Brown and Ernest Clark were both scheduled to produce ten units a day for five days, but the completed chart shows the daily and cumulative variations from this level of expectation.

Figure 18.2 is a chart used for a different application, which is a better example of the way in which planning can be improved. Eleven activities are listed, all of which have to be completed in the launch of a new product. First of all estimates are made of the time required for each one, four weeks for market research, eight weeks for production planning, and so on. When these activities and time estimates are displayed, there is the opportunity to see how the total time may be truncated. Starting with the assumption that each activity can begin only when a preceding activity has been completed, to trigger it, it is possible to review the starting dates for some of the activities.

It is decided, for example, that design and development can begin a week before market research is complete and that production engineering can begin very soon after the beginning of design and development. By charting the manager can juggle with the interdependence of the various activities and find ways in which time can be saved and completion dates brought forward. There is the same possibility with a range of management plans, where the degree of interdependence between sequential activities becomes clearer and overlapping can be used. The figure also has a vertical dotted line in the middle of March. This is the point to which the chart has been "made up", so that the manager can see that production engineering is a week behind schedule, as is staff training. Is this going to affect the implementation of later phases in the plan? Will production planning be able to begin or will it be delayed? Is the production engineering delay simply a question of being a week late, or is it a major setback that will not be overcome for another four or five weeks? How has the rest of the plan to be modified?

Although such a simple device, Gantt charting has an extensive range of applications, if used with imagination and if kept up to date. It is the most widely used planning aid we have encountered among the managers we have interviewed, although the majority have admitted that the chart is a discipline that they find irksome and often moves from the office wall to the desk drawer after a few weeks because "there are simply not enough hours in the day" to update the information constantly.

Network Planning. A development of the Gantt chart that is intended to emphasise the interrelationship of tasks in a way that Gantt charting cannot achieve. It is especially useful in complex operations where a number of activities can proceed simultaneously but which eventually have to come together. The most publicised form (which has already been mentioned in Chapter 6) was PERT or Program Evaluation and Review Technique that was devised to design the Polaris submarine weapon system in 1958. At the same time a similar method of CPM or Critical Path Method was developed at the DuPont Corporation, also in the United States (Gedye, 1965).

The basis of network planning is to find the chain of events that will determine the overall length of a project, so that particular attention can be given to that sequence, either to reduce it or to make sure it does not get any longer. This is the *critical path* through a network of events and activities. *Events* are milestones or the points at which a set of activities are complete and a following stage can begin. *Activities* are the tasks to be undertaken within a project and the time taken to move from one event to the next. In the building of a house, for example, an event would be the point at which all the brickwork was complete and an activity would be laying bricks before that event.

Review Topic 18.2

Produce a network plan of your activities between waking in the morning and setting out for work. Find the critical path through the network and then see if you can organise that time of your day more effectively.

When events and activities have been identified the planner obtains estimates of the time that each activity will take. This may be a simple guess, but is better done by a calculation that incorporates three estimates: first the most likely time, then a pessimistic forecast and thirdly an optimistic forecast. These three are weighted $4:1:1$ in order to arrive at the *expected time* for the activity. With this data the planner draws a network in which each event is preceded by all the activities that have to take place before the event can materialise. When the network has been drawn, it is possible to decide the critical path by seeing which sequence of events will take the longest. This is where managerial attention has to be focused (Schonberger, 1972).

Appendix A to this chapter sets out a drill for constructing and using networks and Figure 18.3 is a simple network of fifteen events, where the critical path is identified as A–B–C–G–J–M–N. These are the key events in the entire operation, where there is no slack and where deadlines have to be met if the whole project is not to be jeopardised.

In large projects there are other ways in which this technique can be used. Additional resources can be deployed to activities on the critical path and it may be possible to eliminate some activities, or to do them differently, if they are on the critical path but not essential to the overall exercise. Another possibility is that arrangements can be altered so that activities which are planned in sequence may in fact be done in parallel.

The connection with Polaris gave great publicity to this method of planning and it has the considerable merit that it forces planning to take place. There is, however, an overwhelming emphasis on time rather than cost and only recently have more elaborate systems been able to incorporate the cost element.

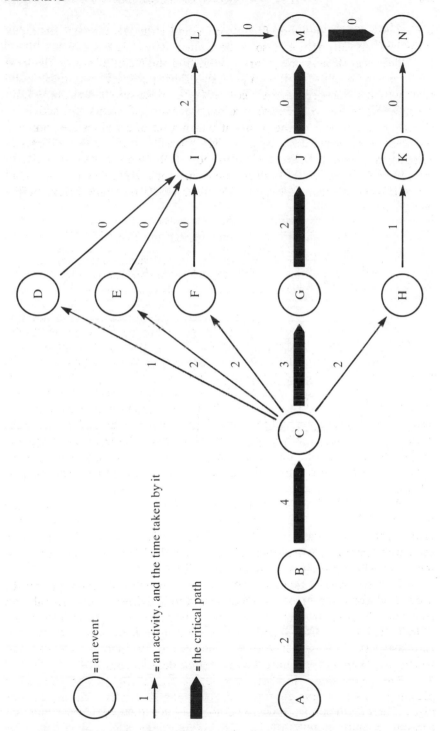

Figure 18.3   Sample of Critical Path Network Planning

Milestone Planning. A method that falls roughly between the Gantt chart and the network. Koontz *et al*. (1980, p. 777) trace a single line of development through the three. The method is quite simply to compile a bar chart of a series of activities, noting the completion date or milestone for each. This is a straightforward way of displaying target dates and showing the time remaining before the date arrives.

Linear Programming. One of the more widely used tools of operations research to decide how scarce resources should be allocated to keep costs at a minimum, or to maximise return. The method depends on the relationships in the problem being precisely proportional: linearity. Although a computer is usually used, a simple graphic method can be used if only two variables are involved. Alternatives include the simplex method, dual simplex method or the MODI method, described in Longenecker and Pringle (1981, pp. 157–60). In Appendix B to this chapter there is an example of the stages in the graphic method. Linear programming has been most used in production planning and transport logistics.

Time Series Analysis. The basic method of forecasting and devising assumptions on which to base plans. A trend line is drawn to reflect the smooth progression of a particular phenomenon into the future. The crudest method is to project a trend line on the basis of a moving average, where the average of, say, a twelve month period is calculated and then a further average of twelve months, dropping the first and adding the thirteenth. The next period is months three to fourteen, and so on. This is illustrated in Appendix C. More accurate methods are to fit a trend line to actual data, and to take account of such influences as seasonal and business cycle variations. The most familiar examples of time series figures are the monthly publications of data such as the retail price index and the employment figures.

Delphi Technique. This is a quite different method which uses a group of experts, each of whom has a different area of specialist expertise. Each is asked to make a forecast about a specific matter, quite independently of the other members of the panel but including reasons for their forecasts. The forecasts and reasons are collected and distributed to each expert, who then makes another individual prediction so that some convergence of the differing perspectives can be achieved. This is intended to make the most of varied expertise and viewpoints by first asking for forecasts that are not influenced by others and only later invoking the differing points of view as modifiers.

Goal Planning. To avoid the difficulty of splendid ideas being too difficult actually to put into practice, there is the simple device of goal planning, based on the assumption that a goal is more likely to be reached if the steps to achieve it are detailed, with target dates, and the goal itself clearly specified. It has many similarities with the method of management by objectives, except that the objectives are for oneself rather than for another, and the goal planning method is most likely to be used only for particular jobs that are difficult. One of the authors has used this method successfully in training staff in the education and health services (see McBrien, 1981). The method is first to specify the goal and then to list *strengths* and *needs* as they affect this goal. Strengths are features of the situation, or in the people involved, that will help in the goal being reached. Listing them is not only reassuring, it also identifies them in a way that is necessary to meet the needs. Needs become strengths once they are met. Some of the needs can be seen and met quite easily, but others are more intractable so the process of meeting them is broken down into smaller steps or subgoals, with methods to be used and dates for their achievement. In deciding the methods to be used the list of strengths is a source of ideas. Appendix D shows how the method is developed.

4. PLANNING AND THE MANAGER

Although managers appear frequently not to plan their activities, it is clear that some organisation of ideas and arrangements for the future are essential in the managerial role. The danger is of being seduced into seeking ever more accurate predictions of the future rather than getting on with the job in hand. The most elegant models and sophisticated statistics can become the purpose of the exercise rather than tools to be used in achieving one's purpose. The growing number of computer terminals and "executive work stations" that are to be found on managers' desks provide a wealth of data and means to manipulate data. There is a risk that planning becomes even more of a managerial game with the use of such facilities. On the other hand there is the possibility that management planning may become more effective. One reason for lack of planning by managers has been the "excuse" of too little relevant information being available. As we move into a situation where we are more likely to have a surplus than a shortage of information, the pressure on managers to take planning more seriously may grow.

There is no point in having elaborate plans if there is no monitoring, or if problem-solving and decision-making are neglected. Also even the most brilliant plans are of no value if there is not the necessary will to make them happen. There will always be the job to be done of getting commitment from others to the plan that has been formulated, winning people round and making it work. People will only commit themselves to what they believe to be right and worthy, with a reasonable chance of success. The more a plan requires people to see things in a fresh light and to alter a way of working with which they are familiar and which they know lies within their capacity; then the more difficult will they be to convince, no matter what the computer printout says.

SUMMARY PROPOSITIONS

18.1.   Planning is a necessary managerial activity that is often neglected.

18.2.   Planning can be divided between that which is strategic — involving the goals and policies of the organisation as a whole — and that which is operational — implementing what strategic planning or policy requires.

18.3.   Operational planning has four logical steps: deciding the goals, defining the present position, identifying what might aid and what might hinder the operation, and working out alternative programmes of action in order to choose the most appropriate.

18.4.   Where managers do not neglect planning (see 18.1. above), they tend to use elementary planning aids, such as Gantt charts, network planning, milestone planning, linear programming, time series, or the Delphi technique.

APPENDIX A

Administrative drill for network analysis

1.   List all *activities* (time taken to move from one event to another) and *events* (completions of activities).
2.   Determine three time forecasts for each activity: most likely, optimistic and pessimistic. Weight these three 4:1:1 to calculate the expected time by the formula:

$$t_e = \frac{4t_m + t_o + t_p}{6}$$

where t_e = expected time; t_o = optimistic time; t_m = most likely time; t_p = pessimistic time
3.   Draw a network containing all the information derived in steps 1 and 2.
4.   Identify the critical path through the network.
5.   See if there are ways of reducing the time involved on the critical path.
6.   Monitor progress of activity to ensure activity times are met, if necessary modifying network and identifying the critical path afresh.

APPENDIX B

The graphic method of linear programming

a. Situation

A small clothing factory has a department that makes anoraks and jeans. The contribution to overheads is £1.00 for an anorak and £1.50 for a pair of jeans. The

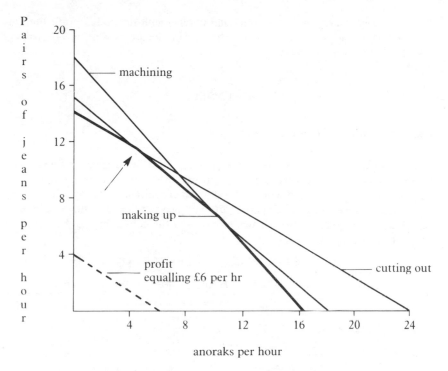

Figure 18.4   Linear Programming Graph for Anorak/Jeans Production

problem is to decide what combination of anoraks and jeans produces the highest profit margin.

b. Constraints

The *cutting-out* section can produce parts for 24 anoraks or 14 pairs of jeans an hour, or some combination of lower figures for each, such as 10 anoraks and 8 pairs of jeans.

The *machining* section can process 16 anoraks, 18 pairs of jeans, or intermediate combination.

The *making-up* section can complete 18 anoraks, 15 pairs of jeans, or intermediate combination.

c. Method

A graph is drawn with the horizontal axis representing the number of anoraks per hour and the vertical axis representing the number of pairs of jeans per hour (see Figure 18.4).

Lines showing the possible mixes for each of the identified constraints are drawn on the graph. Any combination *below* these lines is possible; combinations *above* the lines are not. The area of combinations that are not possible is marked with the thick line.

To decide the optimum profit margin a line is drawn on the graph showing the possibilities; all anorak production, or all jeans production, or a combination. As a starting point, £6.00 an hour can be achieved by either 6 anoraks or 4 pairs of jeans. The line on the graph joining these points also shows the intermediate combinations.

By moving away from the origin and parallel with the dotted profit line, the optimum combination for production is shown with the arrow as being 11+ pairs of jeans per hour and 4+ anoraks.

APPENDIX C

Use of the simple moving average

The moving average provides the most elementary form of illustrating a trend, using historical data to project a trend for the future. In the example below figures are shown of hours lost in a factory due to breakdown of equipment. The moving average is calculated for each three week period, dropping one week and adding one for each calculation. The graph plots both sets of data and the dotted line on the trend line shows the future prediction.

HOURS LOST THROUGH BREAKDOWN

Week	Hours	MA	Week	Hours	MA	Week	Hours	MA
1	212		6	255	231	11	270	253
2	248		7	260	255	12	280	263
3	210	223	8	210	241	13	290	280
4	190	216	9	250	240	14	285	285
5	250	216	10	240	233	15	300	291

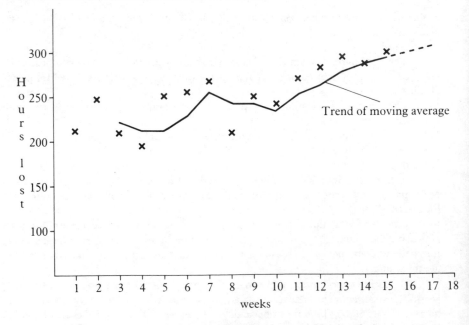

Figure 18.5   Weekly Breakdown Figures and Moving Average

APPENDIX D

Administrative drill for goal planning

Stage 1 Identify and specify goal to be achieved, with target date.
Goal:
Target date: .... *Date done:* ....

Stage 2 List strengths and needs of the situation	
Strengths:	*Needs:*

Stage 3 Divide more difficult needs into sub-goals and specify methods and dates			
Sub-goal	Method	Target date	Date done

REFERENCES

Ansoff H.I., *Corporate Strategy*, Penguin Books, London, 1970.

Argenti J., *Systematic Corporate Planning*, Nelson, London, 1976.

Chandler A.D., *Strategy and Structure*, MIT Press, Cambridge, Mass. 1962.

Drucker P.F., *Management*, Pan Books, London, 1981.

Gedye G.R., *Scientific Method in Production in Management*, Oxford University Press, 1965.

Glueck W.F., *Management Essentials*, The Dryden Press, Hinsdale, Illinois, 1979.

Koontz H., O'Donnell C., Weihrich H., *Management*, 7th edition, McGraw-Hill Kogakusha Ltd., Tokyo, 1980.

Longenecker J.G. and Pringle C.D., *Management*, 5th edition, Merrill Publishing, Columbus, Ohio, 1981.

Macbrien J.A., *Final Report on the EDY Project to the DES*, Manchester University Press, 1981.

Mintzberg H., "Strategy-Making in Three Modes", in *California Management Review*, Vol. 16, No. 2, Winter 1973, pp. 44–53.

Schonberger R.J., "Custom-Tailored PERT/CPM systems", in *Business Horizons* No. 15, 1972, pp. 64–6.

Stoner J.A.F., *Management*, 2nd ed. Prentice Hall International, Englewood Cliffs, New Jersey, 1982.

Chapter Nineteen

PROBLEM-SOLVING AND DECISION-MAKING

When Crawford drove to the beach for some sun and swimming, he found that the car park adjacent to the beach cost £2 a day, while the car park at the top of the hill overlooking the beach cost 30p for the first two hours and 10p for each subsequent hour. He drove uncertainly from one to the other before settling for the first, adjacent to the beach. He found it was full, so he had to go to the hilltop car park anyway.

That sort of elementary dilemma is typical of the situations managers face and is the reason why we combine problem-solving and decision-making in a single chapter. Although Crawford could "quantify" his decision to some extent by calculating how long he would stay, other aspects of the situation could not be so readily assessed: How long would it take him to walk down the hill? How long to walk back up? How tired would he be after swimming? Would he still find a space on the beach if he parked on the hilltop? Did he want to come back to the car before the end of his visit? Could he park in the shade? Many managerial dilemmas have so many considerations that there is only the time or effort available to resolve the question on the basis of balancing one or two. Also the decision to be made is often similar to tossing a coin. It is difficult to see that one alternative is markedly better than the other; so why not toss a metaphorical coin rather than spend hours calculating? Finally, there is not always a choice available, because of some external constraint that was not initially apparent.

Problem-solving is a fascinating activity, as can be seen from the number of people who daily tackle the crossword in their newspaper and who find television quiz games so absorbing. Imaginative people and those with above average intelligence may seek out problems where they do not exist, or give disproportionate effort to a minor matter simple because of the challenege it presents. Problem-solving in management is often of this nature. The job is relatively straightforward and the solutions to problems are seldom obscure, but the effort involved in implementing the solution is considerable. In these circumstances there is a temptation to change the pressing job to be done (implementing a straightforward decision) into a less pressing one (finding a different problem to solve). A meeting to decide what to do is adjourned for more information, or elaborate decisions are made which are easier to implement and more interesting to work out. Here one has the combination of looking for an intriguing problem to solve and shirking a task that might be unpleasant.

A department store was operating on a split site, with one range of goods on one side of the road and others on the opposite side. For a long time the business flourished but eventually there was the need to retrench as the vogue for general department stores began to wane. The directors discussed at great length the steps that needed to be taken. They quickly dismissed the suggestion of concentrating the business into one of the two buildings and selling the one not required. This was described variously as "defeatist", "not the answer to our problems", "counterproductive" and "cutting off our nose to spite our face". The difficulty of having to dismiss loyal, long-serving staff was never mentioned. For three months there was redoubled market research, working parties, consultations and informal meetings of board members. Alternative strategies were considered and costed, but still the difficulty of having to dismiss long-serving, loyal members of staff was not mentioned and no calculation was made of the cost of redundancy payments. Turnover dropped further as costs edged higher, and it was decided to call in external advice. A deputy chairman was appointed at a substantial salary and suggested, after six weeks, that the only logical strategy was to sell one of the buildings and concentrate all the business in the other. The immediate response from his colleagues was that they could not dismiss loyal and long-serving staff, so the deputy chairman said, "You may be doing it, but it's all my fault. Anyway you will be able to afford very generous settlements on those who have to leave." The obvious, straightforward decision was taken at last. Some painful sacrifices had to be made if anything was to be saved at all for the benefit of the majority who would remain.

Part of the art of management is not to see problems where they do not exist, and not to dither so that something that is straightforward becomes problematical through prevarication. Occasionally, of course, managers have real problems to solve. Chapter 6 was called organisational politics and politics is described in folklore as the art of the possible. Russell Ackoff (1978) describes problem-solving as the art of the *im*possible:

> The possible, as conceived by most politicians and those who serve them, is seldom enough to solve the important problems in hand. What they consider impossible is required to solve these problems. …Politicians should employ *the art and science of the impossible* — of making the apparently impossible possible. To practice planning and problem-solving as the art of the possible is to play politics and call it something else.   (p. 29)

Problem-solving for managers can be spectacular and exciting, but not often.

1. CRISES, PROBLEMS AND OPPORTUNITIES

Mintzberg, Raisingham and Theoret (1976) provide a helpful distinction between crises, problems and opportunities facing managers. A *crisis* is a sudden, unexpected event requiring immediate action. The premises are burned to the ground, someone makes a bid for the company equity, the marketing director resigns, or some similar quite unexpected event requires a rapid decision or set of decisions. A *problem* is something of which there is warning in that it becomes apparent gradually, through clues from various sources, and is not initially clear-cut. Examples would be poor morale among the staff of the organisation, the influence of a competitor, or uncertainty about product quality. An *opportunity* is the chance to do something that is created by a single event and often needing swift action (opportunities are "grasped" or "seized" rather than "taken", or "missed" rather than "ignored"). A small change in tax laws provides opportunities for the person shrewd enough to see how that can be exploited, a spell of bad weather provides an opportunity to sell umbrellas. Crises often also provide opportunities, and some languages use the same word for both. The example of the crisis caused by the resignation of the marketing director may provide an opportunity for reshaping the organisation and distribution of responsibilities.

Crisis, problem and opportunity all have in common the need for a decision to be made and all are *unprogrammed decisions* that are not dealt with by routine, procedure or habit. Some events that have all the hallmarks of crisis can be classified as *programmed decisions* in that they have been anticipated and the appropriate action prescribed. If a factory catches fire and is destroyed, the managers will have moved through a series of programmed decisions, as there will have been a procedure to be followed in the case of fire. When those procedures prove inadequate to prevent the disaster, there is a whole series of unprogrammed decisions to be taken. Most people have plans to deal with the onset of misfortune, but few have procedures to deal with the aftermath if the preventive routines fail.

2. REACTING TO PROBLEMS

We have seen that problems become apparent rather than suddenly popping up in sharp outline and this requires a manager to make a preliminary decision about how to react to the problem he thinks he sees emerging. He

---

Review Topic 19.1
A crisis can create an opportunity. How else can opportunities arise?

---

has spotted it early; now what should he do? There are five alternatives.

Deal with it. In most cases the manager will deal with the problem himself, by finding out further information, pondering it, defining the problem more clearly and deciding between alternative ways of dealing with it.

Passing it on. Just because a manager perceives a problem, he should not necessarily deal with it. It may lie outside his competence or his responsibility, so that he may make things much worse if he tries to deal with it. He can pass it to a superior if he feels that it is too big for him to deal with and that he does not have the power or resources to deal with the matter himself. He can delegate it to a subordinate if he feels that the subordinate will have better detailed knowledge of the situation and will thus be able to handle it more effectively (as well as being resentful if "his" problem is taken away from him); or he could pass it to a peer, elsewhere in the organisation. Deciding what to refer is a matter of nice judgement.

A general rule of thumb appears to be that one passes down as many as possible and passes up as few as possible:

> When confronted with an important problem requiring a decision, a manager must determine if he or she is responsible for making the decision. Here is a general rule that can be of help: The closer to the origin of a problem the decision is made, the better. This rule has two corollaries: (a) Pass as few decisions as possible to those higher up, and (b) pass as many as possible to those lower down. Usually, those who are closest to a problem are in the best position to decide what to do about it.
>
> (Stoner, 1982, p. 168)

Referring a problem to a peer elsewhere in the organisation can be seen as avoiding proper responsibility, but failing to do it can cause ructions. An example might be dealing with the problem of an employee who is suspected of stealing. Should this be done by the immediate superior, or should he refer the matter to the security people or to the personnel department? If he refers it to security and the suspicion is groundless he has probably destroyed the working relationship he has with the suspect. If he fails to refer it and the suspected employee then has time to remove confidential documents of great value to a competitor, then he has contributed to that loss by his negligence.

Taking advice. A variation of the first alternative is for the manager to deal with the problem himself, but defer action until he has taken advice from those with specialist knowledge or skills that help him understand the problem. This can also be a preliminary to deciding to refer the problem elsewhere.

Working party. Remitting a problem to a working party or similar group for consideration is fraught with difficulties and dangers. The issue can be "blown up out of all proportion" and made more difficult to deal with rather than easier. Despite this, there are clearly situations in which a complex problem can only be approached satisfactorily by convening a group of people with varied expertise to examine the matter from different perspectives, providing that they all have the degree of commitment that will obviously be needed to solve what is such a difficult problem.

Ignore it. An even more dangerous strategy for a problem is to ignore it on the assumption that something will turn up to deal with the difficulty or that the passage of time will make it obsolete. This seems to most enthusiastic managers a shabby strategy and not facing up to the demands of the job. It is interesting, however, to think of what happens when you go on holiday. During your absence a number of problems will emerge and when you return you find that some of them have been dealt with by other people, but only because you were away. Other problems await your urgent attention, and others have stopped being problems at all. No manager will survive long if he ignores all the problems that occur, but with some it is a wise strategy to leave the matter to resolve itself.

3. THE PROBLEM-SOLVING PROCESS

Figure 19.1 illustrates a straightforward problem-solving process and is adapted from Stoner (1982). There are four stages.

Stage One. Definition and Diagnosis

As problems emerge, rather than presenting themselves with sudden, sharp clarity, they first need to be defined. Is it the right problem? Is declining sales turnover a problem of pricing, or quality, or delivery times, or poor advertising, or an inappropriate product line, or something else? Getting to the correct problem among various possibilities is the first aspect of definition. The second is to question whether it is a problem at all. A taken-

Stage One	Stage Two	Stage Three	Stage Four
DEFINITION & DIAGNOSIS	*GENERATING ALTERNATIVES*	*DECIDING BETWEEN ALTERNATIVES*	*IMPLEMENTATION*
Define problem	Generate alternative solutions	Consider available resources	Check availability of resources
Test definition	Defer judgement	Evaluate alternatives	Check understanding of those involved
Specify appropriate solution		Select most appropriate	Implement Monitor

**Figure 19.1   The Problem-Solving Process
(adapted from Stoner, 1982, p.170)**

for-granted assumption in management circles for many years was that one should try to reduce staff turnover; if a large proportion of the employees left

---

Review Topic 19.2

Small, everyday decisions are often of the "Yes, let's ..." or "No, I think not ..." type.

How many small decisions did you make yesterday at work and at home? How many big decisions did you take, affecting future action over the next six months?

---

the organisation this was "a bad thing". The assumption was underpinned by calculating joining costs, leaving costs, training costs, advertising costs and so on. Although these could be calculated and added up to provide a hefty sum, there was no consideration that turnover among staff employees could also avoid some people lingering on in dissatisfaction, could introduce new blood, could save on payroll costs through having some people at the bottom of pay scales instead of everyone being at the top, and could open up career opportunities for younger employees. Changes in the labour market have recently tended to produce an opposite assumption: that turnover is much needed to prevent a growing sense of frustration. The most useful approach to defining a problem correctly is to assess it in terms of what the organisation is trying to achieve and the extent to which the achievement of those objectives is being hindered by the existence of the supposed problem.

If the problem can be satisfactorily defined, it is then necessary to determine what would be an appropriate solution. If, despite the comment in the last paragraph, staff turnover is accurately defined as being too high, what would be a satisfactory solution? An example could be where a department has an establishment of fifty posts and an annual turnover of 200 per cent, made up like this:

Total number of posts	50
Semi-permanent job holders	25
Unsettled job holders, each staying an average of only three months	100

There is an underlying stability of 50 per cent, as 25 of the posts are held by people whose attachment to the company is settled. Without defining the problem satisfactorily the solution may be inappropriate, such as blanket attempts to persuade everyone to stay longer. These could be wasteful and might unsettle the semi-permanent job holders, who had not previously realised there was anything wrong. What is the problem here? Do we want the short-stay employees all to stay a little longer, or some of them to stay a lot longer, or is it a reasonable mix already? If short-stay employees were to stay for an average of six months instead of three, labour turnover would halve. If ten of the short-stay employees were to become semi-permanent and the remaining fifteen posts still occupied by people staying only three months, the turnover would drop to 120 per cent. Different strategies would be involved according to how the problem was defined. It is always necessary to diagnose what has caused a problem by obtaining information, analysing it and — probably — discussing it with others.

By now the manager knows his problem, what he wants to achieve as a solution and how the problem has been caused. Now on to stage two.

Stage Two. Generating Alternatives

The more complex the problem is, the more alternative solutions there are likely to be. The more intractable a problem has proved to be, the more alternative solutions are needed for consideration. The second stage is one of looking for alternative strategies, possibly using the brainstorming method that is described shortly, or one of the other techniques that have been devised. One system is that of the Americans Kepner and Tregoe (1982) who first promulgated their method in 1965. Better known is the lateral thinking approach, described by Edward de Bono (1982) which enables people to generate new ideas and to escape from old ones by attempting radically different methods of thinking and approaches to problems. He proffers an intriguing example:

> In a singles knock-out tennis tournament, there are 111 entrants. What is the minimum number of matches that must be played? It is easy enough to start at the beginning and to work out how many first-round matches there must be, and how many byes. But this takes time. ... Instead of considering the players trying to win, consider the losers after they have lost. There is one winner and 110 losers. Each loser can lose only once. So there must be 110 matches.
>
> (de Bono, 1982, p. 7)

Lateral thinking claims to do more than develop alternative solutions to problems, but it can be a useful approach at this phase of the problem-solving process.

It is important to defer judgement on which solution is best until a number have been propounded. If alternatives are considered as they emerge, that act of consideration and evaluation can inhibit the generation of more alternatives. Either there is an early commitment to one that sounds attractive, and the effort of shifting one's allegiance is too great, or subsequent alternatives are conceived within the constraint of meeting only the shortcomings of what has already been proposed.

Stage Three. Deciding Between Alternatives

When a range of options have been laid on the table for consideration, there is the stage in the process of choosing between them. There are two interrelated questions to be asked of each alternative. Can we do it? Will it work? First is the question of whether or not the strategy can be put into operation with the resources that are available. Many possibilities cannot be used because there is not the time, or manpower, or finance to mount them. Also some strategies might tackle the problem but cause another, equally or more serious. The second question of whether or not a proposal will work concerns whether or not it meets the criteria set in stage one of being an appropriate solution to the problem defined.

Sometimes there is a clearly preferred solution that is not immediately apparent, but which becomes unequivocally right through the problem-solving process. More often there are a number of inadequate solutions and the decision between alternatives is much more difficult.

Stage Four. Implementation

Because problem-solving is fun, people often lose interest once the nut is cracked, just as many of the people who complete crossword puzzles cannot be bothered to send up for the prize. The road to bankruptcy is paved with the gravestones of those who solved problems beautifully, but did not make the solutions work. Aspects of implementation are making sure that the necessary resources are available and that those who are to be involved in the implementation understand what they have to do and will do it. Later the managerial problem-solver has to monitor developments to see if the solution is working. Unless the solution to the problem was so obvious that the ratiocination described here was superfluous, there must be a good chance that the solution will be different from that anticipated; so the monitoring of implementation and its effects is essential.

4. AIDS TO PROBLEM SOLVING

Various ingenious methods have been devised to stimulate creative thinking and to aid the problem-solving process in which managers engage. The methods of de Bono and Kepner and Tregoe have already been mentioned, but a familiar simple technique is *brainstorming*, in which a group of people discuss a problem in a freewheeling, unstructured fashion. All members are encouraged to say whatever comes into their heads about a specified topic or aspect of a problem, with the contributions of each stimulating the thinking of all. Then the group discusses general ideas that have been mentioned to choose some for further development by the same freewheeling method. Gradually the focus becomes more and more precise and the group has generated a short list of possibilities.

An example of brainstorming is the members of a research and development department who were trying to reformulate a range of household products. They were getting stale and decided that brainstorming might help them to be more creative. Not only did they include all those working on the products, they also invited other senior staff who had the relevant qualifications and experience but had moved on to other areas of work in the organisation. The training manager and the marketing director both came and the meeting produced a number of promising ideas for development.

It is important that there is no evaluation of the ideas being offered in the early stages, so as to reduce the inhibition that group members may feel about the possibility of making a contribution that will be derided by their colleagues. Despite this there is some evidence to suggest that more and better ideas are produced by individuals brainstorming alone than by groups (Rickards and Freedman, 1978) because of the inhibition problem.

A modification of brainstorming is *synectics* (Prince, 1970) in which the discussion is led and organised by a leader who is the only one knowing the precise nature of the problem to be solved, so as to avoid too much divergence. If, for instance, the leader is looking for an idea for a new breakfast cereal, he might ask his colleagues to discuss first what proportion of the population had to rise and leave their homes relatively early in the morning compared with the proportion that were able to rise at their leisure. He might then broach the question of what the implications of varied practice were for the form that breakfast could take. The reason for concealing the precise problem is that group members do not then champion their own particular idea.

Some problems can be solved by mathematical modelling, providing that all the significant variables can be isolated and analysed in order to determine the optimum solution. One of the best known techniques of this type is the formula for determining an *economic order quantity*, so that material for stock is ordered at the frequency and in the quantities that are most economical and efficient. The method of doing this is shown in Carter (1982, p. 136).

5. DECISION-MAKING

Many decisions that managers have to make are limited in their problematic component, and the challenge is not the intellectual question of what should be done, but other questions such as: Who should decide? What will be the reaction of the employees? How do we make it work? It is important to emphasise the aspect of decision-making that requires confidence, courage and skill in winning commitment from others. An elementary rule is that people will support that which they have helped to create, and this proposition supports the process of consultation and participation, but not all decisions are susceptible to such treatment. When action must be taken quickly, there is no time for consultation and a need for someone to say firmly "We will do this". When decisions are going to be unpopular, some aspects may require consultation and others may call for straight executive action. An example might be the decision to close a factory, which has within it a series of components. There is first the business decision that the factory is to be closed because demand for the product has collapsed or because the costs are too high. There is the employment decision about what should happen about the employees generally, and there is the set of individual decisions about each employee personally. There is usually extensive consultation about the second of those three and less about the first and third.

The Americans Vroom and Yetton (1973) have produced a classification of management decision styles, ranging from authoritarian, through consultative to fully participative, set out in Figure 19.2. They then suggest the circumstances in which different types of decision would be preferred or inappropriate. AI and AII would not be appropriate for decisions where the acceptance of subordinates, or other people involved, is crucial to success. AI would also be inappropriate if the manager lacked the information or skill to make the decision on his own. CII or GII would be preferred in situations where all the required information is not yet known and where there may be uncertainty about how to obtain it. If subordinates are likely to disagree about the most suitable decision to make, and if their acceptance is important, then CII and GII are preferred as differences of that sort can only be discussed and ultimately resolved by discussion among group members. If the decision to be made is difficult, and one with which subordinates are likely to disagree, then GII would be inappropriate as the "right" decision could not be made by the manager relinquishing his authority to decide and passing it to the group who would not be able to decide objectively.

Those suggestions all assume that the manager can decide in each situation which decision-making style to adopt, but an underlying consideration is the extent to which his freedom to choose is constrained either by organisational practice or by his own precedents. If he consults widely on one matter and receives commitment from those with whom he consults, they will expect to be consulted the next time that matter occurs. Having been involved once, they will not want to be excluded the next time. The management of an organisation that readily consults with employees and divulges lots of information prior to pay negotiations in a year when profits are low or non-existent will have some difficulty in not being equally open and consultative the following year, when their affairs may be better.

Review Topic 19.3

"Too many decisions, too fast, about too many strange and unfamiliar problems – not some imagined 'lack of leadership' – explain the gross incompetence of political and governmental decisions today. Our institutions are reeling from a decisional implosion."

(A. Toffler, *The Third Wave,* Pan Books, 1980, p. 421)

Does this apply in the organisation where you work?

A I	Managers solve the problem or make the decision themselves, using information available to them at that time.
A II	Managers obtain the information required from their subordinates and then make the decision themselves.
C I	Managers share the problem with subordinates one by one, without bringing the subordinates together as a group.
C II	Managers share the problem with subordinates collectively in a group for them to make suggestions and offer ideas. The managers then make the decision.
G II	Managers share a problem with subordinates as a group, with managers and subordinates both making suggestions and ventilating ideas, which are then evaluated to reach a consensus.

**Figure 19.2   Management Decision-Making Styles
(from Vroom and Yetton, 1973, p.67)**

One useful aid to decision-making is the *decision tree,* an example of which is in the article by Vroom and Yetton referred to above, and the method is set out in the appendix to this chapter. The advantage of a decision tree is that it helps identify alternative courses of action and assess the probabilities connected with them so that the optimum course of action can be chosen. It is not a method that provides definitive answers, but it clarifies the issues on which a decision will finally have to be made.

6. PROBLEMS, DECISIONS AND MANAGERIAL LIFE

The attractiveness of being a problem solver and a decision maker is such that it features largely in management books and in discussions with managers. The need to solve problems emphasises the intellectual challenge of the management job and the need to make decisions underscores his status. Increasingly, however, the really complex problems facing management in organisations can be remitted to non-managers for evaluation. The range of mathematical models and computer simulations is such that groups of specialist advisers (variously known as corporate planners, think-tanks, policy review groups, management services etc.) can manipulate all the variables and reduce the elements of the decision to be made to very simple terms. This means that the manager then chooses between a small range of options, deploying those qualities that the specialist advisers either do not have or do not want to deploy: judgement, intuition, experience, political nous, courage or simple authority. It also means that the manager has to define his problem in precise terms for his advisers or for his desktop computer terminal. The greatest advantage of the computer to managers may well turn out to be the fact that it requires its tasks to be precisely formulated.

SUMMARY PROPOSITIONS

19.1. Many decisions for managers to make are simple, requiring speed, firmness and conviction rather than careful analysis to find the right answer.

19.2. Some of the biggest problems managers have to solve are those that require breaking out of what is politically possible to find a strategy which initially seems *im*possible.

19.3. Alternative ways of reacting to a problem are dealing with it, passing it on, taking advice, referring to a working party, or ignoring it.

19.4. The four stages of the problem-solving process are definition and diagnosis, generating alternatives, deciding between alternatives and implementation.

19.5. No one management style in problem-solving is invariably right: authoritarian, consultative and participative styles can each be appropriate in different situations.

APPENDIX

Administrative drill for a decision tree

a.   Identify:

> Decision points, represented by □
> Chance events, represented by ○
> Probabilities, represented by ( )

b.   Develop a decision tree as a graphical representation of alternative strategies, considering chance events and probabilities, as well as outcomes.

In the example below a comparison is made between two strategies for a company, whether to invest in new plant to produce a new product or to contract out the manufacture to a supplier. By multiplying the possible outcomes by the probabilities, three different cash sums are produced. The addition of these suggest that one alternative is much more likely to be worth pursuing than the other.

REFERENCES

Ackoff R.L., *The Art of Problem Solving,* John Wiley, New York, 1978.
de Bono E., *Lateral Thinking for Management,* Penguin Books, Harmondsworth, Middlesex, 1982.

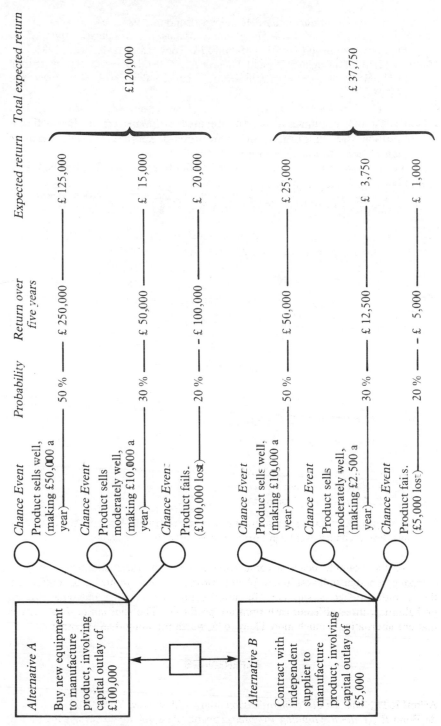

Figure 19.3   An Example of A Decision Tree

Carter R., *Business Administration*, Heineman, London, 1982.

Kepner C.H. and Tregoe B.B., *The Rational Manager: a Systematic Approach to Problem Solving and Decision Making*, McGraw Hill, Maidenhead, 1982.

Mintzberg H.A., Raisingham D., and Theoret A., "The Structure of 'Unstructured' Decision Processes", in *Administrative Science Quarterly*, June 1976, pp. 246–75.

Prince G., *The Practice of Creativity*, Harper and Row, New York, 1970.

Rickards T. and Freedman B.L., "Procedures for Managers in Idea-deficient Situations: an Examination of Brainstorming Approaches", in *Journal of Management Studies*, February 1978, pp. 43–55.

Stoner J.A.F., *Management*, 2nd edn, Prentice-Hall International, Englewood Cliffs, 1982.

Vroom V.H. and Yetton P.W., "A New Look at Managerial Decision-Making" in *Organizational Dynamics*, Spring 1973, pp. 66–80.

Chapter Twenty

BUDGETS AND RECORD-KEEPING

Budgets and record-keeping are two sides of the same coin. Budgets are part of planning and express in numerical detail the expected investment of capital and personnel in the various parts of the business over the next month or year. Records are kept in order to track what investments of resources, time and money are actually made and what the results are of these investments. The record of what has happened is part of the basis on which future planning — and hence budgets — is built.

1. NATURE OF BUDGETS

Budgets begin with those who devise future plans. They are normally handed down the hierarchy: head office issue divisional budgets, divisions issue departmental budgets, departments issue section budgets and sections issue personal budgets. The process is more elaborate in practice than it seems in theory and the control of subordinates that the handing down process implies is accompanied by protracted political negotiation, assertions of authority, challenges to authority and demands for figures to be justified.

Richard Coleman is a divisional accountant and has described to us the broad steps in his budget procedure:

a. He and his colleagues prepare their plan and send it to headquarters.
b. Headquarters responds with guidelines such as "We are not happy with an expected profit of £10 million in two years; try for £11 million" or "Administration costs should be 19 per cent not 20 per cent of the budget".
c. Richard responds by agreeing with some points and resisting others by further justification.
d. Headquarters agrees the divisional budget.
e. Richard now "cascades" the same process down to the departments in the division.

Steps *b* and *c* may be repeated several times before *d* is eventually reached, but Richard finally has not only a series of financial yardsticks against which divisional performance will be measured, but also a substantial degree of latitude: autonomy to exercise discretion and initiative within an agreed framework. The reason for the protracted negotiations is to ensure that the framework is acceptable to those operating within it, so that they cannot claim an unreasonable budgetary constraint as a reason for failure.

> Management control is a systematic effort to set performance standards with planning objectives, to design information feedback systems, to compare actual performance with these predetermined standards, to determine whether there are any deviations and to measure their significance, and to take any action required to assure that all corporate resources are being used in the most effective and efficient way possible in achieving corporate objectives.
>
> (Mockler, 1972, p. 2)

Tying people down as precisely as that will always produce defensive behaviours unless the detail of the controls are worked at to make them mutually acceptable as a framework.

The variety of plans made by an organisation is reflected in the range of budgets that are in use. Koontz, O'Donnell and Wehrich (1980, pp.45–6) list six types:

Revenue and expense budgets,
Time, space, material and product budgets,
Capital expenditure budgets,
Cash budgets,
Balance sheet budgets, and
Budget summary — the complete balance sheet.

All control through budgets requires the determination of *key result areas*. These are aspects of the organisation that produce the performances on which everything else depends. The obvious key result areas are sales, output, stock levels and cash position, but each individual organisation will have one or two that are special to its setting or to its mode of operation. One organisation may have 10 per cent of its sales volume taken up by the sales of one product which produces 50 per cent of the gross profits. Television companies watch the viewing levels of their programmes very carefully. A car manufacturer may have one department where a strike or other form of industrial action would have repercussions elsewhere in the organisation far greater than would be assumed. Identifying these key result areas makes it possible for managers to monitor closely a selected number of performance indicators whilst allowing maximum discretion elsewhere.

2.   THE BALANCE SHEET

An organisation always has some *assets* and some *liabilities*. Those which are tangible and measurable by cash values can be arranged on a balance sheet to show the financial situation of the organisation at a specific time. Figure 20.1 shows a simplified balance sheet. The left side lists assets in descending order of liquidity. Current assets are those such as cash and marketable securities that could be turned into disposable cash at a reasonably predictable value within a relatively short time. Fixed assets show the monetary value of the company's plant, equipment, property and other items used to produce its goods or services. After liabilities have also been listed, the company's net worth is calculated by subtracting total liabilities from total assets. The balance sheet is used, with a profit and loss account and a cash budget, as part of the strategic financial control of the business.

3.   BREAK-EVEN ANALYSIS

The importance of break-even analysis is to determine when a product or service will begin to be profitable after an initial period when income is being used not only to pay variable costs, but also to pay off fixed costs in setting up the venture. The break-even chart in Figure 20.2 is for a company selling home computers at £100 each. The fixed costs are £250,000 and the variable costs are £50 per computer. It is now possible to see the point at which the project breaks even, and to illuminate other points.

4.   PROFIT AND COST CENTRES

The use of profit or cost centres is a means of providing autonomy to departments or sections of a business at the same time as providing a basis for management control of operations that are decentralised. The method is to set targets for a division or department in terms of profits or costs that have to be achieved and then to measure the results obtained. It is thus a form of management by objectives using a single criterion of success and — at least theoretically — providing those in the cost or profit centre with greater scope for deciding how their objectives are to be reached. It is also a different form of using key result areas than have been mentioned earlier.

Review Topic 20.1

How can the use of profit or cost centres provide both autonomy to departments and a basis for management control of decentralised operations?

ASSETS

	£ thousand	
Current assets:		
Stocks	4,784	
Debtors	4,865	
Marketable securities	324	
Cash	102	
		10,075
Less Current liabilities:		
Creditors	3,133	
Bank overdraft	1,430	
Taxation	803	
Dividends	367	
		5,733
Net Current assets		4,342
Fixed assets:		
Land and buildings	3,312	
Plant and machinery	4,675	
		7,987
Investments		867
		13,196

LIABILITIES

	£ thousand	
Ordinary share capital		5,492
Reserves:		
Capital	706	
Revenue	2,631	
		3,337
Ordinary shareholders' equity		8,892
Long-term liabilities:		
Debentures	2,552	
Loans	1,424	
		3,976
		13,196

Figure 20.1   Simple Balance Sheet

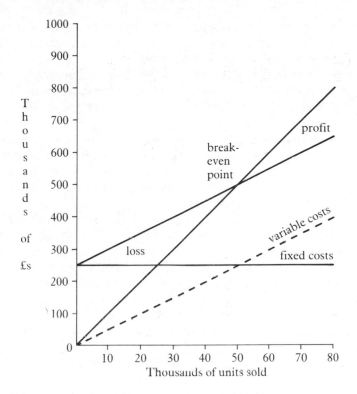

Figure 20.2   A Break-even Chart

In practice individual managers seldom enjoy the complete autonomy that the use of profit centres implies. Organisations are entities, no matter how attractive is the idea of decentralising, so that managers in individual cost or profit centres have to work within quite tight limitations. If there is a national agreement on wages and salaries, managers in the cost centres will have to accept that constraint all the time that the agreement is accepted. Managers will also be required to use some central services, even if they do not want to, as there are economies of scale for the organisation as a whole in working this way.

Central overheads, like head office and general service departments, can be apportioned between cost centres or regarded as separate, but problems arise if a department that is a cost centre wants to reduce its overhead burden by not using a central service department such as personnel, purchasing or management services. A manager may review the use made by his centre of management services and decide that his level of use is so low that he could make a useful saving by doing without the services altogether or using the occasional services of a consultant. Although there has long been reluctance to encourage competition for internal services, some organisations have begun turning central service departments into cost centres that have to survive by selling their services to client departments within the company and in competition with suppliers of similar services from outside the organisation. The next step can be to close the central service department altogether and depend on outside suppliers.

A necessary feature of cost or profit centres is to determine the prices at which goods and services are transferred from one department to another. One option is to use an open market price, so that the internal client pays the same price for internally supplied goods and services as he would pay for those same services supplied from outside. If, however, the internal client is free to buy externally as well as internally, then the internal supplier is at a considerable disadvantage as he does not have the same freedom to sell his services. It is therefore more common for some lower value to be determined, but the precise level is problematical.

The reason why managers in senior positions use the device of profit or cost centres is to try and make the organisation as a whole more efficient, by providing control information on unit performance, and to provide job satisfaction for subordinate managers, by supplying feedback on the progress of their operations. If they are to achieve both objectives the degree of competition between cost centres has to be kept at a healthy level, without allowing it to become so strong as to be destructive.

In producing annual budgets it is most common for the budget of the previous year to be used as a basis, with modifications made in the light of circumstances that have changed in the intervening twelve months. *Zero-base* budgeting is an alternative approach that can be more searching, as each manager has to work from a zero base and justify his entire budget without depending on the events of the previous year as a large part of his justification. The process involves three major steps:

1. *Break down each of an organization's activities into "decision packages".* Each "decision package" includes all the information about an activity that managers need to evaluate that activity and compare its costs and benefits to other activities, *plus* the consequences expected if the activity is not approved and the alternate activities that are available to meet the same purpose.
2. *Evaluate the various activities and rank them in order of decreasing benefit to the organization.* Usually each manager will rank the activities for which he or she is responsible. Rankings for all organizational activities are reviewed and selected by top managers.
3. *Allocate resources.* The organization's resources are budgeted according to the final ranking that has been established.

(Stoner, 1982, p. 631)

5. SPREADSHEETS

The impact of the computer on managing is varied, but one of the significant innovations has been the spreadsheet, which is probably the most popular piece of computer software among managers. The first of what have now become known as spreadsheets was Visicalc (1980), although that has been followed by many others both simpler and more elaborate. The spreadsheet is a computer program that provides a display of data relating to income and expenditure over a period of, say, twelve months. Each item of information is metaphorically in a box, with the boxes arranged in rows and columns. The row is the category of information running across each of the twelve months and the column is of the different categories of information for a single month. The computer program then enables a series of calculations to be made that link one box to another, one row to another or one column to another. In this way it is possible to enter in the figures of expected income and expenditure for the forthcoming twelve month period and then calculate the effect of changing different variables. One can, for example, change one feature of income in month one and ask the computer to calculate the effect of that single change on all the following months, making all the necessary additions, subtractions and other calculations so that there is still a calculated figure for each row and each column with all the cumulative effects accounted for. This helps the initial budget preparation to be more carefully worked out by considering a wide range of possible strategies. It also makes it possible to assess quickly each month what the effect of that month's performance will be over the remainder of the year. Figure 20.3 shows a typical spreadsheet format.

6. RECORD-KEEPING

So far the computer has made its biggest impact in organisations on record-keeping and filing, so that some of the drudgery and routine of manual record-keeping has been overcome. The computer can store so much

	January	February	etc ...
SALES	42,000	42,840	
COST of Sales	28,560	29,131	
GROSS PROFIT	13,440	13,709	
less			
Wages	7,800	7,800	
Rent	2,050	2,050	
Other	1,500	1,800	
TOTAL EXPENSES	11,350	11,650	
TRADING PROFIT	2,090	2,059	
Less interest	800	850	
NET PROFIT	1,290	1,209	

Figure 20.3   A Typical Spreadsheet Format

information and retrieve it with such ease that there is a danger of records being expanded unnecessarily. We need to review why records are needed.

Keeping records is part of the feedback process about the effectiveness of plans and budgets. As the priests of ancient Sumer demonstrated (see Chapter 2), records are needed to measure the contribution made by departments and by individuals. Without a record of how many bandage packs have been issued this month, it is not only difficult for the hospital administrator to know how many to order, it is also difficult to know at what point to argue for more funds for bandages and at what point funds should be diverted from bandages to laundry. Similarly personnel department need a record of those off sick, and working overtime in order to make the correct calculations for paying people. Employment legislation has made it necessary to keep records of warnings to employees about incidents of misconduct which might lead to dismissal. Records of all types provide information to aid decision-making and to monitor performance.

There is a danger that the keeping of records becomes a burdensome administrative activity that is neither accurate nor useful, with the activity becoming an end in itself. One high-tech company we worked in had a system of wall charts on which engineers recorded the number of hours spent on each of several different parts of a project and on each project for different clients. The reason for recording this information was to provide a basis to work out costings for future projects. In practice, however, the records were made nonsensical by the fact that engineers often had to spend more time on an assignment than was anticipated. It would have been sensible to record the extra hours against the project that had been underestimated. In fact the engineers were asked *by their managers* to record the extra hours against a

---

Review Topic 20.2

Why was the use of wall charts (described on this page) made nonsensical and how could the problem have been avoided?

---

different project where there was still space on the chart, as they did not want to give the impression that they had estimated incorrectly in the first place. Nor did they want it to seem that they had lost control of the operation! This is an extreme example of how individuals make nonsensical those records that prescribe their activities too closely. There is particular suspicion of records that are maintained so that an individual manager can keep personal control of the activities of subordinates rather than the records needed for organisational control. To avoid these problems, we suggest three simple rules:

a. Records should be justified in terms of the stated task of the department or organisation;

b. Records should be entered on simple forms; and

c. Records kept should only be those essential to running the unit.

Barbara Dyer (1983) suggests four types of purposes for *personnel* records. First there is information about individual employees as individuals, which she describes as *item* information. Second comes *feature* information, which is mainly statistical and used to aid decision-making by providing a profile on some aspect of the business, such as the age profile of employees. Essential information to meet the requirements of *legislation* covers not only the incidents connected with individuals that have already been mentioned, but that required by the Department of Employment and other outside bodies each year. Her fourth category is *indicator* information, using records to monitor trends such as labour turnover, sickness and absence, as well as providing the basis for prediction and planning, like salary modelling.

All kinds of information circulate in an organisation and there is always the risk that one piece of information suggests the need for another, especially as most managers appreciate the way in which knowledge is power. The challenge to managers, therefore, is to *reduce* information and record-keeping to the necessary minimum and not to let each answer generate more questions. A test is to pose the question "What will you do with the information?" Frequently informal records, that are the basis of action, are kept in notebooks alongside some formal system that is seen as time wasting. Perhaps the notebook is sufficient?

7. RECORD-KEEPING AND THE COMPUTER

Few portents of a new golden age have been welcomed with as much enthusiasm as the advent of cheap computing, which we are told will revolutionise managerial decision-making, make middle management redundant and produce a new era of organisational efficiency. These prophecies may come true, at least in part, but one aspect of the computer revolution that is now widespread is the use of computer memories to store data, so that record-keeping is becoming progressively more electronic. This can make the retrieval of data simpler and eliminate much of the tedium in record-keeping, *once the data are in.* Putting data in (or inputting data, as the computer buffs describe it) remains tedious and can be so tedious that the records are not up to date. This can be overcome only by taking the bold step of developing the computerised system so that data are collected *at source* by linking the production of documents that have to be provided anyway with the up-dating of a data file that might otherwise be overlooked.

If a new employee is to start work next Monday, he will need a letter of offer and a contract. It will also be necessary to add his personal particulars to the aggregate data kept of organisational manpower. One way to do this is to type out the letter and the contract, and later to put the salient information into the computer memory via its keyboard — when there is time. Another method is to produce the letter and contract on the word processor which is linked up with appropriate software so that the records are updated automatically.

It is only by interconnecting the computer and word processor systems with the operational *and* record-keeping systems of the department that the potential of the electronic hardware can be realised.

8.   BUDGETS, RECORDS AND THE MANAGER

In the next section of the book we have material about the manager and his personal organisation. That operation is set within a framework of departmental data and organisational controls. The operating budget is the most familiar form of describing objectives that managers have to reach. It is also the most elementary of procedures, despite the fears that so many laymen have about the expertise of accountants. To monitor his own performance within those guidelines and to give others the chance to review the performance with him, there are records. Together records and budgets are useful tools of management control, providing that they do not become ends in themselves:

> ... so complex, detailed, cumbersome, meaningless and expensive that they become dangerous ... goals may come to supersede organisational goals, requiring care in using (them) as a *means* and not an *end*.
>
> (Shaw and Day, 1978)

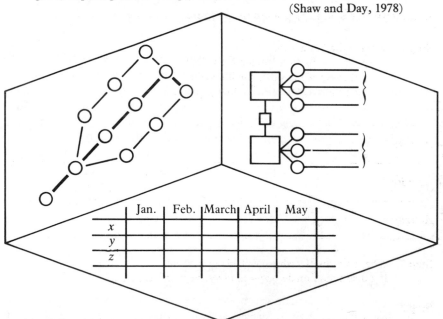

Planning, decision-making, budgets and record-keeping: different dimensions of management control.

Figure 20.4   The 'Control Cube'

SUMMARY PROPOSITIONS

20.1. Budgets and records are the tools of management control of organisational performance.

20.2. Control is made more effective by identifying key result areas and profit or cost centres.

20.3. Records can become neither accurate nor useful unless they are kept simple; are essential to the running of the business; and are justified in terms of the stated task of the department or organisation.

20.4. To make best use of the computer in record-keeping, records should be up-dated by the same process as is used to generate operational documents.

APPENDIX

Administrative drill for drawing up budgets

Step 1 What is the budget for?
    a.   What are the unit's main activities?
    b.   What is the period of the budget?
    c.   List the activities for the budget period:

Activity 1

Activity 2

Activity 3

Step 2 What amount of cash is available to the unit?
Is a distinction made between investment and expenses?

Step 3
    Work out the expected expenditure for each activity for fixed costs, variable costs and investment. Sources of information are: suppliers, other departments, similar job holders, previous experience, last year's budget, formal estimates. Put the figures in the table:

	Fixed costs	Variable costs	Investment
Activity 1			
Activity 2			
Activity 3			

add the totals and see where the difficulties lie.

Here is a simple example of how this could be applied to household expenses with an overall budget of £5,000 after allowing for food, clothing, holidays etc.

	Fixed costs		Variable costs		Investment	
Activity:	Rates	£500	Electricity	£100	Replace bathroom	
Household	Mortgage	£3,000	Gas	£500	fittings	
Expenses			Telephone	£200	Decorate living room	
		£3,500		£800	Available:	£700

Can the money available for investment be increased by reducing gas usage or cancelling holiday in order to raise the total budget to £6,000?
What are the possibilities of the mortgage rate rising, or falling?

REFERENCES

Coventry W.F., *Management,* Heinemann, London, 1981.
Dyer B., "Developing and Maintaining Personnel Records", in *A Textbook of Personnel Management Strategies and Techniques,* edited by Guest D. and Kenny T.P., Institute of Personnel Management, London, 1983.
Koontz H., O'Donnell C., Weihrich H., *Management,* 7th edition, McGraw-Hill, Kogakusha, Tokyo, 1980.
Mockler R.J., *The Management Control Process,* Prentice-Hall, Englewood Cliffs, New Jersey, 1972, p. 2.
Shaw W.C. and Day G.J., *The Businessman's Complete Check List,* Business Books, London, 1978.
Stoner J.A.F., *Management,* 2nd ed., Prentice Hall Inc., Englewood Cliffs, New Jersey, 1982.
VisiCalc, Software Arts Inc., 1980.
Vu-Calc, Psion Ltd., 1983.

Part V

PERSONAL EFFECTIVENESS

Within the communications network and the web of relationships is the manager himself. Having understood the organisation in which he is set and organised the activities of those who make up the team he leads, how well is he organised, personally? How well does he communicate and how convincingly does he perform in generating innovation?

Organising oneself involves analysing what one does, deciding how it can be made more efficient and then imposing the discipline needed to make and sustain the changes. Being an effective communicator is how the manager spends most of his time and his effectiveness increases as he manages the impressions he creates and his understanding of the material he reads and the messages he sends. Innovation is one of the manager's more exciting areas of work, but it involves working with — and making decisions about — the unfamiliar. This requires courage to experiment and due concern to preserve the quality of what is both familiar and sound.

Chapter Twenty-One

ORGANISING ONESELF

Most advice to managers, like the other chapters in this book, is about how to understand the organisational context one is in, or how to organise other people and materials. At the centre is the manager himself: how well organised is he? Understanding the context and organising subordinates, or the decision-making processes, or the performance appraisal procedures is of little avail if the person taking initiatives is not sufficiently well organised to push those initiatives through to successful completion and to exploit successfully whatever responses he receives.

Poorly organised managers are a major impediment to organisational efficiency, slowing things down, producing errors and generating dissatisfaction. Among the clues are the comment "I just have not had time". The workload for any manager inevitably varies, from day to day, from week to week and — for many people — from season to season. The manager who "has not had time" usually is not able to deal with that fluctuation. It may also be that he accumulates arrears of work as a justification for concentrating on those things that interest him and passing over those that are unwelcome. He knows that some of the less interesting things will be dealt with by someone else or overtaken by events, as we saw in Chapter 19. Arthur Brown was a Sales Manager who enjoyed a deserved reputation as a brilliant salesman and a very nice man. He was also known as not being keen on office work and he had three filing trays on his desk: "In", "Out" and "Too Hard", with the third being used for all those matters that could not be dealt with straight away. A mischievous colleague altered "Too Hard" to "Too Dull", and that is all too true for many prevaricating managers.

Another clue is the phrase "Let's play it by ear". Here we see lack of preparation, lack of initiative and a mode of operating that is doomed to be responsive to the initiatives of others rather than creating initiatives of his own. A somewhat similar clue is "I'm still waiting for... (the boss)". Although some periods of waiting are inescapable, there are occasions when managers await instructions because they are unsure of what to do, or because they believe that having passed a matter to the person next up in the hierarchy, they then forget about it until it returns, because theirs is a dependent role.

Finally there is the clue "Really? I don't remember that at all". Managers have to organise their memory and recall to cover a wide range of matters, moving between those matters quickly and effectively. Not for them the purposeful single-mindedness of, say, the sculptor or the research physicist who can concentrate on one task for weeks and in whom absent-mindedness is either a beguiling eccentricity or an indication of absolute, unswerving dedication.

Review Topic 21.1

If you were able to organise yourself better,

(a) Do you think your overall management performance would improve?
(b) Do you think you would enjoy life more or less?
(c) Do you think you would be a more or less stimulating and interesting person to work with?
(d) Do you think other (less well-organised) people would become more reliant on you?
(e) If you say 'yes' to the last question, in what ways would this enhance, and in what ways weaken, your managerial and administrative effectiveness?

In the next few pages we consider how managers can achieve the type of personal organisation that will protect them from giving these damning clues to perceptive observers, and which can greatly enhance their job performance and job satisfaction. As with other features in the book, we are not advocating the *only* ways in which things can be done, as one man's organisation can be another's straitjacket, but even grandmothers can learn to suck eggs better than they used to.

1. ORGANISING ONE'S TIME

One method of organising one's time is to analyse how it is spent by using a temporary diary method like that provided at the end of Chapter 5. With such an analysis it is possible to review the proportion of time spent on various activities and to decide whether or not this is how the time should be spent. Various questions are suggested in the appendix to Chapter 5. Another strategy would be to use Rosemary Stewart's (1982) categories of the demands, constraints and choices of the job to analyse how time is spent. Stewart recommends trying to increase one's choice by rethinking the demands and constraints.

The next step is to decide where changes need to be made, if at all. Are there things being done that could be cut out, or reduced, done differently or delegated? We have found, for instance, several instances of managers keeping careful notes — hand-written in a black book — of figures that are available at the touch of a button on the keyboard of their own computer terminal or workstation. Alternatively there may be some things which should be done and which at the moment are not being done.

The more normal use of the diary is to plan the working day. This is partly an assertion of the individual manager's autonomy, but it is primarily an organising device to fit in various types of meeting. If the weekly marketing meeting takes place at 2 o'clock on Wednesdays and usually lasts all afternoon, that half day is blocked out for other activities. There are normally between one and a dozen such events in a manager's weekly diary: meetings involving a number of people, at a fixed time, mainly at the behest of someone else (no matter how important you are) and these are the immovable blocks in the week, around which other things have to be fitted within the general framework of the working week/day. Although the immovables block out large chunks of available time, they can be used to make good use of what remains. If you need to talk to a colleague who you know to be verbose and indecisive, it may be worth getting the diary out and asking if he could possibly manage 1.30 on Wednesday. .... "It's only half an hour before the marketing meeting, so I'll have to be off like a dirty shirt about five to ... but God knows when the next opportunity would be". One Factory Manager of our acquaintance discovered that the Works Convenor suffered from acute acid indigestion that worsened as meal times approached and was alleviated by eating. Gradually more and more meetings could only be fitted into the diary towards the end of the morning. Although those are two slightly silly examples, they demonstrate how the manager needs to calculate the time needed for different types of meeting and structure the times in his diary according to those estimates. We have already seen that managers spend most of their time talking to other people and these encounters — whether one-to-one or on a larger scale — tend to expand or contract to fill the time available for their completion. If one allows too little time, the meeting is abortive as it has not been possible to deal with the business and if one allows too much time, then opportunities to do other things are wasted.

A refinement of diary usage is to allocate blocks of time to particular activities, just as doctors' surgeries are always at the beginning of the day and in the early evening. Examples of this are doing all the dictation at the beginning of the day, making telephone calls early afternoon (when they are cheaper), reading reports on the train, touring the plant just before lunch. This reinforcement of a habit can make for greater personal efficiency and can make more efficient working relationships with colleagues, who can organise some of their activities to suit. "We'll ask Charlie. He usually comes by about this time".

2. MANAGING THE BOSS

The idea of managing one's boss may sound like a contradiction or a usurping of proper authority, but it is most inappropriate to regard the relationship with the organisational superior as one in which *he* copes with you and you respond with deference or what the Americans call "apple-polishing". It is also insufficient to regard the relationship as one in which the subordinate seeks to comply precisely with what the superior asks for and then awaits further instructions, so that the job is satisfactorily discharged when the wishes of the boss have been met. Virtually all the jobs that people in organisations hold are those in which there are a range of responsibilities, accountabilities and obligations, both formal and informal, and in those the relationship is an aspect both of obligation and resource in managing the complex of relationships. Also all jobs require some skill and some initiative, and the more autonomous a job is the less precise is the nature and degree of the supervision provided by the superior.

Very little has been written on this subject, although there is a helpful article by Gabarro and Kotter (1980) that points out that the relationship with the boss is not only crucial but has to be managed. Such management is not political manoeuvring or apple polishing, but consciously working with him to obtain better results. Alistair Mant (1983) makes the distinction between binary thinking managers and ternary thinking managers. The first are those who see the relationship as that of master and servant, while the second are those who see the relationship as being of two servants, relating to each other via a third point in a triangular affiliation. The third point is the task on which they are both engaged, the customers they seek to serve or the employees they seek to satisfy. Binary thinkers will find it difficult to see how one can manage one's boss; ternary thinkers will be doing it already.

The process is mainly one of mutual accommodation and adjustment, as the two parties find the most effective way of sharing duties between them. They start from the position that the boss has, for instance, more formal power and access to more extensive formal information, while the subordinate may have better grapevine information and a more flexible programme of work. To this will then be added the advantages that each has in terms of personal qualities, qualifications and experience. By discussion and getting used to each other both boss and subordinate can improve their joint and individual results, but it needs initiative from both of them; not just from the boss.

From the point of view of the subordinate alone, it has to be remembered that the boss can influence the promotion and career development prospects of the subordinate, and this can inhibit the degree of candour in everyday exchanges. It also illuminates the need for the subordinate to work within the consent, even if only the tacit consent, of the boss in taking initiatives. In this way there will be support in times of difficulty and a greater likelihood that decisions on action are well judged.

Sometimes the boss has to be used to get things changed. It may be anything from an administrative procedure that is not working or policies about particular clients that need changing to tasks traditionally associated with one's job that no longer seem appropriate. Boursine and Guerrier (1983) make the point that subordinates often assume the boss knows when in fact he does not know what the subordinate's job involves and what is happening within its framework. A useful tactic is to keep the boss advised of what is irritating or frustrating. In doing this, however, it is well to remember the transactional analysis idea that we described earlier. The subordinate is more likely to be successful if the transactions with the boss are adult/adult transactions rather than those of the intemperate child whining to the disinterested parent.

There are also the range of tactics that were described at the close of Chapter 6 on organisational politics: reciprocal support for a patron.

3.   ORGANISING WHAT HAS TO BE DONE

Management jobs inevitably have a delicate balance of long-term and short-term future objectives. Long term considerations are dealt with in our chapter on planning, but there are ways in which managers prepare for short-term eventualities that lie somewhere between the projections of planning and the day-by-day control of diary keeping. In talking with managers during the preparation of this book we have been struck by the difficulty managers have in keeping a number of different issues all in play together. Furthermore this seems to be a growing rather than diminishing problem and was discussed by Kotter (1982) in his study of general managers.

Review Topic 21.2

(a)   List five ways in which you manage the relationship with your boss.*

(b)   Think of three more ways that you have not yet tried.

(c)   Who benefits from the way you have managed your boss so far?

*   For those who do not currently have a boss in the conventional sense, use the example of a parent, a teacher, a sports team captain, leisure activity organiser etc.

One method many managers use is to develop the use of the diary until it almost becomes a timetable. We call this *event anticipation* as people mark in their diary not only the events that are to happen, but also the jobs they have to do in anticipation of those events. A technical manager noted the date of meetings in his diary and then noted three days before the meeting that he had to look through the agenda in order to chase up information or queries. A fashion manager used her diary first to mark the definite dates of fashion shows and similar promotions, and then fixed back in her diary earlier dates for such items as "contact press office", "order invitations". Although this may seem elementary, attendance at any committee meeting shows how few people arrive at the meeting prepared for the proceedings. There are now wallcharts and personal planners commercially available to aid this simple process. For managerial jobs with a strong administrative component and where there is a cycle of seasonal or annual events, the year can be partially mapped out in advance; we looked at the work of one very busy university administrator who had done this several times during the year when the workload was especially heavy. By careful examination she was able to identify a number of jobs that could either be done completely or partly at different times of the year in order to smooth the flow and to improve the quality of jobs done at the peak times.

Similar is the *bring-out system,* long used by private secretaries, in which notes or correspondence about a matter are stored against a date when they will be "brought out" for review. This avoids the pile of papers on the desk generally awaiting attention or the bulging briefcase which is all too often a sign of a manager who reacts to situations instead of being proactive. A familiar comment by a manager asked about the progress of a particular issue is that "it is getting near the top of the pile". This refers to the real or metaphorical pile of papers on the desk and implies that they are being dealt with in strict chronological sequence. Usually they are dealt with only as a result of a query or complaint. With that arrangement everything becomes urgent and other people are always dissatisfied. Jeff Moores is a plant engineer who operated in this way: he dealt with things according to how loudly and often people grumbled at him. It was getting him down, so one week he agreed that he would abandon his standard, defensive, "I'll get to it as soon as I have time. It's getting nearer the top of the pile." Instead he said to each enquirer that he would deal with their query at a specified time, often weeks ahead. All the enquirers were satisfied and he suddenly found the breathing space in which he could begin to control his activities and move into a more satisfying and rewarding way of working. The bring-out system can also be used to prevent other people overlooking things which they regard as too hard or unattractive, like the old Jeff Moores before he took hold of his life.

Many managers keep *lists of jobs* to be done. These are typically kept on odd scraps of paper and reviewed morning and night. This is mainly to keep a check on what has to be done, so that things can be brought to mind in the relative calm of the train journey to the office and later reference to the list can prevent them being overlooked in the rush and bustle of the working day. There is a secondary benefit in running through the list at the end of the day, as it makes one realise that something *has* been achieved, despite the feeling of frustration and lost opportunity. We make no comment about those people who remember something to be done that is not on the list, do it, and then write it on the list in order to cross it off! This is essentially a personal, informal activity, and it changes its nature when it becomes an administrative system. A building society manager had a semi-permanent list of all the routine tasks that had to be done in his branch, and either he or his assistant initialled each item when it was done. It included such items as checking each cashier's till randomly each month, sending returns to regional office, and staff training.

Those especially conscious of the problem of getting things to the top of the pile try different ways of *assigning priority*. On the list of jobs, described in the previous paragraph, one or two would have an * beside them and some might even have ** to indicate that these were things that should be done first, or that should be done even if some of the others were deferred. Less effective is to colour code internal memoranda. One local authority manager had an extremely elaborate system of different colour paper for different types of message:

White	–	advisory
Pink	–	information
Blue	–	interest
Yellow	–	critical for implementation
Orange	–	needs reply

The idea was that memoranda would be sent on paper of a colour to indicate the attention it should receive, with the urgent matters being dealt with immediately and other matters being dealt with later. This seems to be an extreme of administrative precision that does not quite fit in with the vagaries of human nature. Will white, pink and blue be read at all? Is the coding not reinforcing the idea among managers that they are too busy to read all their paper, when the majority of them can probably cope with it easily? Also, if there is this sort of ascending scale of importance, the lower scales are soon abandoned. In the Foreign Office telegrams are marked "Most Immediate", "Immediate", "Priority" and "Routine" and much self-discipline is required to ensure that not everything gets the top two markings.

The chief executive of a medium-sized company was anxious that the memoranda that *he* sent should be acted on quickly and he also wanted to spot easily the memoranda that came in to him from his main colleagues, so a system was introduced whereby all the memoranda from his office were on green paper, all those from directors were on blue, and everyone else had memoranda typed on yellow paper. Quite apart from the explicit declaration of differential status, that caused a lot of difficulty, there soon came the problem that important matters on yellow paper were sometimes overlooked. To deal with this the colour-coding was modified so that non-directors could have their memoranda typed on pink paper if they were urgent. These were soon christened "pink frighteners" and people quickly realised that the way to get a response was to write on a pink frightener. Various people were grumbled at for not treating the system properly, but within a fortnight pink frighteners outnumbered the yellow memoranda being typed and the whole initiative failed.

These last two ideas were used by busy people trying to organise their own work, but the methods they chose depended on others organising their work in a reactive, dependent way. Personal reminders, like the list on the back of an envelope, seem much more effective.

4.   ORGANISING PERSONAL RECALL: MAKING NOTES

As managers have to keep in touch with a range of different matters simultaneously, they benefit from being able to recall quickly and accurately information that they have received. Some they retrieve from files, some they remember, but a preliminary to the first and an aid to the second is the ability to take notes. In meetings, while reading journal articles, while telephoning, while talking with colleagues are all occasions when the manager may need to make jottings of material to be used later.

One method is to use shorthand, which enables the writer to record verbatim what someone is saying. Another is to make a tape-recording, but both of these methods are of dubious value as preliminaries to data storage or as aids to recall. The effort of the writer is in getting the record accurate and the effort of the person using the tape recorder is simply to switch on the machine. The understanding and the internalising, or taking in, of the material comes later as an extra job to be done. It is interesting to consider the experience of researchers and students, who are dedicated listeners. The researcher who is interviewing people at some length, and who uses a tape recorder to make sure that nothing is overlooked, will spend approximately four hours in writing up a one hour interview. That is not transcribing it, word-for-word, but writing a summary of what was said, with nuances, illustrations and some interpretation. Nearly all those who use a recorder for this purpose take notes as well, so that the writing up is based on the notes and the personal recall of the interviewer, with the recording being used only to check details. Students often make tape recordings in lectures in order not to miss anything, but seldom do they persist with the practice after a few weeks because the recorder takes away from them the need to be actively listening during the lecture, and the lecture becomes even more boring as a result, with the added tedium of having to listen to it all over again.

The purpose of taking notes is to record what the listener has understood that he wants to be able to recall as well as specific details that enlighten that understanding. It is always selective and always interpretive.

In taking notes the manager is summarising as much as possible in as few words as possible. An example is the way in which some people make a note at the back of their diaries of funny stories they have heard so that they can recount them on later occasions. The note is seldom more than a phrase or even a single word, even though the story may take five or ten minutes to relate. The funny story has a pattern, so that a few words are sufficient to recall the entirety. In listening to anything that we are being told, we look for a pattern or interconnection of ideas that we will be able to recall. Each of those patterns then produces a note in the form of a *trigger,* either a word or phrase that will be sufficient to summon up the complete grouping of ideas and data we are recording. In this way the listener is working while listening, structuring his understanding and deciding on the triggers.

When it is necessary to record verbatim, there is value in mastering a set of *abbreviations.* The appendix to this chapter has a list that is commonly used, but each individual will have a personal set, linked to the context of his own work. In preparing this book, for instance, we have used the following:

Mgt	–	Management
MM	–	Middle management
Gps	–	Groups
F–to–F	–	Face-to-face
Orgs	–	Organisations

These have been helpful to us, but would be useless to others. There are various ways of adding *emphasis* in notes. Some words are underlined, or have ** put beside them, as in the personal lists we have already described, but another method is to outline items that are to have a special degree of emphasis. A novel device has become available in stationers' shops, which is a text highlighter. This is a broad-tipped felt pen that can be used to paint a band of transparent colour over a word or sentence, so that it is still legible, but is highlighted. This is now much used by people reading reports and memoranda to pick out key words or sections to which they wish later to refer.

5.   ORGANISING PERSONAL RECALL: MEMORY

All of us can improve our ability to recall information from our memory as the potential of the human brain is greatly under-utilised and some individuals who are otherwise perfectly normal are able to recall much more than others. Actors need to memorise their lines and thus develop an ability to recall that is much greater and better organised than that of most other people; some indeed have been able to recall a major Shakespearean role after little more than a single reading. In the 1950s a music hall performer Leslie Welch was known as "The Memory Man" and his fifteen minute act consisted of answering questions from the audience on sporting events and records.

One widely-accepted theory of human memory is that memorising is a two-stage process: a short-term memory and a long-term memory:

> The difference between them is like the difference between recalling a telephone number you just looked up in the directory and your own telephone number. Your own is stored in LTM along with memories of

such items as your name, the words and grammar of the language,
addition and multiplication tables, and important events in your life.
Except for occasional mental blocking on a word or the name of an
acquaintance, these memories are relatively permanent. In contrast, the
telephone number you have just looked up, the definition the instructor
has given you in class, and the name of the stranger to whom you have
just been introduced remain in STM only momentarily. Unless you make
a conscious effort to focus your attention on the information, that is, to
transfer it to LTM, it is quickly lost.

(Hilgard, Atkinson & Atkinson, 1975, p. 236)

Recall is summing things up from long term memory and the
effectiveness of the recall will be influenced by the way in which items were
stored in that memorybank in the first place. Buzan (1977, pp. 35–53)
provides an excellent summary of this process and the possibility of
improvement, but we will here mention only one method of data storage for
effective recall, known as the *method of loci*. In this a series of items to be
learned for recall are identified in the mind of the learner with familiar,
connected locations. The most familiar example being of the shopping list,
which is memorised by identifying each item on the list with a room in the
house. They are not, however, simply identified with the room, but
visualised in it, so that there is a picture of a dozen eggs on the hall floor, a
loaf of bread on the dining room table, breakfast cereals on an armchair in the
sitting room, and so forth. On entering the shop, the items are easily recalled
by summoning up the series of images.

6.   ORGANISING PERSONAL RECALL: FILING

As the amount of information circulating in organisations increases, there is
a growing problem of what to do with it after it arrives. Much can be thrown
away, either because it did not need to come in the first place or because it
will not be needed in the future, but how do you store correspondence,
reports and other items in such a way that they can be found when required?
The average filing cabinet contains material that will never be looked at again
except when you are looking for something else, so that one effective means
of filing is to file as little as possible. This can be achieved either by throwing
away more, more often and more purposefully, or by relying on other
people's files to a greater extent. We realise that some readers will find it
difficult to follow this advice. In visiting different organisations it is striking
to notice the different number of filing cabinets deployed in operational
situations which seem in all other ways to be similar. Some managers are
surrounded by filing cabinets while others seem to manage with only one, so
filing practice is governed as much by the personality and individual methods
of managers as by any objective notion of what is appropriate.

How do you classify what you decide to keep? Most people operate in a way similar to the short-term and long-term memory. Earlier in this chapter we referred to managers who refer to matters "nearing the top of the pile"; nearly all the managers we have spoken to have a "pile". It may be literally a pile of papers on the desk, it may be a bulging briefcase or a dog-eared folder, but it will still have the same characteristics: it contains material that is current and not organised in any particular way. When it ceases to be current, it may be thrown away or filed — transferred to the long-term memory. Once in the filing system, the material is valueless unless you can first remember that it is there, and secondly that you can find it. Both influence how the filing should be arranged.

The most common system of classification is by *subject* and *source.* Some files contain material about a topic, while others contain material received from Mr X or Company A. Other common files are for committees, with all the minutes and papers relating to the Establishment Committee going into a single file. The difficulty of finding material is demonstrated by the way in which many experienced secretaries have a secret "spare copies" file. It contains copies of all the significant letters and memoranda they have typed in the previous six months. When they are not able to locate an item, they flip hurriedly through their spare copies to find the item or a clue to its whereabouts.

The filing system needs a key. The simplest is a typed list of the files that are kept, so that you remember you have a file on a particular subject; otherwise many of the files are forgotten. If you look in your filing cabinet now you will find that fifteen per cent of the files contain seventy five per cent of the filed material, and twenty five per cent of the files are probably empty or contain only forgotten material. The filing system has to match the needs and mental processes of the user, or it is of little value:

> If possible files should be conceptually organised to fit in with the way the users of the files work. Thus project, case and company file names are likely to satisfy the needs of those concerned with research work, litigation and suppliers respectively. If simplicity and comprehensibility are maintained in this way, staff are more likely to use and rely on the filing system.
>
> (Lock & Farrow, 1983, p. 827)

7. SELF-DEVELOPMENT

In this chapter we have reviewed the main ways in which the individual manager can improve the quality of his personal organisation. A more detailed approach to this is to be found in a remarkable book by Pedler, Burgoyne and Boydell (1978) who provide a practical means of self-development. A final consideration is the way in which the manager manages his own career, so that he not only increases his here-and-now competence, but also has a working life that meets his ambitions for variety, challenge and reward.

To do this he should first realise that "up" is not the only way to move. In the early stages of a career it may be more judicious to move sideways, so as to broaden experiences and prepare for a move upwards in a different field. Secondly, the attempt to move upwards is one that few can satisfactorily achieve; most people stop going upwards earlier than they would wish. That is the time when so many managers become bored, frustrated or disillusioned, yet the manager who has developed the substance of his role, rather than always looking beyond it, has the opportunity of deriving satisfaction from doing a difficult job well. Life holds few deeper satisfactions than that.

SUMMARY PROPOSITIONS

21.1.   Poorly organised managers are a major impediment to organisational efficiency.

21.2.   Time can be managed better by using diary sheets to analyse how time is spent, a future diary to plan the working day and the working week, and to allocate blocks of time daily or weekly to specified activities.

21.3.   The working relationship between boss and subordinate is crucial to the effective working of both parties to that relationship, and both of them have to work at managing the relationship.

21.4.   Methods of organising the work that has to be done include event anticipation, a bring-out system, keeping lists, and assigning priority.

21.5.   The quality of personal recall can be organised in making notes, memorising and filing.

APPENDIX

Abbreviations for use in note-taking

= is equal to	+ add or and	& and
≠ is not equal to	∴ therefore	∵ because
> greater than	≯ not greater than	n many
♂ male	♀ female	

acs accounts	ca (circa) about	cf (confer) compare with
Do (ditto) the same	eg (exempli gratia) for example	etc. (et cetera) and the other things
et seq (et sequentia) and the following	ibid. (ibidem) in the same place	ie (id est) that is
no (numero) number	non seq. (non sequitor) it does not follow	NB (Nota bene) note well
op. cit. (opere citato) in the work cited	Pro tem. (pro tempore) for the time being	Sic. so written
Stet let it stand	v. (versus) against	VV vice versa

REFERENCES

Boursine M. and Guerrier Y., *Surviving as a Middle Manager,* Croom Helm, London, 1983.

Buzan T., *How to Make the Most of Your Mind,* Colt Books, London, 1977.

Gabarro J. and Kotter J., "Managing Your Boss", in *Harvard Business Review,* January/February, 1980, pp. 92–100.

Hilgard E.R., Atkinson R.C. and Atkinson R. L., *Introduction to Psychology,* 6th edition, Harcourt, Brace, Jovanovich, New York, 1975.

Lock D. and Farrow N., The Gower Handbook of Management, Gower Publishing Co., Aldershot, 1983.

Mant A., *Leaders We Deserve,* Martin Robertson, London, 1983.

Pedler, M., Burgoyne J. and Boydell T., *A Manager's Guide to Self-Development,* McGraw Hill, Maidenhead, 1978.

Stewart R., *Choices for Managers,* McGraw Hill, Maidenhead, 1982.

Chapter Twenty-Two

BEING A COMMUNICATOR

Communicating with other people is the main activity of managerial life. Mintzberg (1973) was one of many studies that showed managers spending the majority of their working time talking with other people. Some way behind in pervasiveness, but still taking more time than other activities, are reading and writing. To some extent the business of being a communicator is putting on a performance. Erving Goffman (1969) offers us an absorbing account of how all of us are constantly seeking information from each other that is not readily revealed, so that we infer it from a range of cues, like gesture and facial expression. At the same time we are deceiving those trying to obtain the same sort of information from us by the art of impression management, through which we try to create impressions of ourselves that are more favourable than the facts warrant.

Another vogue has been the analysis of non-verbal behaviour. If we are constantly seeking from each other information that is not readily revealed, it appears sensible to try to get behind the impression that the other person is trying to convey. The fruits of this labour have been entertaining but of limited value. Most of the conclusions are either of the obvious, such as the observation that actions speak louder than words, or of the trivial, like the fact that men sometimes scratch their heads when puzzled. Other conclusions that have been announced do not carry sufficient reliability to be adopted as guidelines. Once the code of non-verbal behaviour is cracked, then people can fake the signals. Few signals are more general and unequivocal than the smile, which signals friendliness and pleasure at meeting someone, but because we all know that, we can fake the signal and smile warmly at someone even when that is not really how we feel. The welcoming smile can be as meaningless as the accompanying words "I am pleased to meet you". Impression management has won again.

There are two aspects of the communication problem that are important to mention, from the plethora of comment on the subject produced recently, before proceeding to the main sections of the chapter. First is the simple comment about *the frame of reference*. A Frenchman is alleged once to have expressed surprise that all the monuments in London commemorated defeats, because many of the "glorious victories" for the British have been defeats of the French. Perceptions of an issue will be shaped by the standpoint from which a person views it. When husband and wife separate there will be sharply different interpretations of the reasons for the separation, the truth being somewhere in between. In the words of William Cowper:

> ... differing judgements serve but to declare,
>> That truth lies somewhere, if we knew but where.

In communication we must always remember that out listener will view the matter differently from us, and we therefore have to write or speak with an understanding of his standpoint.

Less familiar is the problem of *cognitive dissonance* which describes the difficulty we have in coping with information that is not consistent with our beliefs. If you wear a beard because you believe that girls are more attracted to men with beards than to those without, you will not readily accept arguments opposed to that belief. Believing requires commitment by the believer, who metaphorically nails his colours to the mast, and information conflicting with the belief is either discredited or manipulated to fit the belief.

People at work have plenty of beliefs that are usually expressed as homespun philosophy and which affect the way they carry out their duties. Here are a few:

"There's only one way to do it, and that's by the book."
"People will do anything if the money's right."
"A machine can never be as good as a skilled man."
"The customer is always right."
"If I say jump, they jump."
"The happy worker is a good worker."
"Women are fine doing routine jobs, but they're too emotional to wield authority."

Those may be accurate or misleading as generalisations, but those who express the beliefs will not readily discard them. An opposing point of view will be met by the cognitive dissonance block, not as a deliberate obstruction but as a genuine attempt to understand the unbelievable, to make sense of what sounds preposterous by reinterpreting it to fit the existing pattern of belief. Every manager trying to persuade people of an argument, or even to convey information, has to remember that cognitive dissonance makes it hard for people to understand new information that contradicts what they believe; it is harder still to believe it if it is understood, and hardest of all to take action based upon it.

1. SPEAKING

It would be unrealistic to suggest how managers should speak to people in their everyday exchanges at work. As we spend a lifetime acquiring and developing this facility, we also develop a high degree of skill at the process. Speaking to groups of people is, however, a much less common activity and one about which many managers are apprehensive, so this section of the chapter considers speaking in public: lecturing, making presentations, offering a vote of thanks, explaining a new procedure to a group of people, addressing a committee, welcoming a party of visitors, or one of the many other occasions when it is necessary to fill the public-speaking role.

Review Topic 22.1

Mr X believes in ghosts and Mr Y does not. Rehearse a discussion between these two in an allegedly haunted house. Which of the comments they produce would you attribute to their different frames of reference and which to cognitive difference?

This is a source of power and manifestation of authority. Most of the best known figures of history have been gifted speakers. Demosthenes, Paul of Tarsus, Martin Luther, Lloyd George, Winston Churchill and Adolf Hitler all had an almost mesmeric power over their listeners, although it was not simply a way with words but also a well composed argument that made them effective. Bowra (1970) describes the effectiveness of Demosthenes:

> Demosthenes had no humour, no lightness of touch, but he had extraordinary oratorical power. Appealing to his countrymen to resist the tyrant who meant to overwhelm them, he stated a powerful case ... driving each point home with relentless force .... He used all his gifts of argument and persuasion ... made carefully considered and practicable proposals.
>
> (Bowra, 1970, p. 144)

Managers do not have the scope of statesmen for their public speaking, but the impact of greater speakers demonstrates the power that lies within the use of the spoken word. Managers may not lead people into battle or initiate sweeping social change, but they can reassure a group of apprehensive employees who are on the verge of industrial action, or gain acceptance for a novel idea, or persuade the members of a committee to back a new proposal because they can produce a convincing case that other people can understand and accept. The emphasis has to be on the way in which the speaker enables the members of his audience to understand. Success is in getting the message understood; not in transmitting it.

Public speaking requires preparation of both the material and the speaker. Adair (1978, p. 73) refers to the first systematic exponent of rhetoric, Quintilian, who identified five phases in a speech: an introduction to gain the goodwill of the audience; a statement of the point at issue; arguments to prove the case; refutations of contrary arguments; and a peroration which either recapitulates the main points or appeals to the emotions of the audience. That remains an admirable *plan* for any speech.

In the introduction the audience have to come to the view that the address will be worth listening to and their attention in the later stages can be helped by explaining the framework of what is to come. If the speaker says that he is going to support his case with three main arguments and deal with two opposing points of view, then the audience will listen for three and two.

In arguing his case the speaker has to remember that he is aiming to get his audience to understand *ideas* rather than facts. Facts are dangerous as they may remain in the mind more readily than the idea that they are intended to illustrate. The speaker is trying to get understanding of the idea that his product is the one the customer should buy, or that output from the factory has to increase rapidly. The facts (such as the price of the product or the percentage increase in production that is needed) are merely indicators, symbols or measurements of the idea. It is like the recipe for a chocolate cake. There is the picture of the succulent cake, with an account of how it will fit specific occasions and appeal to particular palates, then there is the list of ingredients and instructions. Neither is complete without the other, but the list of ingredients is no trigger to action without the picture.

Ideas can be helpfully linked together by a device that will help listeners to remember them and to see their interconnection. One way to do this is to use key words, especially if they have alliteration or an easy rhythm, like "Planning, Progress and Prosperity". Another method is the succinct summary phrase, like "the wind of change" or "keep upkeep down". Where visual aids can be used, a simple system diagram can show the interdependence of ideas being expressed.

Very few people speak well without *notes,* which avoid the dangers of leaving something out, getting a fact wrong, drying up or — most important — wandering from the point. The audience has to work hard to build in their own minds the message that is being conveyed by the speaker. If he wanders from the strait-passage of his message, then they are impeded in trying to hold their own mental picture of the address. The most common form of notes is to use headlines, with the main points underlined and the facts beneath. There may also be a marginal note about an anecdote or similar illustration that would be relevant.

Before speaking the speaker will probably suffer from *stage fright.* This can be useful in putting him on his mettle, sharp and keyed up to produce a good performance, but if the anxiety is too great then the confidence necessary for effectiveness is lost and the audience is more aware of the nervousness than the message. Stage fright can be reduced by deliberate relaxation. On the way to give the address, deliberately walk slower than is usual; concentrate on deliberately relaxing various muscles in the body, especially the ones producing a worried frown on the forehead. Deliberately smiling is relaxing and is also a good mask for nervousness. A simple method of controlling nervous breathing is to breathe in to a steady count of three and out to a steady count of nine; in to four and out to twelve; in to five and out to fifteen. A more elaborate method is advocated by Winifred Marks:

It is relaxing simply to take several long, deep breaths, filling the base of the lungs and activating the diaphragm. More sophisticated techniques have been advocated, such as holding the nose between thumb and middle finger, with the index finger on the bridge and pressing the nostrils in turn to enforce breathing through each one alternately.

(Marks, 1980, p. 51)

Making the speech is putting on a performance and the initial impact on the audience will influence their attitude to what is to be said. The speaker needs to assert himself and display confidence in what he is to do: then the audience will begin to believe that it may all be worthwhile. The attention of the audience has to be won and their attention focused. This is done not only by having good and clear introductory material, as has been suggested above, but also by focusing their attention on the speaker. The best way to do this is to look at them, however daunting the members of the audience may appear. The speaker must also convey *vigour*:

Enthusiasm is contagious. If a speaker wants to convince, he has to believe in the issue himself. His belief helps to get the message across. There is a difference between "We have to do something about wasted materials", said as the speaker picks lint off his trousers, scans the horizon, stifles a yawn and scratches his head, and "We have to do something about wasted materials", said with inflection, pausing, direct eye contact and erect posture.

(Mayerson, 1979, p. 184)

The speaker not only wins the attention of the audience at the outset, he maintains it through the later development of the material:

... interest and motivation should be sustained throughout by the use of material or examples which are intrinsically interesting to the audience, dramatic or simply funny. Concrete examples and stories make the material easier to assimilate, but should be subordinated to the main argument.

(Argyle, 1972, p. 209)

The final point in that quotation is especially relevant to humour. If your preparation reminds *you* of a funny story, which you then tell to the audience, be sure that it will help *them* remember what you are saying. Humour must always illustrate and never distract.

Two general aspects of speaking are *pace* and *language*. Public speaking generally requires a slower pace than normal conversation, which is too quick for the message to be picked up by a number of people simultaneously. Also it is uninterrupted, so that both listener and speaker require more time to cope with forming the ideas for expression and decoding the messages that are received. Variation of pace provides the scope for emphasis and for eliminating the nonsense words that otherwise creep into speech.

When a lawyer was speaking to a lay audience, he frequently used the phrases "you know" and "as it were". Very soon members of the audience were busy noting the frequency and the following coffee break was spent in making comparisons of the different records that were kept. The consensus was that "you know" occurred every sixteen seconds while "as it were" came only at forty-seven second intervals. Few people could remember what he had been talking about. Nonsense words and phrases are used automatically to fill the minute gap when the brain has not got the message through quickly enough to the lips. Varying the pace reduces the number of occasions when such gaps occur. Few people avoid jargon, with the danger that some people will not understand. The words used must lie within the comprehension of all if the communication is to succeed. Even when the words are understood, there can be some resentment when it appears that their use is only to display erudition. Is it necessary to use the word "taxonomy" instead of "list"? Was it necessary to refer at the opening of this chapter to "frame of reference" instead of "point of view"? Many readers will have been irked by the term "cognitive dissonance", even though it is difficult to find an alternative.

The *peroration* (is that jargon for conclusion?) is as important as the opening. The speaker summarises the points that have been made, reinforces them with the audience and prepares for some positive action by audience members. Among the ways in which this can be done are to tell a story that brings together and illustrates the points that have been made, or to raise a series of rhetorical questions to which listeners can now see answers which they could not see at the beginning, or to make a straightforward statement to show the interrelationship of what has already been said.

Any speech can be enhanced by using *visual aids,* as we remember what we see for longer than we remember what we hear, and we sometimes understand what we see better than what we hear. Visual aids are, however, not a substitute for the exposition, and too many can obscure rather than illustrate what is being said.

2.   WRITING

We are all taught to write at school, and some of that teaching appears superfluous in out later working lives as it has a preoccupation with grammatical accuracy or imagery that does not seem appropriate in interoffice memoranda. This may be due to the teaching being unimaginative but it is more probably because at school we are being exhorted to express ourselves; while at work it is important that we get our message across. If our meaning is not clear, it may be misinterpreted. If our writing is vague and muddled, we may be regarded as vague and muddled people. There are many pieces of advice on how to write more effectively, but one of the most helpful is from the advice of Ernest Gowers to civil servants:

> Use no more words than are necessary to express your meaning, for if you
> use more you are likely to obscure it and tire your reader. In particular

do not use superfluous adjectives and adverbs and do not use roundabout phrases where single words would serve.

Use familar words rather than the far-fetched, for the familiar are more likely to be readily understood.

Use words with a precise meaning rather than those that are vague, for they will obviously serve better to make your meaning clear; and in particular prefer concrete words to abstract, for they are more likely to have a precise meaning.

(Gowers, 1948, p. 91)

Following those three simple rules would improve the quality of most writing, making it easier to understand and giving it greater impact upon the reader. If you look back to the paragraph preceding the above quotation, you can immediately see ways in which Gowers would have improved it. Following his first rule would change the opening to: "Some of what we learn at school about writing is superfluous ... ".

Following the second rule would take out the words "preoccupation" and "exhorted". Following the third would improve the phrases "do not seem", "may be due" and "may be regarded as". That paragraph was not deliberately written badly and it is reasonably clear, but writing can always be improved. Here is the rewritten paragraph compared with the original:

Original	*Revised*
We are all taught to write at school, and some of that teaching appears superfluous in our later working lives as it has a preoccupation with grammatical accuracy or imagery that does not seem appropriate in interoffice memoranda. This may be due to the teaching being unimaginative but it is more probably because at school we are being exhorted to express ourselves; while at work it is important that we get our message across. ...	Some of what we learn at school about writing is not needed in our working lives. Accurate grammar and imagery are not important in interoffice memoranda. At work it is important to get our message across, but at school we are also taught to express ourselves. ...
(75 words)	(47 words)

That has saved over a third of the words and is easier to understand, but has anything important of the original been lost? The reference to the possibility that teaching was unimaginative has been removed altogether. That takes away that element, but was it worth saying? It was an unnecessary distraction from the main thrust of what was being said. The reference to grammatical accuracy or imagery is now slightly different in the revised version.

While it is always possible to improve a piece of writing by trimming out what is not necessary and following the general guidance of Gowers and similar experts, there is also the possibility that the resultant material is too terse, with rhythm lost. The reader needs not only accurate writing from the writer, he also needs a style in the writing that makes it comfortable to read.

A final comment on the above revision is that the next passage will now need to be rewritten, possibly using more words. The original finishes with the need to get a message across, so that it naturally leads into the dangers of misinterpretation. As revised there is not that natural link as the finish is about school. How would you rewrite the passage to convey the meaning accurately and clearly?

Every piece of writing needs a framework or *outline* before the writing can begin. This makes the subsequent writing clearer as the sequence of main ideas has been thought out beforehand and the writer does not include in one section material that he already knows will come more appropriately at a later point. The outline can be constructed by analysing the components of the message he wants to convey or the problem that has to be set forth. The components are then subdivided and grouped in a logical sequence. A retailing group was delayed in opening a new store because the local authority refused its planning application. The directors had to decide whether or not to appeal against the decision and asked for a report. The sections of the report were:

a. *Introduction*
   1. Initial decision to build
   2. Site acquisition and development plan
   3. Reasons for refusal of planning application
b. *Alternatives*
   4. Abandon plan, with estimates of costs and lost revenue
   5. Appeal without modifications to plan, with estimates of costs, legal opinion on likelihood of success, and time to complete
   6. Appeal with modifications, including estimates as in 5
c. *Market Research*
   7. Review of latest market research data relating to site
   8. Moves by competitors since initial decision to build
d. *Recommendation*
   9. Summary of alternatives with advantages and disadvantages
   10. Recommended action

Before being used, the outline can be adjusted if the sequence does not seem ideal or if additional material should be included. Short pieces of writing, like brief letters and memoranda, are not usually thought out like this, but may be written to a standard formula or according to a simple outline in the mind of the writer. A checklist for report-writing is in Appendix B of this chapter.

A structural form that helps with the logical development of writing is the *paragraph*, which is the unit of writing for a section of what is to be said. The opening sentence says what the paragraph is about: the topic sentence. This is then developed in following sentences about the single idea or topic that the paragraph represents. The appropriate length of paragraph varies with the type of material being written. The following are some approximate figures:

Understanding Organizations	by C. B. Handy	120 words
Management	by P. F. Drucker	80 words
Emma	by Jane Austen	75 words
Lateral Thinking	by E. de Bono	70 words
The Road to Gandolfo	by R. Ludlum	60 words
Leader article in popular		
newspaper		30 words

As paragraphs get longer, the writing becomes harder to read, as we shall see in the next section of this chapter. It is wise to keep to an average paragraph length of under 100 words in reports and less in letters.

The *active* voice is better than the *passive* voice in most instances. Evelyn Mayerson expresses the reasons succinctly for us:

> The active voice is more vigorous than the passive. *The new polyurethane is believed to be superior by the finisher* is a statement made in the passive voice. It is a timid statement. The finisher is hiding his meaning in clouded syntax. Putting the sentence in the active voice — *The finisher believes that the new polyurethane is superior* — makes the statement bolder. We know without question and very quickly who believes what.
>
> The writer makes a direct statement when he selects the active voice. *Leaking is caused when the roof is rained on* is an example of the indirect quality of the passive voice. As with any indirect route, it takes longer to get there. Notice how much shorter the sentence is when rewritten in the active voice: *The roof leaks when it rains.*
>
> (Mayerson, 1979, p. 307)

A final comment about writing is the piece of advice produced by Winston Churchill in a circular to all Government departments during 1940:

> To do our work we all have to read a mass of papers. Nearly all of them are far too long. This wastes time, while energy has to be spent in looking for essential points.
>
> I ask my colleagues and their staff to see that their reports are shorter.
>
> 1. The aim should be reports which set out the main points in a series of short, crisp paragraphs.
> 2. If a report relies on detailed analysis of some complicated factors or on statistics, these should be set out in an appendix.
> 3. Often the occasion is best met by submitting not a full report, but a reminder consisting of headings only, which can be expounded orally if needed.
> 4. Let us have an end to such phrases as these: 'it is also important to bear in mind the following considerations ... or consideration should be given to the possibility of carrying into effect ...'. Most of these woolly phrases are mere padding, which can be left out altogether, or replaced by a single word. Let us not shrink from using the short expressive phrase, even if it is conversational.

5.   Reports drawn up on the lines I propose may at first seem rough as
compared with the flat surface of officialese jargon, but the saving in
time will be great, while the discipline of setting out the real points
concisely will prove an aid to clearer thinking.

(quoted in Adair, 1978, pp. 114–115)

3.   READING

Being an effective communicator involves not only sending messages
effectively, but also improving one's ability to receive messages from others.
The manager who can cope with a large volume of incoming memoranda,
letters and reports will extend the range of his competence and of his
network.

Quicker reading enjoyed a vogue during the 1960s, when there were a
number of courses provided where those attending could increase the speed
at which they could both read and understand from an average of 200+
words per minute to nearly double that. Some of the methods were based on
false assumptions about how we use our eyes, so that simple increases in
speed due to practice and concentration were attributed to using technical
aids. Manya and Eric de Leeuw (1965) demonstrated the false basis of these
assumptions and produced a manual on how to read both better and faster.
Managers need to develop two different skills; first to read some material
faster without loss of comprehension, and secondly to read some other
material very quickly indeed in order to appreciate the contents superficially
before either discarding it or reading it thoroughly.

To read quickly without losing comprehension one has first to suppress
a childhood habit: *vocalising.* When we are learning to read, our teachers and
parents ask us to read aloud as this is the only way they can easily test our
understanding. That habit dies hard, so that many adults subconsciously
vocalise the words they read. The lips move silently as the eyes move across
the page and the reading speed is thus limited to a speaking speed. If that
habit can be broken, the reading speed will increase. The lips are kept firmly
shut and the reader pushes himself to move along the line quicker,
concentrating on *not* sounding the words as they pass. A habit established
since the age of seven or eight will not easily be eradicated, so it requires
regular practice and concentrated effort.

The second feature of reading more quickly is to persuade the eyes to
be more adventurous. A slow reader will move his eyes across the line of print
fixing on one or two words at a time and with occasional regressions. This
involves the eyes moving and changing focus five or six times in a line of print
as the eyes only *read* while they are still. Speed can be increased by practice
at reducing the number of eye *fixations,* moving the eye more rapidly along
the line to fix on two words at a time, then three, then four.

By combining the elimination of vocalising and reducing the number of fixations per line, the reading speed with comprehension can be increased to double the starting speed. Usually comprehension will improve with quicker reading as the brain is operating at a speed that it can cope with quite easily. Manya and Eric de Leeuw (*op. cit.* p. 29) have found an average increase of 60 per cent in reading speed and 10 per cent in comprehension among those taking their courses.

Reducing vocalisation and fixations both involve moving along the line more quickly. This can be aided by using a pencil or finger as a *cursor* moving along the line in front of the eyes. This focuses attention and leads the eyes to move more quickly and smoothly, providing the pencil is moved steadily and quickly. This method is invariably used by people adding a column of figures and is a simple, practical device for increasing normal reading speed.

Reading very quickly to get a superficial appreciation of contents is usually known as *skimming* and requires a different approach from conventional reading. Many people can read as much as they wish of a

---

Review Topic 22.2

Ask someone to prepare two lists of 20 questions, each about the *main* news items on two separate pages of a national newspaper or magazine. Without looking at these lists, read through the first of the pages as quickly as you can using skimming technique and making a note of the time taken. Then see how many questions you can answer correctly.

Repeat the exercise by reading the second page, this time allowing yourself three times as long as you spent on the first page. Then answer the second set of questions.

How much does your success rate alter and what is the significance for your reading habits?

---

newspaper in less than half an hour because they read superficially. Most headlines are read, but few of the articles beneath the headlines and newspapers have many aids for the superficial reader: there are pictures with captions, blocks of type are broken up with headings or inset quotations from the main text, summary tables are used of football results and share prices, and the column of print is narrow, so that it is possible to skim down rather than across constantly. A more advanced method is to scan the first and last paragraphs of a major article for the introduction and conclusion, or to pick up the opening topic sentences of paragraphs.

A skimming approach to a book is to see first the title and the summary on the flyleaf, then to look for any information about the author. Already there is the beginning of a framework, which can be clarified by looking through the table of contents and the index. Within five minutes you have a general idea of what the book is about, its weight and range. This may be sufficient for you to decide to discard it; it may be a useful preliminary to reading it thoroughly. Buzan (1977, pp. 94–7) has a useful section on this type of reading and Appendix E to this chapter reproduces a summary from de Leeuw.

SUMMARY PROPOSITIONS

22.1. Preliminaries to being effective in communication are: understanding of impression management, the frame of reference and cognitive dissonance.

22.2. Five phases in making a speech are: introduction, statement of the point at issue, arguments to prove the case, refutations of contrary arguments, and a peroration.

22.3. Material can be read faster and with better comprehension by reducing vocalisation and the number of fixations per line of type. This can be aided by using a pencil as a cursor.

22.4. Some reading can be skimming to obtain a superficial understanding only.

APPENDIX A

Interaction guide for public speaking

Before Speaking

Plan the speech	by having an introduction, a statement of the point at issue, arguments to prove the case, refutations of contrary arguments, and a peroration.
Distil ideas	for the audience to understand. These will be the core of your message.
Ration facts	as they are needed to illustrate and emphasise your ideas; they cannot replace ideas.
Connect the ideas	by some device that will show how they are linked: key words, a summary phrase, or a visual aid.
Use notes	rather than memory, to provide the framework for the speech and to recall the details.
Relax	deliberately, to avoid the tension of stage fright while retaining the verve to win the attention of the audience.

While Speaking

Win the audience	by gaining their attention and interest.
Ration humour	so that it is used only to illustrate and embellish; never to distract.
Vary pace	of speaking so as to provide emphasis, to eliminate nonsense words, and to be interesting for the listeners.

Match language to	so that listeners are stimulated to listen, but are always able to
the audience	understand.
Use visual aids	to clarify what is being said, as we remember what we see for longer than we remember what we hear, and we sometimes understand what we see better than what we hear.
Use the peroration	to summarise the points that have been made, to reinforce them with the audience, and to prepare for action.

APPENDIX B

Report writing checklist

A. *Before Writing*
　　1. What is the purpose of writing the report?
　　2. Who will read it?
　　3. How short can it be?
B. *Outline*
　　4. What exactly is the problem the report is to deal with?
　　5. Into how many subtopics does that best divide?
　　6. What order should those subtopics be in?
　　7. Can that order be improved?
　　8. Will the report, as outlined, meet the purpose described in A1?
C. *Writing*
　　9. Keep the average length of paragraphs below 100 words.
　　10. Use no more words than are needed to express your meaning.
　　11. Avoid superfluous adverbs, adjectives and roundabout phrases.
　　12. Use words that are precise and concrete rather than vague and abstract.
　　13. Use the active rather than the passive voice.
　　14. Make clear the source of any facts used.
　　15. Use abbreviations and symbols consistently throughout the report.
　　16. Use numbering and sub-headings consistently throughout the report.
D. *Reviewing*
　　17. Does the completed report meet the purpose described in A1?
　　18. Is anything missing?
　　19. Are any calculations accurate?
　　20. Are recommendations thoroughly justified?
　　21. Is the action to be taken, or the choice between alternatives, clear?
　　22. Is any part of the report likely to offend anyone?
　　23. What objections do you expect, and how do you propose to counter them?
　　24. Can any possible objections be prevented by rewriting part of the report without reducing its effect?
E. *After Distributing the Report*
　　25. Have your recommendations been accepted?
　　26. In what ways have reactions been unfavourable? Could this have been avoided?
　　27. How would you have written the report differently?
　　28. How will you write your next report?

APPENDIX C

Some phrases to avoid in writing

As it were	Afford an opportunity
Be that as it may	Much of a muchness
Attached herewith is	In the near future
At the present time	Owing to the fact that
In respect of	With regard to
I am writing to say	Give rise to
For that matter	Without fear or favour
In such a manner as to	By and large
For the purpose of	Generally speaking
He is a man who	At the end of the day
In a manner of speaking	Arguably

Always remember the advice of William Cobbett (1762–1835)

> Grammar, perfectly understood, enables us not only to express our meaning fully and clearly; but so to express it as to defy the ingenuity of man to give to our words any other meaning than that which we ourselves intended to express.

APPENDIX D

Punctuation

Comma   Makes a logical division within a sentence:
- a.   to separate the subject from descriptive words and phrases (Bob Willis, captain of England, waited ...)
- b.   to separate clauses (If he wins the toss, England will bat)
- c.   to separate items on a list (He came in with his bat, pads, gloves and cap)

Semi-colon   Links two sentences which are so closely related that a full stop would be too great a break (Willis did not open the bowling; Botham did)

Colon   Separates an announcement from what is announced (The batting order was as follows: ...)

Brackets   Used for insertion, additional explanation or oversight (The twelfth man (Foster) brought out drinks)

Apostrophe   *Either* to indicate a possessive (Gower's batting; Jones's bowling; the men's room)

     Or to show a missing syllable in abbreviations (It's Boycott again)

Hyphen   Produces a compound adjective (a well-run single)

Inverted commas   For reported speech or quoted material ("Not out", said the umpire)

Full stop   Used at the end of a sentence which is not a question or an exclamation, after many abbreviations (etc.) and within sets of initials (l.b.w.)

Comprehensive notes on punctuation are in *The Oxford Dictionary for Writers and Editors,* Clarendon Press, Oxford, 1981.

APPENDIX E

Skimming

(This is an extract from the book by de Leeuw (1965, p. 105) summarising how those authors skim.)

1.   There is no conscious direction of the eyes.
2.   The attention is open and takes in the whole width of the page: we find that words near the margins can easily mask each other.
3.   There is a left–right movement to cover the horizontal extent of the page, though sometimes this is so quick that we seem to be going straight down the page.
4.   Within this general movement our eyes, as far as we can judge, behave in an extremely erratic manner, darting here and there as words attract our attention. If a word strikes us forcibly we explore the area around it.
6.   The speed of skimming varies enormously: say from three to twenty seconds a page. There often seems to be a combination of fast reading and short skips. Sometimes there is what amounts to an erratic three-line reading.
7.   When previewing we combine skimming with sampling.
8.   If the meaning is obvious, we skip and skim without compunction, unless we are caught up in the author's mood or take pleasure in the words or situation.
9.   If we want to skip and be reasonably sure of our ground, we often read the first few words of each sentence.
10. Gradually we have become more sensitive to less obvious expressions like "The assumption is", "In opposition to this", "The outcome of this", announcing propositions or conclusions; which is a help both in ordinary reading and skimming.

REFERENCES

Adair J., *Training for Communication,* Gower Press, Farnborough, 1978.
Argyle M., *The Psychology of Interpersonal Behaviour,* Pelican, London, 1972.
Bowra C. M., *Classical Greece,* Time-Life International, New York, 1976.
Buzan T., *How to Make the Most of Your Mind,* Colt Books, London, 1977.
de Leeuw M. & E., *Read Better, Read Faster,* Penguin Books, Harmondsworth, Middlesex, 1965.

Goffman E., *The Presentation of Self in Everyday Life,* Penguin, London, 1969.
Marks W., *How to Give a Speech,* IPM, London, 1980.
Mayerson E. W., *Shoptalk,* Saunders, Philadelphia, 1979.
Mintzberg H., *The Nature of Managerial Work,* Harper & Row, New York, 1973.
Torrington D., *Face to Face in Management,* Prentice Hall International, London, 1982.

Chapter Twenty-Three

INNOVATION AND CREATIVITY

Change was one of the mangerial buzz-words of the 1970s. There was talk about the inevitability of change and its increasing tempo, as well as concern about the unresponsiveness of British industry to its rapidly changing circumstances. Much of the discussion was generated by the influential ideas of Toffler (1970), who argued that change was accelerating to a degree not matched by man's capacity to cope with its challenge. Unless our ability to cope was stepped up, we would suffer from future shock, unable to assimilate and adjust to the changes taking place. Ten years later Drucker (1980) twisted our nerves to a higher pitch by the argument that change had not really begun! Only two new industries emerged in the period from 1947 to 1975: computers, and systemic drugs. In contrast the period from 1856 to 1914 produced a new invention, leading to a new industry, every fourteen to eighteen months. The period after 1975 will see a higher level of innovation:

> ...the period of fundamental technological change is ahead of us. Unlike the quarter-century after the Second World War, it will be a period of structural change rather than one of modification, of extension, or of exploitation. The period ahead will shift technological change to new realms. ... The 1980s are therefore almost certain to be a period of high technological impact and true innovation.
>
> (*ibid.* p. 53)

The initial management reaction to this sort of warning was to try and reduce resistance to change among employees, mainly by exhortation. The working assumption was that *we* (the people doing the talking) understand the significance of change and are able not only to cope with it, but also to turn it to our collective advantage. We also happen to be alert, smart, imaginative, and moving with the times. In contrast *you* (those people being talked at) are living in a comfortable, but unreal, fantasy world, and are not aware of how to deal with this crisis. You also happen to be dull, unimaginative, obstinate and behind the times. It was rather like an evangelist warning the congregation of their sins without explaining the means of redemption.

The effect of this approach was unfortunate. For every one sinner who found redemption there were ninety-nine who were confirmed in their ways, having been warned and disapproved of but without any guidance on what to do, nor any realistic glimpse of what the future could hold.

The next managerial response was to try organisational development initiatives. Here the assumption was that change was here to stay and that the way to cope was to develop the organisational structure and the people manning the organisation, so that the organisation would become less formal and rigid, while the members of the organisation became more adaptable and more open with each other. With those two changes it should be possible to evolve new patterns of organisation more appropriate to change. The success of these initiatives varied. Sometimes there was a new lease of life for an organisation and its people, sometimes there was a fresh impetus that did not survive, and in some situations organisational development became a peripheral activity for detached enthusiasts and was swept away in the first cold winds of the economic recession.

Behind this sort of thinking there were a number of inadequacies. Change was "a good thing" and viewed in an uncritical, unthinking way. Also it was necessary to turn everything upside down to cope with it, so that many people came to believe that anything done differently had to be good and anything that remained the same ought to be shaken up. There was a tendency to make people so insecure that they became defensive and resisted change more grimly. Another problem was that change was seen almost entirely as something to which it was necessary to respond, rather than something to be initiated, and it was usually vague.

Innovation and creativity are terms used not to describe dark forces disturbing our ordered calm, but as interesting activities undertaken by people at work that keep their organisations lively and up to date by exploring possible new activities and changed methods of doing things:

> Innovation and creativity have to do with the development, proposal and implementation of *new* and *better* solutions
>
> (Steiner, 1965, p.4)

Proposals have to meet the criteria of being both new *and* better. When colleagues are reluctant to support innovations, it may be because of lethargy and lack of imagination, but it may also be because the proposed innovation is not a very good one, and not a convincing improvement on present practice. The map of underground railway stations in London is a masterpiece of design, and has remained unaltered for fifty years.

Other inhibitors of change are cost and acceptance. In many ways it would be more convenient if the British were to drive on the right hand side of the road instead of the left, but the cost of the change outweighs the potential benefits. Decimal currency was initially resisted because of the cost of changing, and because of the difficulty of getting acceptance of the change. Both problems were overcome, so that now it is unusual for anyone to think of pounds and pence and then convert their sum to pounds, shillings and pence. Metrication is taking longer. An interesting example of resistance to innovation is the conventional typewriter keyboard. When Christopher Sholes produced the first typewriter in 1874, the keys used most frequently were deliberately spaced wide apart in order to slow typists down; otherwise the keys would jam. The keyboard layout remains the same a century later, not only on manual and electric typewriters, but also on word processors and computers. It would be completely sensible to change the layout, and simplified layouts are available but not marketed because of the difficulty of changing the habits of millions of typists.

In this chapter we are concerned not with change but with *innovation,* which is the whole process from invention to practice, and with *creativity,* which is the initial phase of generating the new idea, product or approach. Both of these have to be viewed in the light of finding innovations that are better as well as new and which are thoroughly thought through to verify their practicability, cost and acceptability.

Pavitt (1979) reasons that technical innovation and industrial development are increasingly important for four main reasons. First because of competition from developing countries who produce an expanding range of standard goods as their industrialisation progresses. Secondly, the taste of consumers and their expenditure level is constantly changing in the advanced countries. Thirdly we have to consider ways of reducing the consumption of energy and the environment: both scarce and irreplaceable resources. Finally there are great possibilities provided by the rapid technological changes in fields such as electronics and biochemistry. These may sound like matters for a few leading figures to consider and develop, but an interest in innovation is important for all members of organisations, especially managers, and it is an important approach to the regular, everyday matters as well as the exciting.

There may be a better way of doing things in the department that will save money, or which will be less frustrating for the members of the department, saving wear on their nerves. There may be a better way of meeting customer requirements or enhancing the quality of the product. The recent interest in quality circles (Bradley & Hill, 1983) is the latest in a series of initiatives to develop employee interest in quality. Perhaps the most important reason for managers being interested in innovation is that it will prevent them from getting stale. Creativity engenders excitement, innovation presents a challenge. It is a risky business as effort and resources are deflected away from the main task and directed to something new and untried. There is no guarantee of success, but only some innovations pay off, others fail, and others again have quite unexpected results. There have been a number of references throughout this book to the balance between the comforting familiarity of administrative work and the challenge and demand of managerial work, both based on technical work and competence. Innovation is the essence of managerial work, as it is replete with decision-making and creating precedents, and it has the added attraction of being seen as the leading edge of managerial initiative in the organisation: creating the future.

We can now review the main stages of innovation: invention or creativity; dissemination and development of the invention; the consequences of the invention in practice.

1. INVENTION OR CREATIVITY

Parker (1978) suggests that there are three theories about invention. The *transcendental model* is the theory that invention depends on individual acts of genius. In the *mechanistic model* necessity is the mother of invention in that inventions are produced to meet problems that have arisen. The *cumulative synthesis* model is one where investigation, thought, analysis and discussion are stimulated by individual acts of insight. These insights are not, however, the quantum leaps of the first theory, but a series of insights that illumine the problem and cause progress.

Review Topic 23.1

Think of examples of:
(a) The demand for a new or revised product providing the push to innovation;
(b) Scientific inventions providing the pull for innovation.

A continuing academic discussion (e.g., Freeman, 1979) is whether the demand for a new, or revised, product is the push to innovation; or is it scientific inventions that provide the pull for innovation? The practical implications of this question for businesses are important as they centre round the issue of where one should look for innovation. Should a company concentrate its efforts on having sensitive feelers out to pick up changes in the market, like teenage fashion boutiques going to discos, or should it invest in speculative research, like a pharmaceutical company investigating pain? The academic discussion will continue for a long time, but the practical answer to the question seems to be that companies will do both, depending on the particular market and product range in which they are interested.

Whichever of Parker's models one accepts, there is always a small number of people in an organisation who produce a large proportion of the initial ideas to trigger the innovation process. Psychologists have tried to distinguish the characteristics of individuals associated with high levels of creativity. Steiner (1965, pp. 7–8) summarises these as:

a.   *Conceptual fluency,* the ability to generate a large number of ideas rapidly:
b.   *Conceptual flexibility,* the ability to discard one frame of reference for another;
c.   *Originality,* the tendency to give unusual, atypical answers;

  d. *Preference for complexity over simplicity,* looking for the
      challenge of knotty problems.
  e. *Independence of judgement,* being different from peers and
      seeing superiors as conventional or arbitrary.

If that listing is accurate, then creative individuals need to be nurtured, as the qualities are unlikely to be warmly welcomed by colleagues and will make it difficult for their possessor to function comfortably in an organisation. He will be regarded as odd and possibly as a nuisance, so he must be identified and his potential contribution channelled effectively.

The organisational setting influences how the creative individual performs, as organisations tend to emphasise an organisational culture and norms: "There is the right way, the wrong way, and our way"; or "In this company we all pull together. Team spirit is our watchword." There may be an emphasis on corporate image through aspects of dress, like the old school tie. Often senior managers in a company all wear the company tie. Organisations acquire a reputation for preferring certain types of skills or personality. Well known bodies like the armed services or the BBC attract recruits with some potential but other people would never apply. The innovatory organisation needs both to attract and to sustain diverse characters in its ranks as a necessary prerequisite for innovation.

Torrance (1970) provides a classic discussion about creative children and how their inventiveness can be encouraged. Creative adults similarly need to be nurtured within the organisation and reconciled to the fact that the world about them is satisfied with its errors. Here are his suggestions of what one can provide for the highly creative:

  a. Provide a refuge;
  b. Become their sponsor or patron;
  c. Help them understand their divergence;
  d. Let them communicate their ideas;
  e. See that their creative talent is recognised;
  f. Help others to understand them.

Little is understood about the nature of invention, but a great deal of effort has gone in to understanding how it can be stimulated. Here are three ways in which an organisation or a department can make inventiveness among its members more likely (based on Paines, 1970).

First, emphasise the importance of keeping *notes.* Workable ideas seldom leap, honed and finished, into the mind. A stray thought comes into focus for a moment but without any apparent connection with anything else, or at least without a complete connection. It beguiles because of its newness and apparent potential, but will drift away when the telephone rings, or a conversation begins. The moment has passed and the idea is lost. These momements of insight (or flashes of inspiration) have to be written down so that they are captured for future examination. Also the act of writing it down will embed it at least slightly in the mind, which may then work on it without one being aware of it. We are all familiar with the idea of deferring an idea until we have "slept on it", often finding that a course of action that was uncertain on retiring is clear on waking. Partly this may be the diurnal rhythm of the body that tires in the evening and is rejuvenated in the morning, so that problems lessen as the sun rises; but it is also due to the fact that our unconscious unravels things for us. The philosopher scientist Arthur Koestler (1964) believed that the great acts of creativity happen in periods of rest after working hard on the problem.

Secondly, there is value in setting *deadlines and quotas* for the production of ideas. This ensures that people attempt to find solutions, rather than putting off the problem till later, like Arthur Brown and his "Too Hard" tray in Chapter 21. Working up new ideas is hard work, and it is all too easy to distract oneself with maintenance activities instead of settling down to wrestle with thinking. One of the authors has over-watered plants and very fat cats!

Thirdly, set aside *a time and place* for generating ideas. As we saw in Chapter 4, managers rarely allow themselves this sort of time, and allow thinking to be squeezed out by the frenetic activity of responding to the demands of others before returning home in the evening having "never stopped". The technique of brainstorming contrives deadlines, quotas, a time and a place to ensure that idea generation happens It is not the romantic view of genius as exemplified by Lord Byron moving sadly from one mistress to another while waiting for inspiration to purge his *ennui,* but it does produce results.

Fourthly, check the *housekeeping* of the organisation. Is inventiveness valued and rewarded, or is it regarded as a nuisance? Are there channels by which the inventive can advance, so that nonconformists can have a sense of career growth because of, rather than despite, their unconventionality? Are the channels of communication reasonably open, so that ideas can be expressed and discussed with a view to finding their merit instead of only finding fault? Always there is the need for balance. The organisation devoid of inventiveness and creative thought will wither through lack of nourishment, but the organisation that is taken over by the creative and where the administrators are suppressed, will probably destroy itself.

Review Topic 23.2

The English novelist George Orwell (1903–1950) wrote in his most famous work, *1984:* "Doublethink means the power of holding two contradictory beliefs in one's mind simultaneously, and accepting both of them."

How is this different from brainstorming?

---

2.   DISSEMINATION AND DEVELOPMENT OF THE INVENTION

The invention has to be disseminated by informing others about it and making them enthusiastic. It then has to be made feasible and put into practice. If that does not happen, the most brilliant idea will be stillborn. Many academic researchers are criticised for not putting sufficient effort into disseminating the findings of their research to those who could put them to practical use. Ralph Waldo Emerson said that the world would beat a path through the forest to the door of a man who could write a better book, preach a better sermon, or make a better mousetrap. The world will only beat the path if they know the better mousetrap is there — and if they happen to want a better mousetrap.

In an organisational context the innovator needs first to influence and persuade his immediate circle that the idea is fruitful. This often happens informally in the office or is a regular part of section meetings, as he tests out the outline of the idea to see the reaction. It is very difficult to get anywhere with a new proposal without the endorsement of the immediate boss and the constructive criticism of immediate colleagues, who will be the first links in the communications network that will be needed to reach implementation. If this group provides its support and commitment, then the next "layer" of boss and colleagues have to be persuaded.

Now all the skills of influence and political manoeuvring that were discussed in Part II of this book become important. First the idea has to be understood as a *better* method than what currently operates (See Chapter 22 on how to prepare a case). Then a commitment has to be won to allocate resources needed to explore the possibilities of the idea. This often involves other departments in the organisation and can seldom be ignored. Too often new ideas are adopted by organisations on face value only and are tried out without being properly tested first, and scarcity of resources is the most common pretext. There is no budget provision for committing money to experiments, so either the proposal is implemented straight away or it is passed over.

Most readers will recall at least one instance in their working lives of an organisational change that went wrong (some may not be able to recall one that went right!). Organisational change is one of the types of innovation that is too often put into operation without being thoroughly worked out first. The broad outlines of allocating responsibility between senior managers are discussed extensively and heatedly, but the nuts and bolts and the ultimate feasibility do not receive the same, necessary, exhaustive examination. Senior managers defend such precipitate action by claiming that organisational change has to be forced in order to overcome the resistance and apathy in the lower levels of the hierarchy. To the outside observer, however, it usually seems more like simple impatience and unwillingness to work through the really difficult problems that can be encountered.

Other types of innovation are also difficult to disseminate and Parker (1978, op. cit.) suggests some factors that influence the success of getting an invention into practice:

a.   Understanding user needs,
b.   Paying attention to marketing the product,
c.   Developing efficiently; not necessarily quickly,
d.   Using outside technical and scientific advice,
e.   Having a senior manager responsible for the innovation.

Langrish *et al.* (1972) studied all the companies that had been awarded The Queen's Award for Industry over two years, and identified the following factors that affected success:

a.   The top person in the company was outstanding and had authority,
b.   There was at least one other outstanding person,
c.   The need to be met was clearly identified,
d.   The potential usefulness of the innovation was realised,
e.   Good co-operation,
f.   Resources were available,
g.   There was help from government.

Those two lists have points of coincidence that are particularly relevant to the dissemination and development of any sort of innovation. The most ingenious idea will founder unless there is a user need to be met. The user may be a customer; it may be a department within the organisation, part of the administrative process linking supply and demand, or some other gap that can be filled. The need does not have to be known to the potential user, but it does have to be a potential need. There will be a potential need for a better mousetrap among people plagued by mice, but the person who invents playing cards that can be used under water is unlikely to find a queue of customers. It also seems to be an inescapable requirement for the innovator to find a patron. The sluggish processes of organisation have to be stimulated not only by the excellence of the idea and the enthusiasm of colleagues, but also the determination of at least one person holding significant position power in the hierarchy.

Langrish and his colleagues also identified the factors that delayed the development of inventions:

a.   Some other associated technology was not sufficiently developed,
b.   No market for the idea,
c.   The potential of the idea was not recognised by management,
d.   Old ideas were embedded and there was resistance to new ones,
e.   Resources were not available,
f.   There was poor co-operation and communication.

Innovations are not automatically understood and passed smoothly into operation. Dissemination and development are harder to manage than the initial creative stage. Lewis Lehr is Chairman of the 3M company and believes that all members of the organisation have to be attuned to the possibilities of a new idea being a winner:

> ... the attitude toward new projects or programs can be very significant. In a company where people at any given time are involved in exploring hundreds of potential developments, it is extremely important that top management do not pre-judge the activities and, for example, identify a group of questionable investment projects under the heading, "problem programs". Some years ago we did this. It was not until we re-named this list — "selected opportunities" — that these programs received the attention necessary to eliminate them as problems and re-direct them as opportunities.
>
> (Lehr, 1982, p. 98)

Invention needs much stimulation and nurture; it is too easy to destroy.

3.   THE CONSEQUENCES OF INVENTION

Like all social action, there are consequences of innovation that are unintended as well as those that are intended, and we have to guard against the assumption, mentioned earlier, that change is automatically desirable. Rogers and Shoemaker (1971, p. 71) provide us with three classifications of the consequences that follow innovation.

First the consequences will be functional or dysfunctional, depending on whether the effects are desirable or undesirable. Secondly, there will be direct or indirect consequences, depending on whether it is an immediate response to innovation or a response to the result of those consequences. Thirdly, the consequences may be latent or manifest, depending on whether or not the consequences are recognised and intended.

Advocates of change usually expect functional, direct and manifest consequences, but invariably some latent consequences are indirect and dysfunctional. An important management activity is to anticipate as many as possible of the unintended consequences, without quashing useful innovation.

4.   MANAGING INNOVATION IN THE DEPARTMENT

Some departments in organisations are set up for the sole, or prime, purpose of innovating. It is the business of the research and development department to introduce, test and develop new ideas. Display and advertising departments need to generate new methods of projection and communication, and other departments are specifically intended to seek new business opportunities and to foster new ventures.

For most departments, however, innovation is more a leavening in the continuing operations to keep excess conformity at bay. A steady stream of new ideas and methods is needed to avoid dullness and to ensure that the department is making its proper contribution within the organisation, but too many innovations may destabilise operations. In the chapter about organisational politics we saw how there is a need to strike a balance between openness and political behaviour among managers. Managing innovation is a similar problem of balance. There must be a co-operative, cohesive working group maintaining an efficient operation, but a part of that co-operative effort is always to encourage and nurture individual creativity so that promising ideas are tested and developed in pushing forward the frontier of what is being achieved. *Managerial* innovation and creativity perhaps begins by setting up that equilibrium.

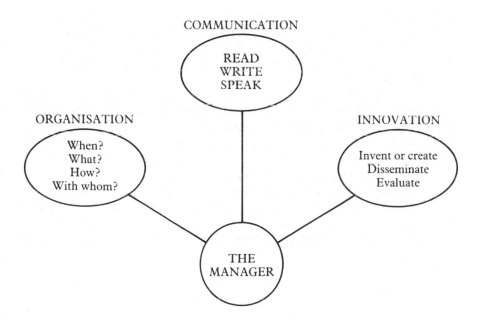

Three ways in which the manager uses his head: getting organised, being a communicator and being creative and innovative.

Figure 23.1   Personal Effectiveness

SUMMARY PROPOSITIONS

23.1. Change is not only something to which to respond, but also something to initiate.

23.2. Creativity is the initial phase of generating a new idea, product or approach; innovation is the whole process from invention to practice.

23.3. The main stages in innovation are: invention or creativity; dissemination and development of the invention; the consequences of the invention in practice.

23.4. Inventiveness among organisation members is made more likely by: the use of notes; deadlines and quotas for the production of new ideas; setting aside a time and a place for generating ideas; checking the housekeeping of the organisation.

APPENDIX

Drill for brainstorming

The technique of brainstorming has been mentioned earlier in the book. Here we suggest a drill for its application in innovation.

Before the session

1. Decide the purpose of the session. Is it:
   a. To find uses for a new idea?
   b. To find a better way of doing something? or
   c. To find a solution to a problem?
2. Make a note of any ideas you have about the subject.

Conducting the session

3. Appoint a note-taker.
4. Ask group members to call out any idea that comes into their heads.
5. Write ideas on blackboard, flip chart or overhead projector, so that all group members can see them.
6. Encourage group members to develop the ideas of others, as well as "sparking" in different directions.
7. Eschew judgement by anyone in the group. All ideas are valid, however, bizzare, and even if they seem to be repeating what has been said already.
8. Generate momentum, so that the group keeps going.
9. Reach a target number — say 75 — ideas in 15–30 minutes.

After the session

10. Classify the ideas generated into five or six groups, possibly adding others that are suggested by the classification.
11. Ask the group to rank the ideas in each classification against questions such as
    a. How new?
    b. How relevant?
    c. How feasible?
12. Decide on action, if any, to be taken to develop preferred ideas.

REFERENCES

Bradley K. and Hill S., " 'After Japan': the Quality Circle Transplant and Productive Efficiency", in *British Journal of Industrial Relations,* Vol. xxi, No. 3, November 1983, pp. 291–311.

Drucker P. F., *Managing in Turbulent Times,* Wm. Heinemann, London, 1980.

Freeman C., "The Determinants of Innovation", in *Futures,* June 1979, p. 206.

Koestler A., *The Act of Creation,* Hutchinson, London 1974.

Langrish J. R., Gibbons M., Evans W. G. and Jevons T. R., *Wealth from Knowledge,* Macmillan, London, 1972.

Lehr L. W., "Entrepreneurs, Innovation and Change", quoted in Wild R. (ed.), *How to Manage,* Heinemann, London, 1982.

Paines S. J., "Education and Creativity", in Vernon P. E. (ed.), *Creativity,* Penguin Books, Harmondsworth, Middlesex, 1970.

Pavitt K., "Innovation and Industrial Development", in *Futures,* 1979, p. 458.

Parker J.E.S., *The Economics of Innovation,* Longman, London, 1978.

Rogers E.M. and Shoemaker F. F., *Communication of Innovation* (2nd ed.), Free Press, New York, 1971.

Steiner G.A., *The Creative Organization,* University of Chicago Press, 1965.

Toffler A., *Future Shock,* Random House, New York, 1970.

Torrance E.P., "Causes for Concern" in Vernon P.E. (ed), *Creativity,* Penguin Harmondsworth, 1970.

Chapter Twenty-Four

THE FUTURE AND THE PROFESSIONAL MANAGER

Few aspects of understanding are sought more eagerly than a look into the future. For centuries people all round the Mediterranean consulted the oracle at Delphi before embarking on any major enterprise. The tragedy of Macbeth is heightened by his reliance on the prophecy of the three witches — using such odd methods as eye of newt and toe of frog, wool of bat and tongue of dog — that he would not be vanquished until Birnam wood be moved to Dunsinane. Today large segments of national newspapers are taken up with predictions based on the position of the stars and planets, while the remaining sections are strewn with predictions about the outcome of elections, sporting events, meetings between statesmen, the durability of marriages between various celebrities, and whether it will rain before breakfast. Having heard our favourite prediction, we then do not exactly ignore it; we interpret it in the way that suits us. Macbeth met his end at Dunsinane, King Croesus went to war against Cyrus of Persia when the Delphic oracle told him that the war would lead to the destruction of a mighty kingdom. Croesus assumed that the kingdom to be destroyed belonged to Cyrus; in fact it was his own.

As we conclude this book with some thoughts about the future, we do so realising that we are probably wrong and that whatever we say the reader will interpret it in the way that suits him, emphasising and remembering what he likes and ignoring what he dislikes. We also realise that some people, browsing in bookshops and libraries, will glance at only this chapter before putting the book back on the shelf. So, with some misgivings and with feet firmly on the mantelshelf, here we go.

1. DECENTRALISATION AND AUTONOMY

The trend towards decentralisation of organisations and individual autonomy will continue. Operational units will be smaller and more manageable by having more scope delegated to them from the centre and less emphasis on conformity to a single pattern. This is not always possible, especially where consumer preference is important. Retail banks cannot vary their operational patterns much as their interconnection is a major feature of their working, but gradually operational units of all types are gaining more independence for their operations. This provides more managers with more scope. Just as management by objectives was a popular attempt to isolate the activities of individual managers so that they could see their performance in isolation from collective performance, so there is growing a more real independence as accountability, responsibility and autonomy are made more feasible through managers being required to conform to organisation-wide norms on a relatively narrow range of activities only but with considerable scope to run the undertaking in their own way.

In Chapter 4, we draw a distinction between the nature of managerial work in senior management posts and those in top and middle management. The decentralisation trend could lead to more people having senior management responsibilities and opportunities. This type of professional autonomy makes the idea of the *professional manager*, who can turn his managerial skills to a number of different situations, a more feasible proposition for the future than it has been in the past. Accountancy and marketing skills have become professionalised and transferable, but managerial skills have been more organisation-dependent due to the "middleness" of most managers. That could now be changing.

This is accompanied by an expectation of greater autonomy among those who do not see themselves as managers. Autonomous work groups received great publicity and scrutiny because they broke the mould of supervision. The pre-existing assumption had been that people at work needed supervision to prevent them from idleness and to avoid their individual efforts being unco-ordinated. By the basically simple tactic of getting (or letting?) work groups to organise themselves and exercise their own responsibility without the yoke of close supervision, it was demonstrated that tight control is not always necessary. Although the speed of movement varies, the general development of autonomy is growing apace, so that the professional manager will be increasingly concerned with a management team or departmental team of other professionals or quasi-professionals, wanting to know what is required of them and then wanting to be left alone to get on with it.

2. THE MANAGERIAL ELITE

In many ways managers as a social grouping are growing apart from those with whom they work. It is not their social origins, upbringing or schooling that makes the difference, but the approach to the job. Most of those at work find their weekly hours slowing reducing, their annual days of holiday increasing and their age of retirement dropping. Paid employment may still be the central organising feature of our society and occupation may still be the main determinant of social status, but for many people work is not as focal as it was and *some* of our human needs are now met not through work but through the twin anodynes of television and do-it-yourself. If even slightly fewer needs depend on paid employment for their satisfaction, then employees become marginally more amenable and less prickly because it means less to them.

For managers it is different. There is a continuing preoccupation with correct dress and correct manners. Smart suits and self-coloured ties are still *de rigueur* for men and women maintain a distinctive convention of dress, even if they are not quite so hidebound. Manners, or styles of behaviour are also distinctive, so that some outside observers regard management as being no more than games playing and posturing. Although this is an exaggeration in most instances, and is much reduced by decentralisation and autonomy, one of the conventional behaviours is "commitment". Managers are expected to be enthusiastic and thoroughly committed to their job and their career in a way that would nowadays seem slightly odd in many other occupational groups. This, of course, is a standard attribute of the professional in other fields. For managers it involves a willingness to travel considerably, day-by-day or week-by-week, so that it must be possible on one day to take the 6.30 a.m. train to London, returning at midnight and on another day to fly to Bahrain for a week. Domestic commitments and family responsibilities do not fit easily into that sort of operating style. For most managers it also involves mobility, which we have already discussed and which presents a different set of domestic difficulties.

Review Topic 24.1

Few managers appear relaxed and their lives are characterised by constant bustle, as we saw in Part I of this book, with hectic travelling a familiar feature of the managerial life-style. To what extent do you think this is:

(a)   Setting a pace for everyone else to follow?
(b)   Inevitable due to the demands of the business?
(c)   Putting on a show, to convince people (and themselves) that they deserve to be well-paid?
(d)   Unnecessary?
(e)   A result of management appealing mainly to people who are hyper-active?
(f)   Changing?

Total preoccupation of this type is relatively easy and attractive to the young and independent. It is tolerable to the married, but problematical for those with families — especially women. Women at the professional managerial level in business have found much improved opportunities in the last decade and have fared better than semi-skilled and clerical women, but for most of them success is gained at the expense of family life. The 28-year-old woman manager who is wondering whether or not to have a baby for the first time will realise that her neighbours who are doctors, barristers, schoolteachers, civil servants, lecturers and solicitors will find it much easier to return to their professional careers as young mothers than would she. It seems to be easier for those who bear their children while they are in their late teens or early twenties and who then begin the assault on the male dominated bastions of management in their later twenties.

3. SOCIAL RESPONSIBILITY

The crude, over-simplified view of management — all that matters is making profits — produces some scepticism among onlookers when managers speak of being socially responsible. Sir James Goldsmith was proud to declare his opposition to the idea of social responsibility:

> Entrepreneurs come in all shapes and sizes. They straddle every class and every system of education. The common theme that links them all together is sound judgement, ambition, determination, capacity to assess and take risks, hard work, greed, fear and luck. The most dangerous entrepreneur is the self righteous one who preaches morality and pretends that he is doing it all for the good of others.
>
> (Goldsmith, 1980, pp. 185–6)

That sort of view would be echoed by many trade union representatives, who would believe that they would be better judges of social responsibility than managers, who should concentrate on being efficient while socially responsible behaviour was imposed upon them by legislation, public opinion or trade union power.

Despite this managers are concerned to behave as human beings and to exercise some social responsibility greater than balancing the books. Even those entrepreneurs whom the reader will have in his mind at the present moment, and who epitomise exactly what Goldsmith was describing, do not operate in a vacuum but via organisational and management processes; they work with other people and those people will seldom share their single mindedness.

There is a wealth of social problems that need the attention of business mnanagers, because the appropriate initiatives cannot readily come from elsewhere. One is some initiative about unemployment, especially hard-core unemployment. We do not have solutions to offer here, but clearly employment comes from employers and managers, no matter how much politicians may nudge, exhort and manipulate. As associated matter is that of equal opportunity. The number of disadvantaged groups grows and the degree of their disadvantage increases. Age for age unemployment among blacks is much higher than among whites. The number of blacks who break out from the lower levels of employment and enjoy the wider prospects of white-collar and management positions remains few. Apart from the privileged minority in managerial posts, the position of women in employment is weak in relation to men. They are still largely found in a narrow range of "women only" jobs with poor rates of pay and limited opportunities, although the female participation rate in employment is higher in Britain than in most of our competitor countries and the unemployment rate among women is lower than for men. Both blacks and women have received much attention and legislative support in recent years, but the employment prospects of disabled people and those who have served terms of imprisonment have attracted less interest and remain gloomy.

A different aspect of concern about unemployment is its effect on the young and the old. The general level of anxiety about unemployment among school leavers is such that there have been a series of quite costly initiatives to mitigate that problem. The Youth Training Scheme that began in 1983 shows signs of potential long-run success. It can, however, only defer the time when those who have been trained seek employment. Job opportunities for the young may mean the loss of employment for those who are older. Workforce reductions are easiest when those who go are volunteers, and many of the job losses in the public sector of employment and in the larger private organisations have been achieved by early retirement, sometimes as young as fifty years of age. In other situations whole organisations and whole industries have closed down, making jobless all employees regardless of age. Here the re-employment prospects for those of forty-five or more have been very poor indeed.

A different aspect of management responsibility is the ecological worry, where business is criticised as much as governments. Technological advance not only accelerates the rate at which we use up our natural resources, such as fossil fuels and iron ore, but the processing of those resources pollutes our delicately balanced ecology and is increasingly resisted. The rain forests of South America have been called the world's lung, yet their extent is being rapidly reduced. We have widespread problems of acid rain, frequent explosions at chemical factories and the occasional calamity like Seveso. Those major problems are reproduced on a smaller scale in many localities and overall hangs the constant fear of a nuclear accident.

4. AGE

Managers will respond to two different challenges relating to age. First will be the age of the customers. The decline in the fertility rate in Western countries has been accompanied by steadily growing life expectancy so that the mean age of the population is rising. We have already seen how managers supplying goods and services have exploited the adolescent market and, more recently, the market among the "mature young" in their twenties and thirties but without family commitments. An expanding market will be among those of advancing years.

Within organisations, however, the situation will be different. At the beginning of this chapter we suggested that decentralisation and autonomy could lead to more managers requiring senior management rather than middle management skills. We have also referred to the shake-out of employment among those who are older. In our interviews with managers while preparing this book we have been struck by how young managers are. This is not just a version of the hoary old comment about policemen getting younger as you get older, it appears to be a clear trend for significant management responsibility to come to younger people.

Partly this is a result of early retirement and similar shake-out strategies. If the "old" people in the organisation are in their late fifties instead of in their early sixties, then the age balance shifts, so that the "middle-aged" are forty instead of 48 and the "young" are 25 instead of 30. Another reason is the growing significance of new technology, especially the computer, which seems to be best understood and developed by those in their teens and early twenties. Also the need to be committed, that we have mentioned, is easier to sustain while young.

The idea of giving real responsibility to young people has been a commonplace for decades, even though it has not often been seen in practice. Now it is becoming much more common, but what happens to older managers? In times of expansion the answer is easy: the organisation grows and more and more people are constantly needed to feed growth. If organisations are getting smaller, or remaining small, that answer will not work. The alternative is that managers move down the hierarchy as well as up. At the moment that sort of move is almost unknown, partly because of the concern with status and partly because of the concern with income level and pension level. The manager at 40 is anxious to maximise his earnings because of his family responsibilities with children and ageing parents. The manager at 50+ develops an anxiety to maximise his final salary, so as to boost his pension. This can produce a number of undesirable effects. One is the manager who is "counting the days" until his retirement but has to cling grimly to a job that he no longer really wants to do, just to maintain his pension. Another possibility is the department or business that stagnates for years because the person in charge is in the run-up to retirement and does not want any innovation or change as he gradually detaches himself from emotional involvement and commitment. A third problem is that of the manager who keeps going at full throttle in the closing stages of his employment, only to find the sudden change to the different pace of retirement very hard to take.

It is unrealistic to think simply of moving people out of the organisation as they get older. First this can be extremely expensive and secondly it reduces the all-round capability of the management, which needs the contribution of older people as well as those who are younger (one of the authors is comfortably under forty; the other uncomfortably over fifty). Shakespeare's seven ages of man distinguish between the soldier and the justice:

... a soldier, ...
Jealous in honour, sudden and quick in quarrel,
    Seeking the bubble reputation ...
And then the justice ...
    Full of wise saws and modern instances.

For effectiveness, management seems to need both sets of qualities. Traditionally the "soldier" is junior to the "justice". Perhaps the time has come for that to change, but we have to find a way of doing this that will ensure the effective contribution of both.

5. INTERNATIONAL OPERATIONS

Despite decentralisation, organisations are getting bigger, so that the multinational is a feature of western societies that concerns some because of the considerable power that such companies are able to wield and concerns others because of the difficulty such companies have in innovating. With the improvements in communications, almost all organisations now operate across national boundaries. If there is not a branch of the business overseas, there will certainly be overseas selling and buying and observation of technical developments.

Underlying this development of the international dimension is the interdependence of western countries and the developing economies of the world. The British buyer of a British washing machine may not realise that the machine may have been partly manufactured in Korea, partly in the Philippines, partly in Italy and only assembled in Britain. The Third World has long looked to the developed countries for technical expertise and investment, even though they have been exploited in the process. More recently the developed countries have shifted manufacturing into developing countries, not in order better to supply *those* markets, but in order to have cheap manufacturing to supply western markets. Pay rates have been low, industrial action unlikely and increased automation has made it possible to produce high quality components.

This transfer of manufacturing operations could lead to a situation where the western nations become more dependent on the developing countries than they have been in the past.

6. THE COMPUTER

One great uncertainty is the influence of the computer. We have plenty of predictions and mostly these are prophecies of what the computer and the microprocessor *can* do and then logically developed to produce a picture of what *will* happen; manufacturing will progressively be taken over by robots, rapid transfer and manipulation of data, the paperless office, people working from home instead of coming into a centre, and so forth: the golden age of the post-industrial society. Our questions about this are first the extent to which the possible will become reality and secondly to wonder what will be done to make up what the computer will take from us.

Managers have long had the opportunity to spend more of their time, and make more of their decisions, by rational planning and operational research methods than in fact they do. There continues to be a preference among managers to spend their time talking with people and to make their decisions as a result of discussion and shrewd judgement. Will managers now begin to eschew face-to-face discussion in favour of face-to-terminal decision-making, or will they continue to confer and keep busy while others feed to them an ever-increasing flow of processed information requiring interpretation, evaluation and further discussion.

Research findings suggest that managers work the way they do at least partly because they like it that way:

> The manager actually seems to prefer brevity and interruption in his work. ...
> Superficiality is an occupational hazard of the manager's job. ...
> Very current information (gossip, hearsay, speculation) is favoured; routine reports are not. ...
> The manager clearly favours the ... verbal media, spending most of his time in verbal contact.
>
> (Mintzberg, 1973, pp. 51–2)

How significantly will managers allow this pattern of working to change and how great will the influence of the computer on managerial work actually become?

Apart from managers, there is then the question about how everyone else will make up for what the computer takes away. If there is a general tendency for people to work at home, taking their terminal with them, how popular will that turn out to be? It is over a century since the household ceased to be the central productive unit and the men, and later the women, began to spend a large part of their waking hours at a different social centre — the factory, shop or office. To be housebound has become a blight. We can see how it used to be:

> In 1810 the common productive unit in New England was still the rural household. Processing and preserving of food, candlemaking, soap-making, spinning, weaving, shoemaking, quilting, rug-making, the keeping of small animals and gardens, all took place on domestic premises. Although money income might be obtained by the household through the sale of produce, and additional money be earned through occasional wages to its members, the United States household was overwhelmingly self-sufficient. ...Women were as active in the creation of domestic self-sufficiency as were men.
>
> (Illich, 1981, pp. 111–12)

Since that time we have dismantled, or allowed to wither, all the social mechanisms that supported that self-sufficiency and developed the social institution of the workplace as the arena for many of our human needs, like affiliation, interaction, team working and competition. If we are about to reverse that trend, we need different arenas to meet those needs.

On a less dramatic level, there is the slightly isolating nature of the work that computerisation produces. The individual employee is not one of many in a crowded workshop, but one of a few scattered around a mass of busy machines. The clerical employee spends more time gazing at his computer terminal and less talking to his colleagues. What employee behaviour will this engender and what attitudes will be associated with that behaviour?

7.   CONCLUSION

In this concluding chapter we have suggested a few possibilities for the future. There are many more and some readers will already have read the best known set of prophecies by Toffler (1980). His predictions and ours may be no more accurate than that of the man who predicted the end of the world at 11.01 a.m. on the 6th November 1882, but they are offered here as they sustain our belief that managers progressively need to develop a personal survival kit that will enable them to be effective in a wide variety of situations, becoming less organisationally dependent and more self-sufficient.

We see the stereotype of the future manager as being younger, better-paid and more autonomous than those of today. To succeed they will need to be mobile and bright. More of them will be women and most will have a strong specialist skill in either accountancy, marketing or a technological area. All of them will need organisational knowledge and a set of operational, managerial skills of the type that we have described in these pages. Finally they will need individual flair, imagination and application. Management is a science: successful management is an art.

Good luck!

REFERENCES

Goldsmith J., "Entrepreneurs, Innovation and Change" in Wild R. (ed.), *How to Manage,* Heinemann, London, 1982.
Illich I., *Shadow Work,* Marion Boyars, London, 1981.
Mintzberg H., *The Nature of Managerial Work,* Harper & Row, London, 1973.
Toffler A., *The Third Wave,* Morrow, New York, 1980.

AUTHOR INDEX

SUBJECT INDEX